DETECTIVE

*The Inspirational Story of
the Trailblazing Woman Cop
Who Wouldn't Quit*

KATHY BURKE

WITH

NEAL HIRSCHFELD

A LISA DREW BOOK
SCRIBNER
New York London Toronto Sydney

SCRIBNER
1230 Avenue of the Americas
New York, NY 10020

SCRIBNER and design are trademarks of
Macmillan Library Reference USA, Inc., used under license
by Simon & Schuster, the publisher of this work.

A LISA DREW BOOK is a trademark of Simon & Schuster, Inc.

For information about special discounts for bulk purchases,
please contact Simon & Schuster Special Sales:
1-800-456-6798 or business@simonandschuster.com

DESIGNED BY LAUREN SIMONETTI
Text set in Minion

Manufactured in the United States of America

1   3   5   7   9   10   8   6   4   2

Library of Congress Cataloging-in-Publication Data

Burke, Kathy.
Detective : the inspirational true story of the trailblazing woman cop who wouldn't quit
/ Kathy Burke with Neal Hirschfeld.
p.   cm.
"A Lisa Drew book."
1. Burke, Kathy, 1943– 2. New York (N.Y.). Police Dept.—Officials and employees—
Biography. 3. Policewomen—New York (State)—New York—Biography. 4. Women
detectives—New York (State)—New York—Biography. 5. Discrimination in law
enforcement—New York (State)—New York. 6. Sex discrimination against women—
New York (State)—New York. I. Hirschfeld, Neal.
II. Title.

HV7911.B86A3 2006
363.20972—dc22
[B]
2006042201
ISBN-13: 978-0-7432-8392-2
ISBN-10: 0-7432-8392-9

For Cathrine, Veronica, Tom, and the rest of my family,
whose faith, love, and support kept me going.
For Janet, who stood faithfully by my coauthor through it all.
For the special fraternity of men and women who work
in narcotics enforcement—and gave me my start.
And for Tony—who made the ultimate sacrifice.

COAUTHOR'S NOTE

About three months after the September 11 terrorist attack that obliterated the World Trade Center, a dozen New York City cops shuffled into a classroom at John Jay College on Manhattan's West Side.

The cops had been among the "first responders" to Ground Zero in the moments just before, during, and after the collapse of the Twin Towers. Some had actually heard calls for help coming over their radios from other cops, twenty-three of whom would not live to see September 12. In the months that had passed since the attacks and the terrible devastation, they had tried to put those awful memories out of their minds. But, to their irritation, they would not be allowed that luxury.

The cops who came to John Jay that day had been ordered to do so by the Police Department. As they entered the classroom, the officers were greeted by three facilitators, also cops, who asked them to sit in a circle and told them they were there to be "debriefed" about September 11. Upon hearing this, most of the cops grumbled. This was, in a word, bullshit. In their minds, the subject had already been talked to death. Any further discussion seemed pointless and redundant, and they resented being forced to take valuable time from their hectic schedules to talk about it yet again.

Undeterred, one of the facilitators posed a question to the assembled group. "You know, I was just wondering . . . if any of you had to pick one thing that happened that day, what is it that continues to trouble you the most?"

Reluctantly, each of them responded. And, to their mutual astonishment, they each gave the identical answer.

It was the memory of Police Officer Moira Smith radioing an urgent 10-13 call for help from Ground Zero, unaware that one of the towers was about to collapse on top of her—and the inability of her brother of ficers to reach her in time. Smith, one of two female police officers to die in the collapse of the towers, had been married to another New York City cop. She was also the mother of a two-year-old daughter.

"She was a damned good cop," said one of the guys who had worked in the same command as Officer Smith, his voice growing raspy with emotion.

All those in the room acknowledged that Officer Smith's radio call, the lone female voice on the airwaves as the World Trade Center calamity was unfolding, had left them haunted by feelings of helplessness. Some were angry at themselves. Others felt guilty that they had survived while Officer Smith and the other cops had perished. And one, admitting that he was still plagued by nightmares about the radio call, actually broke down and began to sob. Once he broke the ice, the others began to reveal themselves as well. Virtually everyone had a story to tell—about waking up in the middle of the night to stare at their kids asleep in their beds, snapping at their wives and friends, becoming paranoid about loud noises, open windows, or unlocked doors, losing their appetites, shunning the violent action movies they used to love, or spending more and more time at the local saloon.

"What you are experiencing is perfectly normal," offered one of the facilitators, a retired detective named Kathy Burke. "You've been though a terrible trauma, and these are the signs of post-traumatic stress. What you need to remember is that it's okay to feel. It's okay to cry. It's okay to hurt. But when it does happen, you need to talk about it. You need to work it out. You need to contact a priest or a rabbi or a counselor or a friend. You need to contact one of us."

Soon, the cops began talking more animatedly, swapping experiences, sharing feelings, revealing their secret terrors. As they did, Detective Burke and the other facilitators took backseats to the discussion. The group was moving along nicely on its own now, no longer in need of prodding or guidance. The cops had begun the long, slow process of healing themselves. The facilitators had simply helped get the ball rolling.

I had seen Detective Burke do this kind of hands-on counseling for other cops and law enforcement officers many times over the past fifteen years. And the skill, empathy, and delicacy she brought to this difficult task never ceased to amaze me. When it comes to getting people to open up about their innermost feelings, cops are not exactly the easiest nuts to crack, especially when the public expects them to be some kind of Supermen in blue.

Detective Burke, however, had an astonishing ability to pierce that macho facade and get cops to talk about their secret hells. No doubt because Burke had been through a secret hell of her own.

I first learned of Kathy Burke in the 1970s, when I was a reporter for the *New York Daily News.* Her exploits as an undercover cop in the New York Police Department were legendary, the stuff of headlines. Unfortunately, at the time, I was not allowed to interview her, since she was still working undercover and her identity was shielded. It was not until the mid-1980s, when she was no longer working undercover, that I finally met Kathy Burke.

We met while I was writing a magazine article about the New York City Police Self-Support Group, an organization for cops who had been shot, stabbed, maimed, or otherwise injured in the line of duty. Burke, who had been badly hurt on the job, had been one of its pioneering officers. Years after her retirement from the New York City police force, she is still one of its most active members.

When Kathy Burke met with that roomful of Ground Zero cops, she was there as a professionally trained trauma counselor. What she did not reveal to those cops was that she was also the victim of a trauma—a trauma so horrible, so profound, and so devastating that few of the rest of us would have survived it, much less gone on to help other victims.

Yet Burke, as readers of her book will discover, did survive. Painfully. Heroically. Incredibly. Kathy Burke survived because of who she was. And who she is today. Which is, quite simply, the strongest, most courageous person I have ever met in my life.

Neal Hirschfeld

What follows is a true story.

However, the names and details concerning some individuals have been changed.

DETECTIVE

CHAPTER ONE

The day I nearly got my head blown off started like any other.

It was August of 1971. And I was worried that I wasn't generating enough drug buys.

Then, out of the blue, a case fell into my lap. It started when a field team from Bronx Narcotics requested a female undercover to make drug buys in the 41st Precinct, or the Four-One as we cops lovingly know it.

Now, most of the field-team cops I had worked with were stand-up guys. Tough, experienced veterans who would go to the ends of the earth to protect your butt. Disguising themselves as plumbers, electrical contractors, city sanitation workers, street sweepers, and, in one elaborate ruse, a watercolor landscape painter in Central Park—complete with beret, easel, canvas, and folding chair—they would blend into the background and keep an ever-watchful eye on you while you made your drug purchases . . . just in case.

But this team in the Four-One was new to me. I had never worked with them before. So I had no idea what to expect.

Just before I was due to join them, I got a strange call from a Bronx detective who was an old pal of mine. "These are not your kind of people, Kathy," my friend told me. "You could get hurt."

This detective felt so negatively about the Four-One field team that he threatened to "burn" me on the street—that is, expose me to the drug dealers and the drug users as an undercover cop—just to keep me from going out with the Four-One field team. He said he'd rather blow my cover than risk letting me get hurt.

But I didn't want to get a reputation as a prima donna or a shirker. That kinda stink could ruin your career, all the more so since I was the rare female in an overwhelmingly male police department. Plus, business had been slow and I was eager to line up as many drug collars as I could before Labor Day. So I tried to smooth-talk my detective friend out of it. "If things don't feel right," I assured him, "I'll shit-can the operation myself. I promise."

My friend was still uneasy about me hooking up with this new crew. But he finally agreed to back off on his threat to burn me. "Just take care of yourself, Kathy."

Lieutenant Ballner, my crotchety curmudgeon of a boss in the Undercover Unit, gave me similar advice. "Just be sure you feel okay about this new team," he told me. "I don't want you futzin' around up there"— *futzin'* being the lieutenant's favorite expression for any sort of behavior that wasn't strictly by-the-book or on the up-and-up.

The day of the buy operation was positively oppressive, with temperatures soaring into the upper nineties. Ten minutes into the drive up to the South Bronx, my clothes were sopping with sweat. The air conditioner in my car went on the fritz. Adding to the misery, my brakes burned out en route. I had to stop along the way and have new fluid put in them. Good omens, these were not.

On my drive through the South Bronx, I got the full measure of the 41st Precinct, and it was not a pretty sight—a 2.5-square-mile moonscape of run-down tenements and burned-out buildings, graffiti-spattered walls and garbage-strewn lots. Developers had tried to pump some new life into the area by erecting prefab housing, but just as quickly as these structures went up, the junkies and squatters would descend on them like hungry piranhas on raw flesh, cannibalizing the contents, sneaking in at night to steal the copper pipes and wiring and fixtures and sell them for quick drug money. Statistically speaking, this precinct had the distinction of being the most violent, the most murderous, and the most drug-infested in the whole city, if not the entire nation. Cops who worked the 41st Precinct likened the place to the Wild West. Taking a cue from their frontier forebears, the cops dubbed the 41st Precinct "Fort Apache" and took to wearing T-shirts and sweatshirts emblazoned with images of a beleaguered Alamo-style fortress flying a tattered flag and embedded with feather-tipped arrows.

No doubt about it, Fort Apache was a no-man's-land.

I met the three field-team guys on the street. And right off the bat, I got a hinky feeling about them. Drake, the guy with the curly blond hair and the flushed, Irish bartender's face, had a nasty attitude toward women. Pisko, who had close-cropped hair, pointy features, and skin so shiny it looked as if it had been spray-painted on his skull, was a scammer, always looking to cut corners and work whatever angle would put money in his pockets, whether it was catching a meal on the arm or saving a few pennies on the tag prices of his shirts and underwear. In his short chino pants, white socks, and penny loafers, he looked like a moldy leftover from the 1950s Public Morals Division. Kenner, who was dark-haired and didn't say much, was pretty ordinary-looking, but smelled god-awful. Most of my other field teams had complemented each other, in experience, in looks, and in personality. But somehow, these three were different. Too different. They seemed all wrong with each other, out of sync—clashing like stripes and polka dots.

A year earlier, Mayor John Lindsay had established the Knapp Commission to begin a far-ranging inquiry into police corruption and official laxity in dealing with it. Eventually, the commission would uncover widespread graft and abuses among plainclothesmen like the ones I now found myself working with, and prosecutors would follow up with indictments, trials, and convictions.

But, at this point, still fairly early into the commission's inquiries, a lot of the rotten apples were still hanging up there in the trees, not yet shaken loose from the branches.

While the three cops in my backup team gave me the creeps, I didn't exactly fall in love with the informant, either.

His name was Billy, and he was a young white kid with long blond hair cut in the style of Prince Valiant. In a place like the 41st Precinct, which was 99.9 percent black and Hispanic, he stood out like horns on a duck. On the street, my undercover alter ego, Marie Martin—that was the name I used when I made my drug buys—was accustomed to hanging out with jive-talking, wisecracking blacks and Hispanics, not polite, clean-cut, white-bread types who looked like surfers from Malibu.

This kid was all wrong. A real three-dollar bill.

I pulled Pisko aside and told him I didn't like Billy, and I didn't think the operation would work. He begged me to go out with the team just this once. They were in a bind. They needed to make arrests. They were desperate to get on "the sheet" for the month.

Still feeling uneasy, I gave in.

Billy and I hit the street later that morning. First, he took me to meet a young Puerto Rican guy who was selling $2 bags of heroin. While I was making my buy—six bags—I looked over and saw Billy shaking like a leaf. At first, I wasn't sure if he was shaking because he was nervous or because he needed a fix himself. Either way, I didn't like it. I had already told him there would be no "copping" (buying of drugs by the informant) while we were working the operation. Whatever the reason for his shakes, my misgivings about this kid were only getting worse. He was supposed to be my informant, my connection, my link to the streets. But he didn't seem to know his ass from his elbow up here. He was a foul ball. Jittery. Clumsy. Dangerous.

When we hooked up again with the field team, I handed them the dope from our buy. We placed it in an evidence envelope, and I signed my name to the outside, in accord with established department procedures for vouchering undercover buys. From here, the drugs would go downtown to the police lab for testing.

I pulled Pisko aside again. "This kid's a lox," I told him.

"Whaddya mean?"

"He's gonna get me burned, I just know it."

"Look, let's not pull the plug just yet. He's got a bundles connection set up for two o'clock."

Now *bundles* were sizable amounts of heroin, costing $55 apiece. For a field team to pull off a bundles bust was like hitting a grand-slam home run. A way to get noticed big-time by the higher-ups.

Pisko kept trying to reassure me. "We'll be right behind you, every step of the way," he promised.

I had about $110 with me, enough to purchase two bundles. I still didn't like the looks of Billy, but I sure as hell didn't want to be the one that screwed up the field team's chances to get on the sheet for a bundles bust. Once again, I let myself be talked into going along with the plan.

I drove with Billy to Hoe Avenue. Now, Hoe Avenue really does exist. It's an honest-to-goodness New York City street name, not some jive for a broad who turns tricks. As we got out of the car and started walking toward one of the buildings, I got a quick handle on the street. Lots of people were milling about, trying to find some relief from the suffocating summer heat. Women with babies. Kids playing hoops or stickball. Men sitting on stoops, swilling bottles of Colt .45 malt liquor and listening to their boom-box radios.

Steam was rising in vaporous puffs off the hot tar. The fire hydrants, opened for the kids, were gushing water into the gutters. The pungent aromas of Latin and Caribbean cooking wafted from the windows of the surrounding apartments. Crushed mango pits littered the curbside. Near one of the buildings, Billy introduced me to his connection, a skeevy black guy named Elton Green. I knew Elton from the streets, and he knew me as Marie. In my hand, I was holding $55. Enough for one bundle.

I was hoping to cop quick, then get the hell out of there. But just as we began to talk turkey, two powerful hands came up under my arms, snapped them upright, and locked my elbows in place so rigidly that my arms were permanently cemented into a raised position, like those of a surgeon who's just scrubbed up for an operation. Suddenly, I felt myself being yanked off the sidewalk and lifted straight up into the air. Then, I felt myself being carted toward a narrow opening between two of the tenement buildings. I tried to struggle free by swinging my feet from one side to the other, but it was no use. My arms were pinned to my sides and I had no footing, no leverage whatsoever. I struggled and struggled, but I couldn't get a grip on anything. In the next instant, I realized that I was being carried away from the street, away from all those people, and down into a darkened alley.

"Oh, shit!" I thought to myself. This was it. The moment I had always been warned about by my first mentor in the Undercover Unit, a detective named Dennis Roberts. I was about to get robbed . . . and maybe worse.

And then I remembered the rest of Dennis's words. "Just remember, kid, you're always alone out there. And you could very easily die."

Another of Dennis's phrases began to swirl around inside my head . . . HE CAN HURT ME NOW.

I kept saying it to myself, over and over and over . . . HE CAN HURT ME NOW. . . . HE CAN HURT ME NOW. . . . HE CAN HURT ME NOW. . . .

I kept saying it not only because I was worried about my survival. It was a mnemonic device that Dennis had made me memorize as a way to picture the bad guys so you could identify them later . . .

HE—Height/Eyes.

CAN—Complexion/Age/Nose. Long, pug, broken, flat, wide?

HURT—Hair/Unarmed or Armed/Right or Left-handed/Tattoos, Scars, Marks.

ME—Mouth/Eyeglasses.

NOW—Nationality/Outfit/Weight.

. . . HE CAN HURT ME NOW.

In the alley, I felt myself being lifted even higher, then hurled through the air like some rag doll. I went head over heels, crashing into some garbage cans. The man who had heaved me, the same man who had sneaked up behind me on the street, turned out to be a 285-pound drug dealer named Stanley Brown. And now, as I lay stunned and sprawled among the piss-splattered garbage cans, the rotting fish heads, the used condoms, and the greasy chicken bones, I realized that he was holding a .22-caliber handgun just under my chin.

"Give it," he said.

I handed over the $55.

"Where's the rest?" he demanded.

"That's all I've got," I said.

His eyes narrowed. "Don't fuck with me, bitch. Gimme the rest."

"I swear to God, that's all I've got."

With that, he smacked me sharply across the face. My head snapped to the side and spittle came flying out. I could feel the warm blood beginning to trickle from my lip. With his free hand, Brown reached across my chest and ripped my shirt open, right down the middle, popping all my buttons. Then he plunged his hand down, inside my bra, looking for the rest of my cash.

But there was none.

Which thoroughly enraged Brown. He shoved his gun into my cheek, and I was certain he was about to pull the trigger. With my right arm, I quickly reached behind me, into my waistband, and pulled out my concealed .25-caliber automatic. Raising the gun toward Brown, I took aim.

But just as I was about to fire, four more hands began to paw at me from behind. One set of hands grabbed for my gun and yanked my right arm back over my shoulder, twisting my wrist into an awkward and painful position and nearly snapping my fingers off. The other set pummeled me in the back and the head, then locked onto my other arm.

I felt something sharp plunge through my flesh. The pointed tip of a knife blade. Sinking into the top of my left shoulder. Then the blood, oozing . . .

Elton Green had stabbed me with the knife. A third guy, Ray Vender, had grabbed my gun, twisted my arm and wrist backward, and prevented me from shooting Brown.

Shit! Now I was really in trouble! They had my gun!

And Stanley Brown, the enraged 285-pound giant, was even angrier than before because I had attempted to use my gun on him. Quaking with fury, he placed the barrel of his own gun against my left temple.

"I'm gonna kill you, you motherfucker. Now gimme the damned money!"

I thought to myself, "Oh, God, don't let me die here, in all this dog shit and cat piss and stinking garbage. Please, God. Nobody will ever find my body."

I closed my eyes.

Brown squeezed the trigger.

Click.

Nothing.

He squeezed it again.

Another click.

Nothing.

His gun had malfunctioned.

Livid, Brown grabbed my .25-caliber automatic from Vender and placed it to my head.

Then he tried to shoot me with my own gun.

Click.

Nothing.

Brown didn't know how to operate the automatic. He'd neglected to release the safety catch.

As I tried to regain control of my rampaging heart, the three men kicked me in my legs, knocking me to the pavement. One of them kicked me in the ribs. Another used a knife to slash open the pockets on my blue jeans, from which the rest of my cash tumbled out. At that point, I heard one of the others—Vender, I think it was—shout, "Hey, man, we got the money. Fuck this bitch! Let's go, man!"

The other two started for the street. But Brown hesitated. He still looked as if he wanted to beat the shit out of me. Suddenly, he bent over me and yanked me up off the ground by my collar. Weighing ninety-five pounds soaking wet, I was little more than a throw pillow in his huge hands. Then, using those huge hands, he drew my face close to his. So close that I could see the gold fillings in his teeth. So close that I could smell the cheap wine and garlic on his breath. So close that I could see the beads of sweat trickling down his upper lip. So close that we were practically kissing. For a moment, he just stared into my eyes, saying nothing. Just staring.

He tilted his head sideways. Smiled. Hawked up a mouthful of phlegm. And spat it right in my face.

"Bitch!" he hissed.

With that, he hurled me back into the trash cans, headfirst. Then he loped down the alley, rejoining his two compadres. All three of them ran toward the street.

For a few moments, I lay on the ground, too stunned to do anything other than try to figure out if I could still breathe. Finally, I wobbled to my feet and tried to dust myself off. My head was sore and bruised, my ankle was swollen, my shoulder was bleeding from the knife wound, and the fingers and elbow on my twisted arm throbbed with pain.

But all I could think of was that these shitweasels had gotten my gun.

If the department got wind of it, I'd be up to my eyeballs in trouble. If I did not get that gun back, I would have to report the loss of it to Lieutenant Ballner, who would probably have a cow. I would be suspended. I was up for a promotion at the end of the year, but with the loss of my gun, that promotion would go right down the crapper. As would the rest of my career. Worst of all, my gun could be used to kill someone. An innocent civilian. A child. Maybe even another cop. Dennis Roberts's cautionary words echoed again and again in my brain: "No matter what happens to you out there, no matter how bad things get, there is one thing you must never, ever let happen. And that is to lose your gun."

I ran toward the street like a woman whose hair was on fire.

The moment I got there, Billy, the informant, stepped into my path and grabbed me around the waist, trying to restrain me. I stepped down hard on Billy's instep with one foot—hell, I would have broken it, if I could—and punched him hard in the stomach. Then I snarled at him, "Get the hell outta my way, you useless piece of shit! You almost got me killed!"

As soon as Billy went down, I raced to my car, jumped in the driver's seat, slammed the gearshift into reverse, and put the pedal to the metal. Around the corner, on Westchester Avenue, I was expecting to find my field team staked out, protecting my back and ready to spring into action if need be. If anyone would know what to do, it would be these guys—they'd bail me out.

But when I turned the corner, there was no sign of them. I looked one way, then the other. Nothing. They were gone. In the wind—those fucking bastards.

"Sonofabitch!" I could hear myself mutter. "Where the hell are they?"

I peeled out and began to look for the robbers. Suddenly, I spotted a black uniformed cop on foot patrol. I pulled my car over, identified myself as a cop, and told him I needed help. He jumped in beside me.

As we cruised the neighborhood, I told him the whole ugly story. I was supposed to check in with the Narcotics Division every two hours to let them know I was okay. Since I had checked in just a little while earlier, I knew I had exactly one hour—one hour—to find my missing gun.

I also knew I needed to get more help, and fast. Stopping in front of a bodega, I ran inside and phoned Detective Ray Sanchez, a former undercover cop who was now working Bronx Robbery. I knew Ray and trusted him. When I told him about my missing gun, he realized the seriousness of my plight. He immediately arranged a rendezvous with me. Then Ray and his partner hit the street running.

Back outside the bodega, the black uniformed cop stood waiting. He was a great big bear of a man—nearing sixty, I would have guessed—trying to just do his time on the job, not make any waves, put in his retirement papers, and get out without any hassles.

"We got some talking to do, Officer," he told me.

"Whaddya mean?" I said.

"Where's your backup?"

"I don't have a fucking clue."

"Alright, then. You got a decision to make. And you better make it now, Officer. You gotta call in soon. What are you gonna tell 'em when they ask you what happened? And you know damned well that's the first thing they're gonna want to know."

"What are you getting at?" I asked.

He eyed me up and down, chagrined to see how ridiculously young I looked, not to mention small, slight, fragile, and helpless. "You don't have much time on the job, do you?"

"Three years."

"Yeah, that's what I figured. So let me explain the facts of life to you about the Police Department, little lady. You go back there and you tell them your partners weren't around when you got ripped off, the bosses'll cut their balls off, pure and simple. They'll probably get thrown off the job because they left you hangin'. But for the next seventeen years, nobody will remember that your partners didn't do their job and that you almost died. What they will remember is that some female cop gave them up. That some broad dropped a dime on them. Ratted them out. So you better make a decision real fast about what you're gonna say when the bosses pop the sixty-four-thousand-dollar question."

This cop had been around. He knew the ropes; I didn't. I thought carefully about what he was telling me.

For the next twenty minutes, we rode around together in my car, looking for the three animals who had ripped me off. We didn't find them, but eventually we came across my missing field team. Cruising around merrily like Keystone Kops on a scavenger hunt, as if they didn't have a care in the world. When I told them what had happened to me, they offered no explanation about where they had been. Nor did they offer an apology. They simply asked for a description of my attackers and feebly promised to join the manhunt. I didn't feel particularly optimistic, especially since Drake was badly slurring his words.

Time was running out. In another few minutes, I would have to make my telltale phone call to the Narcotics Division and fess up about the theft of my gun. And watch my budding police career go straight down the toilet.

With the black uniformed cop still at my side, I drove my car to the intersection where I had arranged to rendezvous with my friend Detective Ray Sanchez and his partner. Once I got there, I parked, turned off the ignition, and tried to sort things out in my mind.

Suddenly, Detective Sanchez and his partner pulled up in their car. Behind them was the car with the three field-team cops, Pisko, Drake, and Kenner. They got out of their car and swaggered toward me, as if they had not a care in the world. But my gaze was quickly drawn back to Ray Sanchez and his partner. I don't know how they had managed to do it, but somehow Ray and his partner had tracked down giant Stanley Brown and arrested him. They had him handcuffed in the back of their car.

Unfortunately, Pisko, Drake, and Kenner had gotten to Brown, too. They had administered what some cops call a tune-up, while others refer to it as a tattoo job, behavior modification, a number, or an attitude adjustment. In short, they had beaten the living shit out of him.

"You want a shot at him, too, Kathy?" Drake belched as I stepped from my car. I had to turn my face away from him. He smelled as if he had spent the rest of his afternoon in some gin mill, sampling the wares.

"No," I said. "Leave him alone already, willya? I just want my gun back."

Drake grunted. He and Pisko shuffled back to their own vehicle.

Meanwhile, Detective Sanchez got into the back of his car along with his partner. Together, the two of them spoke quietly with Stanley Brown for several minutes, explaining to him that he had just unwittingly ripped off an undercover cop, an extremely foolhardy act that would bring him a world of misery—and worse, if he chose not to cooperate. A moment later, Ray stepped back out again.

"Wait for us here, Kathy," Ray told me. "Don't budge."

Detective Sanchez and his partner drove off with Brown still in the back of their car. Within a matter of minutes, they were back again. This time, Detective Sanchez got out of his car and walked back over to me.

"Open your hand," he told me. I did.

With that, he handed me back my missing gun. It had been in Brown's mailbox.

Later, when I called my office and told Lieutenant Ballner what had happened, the first words out of his mouth were "You okay?" followed by "I'm comin' up there."

Ballner put me on the phone with Chief Patton, the commanding officer of the Narcotics Division. And then came the question I had been bracing for. And dreading. "Where the hell was your backup team, Officer?"

I thought a moment, remembering the black uniformed cop's advice to me, and what my answer could mean to my career. It was sound advice, I knew, and intended to protect me. So when I answered the chief, I lied, "We got separated briefly, but subsequent to the rip-off they assisted in the apprehension."

"I see," said the chief.

Apparently, my response was sufficiently ambiguous to allay any suspicion about the less-than-stellar field team of Drake, Pisko, and Kenner. I had covered for them, gotten them off the hook. And, in so doing, I had made my first politically savvy decision about how to get along in the Police Department. But I sure as hell didn't feel good about it.

Not only had the field team escaped getting nailed for disappearing in the middle of a buy operation and nearly getting me killed. These three cheeseballs would actually end up getting the credit for the arrest of Stanley Brown.

And, on top of everything else, they would get a commendation for heroism.

That night, after my wounds were treated at the hospital and I went back home to Queens, I slept fitfully, tossing and turning and reliving the whole nightmarish event in my dreams. It was nothing short of a miracle that both guns had failed to fire and I had come through it alive.

Early the next morning, I was awakened by my mom, who said that Chief Patton was on the phone.

"Yeah, Chief," I said, after my mom handed me the receiver.

"We need you to be down at the Undercover Unit by ten a.m.," Chief Patton said.

"What's up?"

"We'll explain it when you get here." Then, somewhat mysteriously, he added, "Wear a nice dress, Kathy. And bring a wig and dark glasses."

"Sure thing, Chief," I said, wondering why the need for all these elaborate stage props.

Trying to get dressed that morning was agony. Because I had been wearing a brand-new shirt with superstiff fabric, the knife wound to my shoulder had done minimal damage. But my head and neck hurt like a son of a bitch. My ribs ached. My ankle looked like a swollen grapefruit. My elbow throbbed. The fingers on one hand were sore as hell. And so many black-and-blue marks had cropped up on my thighs, legs, and arms that I looked like a dalmatian.

At the Undercover Unit, Chief Patton, a tall man with a Torquemada-like reputation for crucifying cops for the slightest malfeasance, was waiting for me. He asked me to step into his private office. Once I did, he closed the door so that the two of us were alone.

"Let me see your wound," he demanded.

"Unzip the back of my dress," I said. Once he did, he was able to see the bandage that covered my sliced-up shoulder, along with the ugly mosaic of black-and-blue bruises.

Just as he began to zip my dress back up again, the door opened. Unaware that the two of us were inside, one of the other undercover guys popped his head in.

"Whoops!" he said upon catching sight of my half-opened dress and the startled chief with my unlatched zipper in his hand. "Sorry to interrupt." He did a quick U-turn and closed the door again.

For a second, the chief and I just looked at each other. Then we both burst into laughter. "Caught in the act," the chief joked.

Shortly after, we drove several blocks across lower Manhattan to Police Headquarters. Inside the commissioner's office, I walked past all the big oak desks and the heavy wood moldings into a high-ceilinged conference room. Inside the room were Chief of Detectives Al Seedman, Chief Inspector Mike Codd, Deputy Commissioner for Public Information Robert Daley, and a bunch of other department muckety-mucks.

Also in the room were Pisko, Drake, and Kenner, my less-than-illustrious backup team. The Three Stooges of the Four-One, grinning like chimpanzees.

Then, another door opened, and a dapper, white-haired gentleman entered the room. He walked over to me and shook my hand. "Good work, Kathy," said Police Commissioner Patrick V. Murphy. Fair, balding, and round-faced, the commissioner was known around headquarters as Mr. Perdue because of the uncanny resemblance he bore to Frank Perdue, the chicken magnate.

Deputy Commissioner Daley told me to put on my sunglasses and my brown wig. Then I was handed a gauzy, pale blue veil, which I draped mummylike around my face and right over the top of my sunglasses. With all my props in place, I looked like Claude Rains in *The Invisible Man*.

We all took seats along the side of the conference table. The reporters and photographers were ushered inside. Commissioner Murphy explained to the press that I was wearing this disguise because I was an undercover cop and he did not want to expose my face to the public.

He went on to describe the drug-buy operation that had taken me to that grim, trash-filled alley in the South Bronx. I sketched in the details of how I was assaulted, robbed, and nearly killed by the three drug dealers. My backup team was introduced to the press. "Heroes," one and all. Not a word was uttered about their shameful and highly suspect disappearing act. Nor about my stolen gun.

One of the reporters asked me how I felt when Stanley Brown placed the two guns to my head and pulled the triggers.

"Terrified," I answered.

Someone else wondered how I felt about being a policewoman.

"Greatest job in the world," I replied.

Mayor Lindsay had appointed Commissioner Murphy nearly a year earlier, in October of 1970, and given him a broad mandate to clean up the Police Department. With tales of police graft and corruption flowing out of the Knapp Commission and into the city's newspapers almost daily and the stench of negative publicity spreading throughout the entire department, the commissioner had been searching hungrily, desperately, for something that would cast the department in a positive light. The heroic actions of a female undercover cop who had survived a near-fatal assault by three hardened drug dealers provided the perfect opportunity.

The commissioner said he had an announcement to make. With that, he pulled out a gold shield and pinned it to my dress.

"Congratulations, Detective," the commissioner said.

Later that day, back in the offices of the Undercover Unit, Lieutenant Ballner brought me back down to earth.

In typically gruff, brusque Ballnerese, he grunted, "Awright, so now you're a detective. Big deal. Now get back to work. And don't be futzin' around."

CHAPTER TWO

Working undercover was hardly a waltz through the posies.

The hours were grueling. The neighborhoods I frequented were hell-holes. Half the time, my dinner would consist of nothing more than an orange or a banana because, in the kinds of sinkholes where I would make my buys, I didn't dare eat anything if I couldn't peel it. More worrisome than the indigenous cuisine, however, was that I was constantly in danger. Drugs routinely invited assaults, robberies, rapes, and murders. Since I was tiny and female and nobody knew I was a cop, I could easily wind up a victim. What's more, as I had just learned the hard way, if I did go down, nobody would lift a pinkie to help me. Because of the way I looked and what I appeared to be doing, "the street" would step right over my body.

Assuming I must be a junkie or a hooker because of the way I dressed (long pigtails, blue-tinted John Lennon sunglasses, Janis Joplin hat, love beads, knee-high Indian mukluks) and acted (slurring my words and nodding off as if I were strung out on heroin), managers and waiters used to hustle me out of restaurants before I could even finish my meal. While I was waiting on street corners for my backup team or my informant, skeevy-looking greasers would sidle up to me and propose a quick, back-alley fuck. So many times did winos, junkies, and loonies rush up and kiss me on the lips that I took to carrying around an emergency bottle of Listerine in my purse to facilitate rapid-response gargling. Fearful of contracting tuberculosis, I eventually took to wearing a coat with a big floppy hood attached. By pulling the drawstrings tight on the hood, I could keep enough of the fabric in place over my mouth to discourage amorous and potentially infectious suitors.

Lots of times, these same street suitors would pull a pint of cheap booze out of their pocket and offer me a swig. In situations where I did actually have to suck down hard liquor to keep up the appearance of being a party animal, I would dash around a corner or into a nearby ladies' room, jam my fingers all the way down my throat, and make myself throw up before the liquor I had just swallowed could pass into my bloodstream. The alternative—to allow myself to get intoxicated and let my guard down—was just too damned risky.

When I was on the street, even the supposed good guys, the uniformed cops, thought I was a bad guy. On more than one occasion, they busted me while I was in the middle of making a drug buy, and since I wanted to protect my cover, I made it a point to give them plenty of street lip during the arrest, which usually provoked them into slapping me around and roughing me up pretty good while putting the cuffs on me.

The stress of the job was toxic. Sometimes, I would wake up scared and crying in the middle of the night because I had nightmares about being held down by one guy while another one jabbed me with a hypodermic needle full of heroin as the rest of their buddies got ready to gangbang me. And down the line, I knew that all this stress would take its toll. It's no secret that every cop who's ever worked undercover has something wrong with him—stomach problems, ulcers, colitis, nervous tics, irregular heartbeat, hyper personality, paranoia, Napoleonic complex, take your pick.

Nevertheless, I felt more motivated working undercover than ever before. I was a lot more productive in this job than when I was a civilian, stuck in some dreary office, shuffling papers, sharpening pencils, and watching the clock. For the first time, I was accomplishing something worthwhile. Veteran undercover cops who'd been at it a lot longer than me used to say that taking one drug dealer off the street was about as effective as picking one grain of sand off the beach. But I was young, gung ho, and still too innocent to be jaded. I felt I was helping kids whose lives could be destroyed by the ravages of junk. Yeah, yeah, yeah, I know, this all sounds holier-than-thou, maybe a little phony even, but God's honest truth, that's the way I felt about it all. When I saw firsthand what drugs could do to people—the scab-covered young boys loitering on street corners and selling their bodies to chicken hawks to raise cash for their dope, the zonked-out parents who turned their twelve- and thirteen-year-old children into prostitutes in order to feed their own drug habits, the gaunt, malnourished infants left lying inside cribs with mosquito netting over the tops so the rats couldn't gnaw on them while their mommies and daddies were in the next room shooting up—I, too, got religion.

To be perfectly honest, a big part of me also got off on the danger. Working undercover, walking the thin line, making successful buys—fooling the fools, as we used to call it—these were the things that gave me my highs.

Meanwhile, the Undercover Unit turned out to be my home away from home. One big happy family.

Squat, square-jawed, and gruff, Lieutenant Ballner was the boss. The lieutenant looked and sounded like a bulldog. He also was a devout Catholic, and religion was profoundly important to him in all aspects of his life and work. In preparation for my first meeting with Lieutenant Ballner, another undercover cop who had been at the Academy with me, Danny Rizzo, warned me to show real sensitivity to the lieutenant's deep-seated religious convictions. My reaction could determine whether he would let me stay in the squad, Danny advised.

On my first day, Lieutenant Ballner summoned me into his private office and closed the door behind us. Then he looked me up and down, as though he were trying to decide whether I should even be here or if it was all just one colossal mistake.

Squinching up his eyes, the lieutenant gestured to the chair on the other side of his desk. "Have a seat, Conlon," he growled, addressing me by my maiden name.

I sat down.

Lieutenant Ballner studied me for a couple of moments. Then he scowled. Here in his office sat this 5' 1½", 95-pound pip-squeak, saying she wanted to be an undercover cop. Somebody downtown had a piss-poor sense of humor, he must have been telling himself. Suddenly, he swiveled halfway around in his chair, glancing up at the wall behind him. "See that picture?" he asked me.

I looked up over his head at the framed painting. It was a landscape. Or rather, a skyscape. Big, billowing, white clouds floating serenely against a cobalt blue sky.

"Yes, sir," I replied.

Lieutenant Ballner narrowed his eyes into little slits. "Tell me something, Conlon. Whaddya see when you look at that picture?"

I moved my head slightly to one side, then back to the other side, until I could make out the ethereal shimmering image that gradually emerged through the clouds.

"Why, Lieutenant, it's . . . it's . . . it's . . . it's the face of Our Lord, Jesus Christ."

A big, broad grin broke across Lieutenant Ballner's leathery, bulldog countenance. He grunted. Stood up. And thrust a hamlike hand across the desk at me. "You're okay, Conlon. Welcome aboard. Go back outside and we'll get you settled in."

"Thank you, Loo. Happy to be here."

As I left Ballner's office, I spotted my pal Danny Rizzo, sitting at one of the two desks in the office. He shot me a quizzical look. I gave him a thumbs-up. The "cloud" test had gone down exactly as Danny had predicted it would. And, happily, I had passed with flying (and heavenly) colors.

Lieutenant Ballner turned out to be the quintessential father figure. Irascible. Grumpy. Abrupt. And, boy oh boy, could he smother you with his religious devotion. But he sure loved us. And he was genuinely proud of us. He told us what we were doing was important. He always looked for reasons to praise us and pat us on the back. And he took the most incredible care of each one of us, day in and day out. He was never too busy to come up to one of us, put one meaty paw around a shoulder, and quietly ask, "So howya doin' out there, kid? Everything okay? Havin' any problems? Anything I can do to help ya?"

When one of the other cops in the unit, Donnie Doyle, did not immediately get an eagerly anticipated promotion to detective and fell into a funk, it was Lieutenant Ballner who took the initiative to console him. Interrupting his paperwork in the middle of the day, Ballner came up to Donnie and barked, "C'mon, kid, we're goin' out!" With that, the lieutenant grabbed both Donnie and me by the arms and dragged us around the corner to his favorite longshoremen's bar. Once inside, the lieutenant put a consoling arm around Doyle and told him, "Aw, don't worry, Donnie, you'll get it next time." Then the lieutenant started ordering rounds of hard liquor and got Donnie and me shit-faced drunk.

Good old Lieutenant Ballner. He patted us on the back when we did good, scolded us when we did bad, and cried with us when we were in pain. Just as any real dad would.

Often, when you were out in the middle of nowhere, trying to con some seriously dangerous characters into believing you were a bona fide drug user, you'd suddenly catch sight of Lieutenant Ballner turning the corner, wearing one of his goofy old tam-o'-shanters, jauntily sauntering down the sidewalk just behind you and whistling cheerily, as though he hadn't a care in the world. He'd never make eye contact with you, of course, but you knew right away that he was out there to keep an eye on you and make certain you didn't get hurt. Later, when you had to go to court and testify on your case, Lieutenant Ballner would be sitting front and center in the courtroom gallery to make eye contact with you and provide moral support as you took the witness stand. If you had a problem with your field team, he'd be the first one to pick up the phone and give 'em hell. He worried endlessly about his undercovers and gave each of us his home telephone number so we could call him at any hour of the day or night. Though it's been more than three decades since we all worked undercover, to this day every cop who served under Ballner remembers that home telephone number by heart.

Once a week, Lieutenant Ballner would summon all the undercovers into his office for a no-holds-barred heart-to-heart. At these meetings, he'd make each of us talk about what had happened to us on the street. Something funny? Something scary? Something confusing? Something troubling? On several occasions, the undercovers or their field-team backups were involved in shoot-outs. Lieutenant Ballner insisted that we talk about those, too. What did we feel after it had happened to one of us? And what did the rest of us feel on hearing about our comrades' close calls? What Ballner knew, and the rest of us had to learn, was that it was okay to talk about being afraid. In fact, it was damn good to talk about being afraid. Because the guy next to you was probably just as afraid as you were. From his personal experience, the lieutenant knew what it was like to wrestle with these feelings—along with what it was like to see another cop die. Years earlier, when he'd been working as a detective, Lieutenant Ballner and his partner had chased a bank robber. During the chase, they'd become separated, and the partner had been gunned down and killed. And Lieutenant Ballner had been forced to live with that awful memory for the rest of his career. So, by holding these group meetings with the undercovers and forcing us to talk about our deepest feelings and our innermost fears, Lieutenant Ballner was doing something extremely beneficial for the rest of us, something cathartic, even therapeutic. Though he was not a trained psychologist, this guy knew how to deal with "stress" and "trauma" before the words were even invented.

At these meetings, the lieutenant's advice to us was simple but invaluable. Live a clean life. Don't go bouncing around in our off hours in places that were frequented by known criminals, especially places where drugs might be found. Always be prepared to bump into a defendant on the street. Be truthful about our cases and report back everything that happened, no matter how seemingly insignificant the details. Treat every case as if that were the one that would go to trial, for that way we could never go wrong. And if something did go wrong, never, ever, try to cover it up. Call him immediately and give him the straight story. At the end of these sessions, the lieutenant would close with words of praise for our bravery and dedication, a blessing for our safety, and the cautionary message that "the only thing certain about under-cover work is the uncertainty."

Lieutenant Ballner's concern for us did not end with the job. If he sensed that you were having a rough time in your personal life, trouble at home with the family, a spouse, or one of your kids, he'd make you come with him to noon mass for a little spiritual tune-up. Didn't matter whether you were Catholic, Protestant, or Jewish, you'd still end up get-ting dragged to mass. Then he'd bring you over to the local greasy spoon and warm you up with a big bowl of hot soup. Once a year, the lieu-tenant would take all the male undercovers away for the weekend on a spiritual retreat. At our annual undercover dinner-dances, he would al-ways play host and master of ceremonies. And on Thanksgiving morn-ing, he would greet all the cops who were stuck working that day with bottles of champagne and a buffet breakfast. Then, later in the day, he would send us home early to our families, telling us to remain on standby.

Sometimes, just for fun, we used to pull Lieutenant Ballner's leg. At our weekly meetings, we would make up wild, off-the-wall stories about our experiences on the street. The lieutenant would roll up his eyes and sigh, "Lord have mercy, they're at it again." The next minute, we'd sit cross-legged on the floor—there were never enough chairs in the room—and start nodding off like stoned-out junkies.

Seeing us strung out, the lieutenant would grow highly agitated. "Whatsamatter with you!" he'd suddenly blurt out.

Drooling and slobbering, we'd answer, "Nuttin', Loo," then keel over unconscious.

Not realizing that it was just an act, the lieutenant would throw a shit-fit. "Stop that!" he'd shout. "Get up! Get up! Get up!" Finally, when he caught on that it was just a joke, he would chastise us, "Aw, don't be futzin' around."

Danny Rizzo and I were the worst of the pranksters. Knowing of Lieutenant Ballner's deeply rooted religious convictions, we loved to tease him by genuflecting whenever we passed in front of his desk. In exasperation, the lieutenant would repeatedly kiss the miraculous-medal ring he wore on his pinkie, as though hoping for some kind of divine guidance to help him deal with his unruly undercovers.

Because of his religious devotion and his almost prudish propriety when it came to sex, Lieutenant Ballner would also go nuts whenever any of us came back with stories of lewd or suggestive behavior out on the street. Now, I myself was constantly getting into scrapes where drugged-up characters would be buck naked or half-dressed and try to get into my drawers or offer me money to drop my drawers for their buddies. (Hey, as the expression goes, if you're gonna lie down with pigs, you better expect to get some pigshit on you, right?) And, in time, I simply came to expect it. But the lieutenant didn't want to know about it.

Once, when I told the lieutenant that I had made a buy in an apartment where a bunch of guys were wearing only T-shirts, no underpants, he went bonkers.

"Don't tell me these things!" he shouted. "I don't wanna hear this!"

On another occasion, as he read aloud from one of my DD-5 reports, he came across a detailed description I had written of a suspect who had sold drugs to me.

"Whaddya mean, this guy had a hernia?" he asked.

"The guy had a hernia," I answered. "He had a scar from surgery."

"How do you know?"

"Well . . . read on, Loo."

The lieutenant looked down again at my report. And then he nearly rocketed through the roof. "He was naked? He was naked! Whaddya mean, he was naked!"

"Well, Loo, he answered the door, he had a towel on, he invited me inside, and then he took the towel off."

"That's it! That does it! You're not goin' back there!" he shouted.

"But, Loo, I gotta go back to make a second buy."

"You're not goin' back there!" he thundered. "Jesus, Mary, and Joseph! This guy was naked! I don't want you in places like that!"

The irony of the lieutenant's prudish outrage was that, as undercovers, we were all in the business of purchasing mind-blowing, life-destroying drugs, the vilest, most self-destructive, most sinful activity I can imagine. Yet that aspect of our assignment was accepted as no big deal, more or less routine. But if somebody had his clothes off when we made the buy, well, that would send Lieutenant Ballner straight to the moon.

My first partner in the Undercover Unit was Dennis Roberts. He was also my mentor and my training instructor.

Now Dennis could have been the poster boy for the Undercover Unit. He was the epitome of a street skell. Long, scraggly, dirty-blond hair. Reddish-blond beard. Leathery, weather-burnished skin. Button-down shirt with both sleeves ripped out at the armpits. Scuffed black chino pants. Muddy, beat-up shoes that had been worn far past their prime. So convincing was his ratty appearance that the other tenants of his apartment building, unaware that he was an undercover cop, actually took up a petition to get him evicted. Similarly, whenever he drove over to my house to pick me up or drop me off, my mother and our neighbors would watch aghast and shiver.

Dennis drove a blue Volkswagen Beetle with psychedelic flowers painted all over the hood and trunk, a nice little touch that added immeasurably to his image as a spaced-out hippie drug user. The car was a rolling garbage bin. In the glove compartment he had stashed a collection of porno magazines. The backseat contained every single styrofoam coffee cup Dennis had ever drunk out of while on a stakeout. Any druggie who ever got a gander at this heap would have to conclude that the owner must be a true soul mate—that is, a fellow drug user, scuzzball, and skell.

On the day I was to go out in the field for the first time, I showed up for work nervous but eager, dressed in a simple skirt, pressed cotton blouse, white sweater, nylon stockings, and flat shoes. I had been to the beauty parlor earlier in the week, so my hair was neatly cut and my nails were nicely manicured. My three-inch Smith & Wesson revolver was tucked safely out of sight, in the pocket of my sweater.

Dennis came into the office a few minutes later. As usual, he looked like an unmade bed. Once he got a gander at me, he gave me a fish-eyed look and sighed. Crooking his finger, he signaled me to follow him downstairs, which I did. Out on the sidewalk, Dennis stopped and turned to face me. "Don't move," he said.

Was there a spider on my shoulder? A wasp? I stood frozen in place as he circled around me, sizing me up like a Greek statue at the Metropolitan Museum of Art, wondering what in the world was about to happen next.

"Okay, let's pretty you up." And then he gave me his version of what you might call the Extreme Makeover.

First, he dropped to his knees and plunged both hands into the muck in the gutter. Then, popping back up again, he smeared his dirty hands back and forth across my cheeks and forehead, giving my face a coating of oozing, dripping sludge. Then he mussed up my hair, making sure to muddy up my scalp.

"What the . . . !" I protested.

Dennis put a finger to his lips to silence me. He studied me carefully from several angles. A work in progress, he decided, but not quite completed. "Better. But not quite right."

So he grabbed the waistband of my skirt and rolled it down into a tight tube around my middle, exposing my bare tummy. Then he yanked the rest of my blouse out of my skirt and tied the ends into a big knot over my bra, near my breastbone.

"Hey!" I barked. "Whaddya think you're doing!"

Finally, Dennis reached down with his filthy fingernails and put several ugly runs in my nylon stockings. Brushing the mud off his hands, he gave me an admiring look, the artist with his creation, pleased as punch with his stylings. "Now we'll take you back upstairs, wipe that lipstick off, clip those nails, and you'll be ready to roll."

"But . . ."

"Listen, kid, you're new at this. Which means that, out on the street, you're not ready to talk the part. So, if you can't talk the part, at least look the part."

He was right, of course. But I felt humiliated. "How come I'm dirty and you're not?" I demanded.

Dennis grinned. "Cause, you're the student. And I'm the teacher."

Once we went out on the street, I quickly realized how much I had to learn. The first time I made a buy on my own was almost the last time. I was working under Dennis's watchful eye, looking to score some marijuana from a local dealer. But as the two of us talked turkey, I stuttered and stammered, "Uh . . . um . . . one . . . how much?"

"A nickle," the dealer muttered.

So naturally I reached into my pocket and came up with a five-cent piece. I handed it to the dealer, feeling pretty damned proud of myself for getting the goods so cheap.

The dealer's eyes widened. "Whaddya, some kinda wiseass? That's five bucks worth, sister, so get it up!"

"Oh," I gulped, suddenly remembering Dennis's admonition about thinking fast on your feet, "I was only joking. Here . . ."

I handed him $5. In return, he gave me the dope. But he wasn't smiling.

Next morning in the squad room, Dennis jumped up on top of one of the metal desks and gathered all the other undercovers around him.

"Quiet down, quiet down. I got an important announcement to make," he said solemnly.

The room went silent as all the cops in the unit took positions around his desk, eager to hear what Dennis had to say. Dennis waited a moment. He looked down at his notes. Then he began:

"I wish to make the following report. Last night, at nineteen fifteen hours, Policewoman Kathleen Conlon of the Undercover Unit lost her cherry."

I turned red as a beet as everyone around me burst into whoops, whistles, cheers, and applause.

Over the weeks to come, as I slowly eased into more challenging and dangerous buy operations, Dennis taught me the real hard-core tricks of the trade. The biggest challenge was how to convince a dealer that you were a user of drugs without actually snorting, injecting, or ingesting them. Dennis encouraged me to keep nodding off and slurring my speech when I was making my buys, as though I were high on heroin. And to wear long-sleeved blouses in the heat of summer to cover up my arms and conceal what everyone on the street would assume were my track marks. And to create fake needle marks by pricking the flesh on my inner arms with bobby pins and applying theatrical makeup to simulate the open sores and bruises.

Sometimes, Dennis warned me, I would end up in situations where everybody around me would be using drugs, and the pressure to join in would simply be too great to sidestep. To weasel out would immediately raise suspicions that I might be "the man" or working for the man. In those instances, Dennis explained, it might be necessary to resort to a little sleight of hand.

For example, Dennis said, if people were passing around a joint, I should take a long drag on my regular cigarette and hold the smoke in my mouth. When the lit joint came around to me, I could then put it to my lips and exhale my ordinary cigarette smoke around it, making the tip of the joint glow red-hot. Too stoned to realize otherwise, the other potheads in the circle would assume that I, too, had just taken a toke.

Dennis also showed me how to convince people I was snorting cocaine. If everyone around me was snorting coke and the others wanted me to join in, I was to dip a fingertip into the powder and quickly bring it up to my nose. But, at the last second, I would quickly switch fingers, diverting my coke-dipped fingertip safely to one side while sticking a clean, undipped fingertip up to my nostril. A couple of loud snorts, a long, slow exaggerated sigh of ecstasy, and the others would surely assume that I had just gotten off, too.

Finally, Dennis showed me how to sweet-talk heroin users. If someone offered me "a taste," I could pull the old switcheroo at the last second before sticking my finger into my mouth. If some guy handed me a set of works to get off right then and there—hypodermic needle, spoon, bottle cap, etc.—I was to tell him that I only had a "chippie." That meant I only snorted the stuff, but did not mainline it. Other times, Dennis said, I could worm my way out of giving a firsthand demonstration by claiming that I only skin-popped heroin rather than mainlined it. If the dealer wanted me to get off in front of him, I could then say I only skin-popped in my hip or my thigh, then add with self-righteous modesty, "And I ain't about to drop my drawers for you, my man!"

The trickiest challenge, Dennis warned, would be one in which I was trying to buy from a woman heroin dealer. Women tended to be more suspicious than men. They always asked more questions: Who's the stuff for? How much do you use? Where are your tracks? Oh, you skin-pop, eh? Well, why don't we go into the ladies' room together, and we can skin-pop there. . . .With a woman, I could not claim modesty about my body as an excuse for not skin-popping in front of her. So with women, Dennis advised me to say that I was just getting over hepatitis, and I didn't want to chance fooling around with somebody else's works or drug paraphernalia. Or that did I not use the stuff myself—but, rather, that I was buying it for my "old man," who was laid up at home and needed a fix real bad, so I had better make my purchase and get my butt back home in a hurry.

Dennis also taught me:

How to "flake" or "baptize" a defendant by planting drugs on him so you could then lock him up for possession.

How to give an informant a "play," allowing him to get a free drug fix in return for fingering a dealer or giving you an introduction to a dealer.

How to "step on" drugs, cutting them or diluting them so they could be repackaged and resold to even more customers.

How to "spike" a buy, mixing a drug with potentially lethal doses of strychnine or arsenic or lye.

How to "skim" drugs or drug money after a bust, holding some back for your own personal purposes rather than officially vouchering them with the Police Department.

How to "pad" a buy, inflating the actual amount when you filled out your report (e.g., you pay $10 for the drugs, you tell the department you paid $15, then you pocket the difference).

All of these things were flagrantly illegal. Felonies, in fact. When I asked Dennis why in the world he was showing them to me, he smiled. "Because, Conlon, if you are ever stupid enough to try them, you'll go directly to jail."

That set me straight in a real hurry.

Some of the other cops in the Undercover Unit also took me under their wing. Dorothy Richardson, my classmate and close friend from the Academy, would often have serious, heart-to-heart talks with me about the perils of working the streets. When Dorothy decided to convert to Catholicism, a bunch of us accompanied her uptown to the church, where two of the other undercovers stood by her side and acted as her godmother and godfather during the baptism ceremony. Another female in the unit, Lacey Mangold, became the object of the ardent affections of the cook at the local diner near the undercover office. Whenever we'd come in for lunch, the cook, a big, fat guy who wore a rolled-up sailor's hat and a long, white, greasy apron, would swoon over Lacey. "Honey, I'm gonna make you something special," he'd always promise her. Then he would serve her up a plate of food with all the mashed potatoes and steamed carrots carefully arranged in the form of a giant phallic symbol.

Danny Rizzo, my other buddy from the Academy, and I would not only discuss the job, cross-referencing our cases and our informants, but would also confide in each other about what was happening in our personal lives. At our annual undercover dinner-dances, Danny would always play his guitar as part of the evening's entertainment. Tad Noonan used to treat me like a kid sister, letting me ride behind him on the back of his humongous motorcycle. Howie Geiss, a frizzy-haired undercover who resembled that kid Epstein from the old TV series *Welcome Back, Kotter,* was the hippie son who regularly freaked out everyone else in the family. It was Howie who convinced a lot of the other male undercovers to get their ears pierced so that they could wear earrings and look less conspicuous when they worked the downtown clubs. Unfortunately, a lot of the guys got the wrong ear pierced, an unfortunate gaffe that resulted in many of them being propositioned by gay men. Cruising through one club in hopes of making some drug buys, Howie himself, to his great chagrin, got kissed on the lips by one guy. He returned to the office completely distraught. "Do I look like I should be kissed by a guy?" he asked the rest of us with dismay. "Do I look lovable?"

And, finally, there was Billy Hannibal, who could have been my wild and wacky kid brother. Billy was a natural jokester, a wild man with a real penchant for the absurd. Blond, solidly built, and usually camou- flaged in an army jacket and jeans, Billy loved to spice up our street buys by pushing the edge of the envelope. For example, if I was talking to him on a street corner, he might suddenly pretend to go mute and start re- sponding to me in a wildly gesticulating sign language that made ab- solutely no sense at all. Or, if I was making a buy, he'd sneak up behind me and start making weird, goofy faces over my shoulder at the drug dealer—crossing his eyes, pulling his lips apart, baring his teeth, or sim- ulating devil's horns atop his head with his index fingers. Billy's attitude was that these antics could only serve to allay any suspicions that he might be an undercover cop, since no cop in his right mind would ever behave like this. Sure enough, most of the drug dealers thought he must be either stoned . . . or barking mad.

Sometimes, however, Billy used to really bug me with his antics. So much so that, at one point, I decided I was going to get even with him. Which I managed to do on the day we were working an outdoor carnival together in Queens, looking to make drug buys from some teenagers. As we meandered through the crowds, with me several steps ahead of Billy, a young woman whirled around suddenly and gave Billy a dirty look. Ever the charmer with the ladies, Billy couldn't figure out why. So, as- suming he must have bumped into her by accident, he apologized pro- fusely and kept on walking. Farther ahead, another young woman turned around and gave Billy a nasty shove. Now Billy was really per- plexed. This time, he knew he hadn't bumped into her. He hadn't even touched her. Nor had he said anything to her. So why in the world was she having this hostile reaction to him? Badly shaken, he picked up his pace. When a third woman turned around, cursed him out, and nearly took a swing at him, Billy begin to think he was losing his mind. What the hell was going on here, anyway?

So that's when I let the cat outta the bag and confessed that I had furtively been smacking these gals on their ass as I passed them, all to make them think it was him. "You want to play?" I said to him. "Well, two can play at this game just as well as one."

With Billy, I eventually got into insane contests, such as which of us could buy from the Ugliest Drug Dealer or the Smelliest Drug Dealer or the Oldest Drug Dealer or the Craziest Drug Dealer. All the undercovers used to dream up these grotesque little competitions to make the job more interesting and keep us on our toes. (Dennis Roberts, my mentor, became the hands-down winner in the Most Pathetic Drug Dealer category when he purchased drugs from a pregnant woman with only one leg.)

Usually, Billy and I would initiate our little matches to break up the boredom. But sometimes we'd do it to get even with a field team that had done something to piss us off. For example, one field team I worked with made an utterly outrageous promise to one of my informants without my knowledge. Now field teams would often reward informants by "deputizing" them, giving them tin sheriff's shields purchased from the five-and-dime or official-looking (and utterly worthless) scrolls or certificates acknowledging their assistance to the police. But this particular team told my informant that the minute he provided me with my thirty-fifth buy— that is, the thirty-fifth dealer from whom I could successfully purchase drugs and set up to be arrested—he was immediately entitled to an all-expenses-paid weekend at the Concord Hotel in the Catskills . . . with me as his romantic companion!

Field teams would promise informants the sun, the earth, the moon, and the rest of the solar system to get them to cooperate and give up drug dealers. But when I found out that this team had offered me up as bedroom bounty to some seventeen-year-old drug-using dirtbag, without indulging in the minor courtesy of informing me, I decided I had to teach them a little lesson.

Now, usually after an undercover made a drug buy, the undercover would never make the actual arrest. The field-team guys would handle that part of the job so that the undercover would not have to reveal his/her identity until—and unless—the case went to trial. After the initial arrest, the booking and arraignment could be quite time-consuming, taking seventeen, eighteen, nineteen hours or more. And since the arresting field-team officers weren't allowed to take their eyes off their suspect while they fingerprinted, photographed, and arraigned him, they would pretty much have to live with the guy for however many hours this might take. With a defendant who was neatly dressed and practiced some modicum of personal hygiene, this was not terribly onerous. What's more, it usually resulted in a hefty overtime check for the waiting officers.

But with a defendant who never troubled to bathe—well, now you're talking about a horse of a different color. Or, should I say, odor.

So, naturally, after I found out about my field team palming me off to an informant to be his Concord concubine, I retaliated by buying drugs from some old geezer who was on dialysis, reeked of cheap wine, hadn't used soap or water in about five years, had open, running sores all over his body, and stank to high heaven. And, to top everything off, under his filthy shirt he wore a Superman T-shirt! Nineteen hours in court with this overripe coot, and the field team was ready to pass out. But payback, as they say, is a bitch. Meanwhile, the other undercovers readily conceded that I was the uncontested winner in this category of our bizarre drug-buy competitions.

In time, Billy Hannibal and I dreamed up even more outrageous contests. For example, who would be the first one to make a drug buy while holding an evidence envelope from the city's Property Clerk's Office in one hand. (The Property Clerk's Office was where all the cops would go to voucher cash and drugs after they'd made a buy or an arrest.) After that, it was who could make a drug buy while holding an official New York City Police Department envelope in one hand. Then, it was who could make a buy while actually holding a Police Department radio in one hand. And finally . . . who could make a buy with an actual police shield dangling from his or her neck. If some drug dealer asked where you got it, you'd lie and say you stole it off some cop. Or, in my case, that I had swiped it from my unsuspecting cop boyfriend.

By pulling stunts like these, we were taking real risks, no doubt about it. And, sometimes, they were foolish risks, carried out in response to a silly dare. On the other hand, by conducting our madcap little contests we found a way to spice up our buys, keep our instincts sharp, and hone our skills at conning drug dealers. After all, that was the name of the game.

No doubt about it, working undercover was a kick. The other cops were terrific, and I came to love them all. For all his suffocating religious fervor, Lieutenant Ballner watched over me like a stern but doting father. Dennis and Tad were my protective big brothers. Howie and

Billy were my younger, wackier kid brothers. Dorothy and Lacey were my older sisters.

Put 'em all together, and they became my family. Real family.

The family I never had as a kid.

The family I so desperately longed for.

CHAPTER THREE

How she did it, I'll never know. The men in her life were hardly what you'd call heroes or protectors. They were stingy with money, stingier with their affections, and prone to disappearing frequently.

Sent off to live with the nuns in a Boston convent when she was nine years old, my mother, Dorothy Conlon, returned to New York at age sixteen, only to find that nobody in her own family wanted her. By this time, her mother—my grandmother—had remarried and started a second family in the Bronx, complete with a newborn child. Another daughter, my mother's sister, was also living there, so there was no room left for my mother in that tiny Bronx apartment. At the behest of my grandmother, my mother was sent away from New York in 1941 to live with her father in North Carolina.

Her father, my grandfather, was a cantankerous old goat. Born in Holland, he came to America during the First World War. He enlisted in the U.S. Army and served with the cavalry in Panama, assigned to the mule division. After the war, he and his wife, whose family was from Germany, divorced. Then my grandfather remarried and settled in Asheville, North Carolina, where he made his living as a beer-garden owner, pool-hall operator, and wooden-barrel maker. During the Second World War, he worked in a factory that manufactured parachutes for the U.S. Army. He also farmed and raised chickens. (In his senior years, Grandpa became a real eccentric. Once, when he came to stay with me at my house in Queens, he became so impatient when he found the bathroom being used by another family member that he walked into my bedroom, threw open the window, stuck his bare ass halfway out, and moved his bowels right on top of my tulip bed. I promptly kicked him out of my house and packed him off to stay with his sister in Brooklyn.)

Shortly after my mother came to live with him, my grandfather made her take a job as governess at the magnificent Biltmore Estate, built by George W. Vanderbilt, in the Blue Ridge Mountains of North Carolina. But bowing and scraping to rich people was not in my mother's nature, so she soon gathered up all her belongings and moved back to New York City. For a while, she worked in the post office, sorting mail destined for our troops overseas. Later, after renting a furnished room in a cheap boardinghouse on the Upper West Side, she took a job waitressing at a local restaurant. There, she met my father, a long-haul truck driver who became one of her regular customers. A whirlwind romance followed, and they were quickly married in a civil ceremony at City Hall. My mother was sixteen years old on the day of the wedding, seventeen when she got pregnant, eighteen when she gave birth to me. After I was born, the family moved from the boardinghouse on Manhattan's Upper West Side to a more spacious apartment in the Bronx. It had a grand total of two rooms.

About my real father, there's not a whole lot to say. I do know that he was Jewish, though not terribly religious, and that he was born to parents who came to the United States from England. I also know that during the Second World War, he owned several truck cabs and drove tractor-trailers for a living. He even taught my mother to drive an eighteen-wheeler, and working side by side, the two of them used to tootle up and down the eastern seaboard delivering dry goods to stores and factories.

Most of the time, however, my father was on the road and never around. By the time I turned two, he was gone for good. Eventually, he and my mother divorced. Over the years, he would periodically reappear in our lives. But he behaved more like a pal or a big brother than a husband and father. He was known to fancy the ladies, and family gossip has it that he ended up having five or six wives in his lifetime. But being a devoted parent apparently was never part of the deal. Sad to admit, I do not remember ever receiving a single card or letter from my father that said "Dear Daughter" or "Love, Daddy."

After he left my mother and remarried, my father never told his new wife about his prior marriage to my mother. Nor did he tell his new wife about the child they had had, me. Why he kept it a secret, I never knew. Perhaps it was the shame he felt over having abandoned us; perhaps he feared that his new wife might become jealous. Whatever the reason, to this day the woman he married has no idea that her husband had a daughter named Kathy by an earlier marriage. Oddly enough, after his new marriage, my father continued to maintain a cordial relationship with my mother and me, dropping by the apartment from time to time to visit and chat over coffee, taking us for day drives in his roadster, organizing little outings or picnics. Sometimes, he would even bring his new wife along. As far as she ever knew, my mother and I were simply old family friends. My mother never revealed the secret.

Dad's new wife nearly guessed the truth anyway. Once, when she and my father accompanied us to help me buy a new car, she noticed that my father and I walked with an identical gait. "Look at that!" she exclaimed to my mother. "You'd think they were related!" As usual, Mom kept mum. Later, after I became a cop and my father spoke with great pride about my accomplishment in making it onto the force, his new wife again became suspicious. "Hmph!" she sniffed. "The way he talks about her, you'd think he was the father." Even after both my mother and father had died, I kept the truth from his new wife. There was nothing to be gained by spilling the beans. Her husband had never treated me like a daughter; I had never known him as Daddy. So what was the point of causing her grief by revealing my father's dark secret?

In 1949, my mother married Irish Jack Conlon, who owned and operated a gin mill in the Bronx. After the ceremony in City Hall, the newlyweds took me to the Statue of Liberty, where my new stepfather bought me a doll. For their honeymoon, my mother and her new husband went to visit my crazy old grandfather down in North Carolina.

Six feet tall, trimly built, with dark eyes and dark hair, John Conlon had come to this country from County Cavan, Ireland, and spoke with a brogue as thick as chowder. His bar, the Little Tavern, was at 169th Street and Third Avenue, across the street from the Rupert Beer Brewery and equidistant from two Bronx police precincts. Along with being the favorite watering hole for all the brewery workers, the tavern also drew plenty of thirsty cops who wanted to bend an elbow. But while Irish Jack Conlon was only too happy to take their cash, he absolutely detested those policemen, because back in the old days, many of New York's Finest were also New York's Greediest. Whether it was money, free drinks, free food, whatever, these lawmen were always looking for some kind of handout in return for letting Irish Jack stay in business. And Irish Jack hated them for it. He also hated the alcoholic beverage inspectors who would try to catch him in one petty violation or another, then threaten to slap him with stiff fines unless he greased their palms. One of the inspectors' favorite ploys was to sneak into the tavern's bathroom and glom the bar of soap on the sink. Then they would turn around and accuse Jack of violating the city's health code because there was no soap on the premises for customers and employees to wash their hands. Time and again they used this scam to shake him down for payoffs. But, eventually, Irish Jack would have his revenge.

The first time came when one greedy inspector dragged Jack into the bathroom and started to write him up for not having a bar of soap (which, of course, the inspector had conveniently stuffed in his pocket just a few moments earlier).

"Ah, but me soap's here, alright," Jack Conlon insisted.

"What the hell you talkin' about!" sneered the inspector. "I don't see no soap in here."

"Why, it's right there, me friend," replied Jack, pointing a long, bony finger skyward. The inspector slowly raised his eyes to see that bar of soap plain as day—nailed to the ceiling and far out of reach of the pilfering hands of thieving inspectors. Dumbfounded, the inspector stared at my stepfather. Irish Jack gave him an impish little smile, knowing that while the health code certainly did require a tavern owner to keep a bar of soap in his bathroom, it did not specify where that soap had to be placed.

Jack had his dark side, for sure, and it usually emerged after he'd had too much to drink. Which was pretty much always, since Jack was a raging alcoholic. Half the time he'd be working the bar in his Bronx tavern, he'd consume more booze than his patrons. After working the night shift, he'd come home at five in the morning, completely stinko, and go berserk. First, he'd start throwing dishes. Then, he'd start smashing the furniture. Finally, when my mother tried to calm him down, he'd start hitting her with his fists, beating her black-and-blue. Several times, I actually had to summon the police to our house to break up the fights. By the time the squad cars arrived, however, Mom had usually managed to turn the tide and was pummeling Jack senseless with one of her big frying pans.

Jack was also a miserable cheapskate. No matter how much Mom begged him, he would never give her enough money for food, clothes, utility bills, or other household necessities. He was always crying poverty (crocodile tears, as we would later learn). Many a Christmas Eve, my mother would be out until the last possible moment, scrambling to buy clothes for me with her puny savings because Jack had refused to give her enough cash for gifts. Twice when I was a little girl, I had to be hospitalized for illnesses. On both occasions, Jack whined and moaned for weeks on end that he didn't know how we would ever be able pay for the doctors. This would go on right up until the moment that the hospitals would present us with the final bills. Then, at the eleventh hour, Jack would miraculously show up at the hospital with a shopping bag full of cash.

Jack was such a skinflint that every time he would trek down the stairs into the basement of his Bronx tavern, the regulars used to joke, "Uh-oh, Conlon must be burying his money again!" Then, after his death, we found out it was no joke at all. That's exactly what Jack had been doing. For years, he'd been keeping his bankbooks in a hole he'd dug in the basement, which he'd cover up with cement. Every year, at tax time, he would break through the cement with a pickax and dig up his bankbooks to do his taxes. Then he'd stick them back in the hole and re-seal them with fresh cement.

Jack died in 1954, after a bizarre accident. While repairing the roof of his tavern, he tumbled headfirst through the skylight and broke several ribs. In the hospital where he was being treated for the injuries, the doctors discovered that he was also suffering from terminal cancer. Six weeks later, as he lay dying, he revealed to my mother his little secret about his buried bankbooks, promising that there was enough cash squirreled away in his accounts—some $60,000 to $80,000—as well as his other his secret hiding places in the tavern to take care of my mother and me for several years.

The only problem was that Jack had never bothered to change his original will, which left virtually all of his assets to his two sisters. In his naïveté, Jack honestly believed that simply by telling my mother where his precious bankbooks were hidden he had faithfully discharged his fiduciary responsibilities to his wife and stepdaughter. He did not realize that, once you make a will, you may very well have to change it. When my mother found out about the will, she hired a lawyer to contest it. The result was an ugly, seven-year court battle that pitted my mother against Jack's family, along with various shyster lawyers, and created bitterness and resentment on all sides.

The bar was losing money, so eventually my mother sold it—but at a steep loss. Sometime later, she learned that one of Jack's nephews had filched $22,000 in cash that Jack had hidden in a cigar box in the liquor closet. Undeterred, my mother pressed on with her legal challenge to the will.

One day, as my mother and I were driving across the Triborough

Bridge, riding in the big black convertible that Jack had left us, the steering wheel suddenly popped loose in my mother's hands. Somehow, she guided the car to a stop without either of us being hurled to our deaths in the East River. But when the convertible was towed to a service station, the mechanics discovered that somebody had used a file to sever the steering column. My mother always suspected it was someone in Jack's family. Later on, she learned that one of the attorneys who had been handling Jack's estate had quietly been helping himself to much of the money.

Financially speaking, Jack's death pushed us to the wall. With mounting debts, ongoing household expenses, and no steady source of income as long as Jack's will remained tied up in probate, my mother had to take a job parking cars at the old Jamaica Racetrack. I was about ten at this time, and each day when school let out, I would stay with neighbors until my mother returned home that night from her racetrack gig. At one point, the Children's Welfare Society showed up to notify us that it was investigating complaints that Dorothy Conlon was abandoning her young daughter each day and leaving her unsupervised. My mother immediately suspected that one of Jack's spiteful sisters had dropped a dime on her. Bur fearful of losing her child to the authorities, Mom quit her racetrack job to stay home and care for me, even though it meant we would be even more strapped for cash.

Our total monthly income, in the form of two Social Security checks, was less than $200. Every week we would be deluged with threatening letters and phone calls from one creditor or another, and it seemed as if my mother were always going down to the bank to try to bargain for a little more time on our mortgage payments. Her method for deciding which of the many bills we should try to pay was to throw the whole stack up in the air at once and let them flutter to the floor. The ones that landed faceup would receive her immediate attention. The others would be held over until the next month.

In the face of these hardships, my mother displayed the grit and fortitude of a pioneer woman. With indefatigable spirit and remarkable ingenuity, she performed near miracles to keep us afloat. An excellent cook, she would prepare hearty but inexpensive meals consisting of soups, stews, and casseroles that could be doctored up, watered down, and stretched out for days on end to provide us with nourishment. Meat and fish became rarities, potatoes and bread staples. To cut back on our fuel oil bills, she'd turn on the gas stove in the kitchen and cover the walls and windows in our Astoria house with heavy wool blankets to keep the heat in and the cold out. Rather than use the oil burner when we needed hot water to wash and bathe, she would attach an electric heating coil to the kitchen-sink faucet. Finally, when the water main under our house ruptured and we could not afford to hire a contractor to repair it, she recruited a bunch of my friends to burrow under our front lawn and make the necessary plumbing repairs.

Sadly, my mother's greatest sacrifices were made at the expense of her own health. While she made certain that I saw the doctor or the dentist regularly, she rarely took such precautions for herself. Her excuse was "Aw, those people are just plain full of malarkey anyway; they don't know what they're talkin' about." The truth—and this was the part she was just too damned proud to admit—was that she simply did not want to spend the extra money.

Consequently, she did her own doctoring. When she got a toothache, she would gulp down a couple of shots of Scotch and yank out her own teeth with a pair of pliers. When she slipped in the doorway of our house and broke her ankle, she lay on the sofa and had one of her girlfriends stretch out her leg to set the fractured bone ends in place. Then the two of them wrapped Mom's badly swollen ankle with wet strips of plaster of paris, letting them harden into a makeshift cast. Over her life, my mother suffered a seemingly endless variety of physical ailments—diabetes, asthma, chronic bronchitis, a heart murmur caused by a childhood bout with rheumatic fever, a thyroid condition, obesity, and high blood pressure. While married to my stepfather, she also endured five miscarriages, which undoubtedly caused her some serious and lasting internal damage. Yet she never complained. And as far as I can recall, she never received regular checkups or treatment from any doctors. Small wonder she would end up suffering a massive stroke, dying at age forty-eight.

Spurned by both her parents, let down by the men in her life, my mother suffered one more crushing disappointment that had a profound impact on her life and her outlook. And that was at the hands of the Catholic Church. When I was born, she brought me to St. Patrick's Cathedral in Manhattan to be baptized. But because my mother had not married my real father in a church, the priests turned us away. And my mother never forgot the slight. "How could they take it out on a little baby?" she would often ask aloud over the years to come. "Men of God, hah! The nerve of them."

While I was still an infant and we were living in Manhattan, I contracted pneumonia. For days, I ran extremely high fevers and my mother actually thought I might die. In accord with the dictates of Catholicism, which permits a layperson to baptize someone under "extreme circumstances," my mother took it upon herself to baptize me at home, in our apartment. Years later, after my mother had married Irish Jack Conlon and we had moved to our house in Astoria, I was formally rebaptized by the priests at our local parish, St. Francis of Assisi, who seemed a lot more tolerant and understanding of our struggles than the priests at St. Patrick's. My mother, however, could never forget that we had been cast out like heathen by those uppity folks there. Though I myself would end up becoming a devout Catholic, and even attending parochial school with the nuns, my mother never set foot in church again.

"Ah, Kathy, my heart just isn't in it," she'd sigh.

To bring a small measure of joy and beauty to our grim, subsistence lifestyle, my mother filled the house with the sound of music. If she wasn't playing records or listening to the radio, she would merrily be singing and dancing around the kitchen. She especially loved the big-band sounds and the old Broadway show tunes. She herself played the drums, and with her perfect sense of pitch, she also taught herself to play the organ. When I got older, she would throw lively dance parties in our basement, where she would turn up the volume on the record player and teach all us kids to do the Lindy, the fox-trot, the waltz, and the other ballroom steps. One of her Halloween costume parties went on for three days running.

Because my mother was only eighteen years older than I was, she often seemed more like my older sister than my parent. She had a magnetic, larger-than-life personality, and all the kids in our neighborhood adored her. Whenever they were down in the mouth about something or other—fights with their parents, problems in school, difficulties with boyfriends or girlfriends—they would always look to "Ma Conlon" to cheer them up. Our home became a kind of clubhouse for the local kids, open to all comers twenty-four hours a day. At Christmas, no matter how poor we were, my mother made certain that each of them received some little gift or trinket—a spiritual bouquet, a hand-scripted mass card, a black-and-white photo that she had decoratively colored with her water paints. When my friends began to throw dance parties of their own, they would make it a point not only to invite me, but also Ma Conlon. After all, she'd become as much a part of our gang as anyone else.

My mother had a terribly hard life, a never-ending saga of disappointments, pain, and heartache. The most remarkable thing about her was how well she managed to mask all the misery. Mom's flaming red hair and boisterous manner gave her the outward appearance of somebody who was a free spirit, always playful, often raucous, a little bit wild even. Four-letter words were mainstays of her vocabulary, and she would curse like a truck driver (which, after all, she had actually been when she was still with my real father during World War Two). You name it, she'd say it. (Just like me.) To the world at large, Mom always seemed to be of good cheer. In time, I realized that a lot of Mom's brash and bawdy cheeriness was a veil, a facade she carefully concocted to conceal the hurt and disappointment she had experienced in life. As I grew older, she would talk about this deception. It was her way of preparing me for the harsh realities of the real world. Especially when it came to being a woman and trying to make it on your own.

"Be your own person, Kathy," she'd tell me. "Have your own life, your own career. Don't ever become dependent on anybody for anything, especially a man. And, last but not least, no matter what, no matter how bad you hurt . . . never, ever, let 'em see you cry."

Mom was certainly one to practice what she preached. After Irish Jack Conlon died, Mom became the target of a lot of nasty rumormongering and backbiting in our Astoria neighborhood. Back in the 1950s, when church, work, and family were absolutely sacrosanct, it was not considered proper or dignified for a single woman to be raising a young child on her own. I guess it just didn't coincide with everyone's stereotypical Norman Rockwell image of both mom and dad standing by the dining room table, carving up the Thanksgiving turkey, while their apple-cheeked kids happily awaited their drumsticks and candied yams. Unfortunately, in those days, anybody who did not fit neatly into this rosy tableau was considered suspect or of weak moral fiber. People felt free to pass snap judgments on their neighbors and spread malicious rumors. And children, undoubtedly taking the cue from their parents, would blurt out things that were downright cruel.

On the Easter Sunday immediately following my stepfather's death, I wore a pretty, new yellow dress to mass. I knew I was supposed to take extraspecial care of this dress since my mother had dipped deep into her meager savings to buy it for me. It was meant to be my Sunday dress for many, many months to come, and God forbid that anything should happen to it. But on my way home from church after mass, I got into an argument with one of the older neighborhood boys, who promptly smeared grease and dirt all over my new yellow dress and ruined it. For good measure, he also poked me in the face a couple of times and gave me a fat black eye. When I began to cry and scream, he taunted me mercilessly, "So whaddya gonna do about it, Conlon? You don't even have a father!"

When I ran home and told my mother the story, she narrowed her eyes. A moment later, I could see her jaw muscles working as she ground her teeth. It was as though someone had just waved a red flag in front of a bull. "Where's this kid live?" she demanded. I told her. His house was just a few blocks away from ours. Grabbing my hand, my mother dragged me out the front door and up the street, toward the house.

"Don't you worry, young lady," Mom told me as she bounded along the sidewalk, a look of fierce determination on her face. "Everything's gonna be just hunky-dory."

When we arrived at his house, my mother began banging loudly on the front door, which was eventually opened by the kid's mother. "Yes?" the woman asked, giving my mother the kind of down-your-nose look you might reserve for a leper or a beggar. "Can I help you?" Behind her, I could see her stupid, snot-nosed bully of a son, snickering and making faces at me.

Mom arched an eyebrow. "Your husband home?"

"Who wantsa know?"

"Dorothy Conlon wantsa know, that's who."

The woman turned and shouted back into the house, "Harry! Some lady named Conlon wantsa see ya!"

A moment later, her husband, clad in his undershirt and shorts, his beer belly hanging over his waistband, waddled up to the door. Recognizing my mother—that "woman" who had the nerve to raise a young daughter on her own—he gave her a hard, cold stare, dripping with contempt. "So whadda you want, lady?" he sneered.

With that, Mom reared back with one fist, uncorked a solid roundhouse to his jaw, and knocked him flat on his ass. He was out cold.

As his wife gasped and his sniveling son stared down at him aghast, my mother announced to them, "She don't need a father. She's got a mother." Then she marched me back to our house to celebrate her knockout punch.

From that point on, whenever I would come home complaining that somebody had threatened to pick a fight with me, she'd wave me off. "Aw, stop your bawlin', none of this poor-me crap," she'd scold. "Never let 'em see you cry." Then, kicking my fanny out the door, she'd tell me, "G'wan and get back out there. You're big enough to fight your own battles now."

It was a crucially important lesson for me, and one I badly needed to learn if I was going to make my own way as a woman in the world.

It was also one of the main reasons I ended up becoming a cop.

CHAPTER FOUR

If Mom was the inspiration, Taylor set the example.

Bill Taylor. What a piece of work.

Tough as nails. Nerves of steel. A man of many strengths, but few words (*yup, nope,* and *could be* being pretty much his entire vocabulary). He rode a motorcycle. He was married to a beautiful woman with long blond hair, who looked like a fashion model. Five foot ten, muscular, with close-cropped, curly blond hair, he could have passed for a beefier version of Steve McQueen.

Bill Taylor was the beat cop in our Astoria neighborhood. And for most of my childhood, he was my hero.

When Hurricane Hazel slammed into our block in 1954 and nearly sent a huge sycamore tree crashing through the roof of our house, Taylor used a rope to shinny up the teetering trunk, nail planks into its side, and redirect its fall—so that when it did uproot, it toppled into the street and not onto our heads. When a plane crashed into Jamaica Bay, Taylor donned scuba-diving gear to plunge into the icy waters and help rescue survivors, then stopped by our house still in his wet suit to have coffee. And when Taylor was out for a casual stroll one night with his gorgeous wife, he interrupted their evening to scale the side of a five-story building, foil a burglary in progress, and nab the burglar.

Years later, when I was at the Police Academy, I heard even wilder stories about Bill Taylor. Veteran cops said he had shot seven people. That he was a black belt in both karate and judo. That he had single-handedly held entire gangs of thugs at bay while administering bone-breaking blows to the perpetrators. At the Academy, Taylor's exploits were so ingrained in the department's mythology that the instructors would routinely advise new recruits who might find themselves in a jam to think fast and "pull a Taylor." For example, if some thug rushed at you with a bone-chilling karate yell—"Aiyeeeeeeah!"—you could pull a Taylor by responding with an equally bone-chilling yell—"Garbage can!"—and bashing him silly with the lid of a trash receptacle.

While Taylor could be an absolute beast in a street fight, when it came to little kids, he was an absolute softy. One summer, he actually took it upon himself during his off-duty hours to give me swimming lessons at the local pool. While he was patiently explaining the finer points of the Australian crawl, some brat got his head stuck between the bars of the iron railing and began bawling his eyes out. Everyone else got hysterical and began screaming about whether to call the police, the fire department, the medics, or the parks department. But Taylor, sauntering calmly up to the scene in his bathing trunks, plucked the kid off the ground, turned his little body sideways, and popped his head back out like a champagne cork. Everyone applauded. Nobody except me knew that the hero of the moment was actually a cop.

One day, while I was a pupil at the St. Francis of Assisi School, about forty-five of us kids were down in the basement, waiting to begin choir practice. Sister Doretta hadn't shown up yet, so naturally we capitalized on her absence by giving each other noogies and wedgies, throwing paper planes, and making a loud ruckus. Suddenly, the looming, uniformed figure of Officer Taylor appeared in the doorway. Hearing all the noise outside on the sidewalk, he had come into the school to investigate.

"Hey!" he barked at us. "What's goin' on here? What's all this noise? Whaddya think you're doin'?"

At the sight of this big, strapping police officer in his dark blue uniform, all of us little kids went mute. Finally, one of the boys got up the courage to tell Officer Taylor that we were there for choir rehearsal.

Taylor cast a beady eye around this room full of sawed-off troublemakers. "Choir rehearsal, eh?"

With that, Taylor gruffly ordered all of us to form a circle around him, sitting cross-legged on the floor. Then, after removing his peaked policeman's cap, he began to sing "The Lord's Prayer" in a perfect, honey-pure tenor. That was followed by a haunting rendition of "Ave Maria." And let me tell you—the sight of this tough street cop singing these beautiful hymns to all us little kids was something I shall never forget. When Sister Doretta finally showed up, she stood in the doorway and listened quietly. Tears welled up in her eyes. At the end of Taylor's performance, she began to applaud. All us kids did, too.

No doubt about it, Bill Taylor was my role model. Who knows, maybe I even had a girlish crush on him. More than likely, he filled a painful gap in my life, becoming the father I never had. It was obvious that he loved little kids, and they loved him right back. Whatever the reason for my great and enduring fascination with Officer Taylor, I decided that one day, when I grew up, I was gonna be just like him.

The thing that I envied so much about the guy was the way everyone else in the neighborhood looked up to him. I wanted the same kind of respect, the same admiring looks. Maybe it was because I came from a background that didn't give me a whole lot to feel proud about. We were dirt-poor. We were not about to make big headlines or win great prizes. There were no famous lawyers, doctors, athletes, scholars, or captains of industry in our family. Hell, I didn't even have a father. And my mother subsisted (just barely) on Social Security checks. So, if one of the Conlons was ever gonna make people stand up and take notice, it would have to be me. And if I wanted to get the kind of respect and admiration that Bill Taylor enjoyed, I'd have to do it by helping people. Just like him.

I started young, babysitting for neighbors or running errands for the elderly. Later, in high school, I tutored other students and did volunteer work in city shelters for the homeless. I also joined the Junior Red Cross and visited veterans or disabled patients in local hospitals, many of which were situated on nearby Roosevelt Island.

In high school, I really got it into my head to become a cop. A bunch of us heard that a couple of Puerto Rican kids in the school band had overdosed on heroin and died. Sitting in a local coffee shop one day and talking amongst ourselves, we became incensed about the dismal state of the world—and convinced that we, unlike all the other millions upon millions of young people who had come before us, were the ones who would finally fix it. Hell, we were teenagers. Full of piss and vinegar. So, naturally, we had all the answers.

One of my buddies, Al Beddy, turned to me and said, "Hey, kid, why don't you and I become cops? The two of us will take on the system!"

In a flash, I thought of my hero, Bill Taylor. "You know something, Al?" I said. "That's not a bad idea. Not a bad idea at all."

And, thus, the plan was born.

In our high school yearbook, where the other girls wrote under their photos that they aspired to become nurses, teachers, or housewives, I was the only one to put down "Police Department." I began to research the application process, learning that if you wanted to become a policewoman, you had to take a civil service test. And while you might pass that test and get your name on an appointment list, you might have to wait years before your name was actually called. Moreover, once the Police Department started to call the names and make the appointments, only a limited number of people got them. In other words, there would be a quota. So, if your test score was too low, you might not make the cut. Then you'd have to start from scratch and take the civil service test all over again.

But I was determined. No matter how long it was gonna take.

After I finished high school, I could not afford to attend college full-time, so I took a job as a clerk with the Bulova Watch Company, working on statistics and sales analysis. I also enrolled in night-school classes—one in business administration, the other to prep myself for the civil service exam. For a while I toyed with the idea of becoming a mortician, figuring that learning how to deal with human corpses might make me a desirable candidate for the Police Department's Forensic Unit. But a visit to an embalming school in the subbasement of the old Bellevue Hospital quickly cured me of that idea—especially when I observed the students during their lunch break, blithely noshing on meatball heros while sitting next to the splayed-out cadavers.

For two months I attended twice-weekly night classes at Delehanty Institute in lower Manhattan to prepare myself for the civil service exam. The classes familiarized the students with the state penal code, the structure of city government, and the kinds of English and math questions that were likely to be asked.

In 1964, along with five thousand other women, I took the three-hour civil service test to become a policewoman and passed with a score of 89, which placed me 118th on the list of 750 female candidates deemed acceptable for hiring. Less than a week later, I was called into my boss's office at Bulova and fired for failing to tell him that I had intentions of joining the Police Department. Knowing it could still be years before a spot might open up on the force and that I still needed a job while I waited, I found a position as a clerk with Squibb Pharmaceuticals in Manhattan.

In 1965, I got the first call to take the city physical for the Police Department. But, to my great dismay, my physical turned into a debacle. On my application, I had written that, as a child, I had been diagnosed with anemia. The doctors at the city's Personnel Department immediately red-flagged that entry and warned that if my iron levels, already low, could not be boosted, I would be disqualified for the force. More troublesome, however, was the Police Department's height requirement. You had to be at least five feet two inches tall to become a cop, and shorter candidates often resorted to tricks to get past this hurdle. Guys would stick pads inside their socks or wear toupees to add fractions of an inch to their height. Women would attach buns or hairpieces to the tops of their coiffures—rats, as we used to call them. To catch the cheaters, the doctor would examine both your hair and the bottoms of your feet while you were on the scale. What's more, the scale itself had been rigged up with a light that would go off if you tried to inch up off your soles and sneak up higher on your tippy-toes.

The first time I stood on the scale, I measured five foot two.

But some other woman who was up for a police appointment, a five-foot-eleven Amazon, immediately challenged my readings. "Hey, that squirt ain't no five foot two!" she bellowed. The doctor decided to re-measure me, and the second time, the scale malfunctioned. The doctor said I stood only five foot one—and immediately disqualified me, saying I would have to return at a later date to be retested. But how in the world do you make yourself grow after you've already reached your twenty-first birthday? I didn't have a clue. What's more, with the current list of suit-able female applicants about to expire, I would have to wait until the Po-lice Department called for a whole new class of women recruits, and there was no telling when that might happen. Could be months, could be years. For now, however, the door was closed. I was devastated.

I returned to work at Squibb Pharmaceuticals and tried to keep my mind off this setback. Eventually, I was promoted from clerk to secretary, then moved to the accounting department, and finally upped to executive secretary to the director of veterinary research. A whole year went by with-out another call to come down and take the physical for the Police Depart-ment. During that waiting period, I did everything I could to prepare myself for the retesting. To beef up my hemoglobin count, I took massive amounts of vitamin B_{12} and iron supplements, while consuming daily por-tions of leafy green vegetables, peas, lima beans, eggplant, beef tea, and protein-rich nuts. At night, I took phys ed classes to boost my stamina. To improve my posture—and hopefully add a fraction of an inch to my height—I did constant stretching exercises to straighten out my spinal col-umn and slept on the hardwood floor of my bedroom, using nothing more than a quilt for a cushion. My Saint Bernard puppy, Sneakers, used to lie on top of my bed and look down at me dolefully, as if I were nuts.

One more year went by without a call from the department. And then, another. Finally, in May of 1968, I received a phone call from a Police Department investigator alerting me that a new class of policewomen would be appointed on June 7. It would be a small group, only ten females (along with 940 males). It was now or never. If too much more time went by, I might never get my shot. Immediately, I called the city's Personnel Department and asked to be scheduled for a new physical. Toward the end of the month, I was given an appointment.

When I entered the medical office, wearing my shorts and sneakers, I was greeted by a chorus of loud wolf whistles and appreciative but graphic comments about my ass from the thirty prospective firemen and sanitation men who were already sitting inside, waiting for their physicals. As the only woman in the room, I felt conspicuous and exposed.

But the reception I was given by the Personnel Department's examining doctor was a whole lot chillier. Exiting his office, he eyed me up and down, looking like a man who had just sucked on a lemon, and said, "Oh, you must be Conlon."

In those days, women cops were a rarity in New York City (only 338 in 1968 versus more than 6,000 now), hardly ever seen in public. None were assigned to work on patrol—that would not happen until 1972—so they were almost never out on the street where they could readily be observed by the citizenry. Most were consigned to matron duty—doing clerical work, answering precinct switchboards, or searching female prisoners in the precincts, or female corpses for valuables. A handful had been promoted to detective, but they were usually stuck doing the typing and answering the phones in squad offices. Few went out in the field to work cases and interview complainants or witnesses. Consequently, to many old-timers in the department, the notion of women even becoming cops was treated like a bad joke, and the women applicants who came down for physicals were regarded as nuisances.

This doctor, an unabashed sexist, did not want to be bothered examining me. He saw it as a waste of his valuable time and was eager to chase me out of the examining room as quickly as possible.

When I handed him the medical reports from my private doctors, attesting that I was no longer anemic and my blood work was within the norms, he did not even inspect them. On general principle, he was ready to throw me out, without even retesting me. I began to plead with him. "Please, Doc, just let me go the next step. If I'm going to bomb out, at least let me make it to the Police Department before I get the boot."

The doctor seemed indifferent to my pleadings. "Well, Miss Conlon, I'm really sorry, but these reports you've brought with you are totally insufficient. You're going to have to bring me additional documentation. And you'll have to have more blood work done. And, of course, fresh tests on your hemoglobin count. And then, after all that, you'll have to be completely retested for—"

I interrupted him, "Doc, please! I don't have time. The new class begins in just two weeks. I have all the letters and documents you people asked me for the first time. If I don't make it now, I'm going to have to start from scratch. And then I may never make it."

"Well, I'm sorry, Miss Conlon," he sniffed, "but regulations are regulations."

So, I did exactly what he would have expected me to do: I began to cry. And with that, all the burly firemen and sanitation men who had been making catcalls because of my bare legs suddenly took pity on me. In unison, they began to chant, "Let her go! Let her go! *Let her go! Let her go!*"

With their booming, rhythmic refrain echoing incessantly in his ears, the doctor finally waved the flag of surrender. "Alright, Miss Conlon, I'll accept these documents for now. But if they turn out to be false, you'll be in hot water, I assure you. Now get on that scale over there. We have to measure your height again."

I took a deep breath, crossed my fingers, said a prayer, and stepped on the scale. The doctor adjusted the gauges. Then he adjusted his bifocals to make sure he was reading the gauges correctly. This was it. The moment of truth. It was now or never . . .

"Five foot . . . two," he said. "You pass."

I grabbed his face with both my hands and kissed him on the cheek. "Doc, you're the greatest!" I told him. He blushed red. All the sanitation men and firemen in the back of the room burst into hoots and whistles and cheers. They began stamping their feet and applauding.

I telephoned my mother to give her the good news. After four years, four interminable years of waiting for this to happen, she couldn't believe it. "Oh, my God!" she kept saying over and over. "Oh, my God!" Later, when I returned to my office at Squibb, I typed up my resignation. My boss, who was sympathetic to my quest, congratulated me and told me that, for now, he would simply hold it in a corner of his desk drawer, just in case. That night, I gave myself the biggest treat of all. For the first time in two years, I slept in my own bed!

Two weeks later, I went down to the Police Academy on East Twentieth Street along with 949 other recruits. There, we went through the final battery of physical exams (getting chest X-rays, peeing in a bottle) and psychological tests (e.g., "What's your favorite color?" "Do you have weird dreams?" "Do you like to tell dirty jokes?" "Do you like to hear dirty jokes?"). We filled out a million and one different forms. Then we were taken down to the equipment section, to be measured for gun belts, raincoats, hats, ties, and tie clasps (all of which we would have to pay for out of our own pockets).

Given that I was so tiny, nothing fit me properly. The smallest size they had in stock was size 12. I wore size 5. When I squawked to the equipment guy, a real grizzly old-timer of a cop, that the sleeves on my raincoat dangled about six inches below my hands, he told me: "Don't worry about it, kid, you're gonna grow into it."

I continued to bitch and moan. "This raincoat's too damned big for me, and I'm not going to take it, I tell ya!" I kept shouting at him. Finally, the equipment guy rolled his eyes up and walked back behind the counter to get something. When he came back out again, he told me to open my hand. "Here you go," he said, dropping something into my palm. It was an insignia, consisting of a pair of stripes.

"What's this for?" I asked.

"Hey, kid, you ain't even started yet, but you're a corporal already, the way you're givin' orders. You got the biggest mouth I ever seen coming through here!"

As the day wore on, I made friends with another young police recruit, Danny Rizzo (who, as I mentioned, became one of my pals in the Undercover Unit). At the end of all the testing and measuring, all the approved candidates were brought into the auditorium. The chief clerk of the City of New York ascended the stage and stepped to the microphone. He asked us all to stand, raise our right hands, and repeat his words. Then he gave us the New York City Police Department's official oath of office.

As soon as the swearing-in was finished, a uniformed lieutenant stepped to the dais. "All recruits are to report here Monday morning at oh seven fifteen hours," he barked gruffly. "Disssss-missed!"

Danny and I looked at each other. I bit my lip. I could no longer hold back the tears. It had taken me four years to get to this moment.

As soon as we got outside the Academy building, Danny and I went straight to the corner candy store and bought ourselves double-scoop ice cream cones, chocolate sprinkles on top. Then we started running down

East Twentieth Street, shouting and giggling like little kids, leapfrogging in tandem over all the fire hydrants.

It was official now. And we couldn't contain our jubilation any longer. Other people might continue to get their impressions of what police officers looked and acted like from fictitious TV shows such as *The Mod Squad, Hawaii Five-0,* and *Adam 12.*

But we were the real deal.

We were New York City cops!

Kathy in her high school commencement gown with her mom, the woman who inspired her to become a police officer, outside their Astoria home in June 1961. (Photo courtesy of the author)

Kathy (top row, second from left) stands with nine other women recruits in her class at the Police Academy in June 1968. (Photo courtesy of the author)

Kathy, three months into the job, working in the Police Department's Office of Community Affairs, a job she sought to escape to do some real police work. (Photo courtesy of the author)

LATE CITY EDITI•

The New York Times

nt"

Weather: Sunny, pleasant to fair and pleasant tonight, tomor Temp. range: today 60-78; Tue 68-76. Temp.-Hum. Index yeste 72. Full U.S. report on Page

© 1971 The New York Times Company   *NEW YORK, WEDNESDAY, SEPTEMBER 1, 1971*   15 CEN•

Ackley Calls for 'Compact' On Pay-Price Stabilization

Gardner Ackley before the Joint Economic Committee

By PHILIP SHABECOFF
Special to The New York Times

WASHINGTON, Aug. 31 — Gardner Ackley, a former chairman of the Council of Economic Advisers, called today for a "social compact" among labor, business and other groups to support a permanent system to stabilize wages and prices after the 90-day freeze expires.

Mr. Ackley, a top economic strategist for the Democratic party, said in testimony before the Joint Economic Committee of Congress that the problem

management "climb off the treadmill" of inflation.

But he added, "The next immediate step must be to replace the freeze with an effective incomes policy. Beyond that, an incomes policy must be buttressed by a whole range of further institutional changes."

Mr. Ackley firmly opposed any limitation on profits and, in fact, said that profits had been excessively low and should be allowed to rise. He

PRESIDENT DENIES ARMS-AID PLANS TO SENATE PANEL

Invokes Executive Privilege to Block Fulbright Group's Bid to Halt Military Help

By MARJORIE HUNTER
Special to The New York Times

WASHINGTON, Aug. 31—President Nixon refused today to disclose to the Senate Foreign Relations Committee the Administration's long-range plans for foreign military assistance.

With his action—the second time Mr. Nixon had invoked information to Congress—the President forestalled a threatened Congressional halt in all foreign military aid.

The Foreign Relations Committee voted, 15 to 0, on July 29 for suspension of all foreign military aid unless the Pentagon supplied its five-year plan for military assistance, or unless the President forbade making the information available.

Move Disclosed by Laird

The President's decision was announced in a memorandum made public late today by Sec-

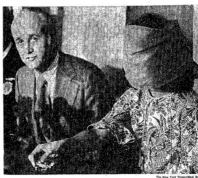

The New York Times/Neal Boenzi

POLICEWOMAN IS PROMOTED: Kathleen Conlon, masked to protect her undercover role, at news conference with Commissioner Patrick V. Murphy. Attacked and threatened with death Monday, she was promoted yesterday to detective. Article, Page 44.

Commissioner Is Calm in Hectic Days

By MARTIN ARNOLD

Through it all, through those two days that convulsed the Police Department, Police Commissioner Patrick V. Murphy moved with the hours of change calmly, with

To a reporter who had been accompanying him during the past two days, it seemed as if the men he conferred with could not speak fast enough in giving him the information he sought.

sioner had appointed a new chief of patrol—jumping him over 72 more senior officers —had removed six captains —not because they were corrupt, but because, he said, they allowed men in their

MURPHY RELIEV 6 POLICE CAPTA FOR LAXITY ON

Men Under Their Comn Reportedly Found As• by Investigators

5 WERE PRECINCT H

Commissioner Says Ch Will Be Made Agains Members of the For

By DAVID BURNHA

Police Commissioner • that he had relieved si• tains of their commane cause investigators had repeated instances of •men under their supe •sleeping on duty. Five o headed precincts.

The Commissioner, mo achieve what he called police standards," also ing prepared against lieutenants, four sergear 18 patrolmen because investigation.

Mr. Murphy, who said

Front page of *The New York Times*, featuring photo of a hooded and masked Kathy taken on September 1, 1971, when she was promoted to detective at Police Headquarters by Police Commissioner Patrick Murphy. She needed to be disguised because she was still working undercover. (Copyright © 1971 The New York Times Company. Reprinted with permission.)

The phony student ID card that was made for Kathy so she could pose as a college coed to make drug buys on campus under the name of "Marie Martin" in the early 1970s. (Photo courtesy of the author)

Kathy, working undercover in the park outside New York's City Hall where she and other detectives from Brooklyn North Narcotics were doing photographic surveillance on suspected drug sales. (Photo courtesy of the author)

Photo of a hooded and armed Kathy that appeared on the front page of the *New York Post* on June 22, 1972, after she testified in Washington, D.C., before a congressional committee that was investigating drug use in the nation's schools. (Reprinted with permission from the *New York Post*, 2006, Copyright NYP Holdings, Inc.)

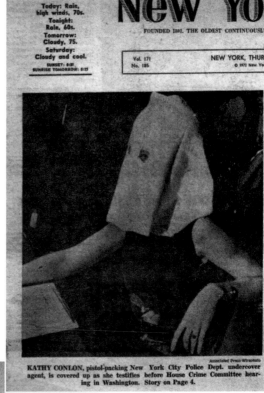

Today: Rain, high winds, 70s. Tonight: Rain, 60s. Tomorrow: Cloudy, 75. Saturday: Cloudy and cool. SUNSET: 8:31 SUNRISE TOMORROW: 5:25

NEW YO

FOUNDED 1801. THE OLDEST CONTINUOUSLY

Vol. 171
No. 185

NEW YORK, THUR
© 1972 New Yor

KATHY CONLON, pistol-packing New York City Police Dept. undercover agent, is covered up as she testifies before House Crime Committee hearing in Washington. Story on Page 4.

Kathy stands with a shotgun during a break from target practice at the Police Department's shooting range in 1975. (Photo by Bruce Curtis for *Parade* magazine)

Kathy, her husband, Bob (right), and her daughters Cathrine (left) and Veronica (right) stand with Police Commissioner Robert McGuire at Police Headquarters after McGuire promoted Kathy to detective second grade in December 1983. (Photo courtesy of the New York Police Department)

Six-foot-nine bank robber William Breckner was arrested on two different occasions by Kathy for stickups. Here, she takes Breckner and an accomplice into the station house after she and partner John Gaspar had collared them on Manhattan's Upper West Side. (Photo by David Bookstaver for the *New York Post*)

Kathy and her partner in the Major Case Squad, John Gaspar, with a bank robbery suspect they had just arrested in 1984. (Photo by David Bookstaver for the *New York Post*)

Mayor Ed Koch places the Medal of Honor around Kathy's neck in a ceremony outside New York's City Hall in June 1987. (Koch Collection/N.Y.C. Municipal Archives)

Kathy with Lillian Braxton, president of the Policewomen's Endowment Association and a major supporter in Kathy's sexual discrimination lawsuit, standing outside New York's City Hall on the day Kathy was awarded the Medal of Honor. (Photo courtesy of the New York Police Department)

"Cagney" and "Lacey" meet some *real* New York detectives, including Kathy (top row, third from left). (NYC Detectives Endowment Association)

Kathy is overcome after receiving the Medal of Honor from Mayor Koch in June 1987. (© New York *Daily News*, L.P., reprinted with permission)

CHAPTER FIVE

The noise from the fusillade was deafening. And the amplified barking coming over the public address system added to the earache.

"Low to the left! Adjust your stance! . . . High to the right! Realign your sights! . . . Don't look left! Don't look right! Just listen to the instructions from the tower! . . . Stop jerking your hand! Support the wrist! . . . Rapid fire! Fire three! Reload! . . . Fire three more! . . . Reload! Rapid fire! Fire five!"

I had never handled a gun before. And when I finally got the opportunity up at Rodman's Neck, the Police Department's firing range in the Bronx, I was jittery as hell. The jolt of the recoil took my breath away. Most of the male recruits had been in the military, so they were up to snuff on firearm usage. But few of the ten women in my class knew which end of the gun was up.

The male instructor didn't make matters any easier. After showing us training films of people inadvertently shooting themselves, he declared, "Most of you women don't have the hand musculature to fire a gun."

Then, in another confidence builder, he admonished, "If you turn around an instant too soon, you ladies may blow away one of the instructors or another cop on the firing line."

All of us, men and women recruits, were required to fire six rounds at a clip. While the men's guns held six rounds, the smaller guns used by the women held only five rounds, which meant that the women would have to stop and reload to get off that sixth and final round. All of this time-consuming reloading by the females thoroughly pissed off the male cops who were on the line.

And there was another problem. The paper targets we fired at bore the likeness of a stocky, dark-haired, pug-nosed assailant in a white-on-white track suit who was aiming a handgun right at you. Nicknamed the

Thug, he was meant to look like a murderous assailant. When the male cops went into a crouch to fire, their average sight line would be center mass on the Thug, and their rounds would land in the chest region. But the women cops were considerably shorter than the men. So when the women went into a crouch and fired, their average sight line was several inches lower on the Thug and their rounds landed lower. When the firing ended, the Thug would be reeled back with bullet holes across the groin of his silhouette. Which, naturally, gave the instructor even more reason to give us digs for being females.

"Ouch!" he exclaimed with glee. "What's with all you women? You got something against men?"

Sniffed another male instructor, "They only want the job so they can get the gun. With a gun, they can feel equal. To them, having a gun's like having a penis."

This gender trashing continued nonstop. We had been ordered to fire 150 rounds with our revolvers. After the seventy-fifth round, my gun jammed. I could not eject the empty cartridges. I raised my free hand and called the instructor over to help me. All the firing around me immediately ceased.

"What's your problem, Conlon?" grunted the instructor with obvious impatience.

"I can't eject my rounds."

"You women are all the same," he said, loudly enough, of course, for all the male cops to get an earful. "You're too weak. You don't have the muscle in your arm to fire a gun."

"But the gun's broken," I insisted.

"Bullshit. You're just not strong enough to fire it. I don't know why they even make you cops."

I started to do a slow burn. "Well, if you think you can do it, then go ahead," I snapped.

"Gimme that, Conlon," he barked. He took my gun. Smirked. And tried to eject the casings. But he couldn't do it either.

Lowering his voice so it was barely above a murmur, he said, "Hmph, something wrong with this one, I guess."

But of course, none of the male cops heard that part. All they heard was his rant about women being too weak to fire their guns. And his conclusion that something was wrong with the shooter, not the weapon. Unfortunately, that's the part all the male cops would remember when they went out to work in the precincts. Women were not cut out to be cops . . . and God have mercy on the male cop who had to work with one.

Even at the Academy, I had gotten into dustups because of my sex. When the men were sent to the gym for lessons in judo and self-defense, the women were relegated to typing classes. Naturally, I was the one who made a stink.

I immediately asked to speak with my PBA delegate so I could file a grievance. One of the instructors warned me that I was still on probation, so I had no right to file a grievance. Undaunted, I marched right in to see the commanding officer of the Police Academy. At first, he was not at all happy to see this grousing pip-squeak female in front of him. But gradually, as I spelled out my beef about the lack of physical training for the women, he smiled. "Took a lotta guts for a young cop like you to come up here to talk to me," he said.

He promised to begin giving the women physical training along with the men. Choke holds, self-defense, judo, subduing prisoners, the usual stuff. However, when our training began, we found ourselves stuck down in the motor pool. The Academy's garage. The floor was covered with oil slicks, and the smell of gasoline was so pungent we nearly puked. So I made another stink. This time, one of the instructors told me to just zip my lip and pay my dues. "Conlon," he said, "you've done enough complaining for your first two weeks on the job. Now it's time for you to learn how to do your job."

When I got shipped out to my first precinct, the 103rd in Jamaica, Queens, the sexual hazing continued. Because I was a woman, they always assumed they could put one over on me.

One day, I drove my own car, a canary-colored Ford convertible, to the scene of a labor protest by public-school teachers, where I had been assigned to monitor the picket line. When my tour ended, one of the inspectors, a notorious skirt-chaser with a reputation for making lewd and suggestive remarks to women cops, ordered me to drive him back to the precinct. Since my car had no muffler and the interior was full of clumps of loose hair from Sneakers, I suggested to the inspector that he would be better off catching a ride with one of the radio cars. But being a boss and being a male boss, the inspector was not about to take any guff from some tiny woman cop.

"Don't tell me who I wanna ride with," he snapped. "You're taking me back, and that's it."

"You're the boss," I said.

As we drove back to the precinct, enveloped in clouds of swirling dog hair, noisily varooming and spewing tailgate smoke like a hot-rodder, the inspector fumed, "What the hell kinda car is this! Don't you know you're in violation!"

"I warned you, Inspector," I said.

By the time we arrived at the station house, he was talking to himself. Coated with dog hair, looking like bigfoot, he marched angrily toward his office, leaving a trail of laughing male cops.

Sometimes I worked the precinct switchboard, where I would munch on sunflower seeds as I took calls from the public.

One of the young male cops who worked the switchboard with me was funny and cute. There was a vibe between us. We started to schedule our meal breaks simultaneously, so we could spend more time together.

Just to be on the safe side, I went back into the records room one day and took a look at his personnel card. It said he was single and lived with his mother. All good.

In time, he started to drop by my house after work. Met my mom. Made a nice impression on her. This was good, too.

Back at the precinct, he asked me what tours I would be working, so he could arrange to work the same ones. But I started to wonder why he never asked me which days I had off, so he could arrange similar days off and we could finally have a real date. For some reason, he kept tap-dancing around the subject, never quite giving me a straight answer. A red warning light went off in my head.

"Tell me something," I finally said to him. "Just who do you live with?"

"My wife and my children," he fessed up. And suddenly, it hit me. This guy had sneaked into the records room and erased that part of his record from his personnel file so I would never know the truth about his marital status.

In full view of all the other cops in the station house, I picked up my bag of sunflower seeds and dumped them over his head.

Teddy Roosevelt was the first police commissioner to open the New York

City Police Department to women, back in the 1890s, and Minnie Gertrude Kelly was the first woman he hired to work in Police Headquarters. But for many, many decades afterward, women were relegated to doing jobs that the male officers would not do.

One such job was to search female cadavers for concealed valuables. The rule was that whenever a female corpse was reported, a female officer would have to do the search. To have a male officer run his paws over the body of a deceased female was considered inappropriate.

I knew I could handle these DOA searches without tossing my cookies. But few of the male cops seemed able to accept my aplomb in the face of death and the company of corpses, many of which were badly mangled or decomposed. Because of my size—I was now being dubbed Super Gnat and Mighty Mite—they assumed I must be a fragile little buttercup.

"Now look, dear," one of the more condescending male sergeants told me over the phone prior to one cadaver search, "this is not gonna be easy for you."

Some of the other women had already warned me to watch out for this guy. He had a reputation for breaking chops, especially if you were female.

"Don't worry," I told him. "I can handle it."

But he wouldn't let up. "Now I know that you gals are real eager, but this is a pretty ugly situation, and I don't know if you're really up to it, so if you'd rather I find someone else, I'd be more than happy to do it."

I was starting to get pissed. Finally, I told him to just send his driver over to pick me up.

"Okay, doll," he said, "but remember, I warned you. It's your funeral."

On the way to the scene, I kept stewing about this sergeant's dismissive and patronizing attitude. Sure, I was new on the job. Sure, I was a woman. Sure, I was small. But I had to nip this kind of crap in the bud if I was ever going to be accepted as an equal in the ranks. It was difficult enough to prepare yourself for what you might find when searching a cadaver. To have some clown adding to all the stress by exaggerating the grisliness of the scene before you even got there only made your job that much tougher.

In all likelihood, this would not be the last DOA I would have to search for this sergeant. So I decided I had to set him straight from the get-go. I told the sergeant's driver to pull the car over, while I dashed into a local supermarket. "I just need to pick up something," I explained.

"Sure, you do," he smirked, probably assuming I was running in to buy tampons or Midol tablets.

When we arrived at the scene, an apartment building, the sergeant was waiting. And smirking. Fiftyish, six feet tall, graying, with a real Irish chowder face. As soon as he saw me, he started in again with his condescending sexism: "Now listen, little lady, if you can't handle this, I'll be more than happy to call for a more experienced officer—"

I cut him off. "No problem, Sarge." Before he could utter another condescending word, I ducked into the building to deal with the corpse.

The search went off without a hitch. When I came back out, I handed the sergeant some rings and a necklace I had removed from the cadaver. All in accordance with proper police procedure.

"That it? Anything else?" he asked.

"Oh, yeah, I almost forgot," I said. "Open your hand."

When he unfurled his hand, I dropped a clump of bloody, slimy, quivering organs into his open palm. The sergeant took one look and nearly blew his lunch. His face turned pea-soup green. "Jesus! What the hell you giving me these for?" he blurted out. For a moment, I thought he might actually faint.

His driver and another officer who was standing nearby burst into laughter.

Baffled, the sergeant looked down more closely at the dripping organs in his palm. And realized he was holding a handful of fresh chicken livers and chicken gizzards. And that's when I lit into him.

"Listen, Sarge, don't you ever, ever patronize me again! Just because I'm a woman and I'm small doesn't mean I can't do the same job anyone else around here does. So I want to be treated the same way every other cop is treated. With respect."

I knew if this sergeant tried to retaliate for my prank, it would only make him look ridiculous in the eyes of the other men. To save face, he would have to keep his trap shut.

Score one for the girls' team, I thought.

At that moment, it probably did not occur to me that I had added my name to the shit list of one more male boss.

Despite the hustling, the hazing, and the harassment, I still felt exhilarated by the job.

The city was brimming with turmoil and upheaval—antiwar protests, campus seizures, myriad bombing plots, attacks on cops and police precincts by black militants, even a notorious police raid on a gay bar in Greenwich Village.

The 103rd Precinct—or One-Oh-Three as the cops called it—was home to many of the radical, cop-hating Black Panthers, some of whom had taken to throwing Molotov cocktails at passing radio cars. My first winter in the precinct we had to install iron bars in the station-house windows because of an intelligence report warning that the Panthers might try to blow up the building on New Year's Eve.

The station house looked like a prehistoric fossil. On the back wall, they still had fully functioning gaslights. The top of the front desk was so high that shorter cops, such as me, couldn't even reach it to sign the duty roster. The guys had to put a two-step wood box next to it to help me get up there. It wasn't long before they dubbed me Peter Pan.

There were no separate bathrooms for women. So, if you had to pee, you better be damned sure you rapped loudly on the door before you stepped inside to take care of business. Nor were there any lockers for the rookies, which meant you had to wear your gun at all times since there was no place to stow it. A lot of the other policewomen cringed at wearing their weapons. They felt that the gun made them look too tough, too masculine. Me, I couldn't have cared less. Hell, if I was gonna be a cop, I figured I damn well ought to look like one, too. Actually, I was the only woman in the female contingent who enjoyed wearing my gun. Which didn't endear me to the others.

But, if I harbored hopes of seeing any real police action, I was in for a rude awakening. On my first day of work at the precinct, a senior policewoman handed me a mop, a bucket, a pair of rubber gloves, and told me to go clean the female prisoners' cells. Since prisoners had a habit of stuffing up the toilets, puking, or defecating right there on the floors of their cells, this was not exactly what you'd call a plum assignment.

When I came home that night and complained to my mom, she had no sympathy at all. "Hey, for a person who would never clean the toilets at home, you're gettin' just what you deserve, kiddo," she told me.

"There's gotta be more to the job than this," I sighed.

Indeed, there was. From cleaning up after the prisoners, I graduated to strip-searching them.

One day, a cop brought in a hooker he had just arrested and asked me to do the body search. Black, about five foot ten, miniskirt, knee-high leather boots, thick black wig. Not bad-looking, in a rough-around-the-edges sort of way. But something about this broad gave me the willies. Her Adam's apple was too prominent. Her hands seemed unusually large. Her forearms were a little on the muscular side.

"Are you a woman?" I finally asked.

She was highly indignant. "How dare you! Of course, I'm a woman!"

Politely, I asked her to remove her wig. The wigs were extremely dear to these gals, their pride and joy, so I tried to show some modicum of respect.

"Thank you, dear, " I said, after she had surrendered her headgear.

From experience, I knew that there was a real etiquette to dealing with the hookers. If you respected them, they respected you. If you didn't give them grief, they wouldn't give you grief back. On the other hand, if you tried to play the hard-ass, the hooker might retaliate by yammering endlessly inside the holding pen for blankets or coffee or cigarettes or sodas. Or you'd get the usual earsplitting litany: "Fuck the police! Fuck the judge! Fuck the DA! Fuck the system! And fuck you, too!"

If that didn't rattle your stones, the hooker would brazenly taunt you about being a female cop. "Honey," she'd sass, "you wastin' your time in here. You got yourself a nice ass. You oughtta try peddling it out on the street. You'd make five times as much money as you do being a police-woman!"

God knows, I didn't need those kinds of hassles.

So with this particular hooker, I tried to be as genteel as possible. Emily Post, all the way. When she handed me her wig, I asked, "Am I gonna find a weapon in here?" I wasn't in the mood to get stuck with a concealed hypodermic or slashed by a hidden razor blade. "You give it to me now, I promise there won't be any charges."

No, she assured me, no weapons. No drugs, either. I searched the wig myself. I always wore plastic gloves for these searches, knowing that these things could be veritable anthills and roach colonies, crawling with lice or bugs or God knows what else. To my great relief, this wig was weapon-free, drug-free, and insect-free. Ever so delicately, I placed it on the plastic head dummy we kept on the windowsill. One more gesture of respect and consideration for our bewigged clientele.

Now, this hooker wore a tight, low-cut, spandex blouse and was showing plenty of pushed-up cleavage. So I asked her to remove the blouse. Underneath, she sported a well-developed pair of breasts. With my hands in my protective gloves, I checked delicately under her breasts and armpits and in the cavities of her back for concealed weapons. Once, I had come upon a small handgun taped under a hooker's breast. Fortunately, this babe was clean.

Next, I asked her to remove her miniskirt and her boots, another favorite hiding place for knives and ice picks. Nothing down there either, thank goodness. Finally, I asked her to remove her red bikini panties. Slowly, she stepped out of them and spun around to give me an unobstructed full frontal. To my great relief, everything still looked in order.

Then I asked her to put one foot up on top of the slab seat in the cell, bend forward, and spread her cheeks wide while I played submariner and did a visual scan of her body orifices. Amazing, the stuff you might find squirreled away up there—ice picks and razor blades wrapped in tampons, balloons filled with cocaine, condoms stuffed with heroin. Before I had joined the Police Department, I used to think my mother had taught me everything there was to know about sex. After my first week in the holding cells, searching the hookers—learning about such gross predilections as "golden showers," "brown bonnets," and "meatballs"—I realized I never had a clue.

This hooker obliged my request and propped her leg up. And, bingo, that's when it popped loose. And remained loose, just swingin' free and easy in the breeze. Something that should not have been there. No, it absolutely should not have been there.

"Get dressed," I ordered. "Now!"

I was furious. The male cop who had brought me this prisoner must have thought it was real cute to play this little joke on me. But I wasn't laughing. I could have gotten into serious trouble for searching a male prisoner. What's worse, I could have gotten hurt. Suppose this he-she, who was more than twice my size, had reared back and hammered me. Suppose he had a concealed weapon. I could have wound up hurt . . . or worse. After my fury passed, I realized I was more than just angry. I was damned scared.

I began hollering for the arresting officer. "Hey, Clancy, get your ass back in here! On the double!"

When Officer Clancy showed up, I read him the riot act. "Okay, wiseass, you know better," I scolded him. "Now get your prisoner over to the other side and let the male attendant search him. And don't ever pull that kinda crap again."

* * *

In time, I began to make friends with the designated royalty of the station house, the precinct detectives.

There were thirty of these guys, all men, and they ranged in age from their late twenties to their fifties. I was always asking them questions about how they investigated their cases. Impressed by my eagerness to learn, my pluckiness, and my willingness to wear my gun on the job, the inspector who commanded the precinct encouraged the detectives to take me along on their gambling raids and homicide investigations.

"Teach her something," he'd tell the detectives.

And teach me, they did. How to approach a crime scene without disturbing the evidence. How to make mental observations about the premises you were entering. How to take note of the other tenants peeking out from behind their venetian blinds, people who might well have been witnesses to the crime or gotten a look at the perps. How to draw conclusions based on where the body was found, what position it was in, and what condition it was in. How to remove a chain or a bracelet from a corpse with your pen so as not to smudge any fingerprints. How to bag evidence. How to be aware of smells that might provide clues. Etc., etc., etc.

Not only did the detectives teach me the tricks of their trade; they also threw me into some low-level decoy work—such as having me knock on one door wearing a demure Catholic schoolgirl's uniform while peddling gingerbread cookies, a ploy that helped them surprise a bunch of mugs who were running an illicit gambling den.

I became especially friendly with one three-man detective team. Daniels was a big, burly, light-skinned black dude with freckles. Massey was a squat-looking white guy who smoked cigars, drank too much, and looked like a fire hydrant. Miller was single, in his twenties, not bad-looking. Daniels and Massey were both married, so naturally they kept trying to fix me up with Miller. Their matchmaking efforts were pretty laughable, though, considering that I was barely five feet two, while Miller stood six feet nine. I mean, how do you even kiss a guy like that good-night? My head barely came up to his pockets.

After they finished their tour, these guys would bend the rules for probationary cops like me and take me to their favorite watering holes, including the Rock Garden, the local topless bar. The experience was humiliating on several fronts. First of all, other than the naked performers, I was the only woman in the joint. Second, I was still in my police uniform, so I felt doubly conspicuous and ridiculous. And, third, with all that wiggling and jiggling and gyrating going on, I felt extremely embarrassed and self-conscious. Who knows? The way some of those topless dancers were endowed, maybe I even felt a little bit inadequate.

But I made it a point not to bitch. I recognized these little field trips as a test, a baptism under fire of sorts, so I tried not to overreact. Was it just a case of piggish male behavior, designed to make me squirm and blush and cry uncle? Were they trying to figure out if I was just a prim little Catholic schoolgirl and get their jollies by torturing me for it?

Or might there be something more calculated to their purpose? Such as finding out just how much I could cope with in an uncomfortable and highly unpleasant environment.

A test that anyone, male or female, who ever had ambitions of one day becoming a detective would most certainly have to pass.

The person who most loved to hear about my adventures with the detectives was my mom.

All during my early years on the force, she was my biggest booster and my most ardent coach. She kept my white shirts freshly laundered and my blue skirts smartly pressed. She spent long hours helping me study the department's rules and regulations. She even took part in my physical training by holding my feet to the floor when I did my sit-ups or spotting me when I did my bench presses. She was an absolute stickler that I abide by my official curfew, continually reminding me of the department's "Cinderella Rule," which forbade probationary cops from staying out after midnight or visiting places that served liquor (even though some of my detective pals in the precinct occasionally nudged me to break the rule). She bought me three hundred pairs of disposable rubber gloves to do my prisoner and cadaver searches, a pocket warmer to keep my hands from freezing up before target practice, and a fold-up plastic raincoat to keep me warm and dry when the weather turned nasty.

In a way, Mom was living vicariously through me, savoring my triumphs as her own. Given how little she had found to celebrate in her own life, my budding career as a New York City policewoman gave her a precious reason to feel something she had rarely felt before—damn proud.

Meanwhile, I was starting to become quite the celebrity in my Astoria neighborhood. All my friends and neighbors wanted to hear my stories about "the job." So I'd spin my yarns with relish—about the strip searches, the outrageous hookers, the dead bodies, the gore, the bawdy cop humor, the field trips with the detectives, the topless bars—and they would sit rapt. No doubt about it, I was the local hero. A regular Bill Taylor. And loving every minute of it.

Then, just as I started to get cocky about my budding career in law enforcement, somebody pulled the rug out.

CHAPTER SIX

I sure as hell hadn't requested the transfer. It was done without my knowledge or approval, in the latter part of 1968. And when I found out about it, I nearly had kittens.

The Office of Community Relations was located in a dusty, old schoolhouse on East Twelfth Street in Greenwich Village. Abraham Lincoln had once made a speech from the building's steps. The office was responsible for initiating contact with the community so residents could meet with precinct commanders to air their gripes about crime, juvenile delinquency, and sanitation. The seven cops who worked in the office spent most of their day using scissors and glue pots to clip and paste newspaper articles about crime sprees, protests, vandalism, broken sewer pipes, and unrepaired potholes.

The moment I walked into the office, I got the impression I had entered a funeral parlor, only nobody had bothered to tell the occupants they were dead.

The people who worked there, especially the policewomen, had been cops for so long they were ready to grow moss. Most had been off the street for years and were determined to keep it that way. The last thing in the world they wanted was to have to make arrests. At this stage of their careers, who needed the hassle?

Right off the bat, I noticed that nobody smiled. Nobody schmoozed. Nobody kidded around. And, God forbid, nobody, but nobody, dared to laugh. "Hell," I thought to myself, "if you can't share a laugh on this job, what's the point?" How would you keep your sanity? And, for the life of me, I couldn't figure out why it was a no-no. So I asked one of the other cops.

He explained, "The deputy commissioner doesn't like it if anyone laughs."

"What!" I exclaimed. "Is she crazy?"

The cop turned pale as a ghost. "Shhh!" he said nervously, placing his finger to his lips to silence me. "She might hear you."

The deputy commissioner, whom I had yet to meet, was Theresa Melchione. I had already gone to the public library to get the skinny on her. From the newspapers, I learned that she was a living legend in the Police Department, a former first-grade detective who had worked undercover, testified at congressional hearings, published her autobiography, and risen to become the first female deputy commissioner in the New York City Police Department's history. But the press clippings didn't tell the whole story. The department scuttlebutt was that Melchione was something of a dragon lady, unpredictable and volatile, someone who could be alternately mothering, manipulative, mysterious, or mean.

Suddenly, as I stood talking to the other cop about the edict against laughing, Commissioner Melchione appeared in the doorway. Or rather, I should say, made her grand entrance.

Gliding majestically through the door as if floating on some kind of perfumed jet stream, she pirouetted toward her private office. The long, lightweight dress she wore swirled and billowed around her.

"Good morning, everyone!" she chirped, her voice positively dripping with fake charm.

Noticing me standing by one of the desks, she inquired, "And who might you be, young lady?"

"Policewoman Conlon. I've been transferred to your command."

"Oh, yes, of course. My new secretary. Come into my office. I need you to take some dictation."

Swell, I thought to myself. From doing cadaver inspections, searching real, live prisoners, and hobnobbing with grizzled, street-smart detectives, I had been relegated to the secretarial pool. What a kick in the ass. And suddenly it hit me. My past had caught up with me. I had been sandbagged because of my prior experience in the civilian work world. Because I had been trained as a typist and stenographer and had proven myself competent at both, I was choice pickings for a paper-shuffling operation like Community Relations.

Despondent, I picked up a steno pad and entered the deputy commissioner's office, all my antennae on high alert. The first thing I noticed was the full-length, three-sided mirror in front of which she now stood admiring her designer dress while checking her makeup and her hairdo from three different angles. It felt as if we were inside the dressing room at Saks Fifth Avenue.

While the deputy commissioner was clearly someone to be wary of, it was the job itself that really made me miserable. Day after day, I would spend eight hours sitting on my rump and pushing papers from one side of the desk to the other. Unlike the 103rd Precinct, with its endless parade of colorful oddballs and characters—half of them cops, the other half crooks—Community Relations was deadly, dry, and dull. Everyone behaved like a robot—reading the newspapers, clipping the articles, pasting them in scrapbooks, filing reports.

Outside, the whole world was exploding. "Drugs, crime, campus revolution, racial discord, draft resistance," as Richard Nixon described it in those days. But, as long as I remained entombed in Community Relations, I would never get close to any of it.

Despite the drudgery of Community Relations, I made it my business to return to the Police Academy gym once a week to practice my judo holds. One night, as I went through my paces, an old-time detective sidled up to me. He told me he worked in the Narcotics Division. Crinkling up his nose, chewing on a fat cigar, he looked me up and down, muttering, "Hmmmm." Since I was wearing shorts, I figured he must be admiring my legs.

But then he said, "Hey, kid, how'd you like to work in the Undercover Unit?"

Immediately, my ears perked up. This was exactly the kind of action I was salivating for.

"Sure!" I said.

He handed me a card. "Call this number, and we'll make the appointment for you to see the boss."

The Undercover Unit was housed on Old Slip, at the southern tip of Manhattan, a stone's throw from the Fulton Fish Market. The three-story, rectangular building, which would later be used in the classic Gene Hackman cop movie *The French Connection,* was another one of those turn-of-the-century relics. The outside was a drab masonry gray, the inside a dingy police green. The bathrooms had those giant, old porcelain sinks. The toilets had wood seats and overhead pull chains. The windows were always left open, which allowed great gusts of dust to sweep through the entire building and over the old, gray wood floors, which seemed impervious to any real cleaning despite decades of continuous mopping. The briny smell of the sea and the pungent odor of freshly caught flounder, sea bass, and lobsters wafting over from the Fulton market permeated the air inside every room.

Trudging up the stairs to meet the CO of the Undercover Unit, I noticed half a dozen seedy-looking characters loitering boozily on the stairs. They looked like bikers and dopers out of that year's hit cult film, *Easy Rider*. Torn and filthy jeans. Cutoff shirts stained with sweat. Ratty beards. Long, greasy hair. Bandannas. Mud-caked combat boots or sneakers. Bad teeth. And, Lord, oh Lord, did they ever smell. I figured they must be looking for a place to sleep off their hangovers. Or else they must be prisoners, about to be carted off to a lockup.

Inside the office, I introduced myself to the commanding officer, a stocky guy in his fifties with olive skin and close-cropped, salt-and-pepper hair, neatly trimmed into a Saint Anthony's–styled haircut, bald spot gleaming prominently at the center.

"So, boss," I said, "where are the other cops in the unit? I haven't seen any around."

His eyes lit up. "Oh, yes, you have. You just walked right by 'em. In the stairwell."

"Oh," I said, mustering a feeble smile. I felt pretty stupid. But I was also amazed at how deftly the undercovers had been able to blend into the background, without tipping me off that they were cops.

With that, the CO began to curse me up and down, spewing out the foulest, vilest language. "Fuck this . . . fuck that . . . those fucking sons of bitches . . . fucking drug-dealing motherfuckers . . . fucking pricks . . . fucking shitbags . . . fucking fuckers . . . fuck 'em all . . ."

I sat there, mouth agape, not believing my ears.

The boss suddenly stopped in the middle of this four-letter rant. "That shake you up, Conlon?"

"I can handle it."

And I knew I could. Hell, my own mother talked like a truck driver, and she'd call you "a fucking son of a bitch" as quickly as she'd call you a friend.

"Good," he said. "'Cause that's just the kind of language you'll be hearing on the street. And if it throws you now, you don't belong here. You also better get used to hearing yourself called a pros and a skell by the uniformed cops, 'cause that's what you'll be when you're undercover."

I tried to smile. "Well, it's not exactly what my mother had in mind when she sent me to Catholic school, but I'll try to adapt."

The boss laughed. "So, just what do you know about drugs, Conlon?"

"Something you buy with a prescription from the doctor?"

"Don't worry. We'll teach you everything."

The CO was eager to bring a young, white female on board. He wanted a raw recruit, fresh out of the Academy. Someone who did not use the kind of police lingo routinely mouthed by veteran officers. Words like *pros* for "prostitute," *skells* for "derelicts," *shield* for "badge," *RMP* for "radio motor patrol car," and *going to meal* instead of "going to eat." Casually uttered in front of an experienced, streetwise criminal, words like these could be a tip-off that somebody was working undercover. They could end up getting some cop hurt. Or worse.

I told him I wasn't fazed.

Actually, I would have told him anything I could—the moon is made of green cheese, there is a Santa Claus, and aliens really do exist—if I could be sure it would get me out of Community Relations. So I became even bolder. I told the CO the undercover job was my dream assignment, my life's ambition. And the sooner I could swing it, the better.

But the CO said there were hurdles to clear. Before I could even put in for the Undercover Unit, I would need to arrange a transfer back to a precinct. But before I could request a transfer, I would have to finish my probationary period, which had another six months to go. Meanwhile, I was still exiled to the gulag, Community Relations, under the tight thumb (and sharp talons) of a controlling deputy commissioner.

He sighed. "You're gonna have to pull some strings to get yourself outta there, Conlon."

The CO told me my chances would improve if I continued to keep a low profile, even after I went back into a precinct. "Don't be active. Don't make lots of arrests. Don't do things that will make you well-known on the street or within the department. Don't do anything that could come back to haunt you once you're working undercover."

I thanked the CO and said good-bye. As I headed back down the stairs, one of the scuzzy-looking undercover cops I had mistaken for a doper in the stairwell leered at me. I shuddered.

"Hey, Kath," he said. "Howya doin'?"

I looked more closely and realized that, under the dirty mop of shoulder-length black hair and behind that scraggly, smelly beard, was somebody I actually knew. It was Danny Rizzo, the recruit I had palled around with at the Police Academy. He'd been plucked out of training for undercover work. When I told him I was angling for a spot in the squad, his eyes lit up.

"Hey, that's swell!" he said. "You'll love it here, Kathy. It's a great gig." Danny promised to put in a word for me with the CO.

"Great!" I thought. Now I was really excited. I had a "hook" in the unit, an insider who could give me the seal of approval with his comrades. There might, just might, be light at the end of the tunnel after all.

Back in the stagnant swampland of Community Relations, feeling ever more hopeful, I began making noises about transferring out. And that's when one of the other cops whispered to me, "Yeah, well, you can just forget about it, Conlon. Your tour in Community Relations has been extended. Indefinitely."

That did it.

In I marched to confront the dragon lady, who, Sphinx-like behind her desk, was spritzing herself with Chanel No. 5. "Can I do something for you, young lady?" she asked curtly, breaking into one of her cryptic smiles. "Do you have a problem?"

Commissioner Melchione was not accustomed to anyone coming into her office. For any reason. She was clearly annoyed.

I just blurted out what was on my mind: "When can I go back to my precinct, Commissioner?"

Suddenly, the cryptic smile turned into a menacing sneer. I could see her jaw muscles working. And her mind working, too, as she tried to figure out whether I had somehow snared a department hook or "rabbi" more powerful than she was, with the clout to thwart her. Her eyes narrowed into little slits. "I'm afraid you won't be going back to the precinct."

"But, why, Commissioner?" I demanded.

"It's quite simple. I intend to mold your mind."

I knew it was bullshit. She just wanted to keep me under her thumb, typing up her silly letters and taking her stupid dictation. She wanted a slave, pure and simple. And, for the indeterminate future, I was stuck with the job.

I screwed up my courage. "You're about twenty-four years too late. My mother molded my mind already."

I could practically see the smoke coming out of her ears. Who the hell did I think I was, this twenty-four-year-old upstart, to give her this kind of lip? And yet, it was certainly a milestone in my fledgling career. Now, in addition to all the male bosses I had irritated, I had finally managed to piss off a high-ranking woman in the Police Department—the very highest-ranking, in fact.

Seething with fury, Melchione threatened to pack me off to the badlands of the South Bronx, miles away from my home in Queens.

"I don't care where you send me," I shot back. "Send me anywhere. Send me to the South Bronx. Send me to Kansas. Send me to the moon, if you like. I just don't want to be here. I want to be a real cop, not a typewriter cop."

"Now listen, young lady, you don't know what you're getting into," the commissioner replied in the most patronizing of tones. "You're young. You're small. You're raw—"

"Is that what they told you when you asked to go into the field?"

Her head snapped up. "What's that supposed to mean?"

"C'mon, Commissioner, you were a first-grade detective. You worked the streets. You were undercover. Can't you give me the same chance you had to be a cop? The same opportunities? Or are you determined to deprive me of that?"

The commissioner studied me long and hard. Her expression turned inscrutable. "You can leave now," she said. Then she busied herself with some paperwork.

I got up and left her office.

The next day, I was transferred.

Over my police career, my propensity for confronting bosses would prove to be both a blessing and a curse.

On the one hand, it made them fear me. And in a place like the Police Department, which was so rigidly stratified and inherently unsympathetic, if not overtly hostile, to females, that might be the only power I had to protect myself and advance my career.

On the other hand, it marked me as a troublemaker, a loose cannon, a person who was sometimes a little bit scary to be around. I hadn't been on the force for a year, and already I was developing a reputation as a broad to be wary of.

My need to speak my mind was undoubtedly something I inherited from my mom, who never minced words. Mom was always quick to voice her opinion, probably for fear that if she didn't speak her mind right off the bat, she would never be able to speak it at all. But mom was not the only influence that contributed to my in-your-face style.

When I was still a civilian, working as a bookkeeper and a statistician, I had trained myself to become analytical. I was quick to size things up and assess the situation, and that propensity for snap judgments continued even after I became a cop. But sometimes I spoke too quickly, challenged too hastily, and criticized too readily. I would think aloud, when it would have been better to reconsider my thoughts for a few minutes before actually speaking them. People would be caught off guard by my bluntness and my seeming arrogance. They would immediately feel challenged, maybe even attacked.

Some people in the Police Department found my candor refreshing. But others took an instant dislike to me. When a situation might call for delicate diplomacy and a little strategizing, I would sometimes come across like a rampaging steamroller. Over my career, that aspect of my personality would come back to hurt me. More than once, I regret to say.

Back in 1968, when I was so desperate to get out of Community Relations and into the Undercover Unit, my confrontation with Commissioner Melchione felt like the make-or-break point in my still-young career. So I fought her with every verbal weapon at my disposal.

But many years later, I learned that, in my righteous dudgeon and my all-consuming need to win, I might have missed something important that Commissioner Melchione was trying to convey to me.

We bumped into each other at the John Jay College of Criminal Justice, where she was then holding down a top-level administrative job and I was guest-lecturing. I went up to her and said, "Tell me something, Commissioner, I'm curious. How come you were so tough on me when I wanted to go back on the street?"

Melchione smiled. "You know, Kathy, you were not the first policewoman I had who wanted to transfer out of Community Relations and into Narcotics."

"No?" I said, genuinely surprised.

"Some years before you arrived, I had another young policewoman under my command, very much like you, full of fire and ambition, eager to work the streets and catch the action. Like you, she was desperate to leave Community Relations and move into the Narcotics Division. At the time, I had a bad feeling about the transfer. I thought the woman was too young, too naive, and would get herself into trouble if she left. So I tried to block her transfer, very much like I did with you. Later on, albeit reluctantly, I gave in and approved it. After she made the switch, she ended up having an affair with a married detective in the Narcotics Division, gave birth to a child out of wedlock, and was drummed off the force in disgrace.

"I failed to protect her," Commissioner Melchione told me sadly. "So I was absolutely determined to protect you, Kathy. At all costs."

Her revelation was chilling. I realized that I might have been too quick to go to war with her. I also realized that, in the years to come, I would be well advised to be a little more thoughtful and a little less hasty in rushing to judgment.

And that, down the line, I would be wise to hold my tongue before speaking my mind.

CHAPTER SEVEN

I had just made a heroin buy on the train overpass at Ninety-sixth Street and Park Avenue when the two uniformed cops jumped out of their patrol car and surrounded us. As usual, I looked like your typically skeevy, strung-out junkie pros, trolling for trouble.

The two cops had observed the sale. The first one collared the dealer, a lanky black guy named John Willie, but he was no longer carrying any of the goods. He had tossed his stuff off the overpass before they noticed.

The other cop grabbed me in a way that was not exactly genteel. "Whattya doin'?" he demanded.

"I'm not doin' anything. I just stopped to ask him for the time."

"Bullshit," said the cop. "C'mon, whattya got? Give it up."

"I told ya, I don't have anything."

"We got you for sale, honey. So give it up."

With that, he threw me into a doorway near the parked patrol car. Shoved me up against a wall. Slapped me around a couple of times. Ripped open my shirt. And plunged his grubby hand straight down inside my bra.

"You pig! What the fuck you think you're doin'?" I shouted at him.

"Shaddap!" he said, smacking me in the face. Then, after managing to cop a couple of cheap feels, he pulled out the two bags of heroin I had stashed inside my bra for safekeeping (or the bank, as I liked to call it, the left cup being for my cash and the right cup being for the drugs).

"You're goin' down for sale, honey," the cop said. "And so's your pal over there."

"There was no sale," I insisted. "Those are my drugs. He had nuthin' to do with it."

I was hoping to buy the dealer, John Willie, a walk. If I could keep him from being arrested, I knew he would later vouch for me on the street as a stand-up broad. I had worked this area many times before, bought from some of the regular pushers who worked for the big suppliers in East Harlem. John Willie was one of these pushers, a small cog in a much bigger wheel. If I could keep him on the hook, I might be able to work my way up the ladder to some of the major players in the operation. So I didn't want him to take a burn because of me. Not just yet, anyway. If he did, none of the other people in his operation would do business with me again.

"Alright, sister, you're goin' to the station house," said the cop. Then he slapped his handcuffs on me so hard that one of the cuffs punctured a vein near my wrist, causing it to gush blood. Indifferent, the cop tossed me into the back of his radio car. His partner threw John Willie in beside me.

I knew I had to walk a tightrope here. On the one hand, I needed to play the heavy so I'd look as if I were covering for John Willie. On the other, if I came off as too much of a hard-ass with these cops, I could wind up getting myself seriously hurt. I decided to play a strung-out, psycho junkie, praying that my field-team backups would arrive at the station house before things got out of hand.

"You pigs," I muttered from the back of the radio car to the two cops up front. "I'm bleedin' to death! I need a fuckin' Band-Aid back here."

"Shaddap!" the arresting officer shot back. Using the back of his hand, he feinted a stiff smack to my chops.

At the station house, I eventually persuaded the cops that the drugs were mine and John Willie had nothing to do with them. They'd probably cut John Willie loose, but not right away. In the meantime, they booked me for possession. But this presented a whole new problem for me. Once I was booked, I would have to be searched by a policewoman. Since there were only a few policewomen in the department in those days, the one doing the search might very well recognize me. And if she blurted out my true identity in front of John Willie, I was dead meat. Meanwhile, I had a loaded gun concealed behind my belt buckle. While they had found my drugs, the two cops hadn't found the gun. If I didn't give it up now, and they discovered it on me, they'd probably beat the shit out of me for not telling them about it sooner.

"Officer," I said to the arresting cop, "I have to tell you something."
"What?" he asked.
"I have a gun on me."
"You what?"

"I have a gun on me. An automatic. It's hidden behind my belt buckle."

The cop reached in and pulled out my gun. He studied it. He looked back at me. His eyes were wild, almost spinning in their orbs.

"Why, you fucking little piece of . . ."

He reared back, on the verge of pistol-whipping me with my own gun, when the desk sergeant suddenly stepped into the room. With him were my field-team backups. Quickly, we all moved off to another room, out of earshot of John Willie.

The desk sergeant tipped the arresting officer to my little secret.

The poor cop was flabbergasted. And embarrassed as all hell. "Oh, my God, I am so, so sorry, Officer," he whimpered to me. He quickly began looking around for a Band-Aid for my bleeding wrist.

I tried to let him off the hook gently: "Hey, don't worry. Actually, you did me a favor. You made my credibility out on the street that much better."

I despised the people who sold drugs. They were poisoning others for their own gain. For the people who used drugs, I had nothing but contempt. I felt terribly sorry for their families, their parents, their children, their grandchildren. But for the junkies themselves, I felt no sympathy. They were stealing to feed their habits, hurting other people, living a life of degradation, allowing themselves to be used, abused, and manipulated. On occasion, some of the addicts agreed to become police informants. But I felt no real compassion for them. I knew they could be neither trusted nor saved.

Drugs dehumanized both the sellers and the users. Drugs turned people into savages.

Up in the Bronx one summer night, where I was mingling with a bunch of hopheads, I watched in horror as four stoned-out Hispanic kids doused a dog with lighter fluid and set him on fire. Just for kicks. Because I was undercover and the dealers I was hanging out with thought it was funny, I could do nothing to save that poor dog. It died, screaming, at my feet. Meanwhile, the kids who had torched it laughed their stupid asses off.

Down in Alphabet City on the Lower East Side, I met a young mother, no more than twenty, rail thin, zonked-out on heroin, her arms covered with needle marks. She probably weighed no more than eighty pounds, but she was so desperate for a fix that she was turning tricks in exchange for dope. Or buying it with the money that was supposed to go for her baby's milk. Her apartment in a grubby, urine-stinking, three-story walk-up was a pigsty. A single bare lightbulb hanging from the ceiling, a filthy mattress on the floor, piles of dirty dishes in the sink, Chinese take-out cartons and used styrofoam cups everywhere. Meanwhile, her baby, desperate for nourishment, wailed continually. A mosquito net had been placed over the top of the baby's crib—not to keep out the mosquitoes, but to keep out the cockroaches and rats that scurried freely through the apartment.

To this woman, her baby was not a young life to cherish and nurture. It was a nuisance, an impediment to her drug use. I wanted to choke this woman with my bare hands, then take her child away from her and give it a decent home. But because I was undercover at the time, I had to stuff my feelings. The only thing I could do was report this situation to my backup team and hope that somewhere down the line the child welfare authorities would show up to rescue the infant from his monstrous mother.

Sometime later, I helped arrest an elderly Hispanic dealer who was regularly smuggling heroin into New York from Chicago. This dealer, who was known in his Brooklyn neighborhood as El Viejo, was himself at death's door—partially paralyzed, dying of kidney failure, on dialysis, forced to wear metal braces on his shriveled and virtually useless legs. Acting on a tip, we collared him as he was coming off a Chicago–New York flight at Kennedy Airport. He was being wheeled off the plane in a wheelchair when my field team put the cuffs on him.

A search revealed that El Viejo had stolen the airline silverware right off the plane. More important, it also revealed that his leg braces had been hollowed out. About a pound of heroin was concealed inside them.

As I studied this frail and sickly old man, I noticed the bulging veins in his arm, grotesquely hardened and enlarged because of his weekly dialysis treatments. And I thought, "What a twisted, demented, disgusting human being you are! Here you are, dying a slow and horrible death of your own, yet you're out here peddling death to others. Have you no compassion at all for your fellow human beings? Is this some kind of grotesque revenge on your part, to make you feel better about your own miseries?"

This old man was degenerate, disgusting, despicable, less than human. But his, too, was the face of drugs.

* * *

I'd grown accustomed to playing a druggie on the street, but it was inside Bayside High School in Queens that I gave my finest performance.

I had been posing as a transfer student—Marie Martin—making buys of pot, hash, uppers, downers, what have you, in the halls, the bathrooms, the cafeteria, wherever. But for several days, the school had been rife with rumors that "narcs" had infiltrated the ranks and were trying to ensnare unsuspecting sellers and users. To allay any suspicion that I might be one of them, I decided it was time for me to pull out all the stops and convince everyone that I was a druggie who could be trusted.

One afternoon, I made a show of tiptoeing woozily toward the girls' lavatory. A hall monitor spotted me and assumed I must be cutting class. Staying several dozen feet behind, she trailed me into the bathroom. Inside, the teacher flung open all the stall doors until she found me. At the moment she "surprised me," I was tying a rubber tube around one bared arm. Two glassine envelopes containing white powder and a hypodermic needle lay on top of the porcelain toilet-box cover.

The teacher began screaming at me, "What are you doing in here? Oh, God! Mr. Catania! Mr. Catania!"

As the teacher shoved me out of the girls' room and into the hallway, Mr. Catania, the dean of students, appeared.

And that's when I went berserk. Like a caged beast, I turned my fury on Mr. Catania. "You framed me!" I shouted at him. "You set me up! My parents put you up to this!"

The teacher tried to take my arm. I yanked it away from her. "Get your fuckin' hands offa me!" I hissed. After some quiet pleading by Mr. Catania, I agreed to accompany him to his office.

Once inside his office, I started staring out the window, as if in a drug-induced trance. Mr. Catania called for the New York City police officer who was assigned to patrol the high school. The officer, a large but mild-mannered man, asked me to go quietly with him. I ignored him, continuing to gaze blankly out the window. Again the officer asked me to leave with him. But my eyes did not leave the window. Gently, the officer reached for my arm. And that's when I staged a shit-fit.

Whirling on him, I began to scream, "Let go of me, you fat pig! Don't touch me! You're all against me! I know my parents put you all up to this! They want to put me away! Well, I won't go! You can't make me go!"

The police officer radioed for backup. A few minutes later, two more police officers appeared in Mr. Catania's office. But these guys did not even try to reason with me. Grabbing me under each arm, they began dragging me roughly down the hall. I began to scream at the top of my lungs, "Let go of me, you bastards! You're killing me! I'm not going with you! God damn you pigs, let go of me! You're killing me!"

When I went limp, the two cops yanked me off the ground, leaving my feet to dangle in the air. All around me, students were poking their heads out of classrooms, trying to get a peek at what was going on. I began to thrash and kick wildly, trying to get at the two cops with my pointy-toed leather boots. So they slammed me up against a wall, knocking the wind out of me, and cuffed me from behind. Then, with the third cop pitching in to help, they hauled my ass as quickly as possible toward the exit.

"Let go of me!" I kept screaming. "You bastards are killing me!"

As they neared the large double wood doors, I swung both feet up like a trapeze artist, planted my bootheels against the pillar between the doors, and propelled myself backward with all my weight, stopping the three officers dead in their tracks. The three cops had to backtrack to pry my feet away from the post. As one of them held my feet down, the other two angled my body sideways through one of the big swinging doors.

Outside the school building, the cops dragged me cursing, kicking, and screaming toward their radio car. When I began to fight with them again, they threatened to throw me into the back of the radio car, head-first and facedown on top of a loose metal hubcap, which would probably have put a big fat gash in my forehead. Suddenly, I went limp in their arms. I began to sob. They asked me if I intended to keep resisting.

"No! No! No!" I wailed.

So, taking care not to let me bang my head on the doorframe, they placed me in the backseat and locked the door behind me. One of the cops used the radio to alert the 111th Precinct that they were en route with their prisoner.

As I sat weeping and shaking in the backseat, I peeked out the radio car's windows. Virtually the entire student body had piled out of the school to watch my arrest. Kids were standing on the steps, milling behind the fences, congregating in the park across the street, and watching. And they were damned angry about what was being done to me.

Ignoring their stares, the two uniformed cops piled into the front of the radio car, and off they rode with their drugged-out prisoner. On the way back to the station house, I could hear the two cops talking about me.

"Too bad she's a junkie."

"Probably a nice kid without the junk."

"Not bad-looking, either."

"Yeah, and a pretty good pair of tits on her, too."

"So I noticed."

"Wonder what the hell she's on, anyway."

"Whatever it is, must be real dynamite."

Meanwhile, back at the school, the mood among the students remained tense and ugly. Refusing to return to their classrooms, milling about sullenly, a lot of the kids talked of boycotting classes, even staging demonstrations to protest what they perceived as an overzealous use of force by the uniformed cops. Sensing that the mood was turning ugly, and fearful of possible violence, school officials called the Police Department and asked that even more cops be sent to maintain order. Meanwhile, some of the students organized a march on the precinct.

Over at the 111th Precinct, the radio car pulled up with me slumped in a simpering pile in the backseat. When the two officers marched their strung-out prisoner into the station house, they stopped at the front desk.

"Whaddya got?" asked the lieutenant, peering down over the top of the desk.

"One for possession," sniffed one of the arresting officers. "Probably kiddie court."

A moment later, the dean of students, Mr. Catania, walked into the station house to give the police his account of what had happened inside the school. Suddenly, a bunch of angry students from the school barged in right behind him. They began shoving toward the front desk, demanding to know what I was being arrested for. The cops in the station house quickly surrounded them en masse, then herded them back outside and down the front steps.

Back in the street, the students regrouped for another possible charge on the station house. They began to shout angry slogans, railing against "police brutality," "the pigs," "the administration," and "the system."

Inside, Mr. Catania gave the police a full statement and signed an official criminal complaint against me. He also presented them with copies of my school records. When the police found out that I was, on paper at least, eighteen years old, they realized they would have to process me through adult court, not juvenile court. Which meant, if convicted, I could get serious jail time.

The arresting officers formally booked me. Checking downtown with the Police Department's Criminal Records Section, they learned that Marie Martin was hardly a stranger to the system. She had been busted for prostitution, shoplifting, loitering, resisting arrest, possession of drugs, possession of drug paraphernalia, possession of a switchblade knife, and possession of a handgun. Marie's drug habit had gotten her into plenty of hot water over her eighteen short years. Along with most of the city's three hundred thousand junkies, she had a nice long rap sheet to show for it.

As they finished the processing, the arresting cops figured they knew everything they needed to know about Marie Martin. Now they could really throw the book at me.

There was, of course, one small thing they did not know about me. And right about then, a team of plainclothes officers—my backup team—arrived to clue them in. The plainclothesmen pulled the two uniformed cops into a back room. And shut the door so they would all be safely insulated from the ongoing commotion outside and on the street.

"Better cut her loose, fellas," said one of the plainclothesmen.

"Whaddya, crazy!" protested the uniform cops. "She's a collar!"

"Nah, not today, I don't think so," said the plainclothesman.

"Why the hell not?" protested the arresting officer, who was growing angrier and angrier over the threat of losing a perfectly good drug arrest.

The plainclothesman shrugged. "'Cause she's on the job."

"What the hell you talkin' she's on the job!" demanded the uniformed cops. "This some kinda fuckin' joke? She's a damned hippie hophead!"

All the plainclothesmen chuckled. "Yep, she sure looks it, don't she?" offered one. "Which is exactly why she works in the Undercover Unit."

The uniformed cops whirled around to study me. I'll never forget the looks on their faces. One summoned up the courage to address me.

"You . . . you . . . you're a cop?

I grinned. "Surprise."

Remembering how they had manhandled me inside the school, crudely sized up my physical assets inside the squad car, and hustled me, battered, bruised, and bleeding like a common criminal into the station house, they both swallowed hard.

"Gee," said one, "we didn't know. We're really sorry."

"Forget it," I said. "You made me look good out there."

But both of them still seemed pretty numbed by my unmasking.

I myself was thinking that I oughtta get an Academy Award.

CHAPTER EIGHT

If working undercover gave me a sense of family, it gave me something else that was just as important. My independence.

Up until my late twenties, I had been inseparable from my mom. I lived with her. Supported her. Chauffeured her everywhere. I was her steady date. I had no social life of my own. Even when I was invited to parties or dinners, I would always be invited along with my mom. We were like an old married couple.

It got to a point where I began to feel invisible. I had no identity of my own. Fearful of getting into competition with my mom, who was such a powerful, larger-than-life personality, I buried my own thoughts and feelings. In social situations, I would hide in a corner, allowing her to take center stage and hold court. I would wilt like a wallflower, becoming bland, passive, and noncommunicative. People used to wonder if I even had a personality.

Cursed with a crushing sense of responsibility to my mom, I turned into my own worst censor and disciplinarian. I ended up policing myself. While other kids were going through their "rebellious" phase, wearing hippie clothes, putting up posters of rock stars, and smoking dope, I shunned any kind of acting out because I had to remain an ever-supportive, ever-dutiful only daughter. I never played hooky from school, went to discos, stayed out late, smoked cigarettes, drank hard liquor, wore outrageous outfits, got myself tattooed, or experimented sexually with boys. Even when I first joined the Police Department and was working in uniform, I continued to behave like a nun, which was why some of the cops in the precinct had ordained me Sister Mary Kathleen.

The beauty of working undercover was that it not only permitted me to act rebellious, it encouraged me to do it. As model citizen, demure office secretary, and straitlaced Catholic schoolgirl Kathy Conlon, I had been obligated to be on my best behavior. But as dope-fiend scuzzball Marie Martin, I could finally be the naughty girl I had never been. I could nod off in class, cut school, never turn in any homework, and brazenly flip the bird to my teachers. I could sleep late and drink cheap wine on street corners in the middle of the morning. I could pal around with slick talkers, sharpie hustlers, con men, and fast movers who were smoking weed, snorting coke, shooting smack, and having sex with two, three, or four or more partners at a time. I could hang out in nightclubs or discos or smoke-filled juice bars and dance my butt off till dawn. I could put on flamboyant makeup, outrageous wigs, and totally revealing outfits and flirt my little fanny off. I could wear hippie clothes and boots and beads and dress up like Janis Joplin. I could do everything I was never ever allowed to do before I became a cop.

Meanwhile, back in my Astoria neighborhood, everyone readily assumed I had turned into a wild child. On seeing me each day in my hippie-hooker getup, in the company of a lot of other seedy-looking characters who started to show up at our house (the other undercovers), most of our neighbors figured I had washed out of the Police Department altogether.

Sometimes for my undercover stints, I would wear a wire cage under my skirt to make me look pregnant. Hell, that really gave 'em something to gossip about.

When I first started working undercover, I couldn't believe the kick I got from all this. Best of all, when I came home after a night of wild partying in the discos and clubs—even though it was really just an illusion—there wasn't a damned thing my mother could say. Not one single word of protest or criticism or rebuke. And why?

'Cause it was my job.

Off the job, I felt more at ease in social situations, voicing my thoughts, laughing and joking, actually daring to argue and disagree with other people. Sometimes, I even allowed myself to become the center of attention. "How do you like that!" people would marvel. "She's actually got opinions of her own. She's got a personality."

Not that Mom didn't try to insinuate herself into my strange and exciting new world of police work. She loved hearing about my undercover exploits and my close calls, meeting my cop partners, living vicariously through me. If she could have, she would have joined the team herself to take part in our buy-and-bust operations. And, believe it or not, on one occasion, she actually did.

One night, I was scheduled to make some drug buys inside an upscale dance club in midtown Manhattan. My field team that night was supposed to consist of three older male detectives and one older woman detective who would take up positions where they could watch my back as I bought drugs, while making observations about the sellers that would corroborate my actions and the statements I would later put in my report. When I was safely out of sight, the backups would go back to effect the actual arrests.

Now the guys in this team were not like the hip, young stallions I usually worked with. They were white, middle-aged, and wore suits and ties. And they drove out to my house in Astoria to pick me up for the drive to Manhattan. But when they showed up, it was just the three men. The woman detective had called in sick.

As I was getting dressed for my undercover role, Mom graciously served the three detectives coffee and cake.

Suddenly, one of the male detectives came up with a bright idea. Glancing up at Mom, he asked, "Say, whattya doin' tonight, Mrs. Conlon?"

"Oh, nothing special," Mom replied. "Watching the TV, as usual."

"How'd you like to fill in for Brigid and come along to help us out?"

Mom leaped at the opportunity. "Sure!" she chirped back. And before I could voice any objections, she went barreling right past me into her bedroom to get herself gussied up for her big role.

I was thoroughly pissed. This was my world, and I didn't want my mother crashing in on it. What if I had to do something outrageous to maintain my undercover act? What if I got propositioned or manhandled by some grabby, horny guy? What if there was a raid and I got busted by some unsuspecting public-morals cops? What if shooting broke out?

But the other detectives in the team were convinced that having Mom along was a good idea. She would add to their cover, allay possible suspicions they might be cops. So I bit my tongue and went along with the plan.

A few moments later, I came out in my stiletto high heels, white fake-fur coat, and tight, knee-high black dress, my Vampira outfit as I called it. I resembled a high-class hooker. Meanwhile, Mom reemerged in a smartly tailored dress, pearl necklace, and stylish leather pumps. She looked as if she were ready for a dinner-dance at the Waldorf.

The game plan was for all of us to drive to Manhattan. Then, the leader of the backup team—a jowly, fiftyish six-footer who looked like Ralph Bellamy—would enter the dance club, sidle up to the bar for a drink, and blend in with the crowd. Sometime later, I would enter the club, begin talking to different guys, and try to initiate drug buys. The other two detectives in the team would sit at the bar across the street, trying to observe my comings and goings through the plate-glass window. By sitting with them, Mom would throw off any suspicions they might be undercover cops—and also deter other women who might want to come over and talk to them.

At the entrance to the dance club, I gave the gorilla-sized bouncer a friendly squeeze and a big, juicy kiss, as if we were old pals. Thinking he must know me, he immediately unhooked the restraining rope and ushered me past the rest of the waiting crowd. The interior of the club had soft, peach-colored lighting, plush carpeting, cozy little banquettes and cocktail tables, and a live deejay. The music was softer, too, not the usual pulsating, brain-curdling, overamplified crud you would hear in the kiddie juice bars.

Once inside, I began working the room. I made friends with a black guy, then casually asked, "Anybody holding?" He smiled and nodded over toward the deejay, a twentysomething white guy with a longish, Beatles-style haircut. In no time at all, I managed to line up a speed buy. I gave the deejay the cash. He promised to hand over the goods later that evening, once the club had closed for the night. Meanwhile, I drifted back into the crowd, trolling for more suckers.

At their observation post across the street, the other two detectives sat rubbing knees with Mom, who sipped at her ginger ale while straining for a better glimpse of the action. All the time, she kept peppering them with questions: "What's she doing now?" "When will you have enough evidence to make the collar?" "How many buys are you gonna try to make tonight?" "If the dealers make a move to leave, how are you gonna keep up with them?"

At 7 a.m., I left the club with the deejay. As we got into his car to drive downtown, the detective who had been inside the club got into his own car to follow us. The other two detectives who had been across the street got into their car, along with Mom. On the way downtown, Mom kept up the questioning nonstop: "What happens if you lose them?"

"What happens when we get there?" "When do you know it's time to make the arrest?" "What happens if Kathy gets into trouble?" More and more, she was beginning to sound like a frustrated detective. Or a worried mother.

On the street corner outside his apartment, the deejay finally gave me the drugs. The actual arrest would not be made until several days later. That way, enough time would pass to muddy the waters and cloud the events, and I would fade from his memory. In the next several days, he would probably sell speed to any number of other women. Let him think it was one of them who'd set him up.

After I picked up my drugs, I went around the corner to a nearby diner to rendezvous with my backup team. Everything had gone down without a hitch. Everything except that Mom had become a royal pain in the ass. She would not let up on her interrogation: "Do they all go down like this?" "Do you always work with these guys?" "Are they always inside the building?" "Couldn't you get hurt?" "What would they do to protect you?"

And then, something even worse:

"Well, now that that one's done, what's next up for us?" she asked the backup guys.

This was all I needed: Mom as my regular partner. "Don't get carried away," I told her. "This was a one-shot deal."

Mom was insistent. "Why can't I go again?"

"'Cause you're not a cop," I snapped.

She was highly indignant. For the entire week that followed, she refused to talk to me.

"Thanks a heap," I later told the three detectives in my backup team. "You guys have created a monster."

Notwithstanding Mom's onetime gig, working undercover allowed me to gradually cut the strings, to be my own person. Working undercover was my liberation, my coming out.

Working undercover gave me one other important gift, one I had waited a long, long time—maybe too long—to experience and enjoy.

My first love affair.

In the spring of 1970, I signed on to work a gig at a juice bar on the Upper West Side of Manhattan. I met the field team early one evening at the 34th Precinct in Washington Heights. The field-team leader, a soft-spoken, droll detective named Ron Reilly, had jet-black hair and looked like Humphrey Bogart. Detective Reilly gave me the skinny on the juice bar, which was a thriving bazaar for grass, hash, coke, LSD, uppers, downers . . . and more.

"How many buys you lookin' for?" I asked.

Detective Reilly shot glances at the other four cops in his team. "Well," he said, "we'd all like to get on the sheet this month." In plain English, that meant each of the five cops in the team hoped to get credit for one arrest apiece.

"No problem," I told Reilly. "I'll take everything I can outta there. My objective will be to make at least ten buys. That works out to two collars a man. That way, everyone gets on the sheet twice."

"Hey, that's really swell," said one of the other field-team guys.

"We appreciate you doing this for us," said another.

"Especially on such short notice," Reilly added.

"Just one thing," I said. "I don't care what the other guys are doin', but I need one inside man to keep an eye on me and make sure nothing goes wrong. The inside man takes the last collar of the night."

"That'll be me," said Reilly.

We piled into a couple of unmarked cars and drove down to the target, a notorious dance club on West Fiftieth Street and Eighth Avenue, right across from the old Madison Square Garden. Outside, on a side street, we set up base camp. Then we mapped out a game plan. It would go down like this: As soon as I signaled the inside man that I had made a buy, he would step outside and send in two of the outside men. Upon entering the club, the outside men would arrest the suspect, hustle him out quickly before anyone else noticed, and read him his Miranda rights. Then they would cart him off to the local precinct station house, where he would be locked up in a holding pen to await arraignment in criminal court. Meanwhile, back inside the club, I would wait a half hour before maneuvering to set up my next buy. That way, everyone else in the team would have time to get back into position. And nobody in the club would suspect that any of us had some connection to each other.

As the team leader, Reilly entered the club first. He casually plopped himself down at the end of the bar, ordered a club soda with lime, and tried to blend in unobtrusively with the rest of the party crowd. Then I made my grand entrance. That night, I was wearing my cheap-tart teenybopper ensemble. White hip-huggers that left my midriff bare, see-through, long-sleeved bolero blouse, white patent leather boots, and long red wig. If anyone in that club looked hot to trot, it had to be yours truly.

The music was deafening. The strobe lights were blinding, and they created an eerie, angel-hair effect above the dance floor. The air was thick with the cloying smell of hashish and marijuana. The cotton-candy-flavored punch that everyone sipped instead of hard liquor only seemed to add to the sickly sweetness of the place—and undoubtedly accounted for all the disgustingly sticky tabletops. As I moved through the darker recesses of this den of iniquity, I realized that all around the plush, red- and blue-colored velour lounges and love seats off to the sides, people were screwing their brains out. Bare-breasted women. Bare-butted men. Guys with girls. Guys with guys. Girls with girls. Every conceivable combination of genders, numbers, and sexual positions.

The first thing that went through my mind was what I would put in my report after this Sodom and Gomorrah operation was finished. How in the world was I ever going to explain all this to the ever-prudish, always God-fearing Lieutenant Ballner? And that I had been here in the flesh to witness it? He'd go straight through the roof!

I moved away from all these X-rated contortionists and drifted over toward the dance floor, hoping some guy might hit on me. To get the ball rolling, I started dancing by myself, as wildly and flamboyantly as I could. Actually, I made a damned-fool spectacle of myself. Funny thing about a drug crowd. If you smile at people, flirt with them, maybe give one or two a wink or a playful squeeze, they begin to think they know you from way back when. Suddenly, you're part of the in-crowd, no longer a stranger. While I danced, I made a beeline toward a guy who looked like a flash dancer, a real slick Disco Danny type. Tight-fitting bell-bottoms, polyester huckapoo shirt, long hair, scraggly mustache, utterly convinced that he was God's gift to the female of the species—but, most important of all, a probable drug dealer. And, therefore, a perfect target for us.

As I got closer to him, I began dancing as suggestively as I could, gyrating my hips, shimmying my shoulders, and wiggling my chest under my see-through blouse. Once I had his undivided attention, I got even friendlier. A wink here. A pinch of the cheek there. A couple of playful, come-hither butt bumps. Pretty soon, we were dancing as a couple. With my wild gyrations and my flirtatious come-on, this guy was convinced he was gonna get lucky this night. He just knew he'd be able to get me into the sack.

By the time we finally took a break from the dance floor, we were no longer strangers. We were bosom buddies. The guy felt as if he'd known me for ages. So we started to rap.

"So what do you think of this club?" he asked for openers.

"It's cool," I said. "But the truth is, I'm lookin' to get straight. You know anyone who's carrying?"

"Sure do, dollface." He smiled. "Whaddya need tonight?"

A moment later, standing in the safety of the shadows and out of the limelight, I gave him some cash. In return, he handed me some cocaine. Which I promptly tucked away for safekeeping in the bank, aka my right bra cup. Then he grabbed me by the hand and dragged me back out on the dance floor. Now that we had established a little intimacy, he was seriously itching to get even more intimate. He kept trying to draw me closer to him, pressing us tightly together so he could let his hands wander freely up and down my body. This guy was a regular octopus, all tentacles. I kept pushing him away from me, fearful that he might rub up against the .25-caliber automatic tucked inside my bra. Soon, it became a virtual tug-of-war. The more he pulled, the harder I pushed. I tried as best I could to keep him at arm's length. But he was stronger than me. He drew me in close. He began to nibble on my earlobe. Then he blew in my ear and murmured something about wanting to go somewhere else. Like his place. He ran his fingers through my hair. Then down my back. His hand dropped to my butt. His lips were zeroing in toward my mouth. I knew he wanted to French-kiss me. And he was just about to . . .

So I lit up a Virginia Slims.

Now, you might light up a citronella candle to keep the mosquitoes and the gnats away. Well, I used to light up a Virginia Slims to keep the drug vermin away. With a burning cigarette stuck between my lips, there was no way in hell this slimy slug would be able to suck face with me. And thank God for that. The last thing in the world I needed was to get bussed by some clown who had just swallowed LSD or had smoked a reefer laced with acid. Just from the residue of drugs in his saliva, I could end up tripping, too!

There was another reason I lit up. That was the prearranged signal to Ron Reilly that I had completed my buy—and had the evidence in hand to prove it. Spotting my signal, Ron slipped away from the bar and out the door. A moment later, two of the other cops from the field team drifted into the club. Long-haired, bearded, and dressed like all the other stoned-out weirdos, they blended in perfectly with the crowd. The three of us made eye contact. I kept dancing with my increasingly hot-to-trot, touchy-feely partner, slowly maneuvering him toward the edge of the dance floor where the two other cops stood lurking in the shadows. The moment he was within grasp, they stepped up behind him, grabbing both his elbows in vicelike grips. He was too startled to say anything, much less resist. In seconds, the backup guys whisked him out the door.

But just as the two plainclothesmen got the suspect to the door, they were spotted by one of the bouncers. He grabbed the whistle that was dangling from his neck and began to toot on it loudly—some kind of secret code, we assumed, to alert the other bouncers and the club's management that something bad was going down inside the club. Were the cops on the premises? Was it a bust?

For a moment, the people around us were puzzled by what was going on. I played dumb. "What happened? What happened?" I asked everyone else. "Man, this sucks! I am really bummed! This guy was gonna do me, I was going to get high. Then he just walks away without even saying good-bye! Damn!"

The other dancers just shrugged and went back to their business. Fortunately, owing to the blinding strobe lights, the blaring rock music, and the choking fog of marijuana smoke pretty much obliterating everyone's sensual perceptions, nobody had a clue as to what had just happened. Nor did they seem to care. I myself got swallowed up again by the throng.

Meanwhile, outside the club, the backup team was reading my flash-dance partner his Miranda rights and packing him off to the precinct to be booked.

Yes, siree, the night had started off with a bang. One down, nine to go.

After a few more minutes, I plunged back onto the dance floor and began to troll for new business, dancing up a storm, flirting, chatting guys up, getting introductions to other guys, as well as gals, anyone and everyone who was "carrying" and willing to "do" me. Each time I made a new buy, I would signal Ron Reilly by lighting up another cigarette. Then he would leave the bar. Outside, he would signal the backups to enter the club and drop the net on the bad guy. By 6 a.m., I had made nine buys, one short of my goal. But I was starting to wilt.

Seeing me teetering, Ron rose from the bar. He drifted over toward me. "Dance?" he said.

"Yeah, sure, if you say so," I answered, somewhat puzzled. His invitation to dance was the prearranged signal that we were shutting the operation down for the night. But I still had one more buy to go before I reached my goal of ten.

"You don't look so hot," he told me.

"Yeah, well, I guess I'm kinda tired."

"Actually, you look like you're about to take a header. Let's go outside, get you some fresh air."

"Deal."

Outside the club, Ron studied me in the first light of dawn. "You look sick, Kathy. Green. Like pea soup."

"Truth is I feel like shit. I hate the smell of that damned smoke. It makes me want to retch."

"You got a contact high. All that marijuana and hashish in the air, it got to you."

I laughed. "I think you're right. Plus, I haven't had anything to eat all night."

"Come on, Kathy, let's go get you some breakfast."

"But you only got one collar. All the other guys in the team got their two, and you only got one. I should go back in there and bag one more—"

Ron stopped me. "Hey, don't worry, I can live with it. The main thing is, you got us all on the sheet tonight. The guys really appreciate that."

At a diner next to the West Side Highway, Ron and I sat alone in a booth. He ordered us both toast and tea. His manner was quiet and soothing. He was grateful for the way it had all worked out.

"Think you'd be willing to work with us again?" he asked.

"Sure," I said. "Just let the lieutenant know when you need me."

He smiled. "Great."

While we waited for our food, we looked out over the Hudson River. Big white gulls swooped and screeched noisily over the piers and the pilings. The sun was just inching up over the island of Manhattan, and it looked as if it was going to be a beautiful spring morning. At this time of the day, the whole city looked deceptively peaceful and benign, beautiful almost. For a while, the two of us said nothing, just losing ourselves in the soothing deep blue of the river and the spectacular sunrise. The toast and tea made my stomach feel better. After a while, we began to talk again.

Though he had impressed me during the buy-and-bust operation as a smart, confident, and tough cop, Ron turned out to be remarkably gentle and soft-spoken. Funny as all hell, too. The kind of guy who does not have to boast or showboat to prove he's macho, but conveys it simply and quietly through the force of his personality, just by being who he is. Plus, he wasn't exactly hard on the eyes.

Ron was married and had three kids. But from a couple of remarks he let slip, I sensed that his marriage might be on the rocky side. It sounded as if his wife was something of a ballbuster, always on his back for him to earn more money.

After he was sure I had recuperated from my contact high, Ron paid the bill and drove me back to the undercover office downtown so I could get my own car and drive back home to Queens. On the way, he told me that I had really impressed all the guys in his team because of my willingness to take on the juice bar assignment on such short notice.

"'Cause I got you all on the sheet, right?" I said.

"Not just that," Ron answered. "Truth is, you weren't our first choice among the female undercovers."

"What happened to your first choice?"

"She doesn't like working late-night tours. She's kind of a prima donna. She begged off."

"Well, it's her loss. Hell, nights don't bother me. You got a better chance of making collars, you work nights. And if there's one thing I love to do, it's make collars."

Over the next three weeks, Ron asked Lieutenant Ballner to let me work with his team several more times. All our operations went down like clockwork. The cops in Ron's team were pros. And Ron was a terrific team leader.

One night when I was back at the undercover office finishing up some paperwork, a visitor showed up—Ron. He stopped by to ask if I would like to take a drive with him. "Sure," I said. "Why not?"

Inside the car, Ron and I talked about the job and our most recent buy operations.

Suddenly, he switched the subject. "Listen, I wanna ask you something."

"Shoot," I said.

"How would you feel about you and I getting together sometime? You know, like after work."

"You mean, like dating?"

"Yeah, that's exactly what I mean. Like dating."

I was thrown for a loop. Sure, I was attracted to him. What woman in her right mind wouldn't be? And there was obvious chemistry between us. It had been evident from the first buy operation at the West Side juice bar. But romance was something I hadn't expected. Nor had I been look-ing for a relationship.

(What's more, I had always been leery in general of dating male cops. In the precincts, if a woman was asked out by a cop and said no, she was immediately labeled "a lesbian." If she said yes, she was elevated to the status of "a whore." If she agreed to have a drink with another cop, she was "a drunk." If she declined, she was "stuck-up." Given all the pitfalls, I had refrained from becoming romantically involved with male cops, working hard to preserve the nickname I had been given: Sister Mary Kathleen.)

"Tell me something," I said to Ron. "You're married, aren't you?"

"With three kids," he said, not even skipping a beat. And then he looked at me. "Does it matter?"

I thought about what it would mean to start seeing a married man. About his wife. His kids. And how all of them might feel if they knew Ron was fooling around with someone else. It was not a nice thing to do to them. I also knew that by getting involved with a married man, I would be crossing a line that, as a lifelong Roman Catholic, I had always held sacrosanct.

Then, I considered how my own life was going. And, sadly, had to admit to myself that it was not going anywhere good. My mom's health was falling apart. In addition to all her medical problems, she was start-ing to have sudden outbursts of paranoia that scared the hell out of me. Certainly, I would meet my obligations to take care of her. But since I was still living at home, I had no way to escape the misery, catch a breath of fresh air, enjoy a life of my own. I felt trapped, like a prisoner. A pris-oner who was doomed.

Meanwhile, my undercover work was starting to take a toll. Every night that I went out there, posing as Marie Martin, I was walking a tightrope, between life and death, and the fear was working its insidious poison on both my mind and my body. If I wasn't grappling with insomnia and nightmares, my stomach would constantly be in knots, my digestion would be screwed up, my innards would be inflamed with colitis, and I would be racked by stabbing pains in my neck, my lower back, and my legs.

The job was starting to get to me.

As Marie Martin, I was seeing and hearing things on the street that repulsed me. Ugly things. Vile things. Guys coming to the door naked, expecting to have sex with me. Other guys offering me money for blow jobs or threesomes or gang bangs. Girls offering to take me "around the world." Pimps trying to entice me to work for them by touting the length and girth of their sexual organs.

Was that really all people saw when they encountered me? Was I just a piece of cheap meat for sale on the street? Was there nothing more to me, to my being, than the sleazy character of Marie Martin? I needed someone to assure me it was otherwise. Someone to lean on. I had reached the point where I was unable to separate my undercover persona from my real self.

I was desperate.

So when Ron asked me if his being married mattered, I did not really think about his wife's feelings or his children's feelings. I thought of my own feelings. My desperation to bring something sane and healthy and good into my life. And I gave him a purely selfish answer.

"No," I said. "It doesn't matter."

Since I had absolutely no interest in getting married myself, it actually felt safer that Ron was married. That way there would be no expectations, no strings attached.

Though Ron made it clear he was hoping for more than just a friendship, I was not ready for that. He promised not to pressure me.

With Ron, I sensed that things would be different. Unlike the other cops who had tried to hit on me, there was no deception or dishonesty with this guy, no bullshit stories. He didn't doctor his personnel records or lie about his marital status. He wasn't trying to con me. Nor was he looking to score so he could go boasting to the other guys. He'd been having a tough go of things in his marriage, but I could tell he genuinely cared about me.

We began to see each other in a casual, friendly kind of way. Dinner, movies, tea, picnics in Central Park, walks by the lake, and lots and lots of talking. We would get together after our work tours. Or take a few hours off from the job during the day. On our dates, there was no pressure on me to do anything more than what we were doing, which was simply having a nice time.

With Ron, I felt protected and cared for. Our times together were almost magical—fun, relaxed, easy, calming. And, of course, strictly platonic. They continued to remain platonic for quite some time.

Right up until that day in the Bronx when I nearly got my brains blown out.

CHAPTER NINE

Not long after my brush with death in the Four-One Precinct, Ron Reilly took me out for a quiet, intimate dinner to celebrate my promotion to detective.

After we had downed a couple glasses of wine and chatted a bit, about this, that, and the other, I cleared my throat. My heart was pounding inside my chest. I summoned all my courage.

"Can I ask you something?"

"Yeah, sure. What is it, Kath?"

"Do you remember the conversation we had a few months back, about you wanting more than just a friendship with me?"

"Of course. What about it?"

"Well, I'm ready."

Ron just stared at me. "You're kidding."

"No, I'm not kidding, Ron. The time is now. And it's right."

"Why now?"

"Because, after that incident in the South Bronx, I realize there might not be another time for us. Working undercover, I could die at any moment."

Ron studied me carefully. I could see that he had been caught totally off guard by my proposition. He reached across and touched my hand, gently. He wanted to make absolutely certain I realized what I was saying and wouldn't have regrets about it later.

"Kathy, are you sure you know what you're doing?"

I took a deep breath. "If you've got the time, I've got the place."

"Okay, then."

As part of my undercover work, I had been making frequent use of a small basement apartment in Queens belonging to the Undercover Unit, a place where I could unwind and do all my paperwork. It was nothing fancy, just a couple of modest rooms with a stove, a stall shower, a pull-out couch, a table and chairs, and a TV. Ron and I began to meet at this basement apartment and spend four or five hours together. Our love-making was slow, gentle, tender, wonderful. I was new at all this, and Ron never pressured me to do or try anything I was not comfortable with. He was my protector, as well as my friend and my lover.

And so it was, at the ripe old age of twenty-eight, that I began my first love affair. And my first experience with sex.

It wasn't so much the sex that fueled our affair as it was the emotional bond. The circumstances of "the job" had brought us together. This man was entrusted with my safety when I went into the clubs, the discos, and the parks to make my drug buys. He was my backup. My safety net. My guardian angel. I depended on him for my survival.

And, at a time when my emotions were completely frazzled, he was the guy who helped me put the pieces back together. Time and again, when I would endure the humiliation of being propositioned by junkies or drug dealers, as though I were actually some $10-a-trick junkie whore, he'd remind me, "You have to remember, Kathy, it's not Kathy Conlon they're coming on to, it's Marie Martin. And Marie Martin is not really who you are. Marie Martin is make-believe. Kathy Conlon is real. But these people don't know Kathy Conlon. And, thank God, they never will."

In his strong but quiet way, Ron became my emotional compass. And while we did have sex, it was a very different kind of sex from the cheap, raw, and ugly sex that was being thrown in my face on the street. In a sense, our affair was not so much about having sex as it was an escape from the sordidness, selfishness, and commerce that could be coupled with sex. With Ron, I gained a whole different perspective on lovemaking. No longer did I feel violated or dirty. Ron helped me to feel healthy, sane, and normal again. And, yes, loved.

During the workweek, Ron would send me cards telling me how much he missed me. Or leave little notes in my mailbox. Once in a while, I would find gifts on my desk, like a record album or box of candy or a stuffed toy dog.

During our time together, Ron never talked about leaving his wife. And, frankly, that was an enormous relief to me. We had found incredible joy in just being with each other, without any expectations for the future. Neither of us really wanted to change our lives. Our affair had one cardinal rule: it would last as long as neither of us did anything to cause pain to the other. And that made it a special relationship, indeed.

On my twenty-ninth birthday, Ron gave me a surprise birthday gift. A gold ring adorned with a small diamond and deep blue sapphires. It was breathtaking, truly exquisite.

"This is for living," Ron told me.

I cried. I wrapped my arms around him. And then I practically squeezed every last breath out of that wonderful man.

I had never liked making drug buys in Brooklyn. The Brooklyn DA's office never accorded us much respect. And the Brooklyn DA himself, Eugene Gold, seemed far more interested in putting up big numbers for the press than making quality arrests that would stand up in court. A shameless and egotistical publicity hound, he behaved as though the police were simply accessories to help him generate more positive media coverage for himself.

At one point, by posing as a transfer student, I bought drugs from eight different students at Fort Hamilton High School in Brooklyn. My field team arrested all eight defendants on a single night, plucking them out of their large, comfy houses as their mommies and daddies protested and sobbed. As the arrests were carried out, I sat inside a darkened car, out of sight, watching carefully as each of the kids was marched out and Mirandized.

But soon after the arrests, I received a curious phone call from the Brooklyn DA's office.

"You misidentified one of the defendants," said Assistant DA Mars, one of the bureau chiefs. The defendant in question was a chubby girl who had sold me Seconals, a barbiturate, in the Fort Hamilton High cafeteria.

"No way," I told Mars. "She was the one."

A day or so later, ADA Mars called me into his office, along with the two detectives who were my backups. Tall, crew-cut, and chisel-faced, Mars puffed on a big fat cigar as he spoke to us, choking the room with his smelly smoke. His manner was surly and condescending, as though we existed for the sole purpose of carrying out his exalted orders. "I want all of you to make a photo ID of your subjects," he announced.

"Wait a second," I fired back. "I made a face-to-face buy from this girl. Why do I have to make a photo ID? I've never had to make a photo ID before."

"Because I say so, so just do it, Detective," ADA Mars said stiffly.

Reluctantly, we complied. All three of us picked out the chubby girl who had sold me the Seconals.

"You're all wrong," ADA Mars said. "She was not the one who sold you the drugs."

By now, I was getting pretty pissed. "What do you mean she wasn't the one? I was there. I made the buy. She was the one, no question about it. Let's go to court, Counselor."

"Well, we'll just have to see about that," said ADA Mars.

For several months afterward, I pressed for indictments against the chubby girl and the other seven students who had sold drugs to me at Fort Hamilton High. But no matter how many times I pestered the DA's office to put my cases on the calendar, I could never seem to get them in front of the grand jury. The whole business was starting to smell fishy.

Then, several months later, there was a reorganization in the DA's office, and another prosecutor took over many of ADA Mars's cases. To my great surprise, I got a subpoena from the new prosecutor to appear before the grand jury. As a result of my testimony, the grand jury returned an indictment against one of my Fort Hamilton suspects.

At last! Some action. When I left the courthouse, I felt vindicated.

But the moment I got back to my office, I got an angry telephone call from ADA Mars. "How the hell did you manage to get that case before the grand jury!" he demanded.

"Simple," I told him. "I received a subpoena from Kings County. I answered the subpoena. I presented my evidence. And the grand jury returned an indictment."

"Your indictment is no good," said Mars. "I'm going to have it dismissed. Along with all your other cases."

Clearly, the fix was in. This thing had the stink of politics and favoritism all over it. The DA's office had been bought and sold.

"Tell me something, Mr. Assistant District Attorney," I said, making no effort to conceal my fury. "Just how much did it cost that girl and her parents to get all eight of these kids off the hook?"

Mars tried to dodge the issue. "Er—we won't go into figures or any other matter involving this case over the telephone."

But I pressed the point. "Oh, but there was a contract, wasn't there? A contract did go in, right?"

Mars sidestepped me again. "What I do for one, I must do for all."

When I got off the phone, I immediately reported the conversation to my superiors in the Police Department. "They're selling my cases out for political favors," I told them.

Lieutenant Ballner pulled me aside. "Listen, Kathy, nobody's gonna hold it against you if you lose these eight cases. You got too many years to go on the job to let this derail you. The important thing here is that you don't want to get into a war with the DA's office. That's a whole other can of worms. And once you open it up, it could end up ruining your career. So don't be futzin' around here."

I knew the lieutenant was trying to protect me. Heeding his advice, I decided to let the matter drop.

But from that moment on, I tried to avoid working any new undercover cases in Brooklyn, where I now knew the district attorney's office to be corrupt and compromised. Whenever I did have to make drug buys in Brooklyn, I would ask my targets to get into my car, then drive them across the border into Queens before actually completing the transaction.

That way, when it came time to make the collar, my report would reflect that the actual drug sale had occurred in Queens, and I could be assured of dealing with an honest DA in Queens instead of a dishonest one in Brooklyn.

In June of 1972, the Select Committee on Crime of the U.S. House of Representatives scheduled public hearings on the rampant drug problem in our nation's schools. The committee subpoenaed thirty people from New York City to appear as witnesses.

Including yours truly.

One of the other witnesses it subpoenaed was Louie Luongo, a detective who had worked with me as a backup on my Fort Hamilton cases. Testifying with a black bag over his head to conceal his identity, Luongo flat-out accused the Brooklyn DA, Eugene Gold, of being corrupt and fixing cases for political favors.

Luongo's allegations hit like a nuclear bomb. His testimony exploded in front-page headlines in the *New York Times*, the *New York Daily News*, and the *New York Post* and led the newscasts on all the TV and radio stations. Little wonder that the Brooklyn DA's office dubbed him Louie, World War III. In a desperate attempt at damage control, Eugene Gold, the Brooklyn DA, hastily summoned a press conference and denounced Luongo as a head case.

Now Luongo did have a reputation as a loose cannon. A short, wiry ex-marine, given to wearing pointy leather shoes and skintight pants, he was a bit of a paranoid and an obsessive-compulsive. Terrified of germs, he was known to wash down the telephone on his desk with soap and disinfectant each and every day. But he was also a damned fine cop, utterly honest and dedicated, and did not deserve to be maligned and vilified by the sleazeballs in the DA's office.

I had planned to limit my congressional testimony to my undercover experiences in the city's public schools and colleges. But once Luongo went public with his sensational allegations, I knew I would be dragged into the middle of this imbroglio as well.

Sure enough, within twenty-four hours of Luongo's bombshell, the aftershock hit. I was summoned to Police Headquarters to meet with Chief Garrett, head of the Narcotics Division. The chief wanted to know what I planned to tell Congress.

When I entered the office, I bumped into another detective who was waiting to see the chief. Scruffy, long-haired, bearded, dressed in jeans, he looked more like a bohemian poet or a downtown painter than a cop. I had never met him before, but I would have recognized him anywhere. He was, in a way, a celebrity in the department and the city of New York. But not exactly for positive reasons.

"I know who you are," I told Detective Frank Serpico.

Serpico had been in the midst of testifying before the Knapp Commission about wide-scale corruption in the Police Department. In its final report, the commission would allege that high-ranking police officials had ignored information that some of their men were suspected murderers, extortionists, purveyors of stolen goods, and heroin dealers. It would specifically accuse many narcotics cops of being thieves and shakedown artists, willing to extort and brutalize drug dealers to collect hefty payoffs. In cop lingo, these payoffs were known as scores.

As the star witness to appear before the Knapp Commission, Serpico alleged that most narcotics cops would like to see him dead. And that had really pissed me off.

Now I was no Pollyanna. I knew the department was going through a tumultuous catharsis, a period of painful self-cleansing. I knew there were cops on the take, too many cops. I had seen guys I'd once worked with marched out of precincts and squad rooms in handcuffs. But many more officers, in my mind, were honest, dedicated, and hardworking. Yet Serpico was smearing all of us with the broad stain of corruption.

"I work narcotics," I said to Serpico, "and I take offense that you say all of us want you dead. I don't even know you. It never crossed my mind to wish you dead or hope you got hurt. But now, you're telling me I'm corrupt. You make it sound like all of us are corrupt."

"Well, I really didn't mean it that way," he replied.

"You've made life hell for us," I told Frank Serpico.

There was no time to continue this little debate on police ethics, however. Chief Garrett summoned me inside his private office. Clean-shaven, with clipped blond hair that gave him the look of a senior naval officer and a sarcastic, no-nonsense manner, Chief Garrett was an absolute zealot about ferreting out corruption. He was convinced that everyone was guilty of something and saw scandal everywhere in the department. With that cat now out of the bag thanks to Louie Luongo's testimony, he was fearful that, sooner or later, the whole Police Department would be drawn into a nasty mudslinging with the Brooklyn DA.

He demanded to know what I planned to say in my testimony before Congress. I told Garrett that I intended to tell Congress the truth. He gave me his blessing, but warned me that I would have to stay one step ahead of the Brooklyn DA's office, which was pulling out all the stops to block my testimony.

In fact, the chief had just gotten word that the Brooklyn DA intended to subpoena me to appear as a witness at some half-baked proceeding in Brooklyn Criminal Court. By law, the local subpoena would take priority over the federal subpoena, effectively preventing me from traveling to Washington, D.C., the next morning to make my scheduled appearance before Congress.

However, since I was still an undercover cop, and the Police Department maintained no personnel files on me, the Brooklyn DA could not figure out where to track me down. Chief Garrett told me to stay out of sight and out of reach. So, once I left Police Headquarters, I spent the rest of the day holed up in the Federal Building at 26 Federal Plaza, not returning home to Astoria until late that night.

Bright and early the next morning, I boarded the first shuttle flight out of La Guardia Airport to Washington, D.C. Accompanying me was Detective Luongo. An inspector from the Narcotics Division also made the trip down to Washington, but opted to travel by train since he was afraid of flying. The inspector was a boozy old-timer who carried a small flask of Scotch in his jacket pocket to periodically fortify himself.

After we arrived at the Capitol, Detective Luongo and I rendezvoused with the Narcotics inspector in one of the corridors outside the hearing room. We had some time to kill before I was due to testify, so Luongo went off to get a drink of water. The moment he disappeared, the inspector pulled me aside.

"You know, Detective, you don't have to do this," he told me.

I looked at him. "Do what?"

"Support Luongo," he said, reaching for his pocket flask. He took a deep swig, smacked his lips, then tucked his flask back inside his jacket pocket.

Basically, the inspector was telling me that I could go before the committee and refute everything that Luongo had said. Now Luongo was a wild man, no question. But he had told the truth about our cases. And about the tampering by the Brooklyn prosecutors. He was an honest cop. And I had no intention of leaving him to hang out and dry.

Then it hit me.

If I thought I had eluded the tentacles of the Brooklyn DA's people back in New York, they had just caught up with me in Washington. Somehow, this fat, old drunk of an inspector was in cahoots with them and doing their bidding. The fox had been inside the chicken coop all along.

I fixed the inspector in a long, cold stare. And then I told him:

"Lemme tell you something, Inspector. In five minutes, I am going to walk into that hearing room. I'm not going to volunteer anything. But, if they ask me a question, I'm going to answer it. Truthfully. And if they ask me if anyone tried to get me to change my testimony, your name is the first one I'm going to drop. For the record."

I started toward the hearing room. The inspector tried to block my path. "You know, you're a detective," he said. "You got a lot to lose."

Son of a bitch. Now he was suggesting that if I didn't play ball, I could end up losing my gold detective shield. Well, screw him.

"I got nothing to lose," I told him. "The truth can't hurt me." With that, I pushed past him. "See you in Congress, Inspector." And I walked through the door.

Inside the hearing room, stately and plush with all its dark, polished wood fixtures and red velvet carpeting, I sat down at a table with several microphones on it. Then I donned a white pillowcase, with holes cut into the face for my eyes, to conceal my identity from the press corps and the public, who had not yet been admitted into the room.

The first part of my testimony went fairly smoothly as I described my thirty-eight months working undercover. Detailing my experiences in my undercover persona of Marie Martin, I told the congressmen that, in some schools, as many as 75 percent or more of the students were using drugs. Sadly, I added, most of their teachers didn't give a damn. As a matter of fact, when I showed up masquerading as a strung-out, foul-mouthed doper transfer student, "they didn't even have the decency to throw me out," I testified.

And then, somebody on the committee asked me what I thought about Detective Luongo's allegations that the Brooklyn DA was corrupt.

I thought about the efforts to derail me, both in court and before I could come down to Washington. I thought about Lieutenant Ballner's advice to me to keep a low profile and not tangle with the powers that be. I thought about what that weaselly, booze-guzzling inspector had just told me outside the hearing room in an effort to dissuade me from telling the truth.

I cleared my throat. I took a drink of water. I adjusted my microphone.

"We believe our cases were tampered with," I told the committee.

Then, going into all the gory details, I backed Louie Luongo to the hilt.

On the flight back to New York City, our plane ran into a nasty thunderstorm. As bolts of lightning flashed all around us and we were buffeted by high winds, our plane was tossed around like a toy. At one point, as we hit an air pocket and plummeted several hundred feet, all of the bags came flying out of the carry-on luggage compartments.

I was sure we were going to crash.

Louie Luongo just laughed.

"Musta been arranged by the Brooklyn DA," he suggested.

Now, here's what happened in the aftermath of our testimony to Congress:

Absolutely nothing.

None of our allegations of case-fixing was ever investigated or acted upon.

Detective Luongo became known within the Police Department as a head case. He retired on a disability pension.

One of the assistant DAs whom Luongo had accused of being on the take was arrested, prosecuted, and sentenced to fifteen years in federal prison for heroin possession. He later testified before the President's Commission on Organized Crime that he had done numerous favors for the Mafia while still working in the Brooklyn district attorney's office.

ADA Mars, the Brooklyn prosecutor who had repeatedly sabotaged our eight Fort Hamilton cases, would many years later go on to be appointed a New York City Criminal Court judge.

In May of 1981, Eugene Gold decided not to run again for district attorney. Two years later, he was arrested in Nashville, Tennessee, on charges of raping a ten-year-old girl at a national convention of district attorneys. He subsequently pleaded guilty to fondling the girl, agreed to undergo psychiatric treatment, was placed on probation, and was disbarred. He now lives in upstate New York.

Last but not least, I gained the reputation of being a troublemaker with a big mouth.

Ron had not been happy about my willingness to testify before Congress.

With the Knapp Commission cutting a bloody swath through the ranks of the department, police careers being destroyed left and right, and overzealous prosecutors competing with each other in some kind of frenzied, Inquisition-like witch hunt to see who could crucify the greatest number of cops, even the ones who might be innocent, Ron felt this was the worst possible time for me to place myself in the limelight. Even though I had no intention of exposing a fellow cop, but rather exposing a corrupt prosecutor, Ron worried that I would still end up with a reputation as a rat. And that could put me in peril with my peers, who were paranoid about anybody who might be inclined to spill the beans, whatever the reason, the subject, or the target.

"Don't hurt yourself, Kathy," he told me. "You still got a long way to go yet."

I wasn't eager for a fight, so I let the matter drop. But, deep down, I was gonna do what I had to do. And nothing he could say would stop me. Still, it was disappointing to think that he would even try.

Meanwhile, our relationship began to unravel.

Ron got transferred to a new squad in Manhattan. With his transfer, his hours changed, as did his days off. It became increasingly difficult for us to meet. Our get-togethers became fewer and farther between. And when we did get together, our dates seemed to end a lot quicker than they used to.

Meanwhile, my mom's health took a turn for the worse, and her behavior became increasingly erratic. She spent hour upon hour playing a small organ I had bought for her, rarely leaving the house. When she did go out, she would complain of being followed by strangers. One night, convinced there were armed intruders at the door, she tried to grab my gun away from me to shoot them, and it was all I could do to restrain her. Another night, without telling me, she drove off in my car. She began painting all the rooms in our house in dark, dreary colors. She talked about drinking gasoline and lighting a match.

I tried to convince her that she needed to get professional help, but she wouldn't hear of it. Instead, she flew into screaming rages and accused me of trying to "gaslight" her. During one of her more violent outbursts, she threw me up against the wall and grabbed a butcher knife. I had to twist her arm backward to get the knife away before she could hurt me or herself.

Her chronic diabetes led to gangrene in her big toe. When I finally managed to get her to a hospital, the doctors decided to amputate. After further tests, they also discovered that Mom had suffered a series of ministrokes, which had triggered all her crazy behavior.

Meanwhile, my own health problems—primarily, those painful bouts of stress-induced colitis—began to recur. The night my mother went to the hospital to have her toe amputated, I found myself at home, completely alone for the first time ever in my life. I was physically sick. And absolutely petrified.

Frantic, I called Ron at work and asked him to come over. Pleaded with him, in fact. But when he did show up, he seemed edgy and irritable.

"I really can't stay," he told me. "I've got to get home." I could read the impatience in his eyes, his mouth, the tensed way he was holding his body. Clearly, he wanted to put some distance between us.

And then, just like that, he was gone. Along with our love affair.

There were no tears, no angry words, no emotional good-byes. It ended not with a bang, but a whimper. The gifts and notes stopped coming. The telephone calls ceased.

Both of us had known for some time we were drifting apart. And, truth be told, both of us had known that, sooner or later, it would end exactly like this.

CHAPTER TEN

For a long time after my breakup with Ron, I avoided dating altogether. Even though our split had been inevitable, I was still hurting and needed time to heal. Meanwhile, Mom's declining health was requiring more and more of my attention. I had neither the time nor the energy nor the emotional stamina for any new men in my life. And I began to figure that's the way it would stay for a long, long time to come.

I finally transferred out of the Undercover Unit, to a field-control team in the Narcotics Division, where I was assigned to train younger cops in the fine points of making undercover drug buys (including buys from corrupt police officers, if need be). It was a far less stressful job than working undercover myself. But I still didn't have much of a social life.

Then, totally by accident, I met someone.

It was at a St. Patrick's Day dinner that was held in the banquet room of a fancy hotel on Park Avenue. The dinner was sponsored by the Honor Legion, a group that salutes individual cops for their bravery. Because I had received a medal after my near-fatal rip-off in the Four-One Precinct, I had been inducted into the legion. About three hundred people showed up to feast on corned beef and cabbage. Most of the guests were cops, but there were also representatives from other city agencies and the press.

Usually at these formal dinners and affairs, I would sit with the other policewomen and shy away from making dinner conversation with any of the men. But this night, one of the women had invited several guests and needed some extra seats at our table. The hostess asked if I would mind relocating.

At my new table, I found myself sitting with a bunch of male cops. "Hi," said one of them. "I'm Bob Burke."

"Kathy Conlon."

I gave him the once-over.

Tall, good-looking, a real Irish mug, fashionably dressed in a buttoned-down shirt, silk tie, and tailored three-piece suit. He had a real presence. For the rest of the evening, we bantered playfully, and he seemed totally at ease with me. Plus he had a wickedly funny sense of humor. Notwithstanding my self-imposed celibacy, I found myself growing more and more attracted to him.

Because I had come to the dinner directly from work, I was wearing slacks and a vest and no makeup. My hair was also very short, styled into one of those duck's-ass cuts from the 1950s. I worried that I might look too boyish or butch.

After the dinner, Bob Burke gave me a lift back to Queens, so I could pick up my own car. Still worried about my tough-gal appearance, I kept studying myself in the side mirror.

Suddenly, Bob turned to me and asked, "Tell me something. Are you straight?"

My temperature shot up. "You have some nerve!" I shot back. "Of course, I'm straight."

He smiled. "Great. Let's get together sometime."

Bob Burke was unusual among the men who had wanted to date me. He wasn't the least bit cowed or intimidated by me. And why should he be? I was a detective; he was a captain. He outranked me.

Our dates were low-key. Movies. Dinners. The beach. After-hours get-togethers at an East Side pub near the Police Academy, where he was currently assigned. It was easy to date Bob. We spoke the same language, shared many of the same friends, looked great together at social functions. Because he, too, was a cop, he could accommodate my unusual hours and days off without getting bent out of shape the way a civilian might. Also, he understood my reluctance to go into certain bars and nightclubs late at night because of my fear that either the premises or the patrons might later become targets in my drug-buy operations.

Best of all, he appreciated my sense of humor, which could be pretty darned warped.

Not long after we started dating, I went to meet Bob at the Police Academy for lunch one day. I came to the building straight from work. Because I had been training some younger guys to make undercover buys, I was still dressed like a $5-a-trick whore. Hip-hugger jeans with bell-bottoms, moccasins, ruffled, long-sleeved shirt, bare midriff showing. As I walked into the Academy, all heads turned to gape at me in dismay.

When I got to Bob's office, he was immersed in paperwork and didn't immediately notice me. But an old-time lieutenant who sat at the desk nearby gave me a real fish-eyed look, as if he wasn't sure whether to greet me, handcuff me, or proposition me. Tiptoeing toward Bob's desk, I stopped, planted my feet, put my hands on my waist, and stood with my back to the lieutenant.

"Somebody told me I had a nice pair," I announced loudly. Bob looked up from his desk. "So, you wanna see my nice pair or what?"

With that, I yanked my blouse up high above my belt, revealing even more of my bare midriff.

Sitting behind me, the old-time lieutenant nearly keeled over. But Bob simply guffawed as he gazed down at my belt buckle, which had been perfectly carved into the shape of a giant pear.

Bob also made a big impression on me because of his patience with my mom, who was growing sicker and frailer with each passing day. She seemed to develop a real fondness for him, particularly when he came to visit and showed her a picture of his own mother. "You know, you kinda remind me of her," he said, and she practically melted with pleasure. In the beginning, Mom was Bob's biggest fan.

Later, however, as Mom's various illnesses started to play havoc with her brain, things changed. Feeling increasingly vulnerable and dependent, she was frightened of losing me to some man at a time when her mind and body were failing her. A man who might not look kindly on the extremely close relationship she had always maintained with her one and only daughter.

One morning, I was getting myself ready to go out with Bob. As I was dressing, Mom went into the bathroom. Suddenly, I heard a scream. I rushed toward the bathroom to find her collapsed on the floor, half-conscious and unable to control her bodily functions. I immediately called 911.

As the attendants were lifting her into the ambulance, I tried to reassure her: "Mom, I love you. It's gonna be okay."

"I love you, too," she answered weakly. The attendants strapped an oxygen mask over her face. Suddenly, the demons took over and she abruptly ripped the mask off. "Kathy! Kathy! Don't marry him! Promise me, you won't marry him!"

I scolded her. There was no logic behind her outburst. "I'm not promising you anything. This is ridiculous. Now put that mask back on this very instant!"

By the time she reached the hospital, Mom was in a coma. The doctors concluded that she had suffered a massive stroke. There was little I could do for her at this point except make her comfortable, talk to her, squeeze her hand, just be there for her. In my heart, I knew the end was near.

On Thanksgiving Day of 1973 I came to the hospital to visit as usual, hoping against hope for some improvement in Mom's condition. But she was still unconscious. After a couple of hours of sitting in her room, I went down to the cafeteria to get a cup of tea. When I returned, I found that someone had drawn the curtain around her bed. I opened it to discover that a sheet had been placed over her face. I pulled it down so I could see her one last time and say my prayers. Mom's eyes were closed. After a long and painful struggle, she was finally, mercifully, at peace and at one with God. I kissed her softly on the forehead.

There was no wake. No funeral service.

She was buried in a plain pine coffin.

Bob and I tied the knot in October of 1974.

Seventy-five guests, most of them New York City cops, attended our wedding. The ceremony was performed by the Reverend Bill Kalaidjian, a Police Department official chaplain.

Undoubtedly the most memorable thing about our nuptials was that, along with most of the guests, both the bride and the groom were packing guns. We might be getting married, but we were still cops, whether on duty or off. Bob had his revolver tucked inside the back of his tuxedo trousers, behind his cummerbund. I had my .38-caliber revolver concealed in an ankle holster, which was stylishly covered by the hem of my wedding gown.

We decided to make our home in Astoria, Queens, in the house where I had lived with Mom. We were determined not to mix our professional careers with our home lives. And, for the most part, we succeeded.

For one thing, we tried not to talk too much about "the job" when we were at home. That Bob was a uniformed captain in management and I was a plainclothes detective helped greatly. As cops, we had different sensibilities, different objectives, and different headaches. Bob had spent most of his time supervising cops on patrol; I was an investigator. Bob was a boss; I was an employee and a delegate to the detectives' union, the Detectives' Endowment Association.

Whenever someone would want to know how the two of us could co-exist in a police marriage, I would chirp, "Oh, we never talk shop. He's management, I'm labor."

Occasionally, however, our paths did cross on the job.

In 1976, we both ended up in the 79th Precinct in Brooklyn. Bob was the captain in charge of the patrol cops downstairs. I was assigned to the Brooklyn North Organized Crime Control Unit upstairs. The acronym, BNOCCU, made us sound like breath spray.

One day, the Patrolmen's Benevolent Association staged a protest over a proposed new labor contract. A bunch of off-duty cops were picketing outside the station house. Now, in his heart of hearts, Bob actually felt a great deal of sympathy for these picketing cops. But because he was management, he could not display his sympathy in a public venue or in front of the news media.

I, however, could show it. As a delegate to the Detectives' Endowment Association, and a delegate with a growing profile, I felt it was my duty to join the picket line and wear a big placard showing my support for the rank and file. I had just gotten my hair cut that morning, and I was so closely shorn that I looked like a prison inmate.

Stepping outside the station house to make sure the labor demonstration remained peaceful, Bob caught sight of his wife marching shoulder to shoulder with other off-duty protesters in the picket line.

"Hey, escapee," he teased, "your tour's about to start. Get to work."

At one point, BNOCCU targeted a cheaters' place, a hotel where adulterous wives and randy husbands sneaked off to do the nasty.

One of our undercovers was planning to make a big drug buy inside the hotel. As part of the backup operation, we rented a room just down the hall from the site of the buy. To allay any suspicions among the other guests that we might be cops looking to make a bust, the lieutenant told me and one of the male cops to plant ourselves at the hotel bar, posing as hot-to-trot lovers, before we went up the stairs to our room. As long as the two of us did a convincing act of the preliminaries to passion, he decided, nobody would ever make us for cops.

"You might have to look like you're making out," the lieutenant said.

"Fine, Loo," I told him. "Just as long as you don't send me in there with one of the slobs. I mean, I got my pride. And I am a married woman."

The lieutenant laughed. "Don't worry, you'll be working with Brad." Great, I thought. Brad was one of the younger, more clean-cut cops in the squad. Smooth-shaven, with reddish-blond hair, he favored bell-bottom leisure suits and wild-colored shirts. His breath wasn't rancid and he didn't have BO. I was married. He was married. What could be safer, right?

Before we went out, I phoned Bob. "Listen, you may hear some scuttlebutt about your wife making out with some strange guy in the lounge of the Westway Hotel. But it's legit, all part of the job. And they're not going to send me in there with some randy Andy. So, down the line, if you hear any talk about me swappin' spit with some guy, you know it's on the up-and-up."

"Knock 'em dead," said Bob.

The operation went down smoothly. I sat at a table with Brad and we behaved like a couple of bunny rabbits in heat. We kissed madly and hugged and made it look as if we couldn't wait to get into each other's pants. To me, it was like acting in a movie or playing a love scene on TV. And I gave what I thought was a four-star performance. Then we went upstairs to our rented room and waited for the drug buy to go down. Which it did, without any hitches whatsoever. All in all, the entire operation went off beautifully.

Or so I thought.

Unbeknownst to me, Brad came away with the impression that I wasn't acting—I really was hot for him. Either that, or he had spent too much time hanging around hookers. Because from then on, he began treating me as if I were a hooker, too.

It started when I came into work late one day. Because of a colitis attack, I had needed to take an extra hour at home, to wait for my medication to kick in. I phoned the lieutenant to tell him I would be late.

But when I walked into the office, Brad promptly asked, "What, it's your time of the month?"

Pretty soon, I found myself on the receiving end of all kinds of lewd suggestions and gross innuendos. Now I have no objection whatsoever to cussing. Some of my favorite expressions are four-letter words. Hell, they do the job better than a lot of prettier words, right? But this guy just made everything sound so damned dirty. Such as asking me what kind of birth control Bob and I used. What brand of condom we liked. Or what sexual positions Bob and I preferred. Brad turned out to be something considerably different from the solid, safe, clean-cut guy I had assumed he was. In short, he was a creep.

In the beginning, I tried to ignore him. Whenever he'd start with his locker room filth, I'd tell him, "Oh, grow up!"

But the obscenities and innuendos kept flowing. I hadn't really been looking for a confrontation. But, pretty soon, I realized I would have to deal with this pinhead if I ever wanted to shut him up.

I got my chance shortly before Brooklyn North was due to hold its annual dinner-dance. Cops traditionally invited their spouses to these parties. A bunch of us were riding in a car one day when I turned the conversation to the upcoming gala. Brad was sitting in the front seat with another cop, who was driving. I was in the rear with the sergeant. I leaned forward and put my face close to Brad's ear. Then, ever so sweetly, I inquired:

"Tell me something, Brad. Is your wife coming to the dinner-dance?"

"Yeah. Why?"

"Oh, good. I'm really happy about that. I can't wait to meet her."

"Really? Well, my wife's really a nice person. I hope you sit with us."

"Oh, I intend to, believe me. I mean, the two of us just have so much in common, so many, many things we need to talk about."

"Oh, yeah?" said Brad. "Like what?"

"Like what kinda birth control you use. What kinda condoms the two of you prefer—you know, ribbed, French ticklers, extralarge, lubricated, colored, whatever. And what kinda position you like to screw in. I'm always interested in hearing about that."

Brad's head whipped around. He looked at me with bug eyes.

"And, of course, her time of the month. How she handles that."

All the color in Brad's face seemed to drain. He tried to speak, but his words came out incoherently, like blubbering. "You . . . you . . . you can't talk to her like that! For God's sakes, she's my wife!"

I screwed up my eyes. "Well, I'm somebody's wife, too. Or did you forget?"

From that day on, Brad never bothered me again.

In 1984, Bob and I would cross paths at the scene of a tense standoff with an elderly man who, threatened with eviction, would barricade himself inside his apartment with a gun. Bob was working as the department's liaison with the press corps; I was a member of the hostage-negotiating team trying to talk the perp into surrendering. At one point, we decided to use a robot, equipped with a built-in camera and microphone, to approach the gunman. To dim the illumination in the hallway that the robot would navigate en route to the gunman's apartment, I actually had to stand on the shoulders of another hostage negotiator and unscrew the ceiling lightbulb. The robot was then sent down the hall, toward the gunman, but hours of talking back and forth via its microphone failed to persuade the old man to give up his weapon and come out. When a shot rang out, Emergency Service cops stormed the apartment and discovered that the guy had shot himself in the leg. He was quickly taken into custody.

Back outside again, where the press was now swarming, I started to talk to one of the other hostage negotiators about how it had all played out. And Bob nearly bit my head off. "Hey, cool it!" he snapped, pointing to one of the long-boom microphones the TV crews were carrying. "The press is all around!"

One of the uniformed cops, not knowing about our man-and-wife relationship, turned to me and asked, "God, what did you do to piss that guy off?"

"Aw, nothin'," I said. "I just sleep with him."

CHAPTER ELEVEN

When I had first transferred into the Brooklyn North Narcotics Division, I was thrilled. It was like coming in from the cold. I would be able to act like a real cop. Since I was no longer working undercover and not required to mask my true identity, I could finally wear a shield, make arrests, put handcuffs on the bad guys, and let the rest of the world know in no uncertain terms that I was on the job. No longer would I be a nameless, faceless phantom. No longer would I present to others the face of a petty criminal, a cheap whore, or a strung-out dope addict.

But my euphoria quickly evaporated when I discovered that I was about as welcome in Brooklyn North as a case of poison ivy. In the eyes of the male cops in the unit, I had three big strikes against me. One, I was tiny, and most of the men cops were convinced that I couldn't carry my weight or get physical with the bad guys. Two, I was a woman, the only woman in the whole unit. And three, after leaving the Undercover Unit, I had worked in a field-control unit, sometimes helping to make corruption cases against other cops. So I was labeled *rat squad*.

For the first six months, I was given the cold shoulder. Almost nobody in Brooklyn North would even talk to me, much less work with me. Rarely was I allowed to get involved in any real police work. One night, however, I did make an arrest, the first of my career. A team I was working with stopped a van with two Colombian nationals, a guy and a girl suspected of dealing drugs. I moved quickly to cuff the female. But as I was cuffing her, I glanced around. And realized that my partner had suddenly vanished. Along with all of my backups. On orders of the lieutenant, they had all hightailed it back to the office, leaving me behind to fend for myself with these two dope dealers. Without backup, I was in an extremely perilous situation. The Police Department had instructed officers never to operate solo when attempting to transport prisoners. But, in this instance, I had no choice. I quickly handcuffed the two suspects—back-to-back—then placed them in the rear of my car.

When I searched the female, I came up with a loaded gun. "Son of a bitch," I heard myself say. I coulda bust a gut.

When I got back to Brooklyn North, the lieutenant blithely inquired, "So how'd you make out?"

I looked at him with disgust. "I made out fine, no thanks to you."

I was furious, but not one of the male cops in the unit was willing to acknowledge the dangerous situation they had put me in. When I started to give the lieutenant a piece of my mind, another male detective piped up:

"Look, we don't want you here, lady. We're not gonna do anything for you. You're a woman. Women don't belong on the job. What's more, you came outta a rat squad. So you must be a rat."

With that, I turned on him with both barrels. "Well, don't get in my way, 'cause I'm going to be a better detective than you ever were. You get in my way, I'm going to walk right over your fucking face."

Yeah, I lost my cool. But I wasn't sorry about it, not one damned bit. These guys had jammed me up. I had already had one brush with death because of partners who had abandoned me on the street, up in the Four-One Precinct; I sure as hell didn't need another. On top of that, I was being tagged a rat, even though the only cop I had ever helped lock up was a full-fledged drug peddler and drug user who had actually been growing marijuana plants outside the Central Park station house. And, last but not least, there was that old bugaboo about my gender. "Women can't handle the job."

But, damn it all, I was gonna show these guys once and for all . . . this woman can, can, can.

After my little outburst, my relationship with the Brooklyn North remained icy, at best. Right up until that night we staged a raid on a Rastafarian drug den on Bushwick Avenue.

I was partnering that night with Jimmy Mullahey, a six-foot-four Clint Eastwood look-alike and my only real friend in the squad. Jimmy and I had connected when I was still working undercover and both of us were sent by the Police Department to a training seminar in Virginia. The seminar was sponsored by the federal government's Bureau of Narcotics and Dangerous Drugs, the predecessor of the U.S. Drug Enforcement Administration.

Undercover cops had already made several heroin buys at the Bushwick Avenue location. Now, with enough evidence to make cases in court, it was time for us to shut the drug operation down and lock up all the dealers. The raid began when four beefy detectives swung a heavy metal battering ram—nicknamed Big Bertha—into the front door. Once, twice, three, four times—until the planks splintered, the lock gave, and the door flew wide open. Jimmy and I and the lieutenant were the first to charge inside. The lieutenant had his revolver out. Both Jimmy and I were wearing protective metal flak jackets and toting double-barreled shotguns. As we raced toward the back of the house, the rest of our raiding party poured in behind us. Fanning out, they began searching and securing the rooms. Meanwhile, back outside, other detectives were scampering around the sides of the house, hoping to cut off any of the rats who might be scurrying to make a backdoor getaway.

Bobbing and weaving down the main hallway, our loaded shotguns at the ready, Jimmy and I moved gingerly through the drug den. Through a door. Around one bend. Then another. And another. Suddenly, up in front of us, we saw a blur. A man. Jumping out the open window. Jimmy went racing after him, flying right through the window. I followed on Jimmy's heels. And sailed through that window, as well.

Only to discover, as I came out the other side, that I had jumped not from the first story—but from the second story. "Oh, shit," I could hear myself saying as I looked down with a sickening feeling at the hard, concrete pavement coming up to meet me.

What Jimmy had known—but I had not—was that the back of the tenement was a full story lower than the front. In other words, while the first floor was only one flight up in front, it measured a full two flights up in back. When Jimmy went flying through the window, he had wisely grabbed the ledge with his hands, then done a dexterous hang job before dropping safely to the ground, some twenty feet below.

I, on the other hand, did a full-scale Mary Poppins. And was heading for a nasty crash landing.

Just in the nick of time, Jimmy saw me come flying out behind him. Turning, he caught me in midair, breaking my fall before I broke both my legs. As I dusted myself off, I spotted the drug dealer trying to climb over a fence. "There he goes!" I shouted. Before he could scramble to freedom, Jimmy and I grabbed his legs, dragged him back down to the ground, and cuffed him.

Just then, the other cops in the raiding party came running around to the backyard to see the three of us in a heap on the ground. Seeing me side by side next to Jimmy, helping to put the cuffs on the suspect, they were stunned.

"How the hell did you get here?" asked the detective who had pronounced me "a rat."

"I came outta the second-story window," I said. "Not too smart, huh?"

The other cops looked back up at the window, a full two stories up. Then back down at me, as if I were some creature from another planet. The guy who had been busting my chops for being a female said, "Well, I guess if you did that to save your partner, you must be alright."

"Hey, guys," said Jimmy, "I told you she was okay."

Some of the guys gave me an appreciative pat on the shoulder. Then everyone had a good laugh about my acrobatic prowess.

That night, the ice temporarily thawed.

But one way or another, I knew I would always be tested.

Eventually, toward the end of 1976, I was transferred out of Brooklyn North and over to Queens Narcotics. I was thrilled. Because I had made so many undercover drug buys in Queens, back in the days when I was still Marie Martin, I had gotten to know a lot of the Queens detectives, so it was like a homecoming. Only now, I was coming back to work with them in my new public identity—Detective Kathleen Burke.

Unfortunately, my stint in Queens was short-lived, owing to a sensational tabloid story that mushroomed into a major embarrassment for the Police Department.

What happened, believe it or not, was that the Police Department made a porno movie.

I know this sounds incredible, but it was true. In 1977, four public morals detectives were quietly authorized to use NYPD funds and equipment to set up a bogus film production company, hire a cast and crew, and shoot a series of pornographic "loops" or explicit X-rated films in which the actors engaged in all manner of sexual high jinks. The story lines consisted of three basic porn scenarios: the burglar and his semi-willing female victim, the cheating wife and the handyman, and the honeymoon couple frolicking in the shower. Posing as producers, three of the public morals cops actually stood by and observed the action. The fourth cop who was part of the undercover team—an unmarried female officer—was not permitted on the set.

The object of making this porno movie was to give the "production company," which was called Triple-X Enterprises, an entrée into the porno community. Once they gained credibility, the four cops intended to backtrack the flow of smut, infiltrate the X-rated underworld, and learn who was producing kiddie porn and snuff films. It was a bold and ambitious undertaking, meticulously orchestrated by a smart detective named Phil Tambasco, who passed himself off as Philly Russo, a wiseguy sharpie who was the president of Triple-X Enterprises. What's more, the undercover operation had been given the green light by several high-ranking chiefs in the Police Department, as well as the legal blessing of local, all-powerful prosecutors.

Unfortunately, not all of the higher-ups in the Police Department had been made aware of the porn-movie gambit (or so they would later claim). Somebody leaked word of Triple-X Enterprises to the *New York Daily News*. And when the newspaper broke the story with a blaring front-page headline, "Cops Make Blue Movie," the police commissioner, a devout Irish Catholic and lifelong straight arrow, hit the ceiling. At first, he angrily denied the story. The next day, however, he was forced to do an embarrassing about-face and retract his denial. Yes, he admitted, it was true. All of it. The Police Department had made a porno movie. And he was furious about it.

With characteristic clumsiness, the department decided to deal with this public relations mess by punishing the undercover cops rather than figuring out a way to salvage what could have been a truly productive undercover operation. Triple-X Enterprises was shut down, its records seized, and the film it produced put under lock and key. The four cops in the undercover operation, including team leader Tambasco, were yanked out of their top-secret assignment and more or less placed under quarantine in dreary desk jobs at Police Headquarters.

Soon after, more heads began to roll. Lots and lots of heads. Including my own.

In a silly, shortsighted move, the department's first deputy commissioner decided that a complete shake-up was needed in the Organized Crime Control Bureau, the umbrella superstructure that had sanctioned the blue-movie undercover operation. And just how would he shake up OCCB? Well, the porno movie had been made by senior detectives, people with five or more years experience working public morals. So, in his infinite wisdom, the deputy commissioner decided to get rid of all the senior detectives working in OCCB. I was a senior detective. So, even though I was working out of Queens Narcotics and had absolutely nothing to do with making the porno movie, I—along with nine public morals detectives and sixty-five other senior narcotics detectives—would have to go.

The transfer could not have come at a worse time for me. I had just arrived in Queens, and I was happy there. I had recently learned that I was pregnant with my first child, and working in Queens, close to my home in Astoria, was the best possible place for me to be, given my condition. The lieutenant in charge of the squad was a real mensch, and I was working with a lot of old friends and familiar faces from my undercover years. The guys in Queens were like big brothers to me. They looked upon my pregnancy as a joyous event, worthy of celebration. Every day they used to record my expanding girth by wrapping a tape measure around my belly and making notations on a chart to keep track of my growth. When I started to have weird cravings, they even took me out to eat raw clams for the very first time!

I was crushed when I was told I would have to leave Queens for reassignment elsewhere. But then, word came down that I would be transferred into the Detective Bureau, specifically, the Special Investigations Division, and my spirits immediately perked up. SID, as it was known, included some of the most highly specialized and elite detective squads in the department, including the Safe, Loft & Truck Squad, the Arson-Explosion Unit, the Special Frauds Squad, the Hypnosis Unit, and the Major Case Squad. My transfer began to look like a real step up.

As part of the transfer, I had to fill out a new personnel form and interview with the chief of the Special Investigations Division at Police Headquarters. On the form, you were asked to give a physical description of yourself. I wrote that I was thirty-four years old, stood five feet two, weighed one hundred pounds . . . and was still growing. In parenthesis, I added "three months pregnant."

I thought it was cute. The chief of special investigations, however, failed to see the humor. "What the hell is this supposed to mean?" he angrily snapped as he reviewed my personnel form.

"Exactly what it says," I replied. "I'm three months pregnant."

He scowled. "Well, what am I supposed to do with you then? You're nuthin' but dead wood."

Swell, I thought to myself. One more sexist meathead in a position of power.

"Look," I said, "if that's the way you feel, just send me back to Narcotics. I don't want to be here anyway."

"Oh, yeah?" he shot back. "Well, that's too damn bad, Burke. You're mine now and you're not going anywhere. Report here first thing tomorrow morning."

"Which unit, Chief?"

He looked at me blankly. "Missing Persons."

Oh, shit. Missing Persons.

Of all the places he could have sent me—Safe, Loft & Truck, Major Case, Arson-Explosion—it had to be Missing Persons. The Rubber Gun Squad. The trash heap. The dumping ground for drunks, rogues, losers, and head cases. What a kick in the ass! What an insult! I thought I would die.

Things looked no more promising when I showed up for work the next morning. While some of the cops in the Missing Persons unit appeared to be competent and dedicated investigators, a tiny nucleus of hard workers, far too many others were dinosaurs or has-beens or weren't wearing guns. Some were on modified assignment, pending some kind of disciplinary action by the department. A whole bunch of others had been buried in Missing Persons because they were alcoholics, wife beaters, malcontents, wiseacres, and nonconformists.

Since I was pregnant and the bosses had determined that I couldn't function anymore as a real cop, I was relegated to a desk and told to answer the telephones. I knew I was in for a rough haul when I opened one of the file-cabinet drawers and a half-empty bottle of rum fell out.

My hope was that, as time went on, my initial impression of the cops in the Missing Persons Squad would change. And, as time went on, my initial impression did change. They were even loopier and more pathetic than I had first thought.

The one good friend I made in Missing Persons was an old-time black detective named Ben Lamb, whom everyone used to call Baby Lamb. He was a good cop, a nice guy, and my guardian angel. Baby Lamb used to protect me from all the crazies in the squad. As I got closer and closer to giving birth, he also took care of me, helping me to get my boots on whenever it was raining or snowing, bringing me blankets when it was drafty, and making sure I had my milk and my yogurt each day. "Come on, Mama," he used to say, "you gotta eat for the two of you now."

Baby Lamb and I used to have lunch together in the back room, affectionately known as the Chamber of Horrors. This was the room where the Missing Persons Squad kept hundreds upon hundreds of photographs of unidentified dead bodies. The photos, all of them truly ghastly, were glued inside books, and the books were attached to sliding drawers. Whenever people came in, hoping to track down some lost friend or loved one, we would pull these drawers out for viewing and start flipping up the photos, one by one, hoping that they might assist the visitor in making an identification. In some instances, we were only able to show them photos of body parts—a head here, a pair of legs there, some teeth, a hand—from which to make a possible ID. By matching one missing part to another—say a head with a torso, or a leg with a foot—we could sometimes cobble together a positive identification. Sometimes, just to keep our sanity in the midst of all this grisly carnage, Baby Lamb and I would play a macabre game with each other by attaching these body-part photos together with paper clips, then manipulating them up and down like Punch and Judy marionettes.

Despite Baby Lamb's best efforts to make my life more bearable, I found Missing Persons to be dreary, dismal, and depressing. A graveyard, both literally and metaphorically. Half the time, when you put your lunch in the refrigerator, somebody else would eat it. When the squad organized a Christmas party, only one person showed up for it—the guy who organized it.

After my years of working undercover and narcotics cases—doing major investigations, teaming up with real cops, taking the bad guys off the streets—I didn't feel like a detective anymore. All I was doing was shuffling reports and answering the telephones. What's more, because of my pregnancy, I felt increasingly helpless and hopeless. In the first three months, I gained twenty pounds and resembled a pumpkin with legs. Even though I was thrilled that I was pregnant, my hormones were raging, my chemistry was in chaos, and I turned into an emotional powder keg. Sometimes, for no apparent reason, I would burst into tears and become hysterical. To keep my mind off my fragile state, I started to crochet in the office. Baby blankets, baby bootees, baby hats, baby sweaters, baby buntings, baby everythings.

One day I made an appointment to see the chief of the Narcotics Division. Desperate, I begged him to get me out of the Missing Persons Squad. "How can you do this to me?" I asked him. "I've worked hard for eight years. I've done everything you ever asked me to do. I've gone to places nobody wanted to go. I've made drug buys from people that nobody thought they could make buys from. I've taken my cases to trial. I've taken all the hits along the way. How can you bury me in Missing Persons?"

The chief looked at me with dismay. "What's wrong with Missing Persons? That's an elite unit."

Just then, another chief I knew walked into the office. On seeing me sitting there, he asked, "Hey, Kathy, are you in trouble or something? Are you under indictment? I saw that you went to Missing Persons."

I burst into tears all over again. Clearly, I had been banished to the gulag. But the chief of Narcotics said that the situation was out of his control. I had been transferred out of OCCB, so he had no authority over me anymore. Ultimately, the only thing that would rescue me from this purgatory was that I was due to give birth in a few weeks and would have to stop working altogether for a while.

My last day of work in Missing Persons, just before I began my maternity leave, occurred during a huge snowstorm. Baby Lamb brought in a bottle of Dom Pérignon to celebrate my impending delivery.

"Here you go, Mama. A bit of the bubbly."

"I can't drink that," I told him. "I'm pregnant."

"Well, then I'll just have to drink for the two of us."

As was our custom, we had our last lunch together in the Chamber of Horrors, with its intimate and cheery decor of photos of corpses, heads, and severed limbs. Then, as the snowstorm outside began to intensify, Baby Lamb helped me get my boots and overcoat on. And I caught the last bus back to Astoria before the blizzard shut down the entire city.

Twenty-three days later, my baby was born at Flushing Medical Center. It was a little girl and we named her Cathrine. Because the doctors had to perform a cesarean, I spent ten days in the hospital, much of it zonked out on painkillers. With the exception of Baby Lamb, not a single one of the other cops from Missing Persons ever called me, sent a card or a gift, or stopped by to visit. What a swell bunch.

One morning as I lay in my bed, the nurse informed me, "Oh, dear, it's so sweet—your father's down in the nursery holding the baby."

Now I knew I was still pretty out of it from all the medication, but not that out of it. "My father!" I gulped. "Whaddya talkin' about! Just who's holding my baby?"

"Well," said the nurse, "he said his name was Bill. Isn't he your father?"

I tried to clear the cobwebs from my brain. Bill? Bill? Who in the world was Bill? And then it hit me. Bill . . . as in Bill Ballner. As in Lieutenant Bill Ballner. As in Lieutenant Bill Ballner, my old boss from the Undercover Unit. I knew that Lieutenant Ballner, now retired, was doing volunteer work in the hospital. It had to be him.

"Oh, that crazy person." I smiled at the nurse, remembering just how wonderful Lieutenant Ballner had been to me all those years when I was working undercover. "He's not really my father. He just behaves like he is." And then I drifted back into sleep.

The day I brought Cathrine home from the hospital was bittersweet for the Burke family. On the one hand, we now had a beautiful, bouncing, healthy baby girl in our lives. But on the other, that same day two uniformed cops under Bob's command were ambushed and murdered by the Black Liberation Army. What made those shootings even more painful for both Bob and me was that the wife of one of those murdered officers was eight and a half months pregnant with her own baby. Since Bob had to be with the cops in his command in the immediate aftermath of the shootings, I had to bring Cathrine home by myself.

Little Cathrine was a joy. Giggly, funny, always posing for the camera, and a huge fan of playing peekaboo with both her parents. Unlike a lot of newborns—and much to our great relief—she slept right through the night. Naturally, I wanted to spend as much time as I could with her. It saddened me terribly that my own mom was not alive to meet Cathrine. And because I had no mother, no sisters, and no other female relatives to help me take care of her, I chose to stay out of work for the maximum period allowed by the Police Department, eighteen months. I would receive no pay and no benefits during this leave, but I would retain my seniority. In truth, I opted to stay out the full time for another reason, as well: I planned to get pregnant now with my second child, return to work for several months, then go right back out on maternity leave just before that child was born.

I returned to the job after Cathrine's birth, in September of 1979, I had to go up to the department's Personnel Division to get my credentials back.

"How you feeling, Detective?" the lieutenant in Personnel asked me.

"Great!" I said, carefully neglecting to mention that I was actually three months pregnant with my second child. But I had no intention of informing the department until I absolutely had to.

"Well, you're going back to the Missing Persons Squad," the lieutenant said.

With that, I promptly tossed my gold detective's shield onto his desk. "I tell you what. You keep this. Then you give me one of those nice little white shields you have in the drawer there, you bust me back to police officer again, and you put me on patrol. I've never been on patrol. But I have been in Missing Persons. And, no way in hell am I goin' back there. I will not be a social worker. I will not be a babysitter. I'm a criminal investigator. I'm a detective. I chase bad guys. And I make collars. That's what I do for a living. And I am not—repeat *not*—going back to the Rubber Gun Squad under any circumstances."

The lieutenant got all flustered. "I . . . uh . . . uh . . . uh . . . you better go upstairs to the chief of detectives' office and speak to the personnel officer there."

"Fine. Gimme my paperwork." And off I went.

Luckily the lieutenant in the chief of detectives' office knew me and liked me. "You're right, Kathy," he told me. "You don't belong in Missing Persons." We were kicking around possible alternatives when, suddenly, the chief of detectives himself, dapper, debonair Frank Cosgrove, walked in. In his hand he was holding a list of all the recent bank robberies in the city. There had been a record-breaking number that summer, close to 750, and the squad responsible for investigating them—Major Case— was woefully overworked and undermanned.

"Hey, Kathy," said Chief Cosgrove, barely glancing up from his list and its highly disturbing contents. "Whattaya doin' up here?"

"My first day back, Chief. And I'm lookin' for a new home."

Suddenly, Chief Cosgrove looked up at me. "Whaddya know about bank robberies?"

"Not much."

"Whaddya know about making arrests?"

"A lot."

Chief Cosgrove smiled at me. He extended his right hand. "Then congratulations, Detective. You've just joined the Major Case Squad."

CHAPTER TWELVE

The detectives in the Major Case Squad were considered the crème de la crème of the Detective Bureau, and with good reason.

The squad, which comprised thirty-five detectives, was detailed to investigate the highest-profile cases in New York City. Bank robberies and commercial burglaries in excess of $100,000. Extortion attempts. Murders of police officers. Kidnappings. Black Liberation Army attacks and terrorist plots, both of which were accorded high priority in 1979, the same year in which Lord Mountbatten was assassinated by the IRA, Iranian students seized the U.S. embassy in Teheran, taking sixty-two Americans hostage, and a radical Puerto Rican liberation group known as the FALN, which had already set off terrorist bombs in the mid-1970s, was threatening to set off even more. The Major Case Squad functioned as the chief of detectives' right hand. Or, as the chief himself liked to put it, the chief of detectives' detectives.

The Major Case Squad had the single highest concentration of veteran detectives of any unit within the department. First- and second-grade detectives who earned top dollar. Tough, grizzled old-timers with the kind of savvy and street smarts that came from years and years of experience on a wide variety of investigations. Sadly, I was not yet in their league. After eleven years on the job, I was a good detective. But not yet a great one, like the old salts, the real heavy hitters in the Detective Bureau. I still had volumes to learn. And I knew it.

Unfortunately, when I showed up in the squad, a lot of the old-timers got their noses bent outta joint. They regarded me as a lightweight, with no real bona fide experience in a detective squad, such as homicide, robbery, or burglary. That I had spent nearly eight years in narcotics, and much of that time putting my life on the line while undercover, meant squat to them. To them, working narcotics was bush league, no better than being a school-crossing guard.

Right off the bat resentment toward me began to build because, in detailing me to Major Case, the chief of detectives had overridden the chief of special investigations, the titular boss of Major Case and a lot of other specialized detective squads, who had been planning to dump me back in the quagmire of Missing Persons. Naturally, the old-timers began to suspect "contracts" and conspiracies at work. "How the hell did she get here?" they would grumble. The simple facts of the matter—that the chief of detectives had thrown me into Major Case because of an up-surge of bank robberies and a shortage of personnel to investigate them—were given short shrift. The scuttlebutt was that I must have a "rabbi" or a "hook" in the department who'd pulled strings to get me my detective status and route me into this elite squad.

And, of course, the logical suspect was my husband, Bob, who was a captain. Few of the naysayers paused to consider that I had actually earned my gold detective shield long before I'd even met Bob, much less married him.

Fueling the resentment, as always, was my gender. I was a woman. And an ambitious, aggressive woman who wasn't afraid to speak up. A lot of guys couldn't stomach my blunt, in-your-face style. There had been other women detectives in the squad. But they were more ladylike, demure, and deferential. I, however, had zero interest in being a lady; I wanted to be a cop.

A couple of months after I joined the squad, one of the sergeants, a guy named Burton, started giving me grief about the way I dressed. Black hair, six foot three, paunchy, Burton had a reputation for being hostile toward women. I was still wearing my laced, heavy, black nun's shoes with the two-inch heels, a carryover from my Brooklyn North days of raiding vice and drug dens. Much more practical than high heels, I had discovered, especially if you needed to kick some lawbreaking trou-blemaker in the ass to get his attention. And, I preferred trim pants suits to dresses and short skirts. That way, if I ever had to go rolling in the gut-ter with a perp who was resisting arrest, I wouldn't have to worry about my bloomers sticking out. But Sergeant Burton made no secret of his disdain for my fashion choices.

"You know, Burke," Sergeant Burton said one day, "you wear the ugli-est shoes."

I was completely taken aback. "I'm sorry you feel that way, Sergeant."

Nodding over at the only other woman detective in the squad, who, in between answering the phone, seemed to spend most of her time spritzing herself with French perfume, fussing with her hair and her lipstick, and filing her fingernails, he looked me up and down, then sneered, "Why don't you ever wear nice shoes like Tina over there? And, while you're at it, why don't you try wearing a skirt? It's a lot more ladylike, y'know."

Once Burton had walked away, one of the other male detectives plopped himself down by my desk. Lowering his voice, he looked one way, then the other. Then he leaned across and told me, "You know, kid, if you're ever gonna have any problems with anybody in this squad, it's gonna be that man."

His words would turn out to be prophetic.

In the beginning, they never seemed to give me a regular partner to work with in Major Case. And the ones I was given often seemed to have other things on their mind besides catching cases and making arrests.

For a while, I teamed with a first-grade detective named Liam Flaherty. In his sixties and nearing retirement, Liam had a whole brood of kids, always wore mismatched clothes, and favored straw hats in summer. He also smoked a pipe. But he was so absentminded that he was constantly setting his tie and pants on fire with hot pipe ashes.

Liam had little interest in making arrests. Or, for that matter, being involved in police action of any other kind. One day, we responded to the scene of a bank robbery and began taking statements from all the witnesses. While we were there, a customer murmured to one of the tellers that he was being forced to cash a check by the tall, stocky, mustached man standing behind him. The teller alerted the manager, who in turn tipped us.

"C'mon, Liam," I whispered to my partner. "That guy must be one of the robbers." And even though I was visibly pregnant at the time, I moved in quickly to collar the suspect. Notwithstanding my condition, I actually threw him up against a table to cuff him and search him. But when I looked around for Liam to back me up, he was nowhere in sight.

Suddenly, from the far side of the room, I heard a distant shout: "I'll call the precinct squad!" It was Liam, standing a good seventy-five feet away, doing his best to keep out of harm's way. Needless to say, this kind of head-in-the-sand behavior did not bode well for our budding partnership.

And soon after, things went from bad to worse. We were cruising through Greenwich Village when we caught a radio run on a bank robbery in progress. The bank was in the same direction we were already traveling, just a few short blocks away. I was psyched.

But Liam spun the steering wheel all the way around to the left and made a sharp U-turn, turning our car in the exact opposite direction, 180 degrees away from the bank robbery. Now I was dumbfounded.

"Liam, whattaya doin'?" I exclaimed. "The bank is back that way!"

Liam gave me a wink. "Hey, kid, we don't wanna get there too soon. I only got a few months to go before I put in my retirement papers, y'know."

As other police cars sped past us en route to the crime scene, I did a slow burn. We weren't cops—we were cowards. Puffing contentedly on his pipe, Liam took his time driving us back toward Police Headquarters. When we got back to the office, the first thing he did was troop into the captain's office.

"Boss, I never had a medal in this job," Liam bitched to the captain. "But if I keep workin' with her, I'm gonna wind up gettin' one. And, frankly, I can live without it."

And that was the end of my short-lived partnership with Liam Flaherty.

After a while, finding a partner ceased to be the most pressing priority in my life. Preparing for the arrival of my second child was. I could no longer disguise that I would soon be going on leave to have my baby.

My pregnancy made for some amusing moments. When I brought one kid out of the holding pen at Central Booking to book him on bank robbery charges, the other prisoners started to give him the business. "Man, you let that fat, little pregnant broad lock your ass up? What kinda dumb-ass turkey are you, anyway? You shoulda just run away from her!"

The kid was mortified and humiliated. "Well, at least she didn't hit me," he piped back feebly.

On the way up the stairs, however, the kid, worrying about his macho, turned to me and dolefully complained, "You know, it was bad enough I had to get locked up by a woman. But you hadda be pregnant, too?"

"Hey, life's a bitch," I said, no pun intended.

"Well, what would you have done if I tried to hit you? Or run away from you, like those guys said I oughtta?"

"Shot you."

He swallowed hard. "Oh."

And that ended that.

One of the few people in the squad who showed any interest in my delicate condition was Terry Carey, a detective assigned to working bank-robbery stakeouts.

Fine-featured, muscular, impeccably dressed, with long brown hair, Terry looked a little bit like Tom Cruise. He was a terrific detective, smooth as silk, completely at ease with his investigating abilities. And unlike a lot of the other men in the squad, secure enough about his manhood that he didn't reel from befriending me. Terry had worked Narcotics. So there was an instant rapport between us.

Married and the father of two girls, Terry didn't seem at all uncomfortable with my pregnancy. In fact, he used to comfort me by bringing me cups of hot tea and chatting with me in the office.

Any man who's kind to a pregnant woman can't be all bad, I thought.

Maybe even one who, down the line, would make a half-decent partner.

My pregnancy, however, caused some real anguish at home for Bob and me. It started when the hospital called me back for a second sonogram. "We saw something on the first one," said the technician. "We'd just like to double-check."

After the second sonogram, I went to see my obstetrician. "What are we talking about here?" I asked him.

"I don't know yet," he said. "Left ventricle looks a little enlarged . . . could be some fluid in the brain . . . head's somewhat big for four months . . . really too soon to say, though . . . more tests might clarify the situation—"

I interrupted, "Look, Doc, let's cut to the chase. Are we talking about hydrocephalus or what?"

"Well, I'm not totally convinced yet, but that is what the tests are suggesting."

Hydrocephalus, as I had learned from my own reading of medical texts, was characterized by an abnormal increase in the amount of fluid in the cranium, causing enlargement of the head, wasting away of the brain, and a sometimes crippling loss of mental power.

"Fine," I said to the doctor, "so what am I going to do about this?"

At the urging of my doctor and another female detective whose child had been born hydrocephalic, I visited the Albert Einstein Medical Center in the Bronx. Einstein was doing research in hydrocephalus and had pioneered the shunt, a tube that allowed fluid to drain from the brain. The doctors at Einstein walked me through the clinic where they were treating the hydrocephalic kids. What I saw was heartbreaking. Some of them had been born with cleft palates, facial deformities, or spina bifida. Many were severely retarded. I burst into tears.

And that's when the doctors delicately broached the subject of abortion. It was, they advised, an option.

When I went back to work that day, I could barely keep myself together. I had already gained thirty pounds during my pregnancy. Having now reached the twenty-four-week mark, my baby was big. I could feel it moving, kicking, living, struggling toward its birth. And yet, the doctors were suggesting that I end its life. I just wanted to curl up in a corner and sob. I confided in Terry Carey about my dilemma. He tried to reassure me that everything would be okay. Then he brought me a cup of hot tea.

Later that night, Bob and I had a real heart-to-heart. Both of us knew we could not agree to an abortion. It flew in the face of everything we believed in morally, spiritually, and philosophically. Neither of us could even bring ourselves to consider the notion of arbitrarily snuffing out this baby's life. Rather than dwell on the problems of the present, we tried as best we could to focus on what might be in the future. Perhaps it was my strong religious convictions, my fervent and lifelong devotion to Catholicism.

"Maybe it's God's way of saying our first child, Cathrine, will grow up to be a brain surgeon or a scientific researcher who will find a cure for hydrocephalus," I found myself saying.

Bob and I talked about the big changes that would occur in our lives with the birth of our second baby, particularly if it was born hydrocephalic. We knew we would have to take turns caring for our child, given that it was likely to have extraspecial needs. We would certainly have to stagger our work shifts so one of us would always be at home with our newborn. To give the child the care it would need, I might ultimately be forced to retire early from my police job, even forfeit my pension. Undoubtedly, we would both have to make painful sacrifices. But, with constant prayer, faith, and God's love, we would find a way. We simply had to.

I returned to Einstein for more tests. Each new sonogram appeared to reconfirm the initial findings. There was still something. . . .

I agonized over these reports, wracking my brain for a possible cause. For months, I had taken the most painstaking care of myself and my unborn child. I had shunned alcohol and cigarettes, avoided harmful prescription medications, eaten only the healthiest foods. I had got as much sleep as I possibly could. To keep my stress levels down, I'd practiced meditation. On top of everything else, I had prayed to the Almighty regularly and fervently. Never before in my life had I made so many novenas. And yet, there was still that something. . . .

What in the world could have gone wrong?

"You may have had a virus you didn't know about," my obstetrician theorized. But then he added, "The truth is, we just don't know." For the next three months, I went through the uncertainty of not knowing whether my baby would be born dead or alive, deformed or normal. It was agony.

Back in the Major Case Squad office, I tried to keep my mind off my baby's problems. Now that I was in the advanced stages of my pregnancy, worrying about finding a steady partner was no longer even an issue. Given my condition, I knew I would have no choice but to accept a desk job. The squad analyst was about to retire, and they wanted me to replace him. This meant I would work inside the office, filing folders, answering the phones, analyzing New York City crime patterns, and compiling weekly and monthly crime statistics. This was okay in the short term, but I worried that I could get pigeonholed in this job the way I had in Missing Persons.

Sure enough, one morning the captain called me into his office and told me he wanted me to remain as the squad's analyst. On a "temporary basis," of course.

"Well, sure, okay, boss," I said, knowing full well that nothing "temporary" ever stayed temporary in the Police Department, especially if you demonstrated that you were even barely competent at the job.

So I began to lay the preliminary groundwork for my eventual escape from what looked to be deskbound servitude. "But you oughtta know I'm not real good in math. In fact, I'm absolutely awful with numbers."

"Do the best you can," the captain said. For a while, I did just that. And, sure enough, I began to hear rumblings that he was determined to bury me in this job, even after I returned from my maternity leave.

So that's when I began to screw up each month's crime stats. Deliberately.

When the chief started to get monthly bank-robbery figures that made no sense whatsoever, he yelled at the captain. The captain, in turn, yelled at me.

I became defensive, portraying myself as the innocent victim of my own ineptitude. "I'm so sorry, boss, but I just can't figure out how you get from here to there. And, no matter how many times you explain it, it just doesn't seem to sink in."

Exasperated, the captain finally tossed in the towel. "Alright, alright, Burke, I'm just gonna have to give this job to somebody who knows what they're doing. It's pretty obvious to me you're no damned statistician."

"Guess you're right, boss." I shrugged, carefully neglecting to mention that I had actually been precisely that—a professional statistician—before I joined the PD and was still a civilian.

After my last day of work at the Police Department, I continued to drive up to the Einstein Medical Center for more sonograms, which, to our continuing and mounting distress, indicated that there was still something. And then, incredibly, inexplicably, just a week before I would go into labor, that something mysteriously vanished from the sonograms. Why or how, nobody could say.

Nevertheless, I was not optimistic. We could still be looking at the birth of a hydrocephalic child, with all the attendant problems. So, as my delivery date neared, I prepared for the absolute worst. I told my obstetrician I wanted to sign organ-donor cards in case the baby did not survive after the delivery. I arranged for a neurologist to be in the delivery room and, in the event the baby was born hydrocephalic, for it to be rushed by ambulance to Einstein, where it could immediately be given a shunt. I also arranged to be moved out of the maternity ward as soon as I gave birth, into a surgical ward. If my baby was born deformed or did not survive, the last thing in the world I wanted was to be surrounded by other mothers happily nursing and cuddling and cooing to their newborn infants.

My baby was born in March of 1980. As with my first child, I had to have a cesarean, and it was in the same delivery room at Flushing Medical Center in Queens where I had given birth to Cathrine.

In the recovery room, I fought like crazy to shake off the effects of the anesthesia. Good Lord, I had to know, just had to. Through my fuzzy-headedness and nausea, I buttonholed the recovery-room nurse. "How is my baby's head?" I mumbled to her.

"What?" said the nurse. Not knowing anything about the preliminary sonograms, she didn't have a clue what I was talking about.

"How is my baby's head?" I repeated.

The nurse tried to humor me. "Uh . . . fine . . . I think."

But, somewhere beneath the medication fog still clouding my brain, I could sense that she was being vague. So I forced myself to scream it at her. *"How is my baby's head!"*

Another nurse, who knew me, overheard my lunatic outburst. She approached my bed. She looked down at me and reached for my hand. She squeezed it. Then she smiled.

"Your baby's fine, Kathy. Absolutely fine. There's nothing wrong with her head or anything else. You'll see her as soon as you come out of recovery."

"Thank you," I said. And then, through my tears, I continued to repeat it. "Oh, thank you, thank you, thank you . . ."

And so it was that our beloved second child, Veronica, came into this world.

A child's life is such a precious, precious thing. Shortly after I had returned to work following Cathrine's birth (but before I went back out on leave to have Veronica), I had been thrown headlong into a case that would underscore just how precious.

Etan Patz was an achingly adorable little boy of six years who had bright blue eyes, a blond, mop-top haircut, and a smile that could melt your heart. He lived in a SoHo loft with his parents and his other two siblings. But in May of 1979, after walking to his nearby school-bus stop, he vanished without a trace. At the time of his disappearance, he was dressed in blue—blue pants, blue corduroy jacket, blue sneakers—and carrying a blue cloth bag with an elephant pattern in the fabric.

After his disappearance, nearly a hundred police officers scoured the neighborhood, doing a street-by-street, door-by-door, alley-by-alley search. Friends and neighbors papered the entire city with posters bearing color photos of Etan's smiling face. Newspapers and TV stations, in New York City and elsewhere, bannered the story for weeks and months. But little Etan could not be found.

A year went by. On the first anniversary of Etan's disappearance, a man called the house asking that Etan's mother, Julie Patz, meet him at a location in Chinatown with $25,000 in cash. Fearing that Julie might be exposed to foul play, one of the Missing Persons detectives working the Patz case, Donald Tasik, suggested that the Major Case Squad temporarily detail me to go in Julie's place.

When I met Stanley and Julie Patz at their apartment on Prince Street, I was struck by how much they had immersed themselves in police vernacular when they spoke about the case. Rather than use regular time, they had adopted the police habit of using military time (e.g., "oh seven hundred hours"). Their conversation was peppered with terms that a detective might put in his report ("perpetrator," "apprehend," "location," etc.). After having spent so much time with the police, they had come to sound like the police. I decided it must have been some kind of survival mechanism they had unconsciously utilized to numb themselves to the continuing pain of their lost son.

Back in the offices of the Major Case Squad, I was carefully prepped to play Mrs. Patz and told what to say should the caller make contact. I was wired with a Nagra device to record conversations and a Kel device to transmit those conversations to backup detectives who would be on the street nearby. The chief of detectives' office provided the $25,000 cash, which was to be delivered to the caller in a plain brown paper bag. But just before the cash was inserted, I was instructed to leave my palm print and fingerprints inside the bag, for evidentiary purposes. Then, after the serial numbers on each of the bills were recorded, the $25,000 was tucked inside.

At the appointed hour, I found myself standing on Canal Street, near the jewelry exchange that sits opposite the entrance ramp to the Manhattan Bridge, in the heart of New York's Chinatown. Nearby sat an unmarked van, inside of which two detectives surrounded by a dizzying assortment of surveillance and recording equipment were watching and eavesdropping on my every word and move. Meanwhile, three more detectives from the Major Case Squad had positioned themselves in the doorways or vestibules around me.

As I stood on the corner waiting, I wondered if I might become a walking target. Would the perpetrator show up? Would he be armed? Would there be gunplay?

Rain began to fall, growing heavier and heavier as the minutes ticked off. In no time at all, the downpour had soaked through my wool jacket and shirt and turned my hair into a wet, stringy mess. Standing alone on that street corner, I looked like a homeless person, without a friend in the world.

Suddenly, from out of nowhere, a young white male sidled up to me. He was wearing jeans and a short, zip-up jacket.

"Are you Mrs. Patz?" he murmured, keeping his voice low.

I nodded yes. He quickly plucked the brown paper bag from my hands.

"Where's my son?" I asked him.

Ignoring me, he simply turned and started walking away. He got no more than ten feet before the backup detectives pounced and hand-cuffed him. Fortunately, it all went off without a hitch. As we had feared, this creep had no information whatsoever about Etan. He was just a two-bit extortionist, some amateur looking to cash in on the Patz family's pain.

The night after the Chinatown sting operation, I went home to Asto-ria and made myself a cup of hot tea. I thought about how fortunate we had been that the arrest had gone down without any violence or injuries. I thought about how this would probably not be the last time that some craven bottom-feeder would try to exploit the Patz family for selfish gain. And I thought about the Patzes, how strong and brave and stoic they had been in the face of this interminable torture.

Then I picked up my infant daughter, Cathrine, and gave her a great big hug, thanking God in heaven for keeping her safe and sound.

In the years after I gave birth to Veronica, there would be even more scam attempts on the Patzes, including one shakedown that culminated with the arrest of two extortionists in the parking lot of a sleazy Long Is-land hotel where Detective Tasik and I, pretending to be hot-to-trot lovers, had rented a room in order to observe the exchange of cash be-tween Etan's father, Stanley, and the two suspects.

Sadly, however, none of the arrests of these greedy bloodsuckers ever produced a single useful lead in Etan's disappearance. In 2004, a quarter of a century after Etan had vanished, a Manhattan judge would declare an imprisoned child molester (and onetime boyfriend of Etan's babysit-ter) to have been legally responsible for Etan's murder.

But Etan himself would never be seen or heard from again.

In raising our daughters, Bob and I tried to preserve a delicate balance. While we wanted the kids to know what we did for a living, particularly when we did it well, we wanted to shelter them from the violence and ugliness of our work.

And yet, we were both aware that, on any given day, some of that vio-lence and ugliness could come crashing into our lives, whether we wanted it to or not. So we tried to prepare our girls for that possibility without scaring them to death.

For starters, I tried to make them feel that my job was something routine and natural, not something secret, ominous, and never to be discussed. To create some feeling of normalcy for the girls, I would make it a practice to bring all my detective partners home for lunch so the girls could meet them in person. When they were little, the girls would climb into their laps. My partners, in turn, would ply them with chewing gum or candies or jelly beans.

Whenever I had to work late, I would always call the girls to let them know I was okay and would be home later. I would also tip them off in advance if I knew my picture was going to be on television or in the newspapers as the result of some arrest I had made.

Cathrine and Veronica were the daughters of two New York City cops, and that would make them unique. At the same time, we worked hard to make sure they would grow up just like any other kids.

When they were little, I would always read them bedtime stories and Mother Goose rhymes, play dolls with them, help them do their finger painting, teach them arts and crafts, and sew all their costumes for their school plays. In spring, we'd take the kids to amusement parks and ride the roller coaster. In summer, we'd go shell hunting at Jones Beach. Every fall, we'd drive to a pumpkin patch in the country in time for the harvest. And every Halloween, we'd throw a big party at our house so all the neighborhood kids could dress up in zany costumes and duck for apples. Then, at Christmastime, we'd all drive out to the Westbury Music Fair on Long Island to catch a performance of *The Nutcracker* ballet or the annual *Christmas Pageant*.

As the girls got older, Bob and I took them with us on our vacations. England, France, Holland, Germany, Luxembourg, Belgium, Canada, Hawaii, you name it. Wherever we went, Cathrine and Veronica would come, too.

On one of our trips, to New Mexico, Cathrine accidentally got her hand caught in a slamming car door. Her fingers crushed and bloodied, she began yowling in pain. Fearing she might have broken something, Bob and I rushed her to the local hospital. When we arrived, a doctor in white scrubs and sneakers came out to greet us. Taking Cathrine by her good hand, he began walking her back into the emergency room to be examined. But little Cathrine, intimidated by his strange, all-white appearance and fearful of what he might want to do to her in that emergency room, decided to put him on notice that he better not try anything funny.

"You better not hurt me," she told the doctor through her tears. "'Cause if you do, my mommy has a gun . . . and she'll shoot you."

Cathrine, thank God, suffered nothing more than some badly bruised fingers. The doctor, however, was considerably shaken.

Sometimes, being the children of two cops would add an extra dimension to the girls' lives. On career day at their grade school, St. Francis of Assisi in Astoria, it was their mom who would show up in her dress blue uniform, sit cross-legged on the floor with all the other kids, caution them about avoiding strangers and dangerous situations. Then—and this was the really cool part—it was their mom who would let all the other kids play with her handcuffs and her shield and her police whistle. And it was their mom who would fingerprint the kids in school—all 450 of them—as a way to identify those kids should they become victims of kidnappings, murders, or changes in their identities by their abductors.

While other parents brought their children to their stores or offices to see where they worked, Bob and I would bring the girls to the Police Academy. There, along with the other cops' kids, Cathrine and Veronica would be treated to judo exhibitions and demonstrations of apprehensions or bomb alerts by the department's specially trained police dogs. Later, they would be escorted through the holding pens and allowed to sit in the 13th Precinct's radio cars, on which they could joyfully illuminate the flashers and blare the sirens.

Each day, my older daughter, Cathrine, would help me get dressed for work, handing me my socks, my belt, my shoes, my bulletproof vest. Then she would sit on the bed and watch as I got ready for my tour of duty. One day, out of the clear blue, she asked me, "Mommy, what happens if you get hurt in a place where you don't have the vest on?"

I hadn't been prepared for her question. And, quite honestly, it threw me a little. But I tried to come back with an answer that would be both truthful and reassuring to a child of just four tender years.

"Well, honey," I said, "if that happens, I'll get hurt."

Then, hugging her tightly, I added, "But I'll still be coming home to you. I promise. "

CHAPTER THIRTEEN

Because of a change in the Police Department's rules on maternity leave, which resulted in a drastic reduction in the amount of time you were permitted to stay off the job without losing your seniority, I came back to work only five weeks after Veronica was born. When I returned to the Major Case Squad, I began lobbying again for a regular partner.

Other detectives with less seniority were being assigned partners. Yet I remained the odd man—woman?—out. For one reason or another, whoever teamed with me would get up and walk away seventy-two hours later.

What's more, I knew it was no accident.

The lieutenant in the squad was an old-school veteran named Caro. Bespectacled, bland-looking, and standing five feet ten, he repeatedly told me that I was just a pathetic, watered-down facsimile of a real detective. His rationale was that I had never worked patrol, but I more or less assumed that most of his hostility stemmed from my gender. Like a lot of the other male bosses, he was convinced that women cops just couldn't cut it.

Meanwhile, Sergeant Burton—that crude, self-appointed member of the fashion police—continued to bust my chops. If it wasn't the way I dressed, it was my overtime. He was always convinced I was trying to (a) scam the department and (b) make him look bad.

Notwithstanding their animosity, I did manage to team up for a while with Terry Carey, the detective who had been so kind to me during my difficult pregnancy, and a third detective, a black guy named Cliff Foner. Together, the three of us made an eye-catching appearance. Terry with his fair, Beach Boy good looks; me with my straight, long hair; Cliff with his frizzy Afro—hey, we looked just like Pete, Julie, and Linc from that campy 1960s cop show *The Mod Squad*.

One night when I was working with Terry, some precinct cops called to notify us that they had arrested one of our bank-robbery suspects. A huge black man, he stood six feet five, weighed three hundred pounds, and was as crazy as a loon. When we arrived at the West Side station house to pick him up, the precinct detectives had him locked in the holding pen—but just barely. Swaying heavily from side to side, he kept thrashing about inside the cage, praying loudly to God, ordering the other prisoners down on their knees in supplication, and announcing the imminent arrival of the Messiah, of whom he claimed to be the official emissary.

"The Lord is coming! The Lord is coming! And I am his disciple!"

Pulling me to one side, Terry worried that we'd never be able to get this hulking madman out of his cage to be booked, fingerprinted, and processed.

"Gimme a second," I told him. "Why don't you go down the hall and make sure that nobody else comes back here."

"Okay," said Terry. And off he went.

Quietly, I walked up to the holding pen. "Kenneth, c'mere," I said to the swaying hulk.

He began ranting and raving. "I am the Lord's disciple! Pray to Jesus! He is coming! He's gonna save us all! Pray to Jesus, I tell you!"

"Yeah, yeah, yeah, I know," I said. "Just come over here a second. I got something very important to show you. Closer."

Curious, Kenneth inched closer. He bent his massive frame over to get a better look at me.

With that, I pulled out my rosary beads. "See these? These are my rosary beads. My magic rosary beads. These are a sign I've been sent here by God. He sent me here to help make things right."

"Hallelujah!" exclaimed Kenneth. With that, Kenneth dropped to his knees. "What does God want me to do? Tell me! Please, tell me!"

I looked at him sternly, nose to nose and eyeball to eyeball. Then I said, "God wants you to come quietly with me, let me make it all right. 'Cause, Kenneth, you've done something sinful. And you need God's forgiveness."

"Yes, yes, Lord." Kenneth began to sob. "I pray for His forgiveness."

"Remember now, Kenneth, quietly."

"Praise the Lord!" Kenneth wailed.

"Amen, brother."

From that point on, Kenneth was as docile as a lamb.

During an earlier melee with a couple of street thugs who had tried to rip him off, Kenneth had sustained a broken arm. Before we could take him over to Central Booking, we first had to take him to the hospital to have his arm x-rayed and put in a cast. But when we finally got back to the Major Case Squad, Sergeant Burton looked as if he were about to have kittens.

"You hadda take this guy to the hospital first? You couldn't have taken him straight to Central Booking?"

"Guy's arm was broken, Sarge," I said. "Law says we gotta get him prompt medical treatment."

Suspicious of our motives, Burton sneered derisively, "Yeah, and especially when it means more overtime."

It was pretty obvious that neither Lieutenant Caro, Sergeant Burton, nor most of the other detectives wanted me in the Major Case Squad. And I certainly didn't want to be in a place where I was not welcome. So I began sniffing around for a happier home.

Through the grapevine, I learned that a new robbery unit was shaping up in Brooklyn, and they were looking for an experienced female to work undercover. From my days in Narcotics, I still had a lot of friends in Brooklyn, so this seemed like an ideal fit for me. But for them to bring me onto the new team, somebody would have to put in an official request-for-transfer form, known in department parlance as a 57.

Just as I was about to put the 57 in myself, one of my few friends in Major Case pulled me aside and advised me against it.

"Don't do it, Kath," he warned. "That's just what they're looking for you to do. They'll cut you off at the knees."

"Whaddya mean?"

"Lieutenant Caro is onto you. He wants to stick it to you. He knows you're lookin' to put in a 57. Once you do, he'll kill it. Then he'll bury you forever."

So that was the deal. Somehow, some way, I would have to orchestrate my transfer without actually coming out and asking for it. So I asked the sergeant in Brooklyn Robbery, an old friend of mine, to put in the request instead of me. Politically, it would be a more judicious way to achieve the same objective.

But one day, before the sergeant in Brooklyn had officially requested my transfer, Lieutenant Caro called me into his office and matter-of-factly asked, "Where's that 57 you put in?"

I looked at him. "What 57 you talkin' about, Loo? I never put in a 57." Whoops-a-daisy!

Realizing he had just tipped his hand, the lieutenant turned bright red. He had just made a careless slip of the lip that, in effect, exposed his own treacherous intentions.

Lieutenant Caro uhmmed and ahhed, hemmed and hawed, cleared his throat a few times, then said it was all just a big misunderstanding. But it was too late for that; thanks to his gaffe about my 57—and my quick-jab comeback—he knew that I was onto him and what he'd been scheming to do to me all along.

So, there was no longer any mystery about what was brewing for me in the Major Case Squad. The long knives were finally out in the open. And now, more than ever before, I would have to watch my back.

Shortly after this conversation, the sergeant in Brooklyn Robbery did go ahead and put in a formal request that I be reassigned to the Brooklyn office. But, to my great chagrin, the transfer was nixed by Chief Jackson, the new boss of the Special Investigations Division, the umbrella super-structure over the Major Case Squad.

With his pot belly and white hair, Chief Jackson resembled Santa Claus. But he had an unsavory reputation as a compulsive sneak thief who would snatch away the personal belongings of other cops without even asking. He would steal your newspaper, steal your cigarettes, steal your chewing gum, and steal your lunch right out of the refrigerator and eat it if you weren't looking. Of greater concern to me, however, was that Chief Jackson loathed the idea of women on the force. And he had not the slightest inclination to make it any easier for females to advance through the ranks and succeed. So when the opportunity came up for me to transfer out of Major Case and into a more hospitable environment in Brooklyn Robbery, he quashed it.

"Her clearance rate is too high on bank-robbery cases," Chief Jackson disingenuously told the sergeant in the Brooklyn Robbery Squad. "We can't afford to let her go."

Bullshit.

Somehow, the women haters in Major Case had gotten to Jackson. They obviously didn't want me, but they wouldn't let me go somewhere else where I would be accepted, appreciated, and more productive as a detective. The whole situation was absurd: I wanted out of Major Case, and they wanted me out of Major Case. But partly to spite me and partly to protect their own reputations—it would be hugely embarrassing to them if word got around that one of their detectives had actually asked to get out of such an elite squad—they refused to let it happen.

And then, amidst all this skulduggery and backstabbing, something truly wonderful did happen.

At long last, I found myself a full-time partner.

CHAPTER FOURTEEN

The room was dark, quiet, and serene. The voice was deep, mellow, and soothing:

"At the count of one, I want you to look straight ahead. At the count of two, roll your eyes back as if you were looking through the top of your skull. At the count of three, slowly lower and close your eyelids. Ready?

"One . . .

"Two . . .

"Three."

I closed my eyes, allowing myself to go with the flow. Soon, I could feel my whole body go slack. The deep voice continued:

"Now you are feeling completely relaxed. You are going into a room. A pleasant room. A room you are both comfortable with and familiar with. Here you go.

"Now you are inside the room. And you see a staircase. You walk towards that staircase. You will begin to slowly descend that staircase. Grabbing the banister with one hand, you slowly take the first step down. As you descend down the staircase, you will drift into an even deeper state of relaxation. As I count backwards, you will begin to descend the staircase, one step at a time, first one foot, then the other. And with each step you take, you will feel more and more relaxed.

"So here you go, slowly down that staircase, feeling more and more relaxed with each step down that you take.

"Ten, nine, eight . . .

"Now, you are feeling much more relaxed.

"Seven, six, five . . .

"So relaxed now, so very, very relaxed.

"Four, three, two . . .

"When you get to one, you will feel even more relaxed.

"One.

"You are now feeling totally and completely relaxed. Now that you are at the bottom of that staircase, you see a door. You walk towards that door. And you open it. And walk through it. And you find yourself outside . . .

". . . on a beautiful, sandy beach. With big, lovely palm trees swaying in the breeze. The sun is shining. The water is a deep, turquoise blue. The sky is full of puffy, white clouds floating serenely overhead. A few feet away, you see a blanket. You go to that blanket. And you lie down on it. And close your eyes. Once you are lying down, you let your mind drift. And wander.

"Lying on that beach, hearing the gentle sound of the surf, feeling the warmth of the sun, will make you feel even more relaxed. You are going to rest here. Rest and relax. Until you are totally and completely relaxed.

"Your body is becoming more and more rested. Your strength is beginning to return. When you come out of this hypnotic state, your body will feel as if you've had a good night's sleep. You will be fully rested. And refreshed. Rested and refreshed.

"Now, you are going to get up from that blanket. And walk slowly back through that door. Then back up the staircase. As I count forward, you will move slowly back up the stairs, taking one step at a time. When you get to ten, you will open your eyes. When you do open your eyes, you will feel fully refreshed and revitalized.

"Ready? Here we go.

"One.

"Two.

"Three.

"Four."

When I did finally open my eyes again, police officer John Gaspar was sitting in front of me, studying my face. "How do you feel?" he asked.

"Like Superwoman," I said. "Raring to go."

"Great. Then it worked."

Officer Gaspar was the department hypnotist. I had already borrowed him to hypnotize one of my witnesses in order to glean a more detailed description of the stickup men who had hijacked an armored truck. Then, as I found my own body succumbing to the exhaustion of the grueling, forty-eight-hour tour I had just worked on this investigation, I had asked John to hypnotize me. By putting me under, John was able to trick me into thinking my body had gotten a full night's sleep. When he brought me out again, I felt like a million bucks.

John Gaspar and I next bumped into each other at a hypnosis seminar in Virginia. John was sent there by the department. Eager to learn more about the uses of hypnosis as an investigative tool, I paid my own way. During the training exercises, we decided to team up and hypnotize each other.

Sometime after we returned to New York, John was transferred into the Major Case Squad. I immediately asked him if he wanted to partner up.

"Why not?" he responded cheerily. "We'll stir up some shit. We'll make some collars. And we'll have some fun."

But I was worried. "You don't have a problem working with a woman?" I asked.

"Not as long as you don't have a problem working with a guy who's only a white-shield cop and not yet a detective."

Great! I was ecstatic.

John Gaspar turned out to be a cop's cop. Although not yet a gold-shield detective, John was a superb investigator, plus a guy who loved being in on the action and making arrests. Broad-shouldered and heavily muscled from his days as a champion college wrestler, he ran five miles a day and held a black belt in karate. Personality-wise, he was down to earth, affable, and insanely funny.

Apart from our interest in hypnosis, John and I shared other things in common. Both of us were married. Both of us, at the time, had two kids apiece, and our kids were reasonably close in ages. Both of us loved to ski. Both of us liked to play mind games with our suspects and witnesses. Both of us had worked in Brooklyn North and knew a lot of the same guys out there. And both of us loved nothing more than a rip-roaringly good belly laugh.

John was an incurable prankster. When I'd come into the office, I'd often find that he had used his briefcase, along with an assortment of telephone directories and crime reports, to erect a makeshift barricade between our two desks. Peering furtively around his side of the barricade, John would sniff, "I'm pissed off at you today; I don't wanna see you."

Driving my car home at the end of a tour, I might reach for my sunglasses, only to discover that smiley faces with huge googly eyeballs and big dopey grins had been sketched with a Magic Marker right on the lenses. Opening the glove compartment for a tissue to clean them off, I would find a hand-scrawled note: *Smile! God loves you!* The next day, when I told John he was behaving like a four-year-old, he'd lower his eyes forlornly and apologetically, then pummel me with noogies.

Because I seemed to possess a knack for predicting things—where a street might be located, which boss would praise us versus which one would break our chops, when and where a wanted suspect might show up—John labeled me a witch on a broomstick, with eerie, supernatural powers. So, whenever he got stuck working the overnight tour, I'd pretend to be that TV character Samantha who was played by Elizabeth Montgomery on the show *Bewitched*.

Crinkling up my nose and twitching it witchily, I'd squeak at John, "*Gneeeeeee!* You are gonna have one horrible night in the squad!"

Sure enough, the next morning, a bedraggled John would barely be able to lift his head from his desk. Deluged by a flood of fresh-breaking cases, he had not even had a minute to go to the bathroom. "You bastard," he'd snarl through red and bleary eyes the minute I walked into the office. "You did it to me again. You cursed me. You and your damned nose! You witch!"

I loved to needle John about still being a white-shield police officer. "You're just an embryo detective. You haven't got all your feathers yet. Not until you hatch and get that gold shield will you be the real thing." I also liked to rag him about his temper. For the most part, John was good-natured and easygoing. But when he got mad, boy, did he get mad. He'd fume and rage and bellow, like thunder and lightning. Naturally I nicknamed him Thor, after the Norse god of thunder.

And so was born the crack investigating team of Gaspar and Burke . . . aka Thor and the Witch.

Down the line, John and I would also team up as hostage negotiators. Along with seventy-four other detectives, the two of us attended a two-week training session in May of 1984, during which we familiarized ourselves with the psychology and pathology of hostage takers, the language a negotiator should—and should not—employ with a distraught person, a psycho, or a terrorist, the usage of certain firearms (particularly mini-machine-guns, sniper rifles, and shotguns), working with robots that survey the hostage scene, and how to handle barricade situations. During the second week, we role-played, and I pretended to be a terrorist who killed two cops before taking my own life.

Shortly after graduation, John and I were called to the scene of a real-life standoff in Brooklyn. High on drugs, a young man who had been fighting with his male lover barricaded himself inside his parents' home and threatened to commit suicide. On arriving, John and I positioned ourselves at the foot of the interior staircase and took turns trying to talk him down—first John, then me, then John, then me again. But the distraught young man refused to talk with us. Instead, he began hurling furniture down the stairs at all the police officers who were on the scene.

One of the Emergency Service cops who was working with us volunteered to go up the stairs to remove some of the furniture. Handing me his shotgun, he said, "Cover me."

It was a small gesture, but in my mind it was enormous. In effect, this EMS guy was saying, "Hey, you may be a female, but you are equal to me and I trust you with my life." I would never forget it.

At the time, however, I handed him back the shotgun and told him, "Here, this looks better on you than it does on me. We'll move the furniture."

As we started to clear away the chairs and other debris from the stairs, the young man began pegging shots at us. We quickly pulled back and took cover. Another EMS officer came tumbling down the steps, and at first we thought he had been shot. But, no, it turned out that he, too, had just been trying to leap out of harm's way.

From a protected position out of range of the shooter, John and I kept up a steady flow of chatter, trying to convince the suspect to surrender. But he continued firing down at us. Finally, after one long volley, the shots stopped. When the EMS cops went up the stairs to investigate, they discovered that the young man had gone into the bathroom and killed himself with one shot to the head. A German shepherd that was with him had to be tranquilized before he could attack the EMS officers. Later, the dog was carried out upside down by EMS officers who had tied his four legs to a pole. A photograph of the cops carrying the dog suspended from the pole would appear in all the next day's newspapers.

After it was all over, John and I would shake our heads at the insanity of it all. A disturbed young man kills himself and destroys his parents' lives forever. But the thing that captures the media's fancy is that photo of his doped-up dog being carried out of the house, upside down.

If one event truly cemented our partnership, it had to be the Great Powder Fight.

It happened the night the dispatch desk in the Major Case Squad got a report of a commercial-truck hijacking. John and I volunteered to drive out to Brooklyn, where the looted truck had been found, and do the forensics. In simple English, that meant dusting the entire truck for fingerprints.

Donning protective cotton smocks and using long quill feathers, we jumped aboard the truck and carefully applied black graphite powder to all the exterior and interior surfaces—front, back, top, bottom, all the panels as well as the handles, knobs, locks, and mirrors. Because the truck was so huge, the process was long and laborious. But, in time, we retrieved several readable lifts of prints. These we would eventually turn over to the police lab.

Close to midnight, John and I decided to call it quits. We began to clean ourselves up. Finally, after a full half hour of wiping and rubbing off powder, I declared, "Well, I guess we're clean now."

Unconsciously, I reached up to scratch an itch on my scalp. When I brought my hand back down, my fingers were totally black. My hair was still completely full of graphite powder. Frantically, I tried to shake the stuff out, then brush it out with my hands. In the process, I smeared a huge black streak across the top of my forehead.

"Damn!" I said.

With that, I sneezed. A fine spray of black powder came misting out of my nostrils. *Yucchh!* When I went to wipe my nose and eyes, I blackened the rest of my face. I was beginning to look like some kid who'd just taken a mud bath.

John, meanwhile, was scratching furiously, under his collar, under his jacket, under his shirt, anywhere and everywhere. He might have gotten the powder off the outside of his clothes, but inside it was a whole other story. He was a powder keg, literally. The stuff had even gotten inside his undershorts.

When he looked up and saw my newly blackened face, looking like some kind of old-fashioned minstrel singer's, he exploded in laughter.

"Stop that!" I shouted at him. "It's not funny!"

Which only made him laugh that much harder.

"Stop it, I said!"

By now, John was laughing so hard he was doubled over.

Pissed, I reached for a can of dusting powder, scooped out a nice fat handful, and splattered it across his shirt. "You bastard!" I said.

With that, he reached over, grabbed his own fistful of powder, and bombed the top of my head.

I picked up another handful and threw it all over his trousers.

Pretty soon, powder was flying all over the place as the two of us, reverting to eight-year-olds, flung handfuls of this vile stuff back and forth at each other with lunatic glee. By the time the dust had settled—literally—we looked like a couple of turn-of-the-century chimney sweeps. Completely covered in powder from head to toe, we plopped ourselves down at the back of the truck and let our legs dangle over the side.

Then we just laughed our asses off.

Rest assured, it wasn't just the clowning that made our partnership work. It was also the respect we developed for each other.

I regarded John as a paragon of loyalty and integrity. He was a family man, absolutely devoted to his wife and kids. Unlike a lot of other married cops who were always sniffing around for something extra, he wasn't out chasing skirts. As a cop, he was all business. He loved working cases and making collars. And, although he was physically powerful and possessed the martial arts skills to hurt people with both his hands and his feet, John never beat up his prisoners. Like me, he preferred wits over muscle.

Once we got accustomed to each other's style and rhythm, we became adept at working interrogations together. When it came to playing the game of Good Cop–Bad Cop, we would alternate the roles, taking turns at each.

Meanwhile, on the street, we complemented each other like peanut butter and jelly. When one of us had a gut feeling, the other would never try to second-guess it. From experience, we both knew that instincts could be a police investigator's most valuable weapon in breaking cases.

The long and the short of it was that John and I made a terrific team. Which excited each of us no end. And bugged the hell out of everyone else in the Major Case Squad.

When he first came into the squad, the other detectives began giving John the business because he was not yet a detective. But, pretty soon, they began to rag on him because he had teamed with a woman.

"Whatya wanna partner with her for?" the old-timers would sneer. "You're one of the boys." Knowing that John was half-Italian, another detective who was also Italian told John, "Hey, paisan, you and me should team up, you know what I mean?"

John replied, "Hey, I told her I'd partner with her. She's a good partner. We like working together."

When the subtler approach failed, the old-timers began insinuating we must be sleeping together.

If we were seen talking together in the hallway or eating together in some restaurant, rumors flew. "They must be shacking up." We got so tired of all the innuendo that I finally bought John a T-shirt embossed in big block letters: IT'S OKAY. WE'RE PARTNERS. He wore it proudly to all our Police Department picnics and intrasquad softball games.

The salacious inferences and rumors became so commonplace and so ludicrous that the only way to respond to them was with sarcasm. When one detective began badgering John for the umpteen-thousandth time about whether he and I had "something going," an exasperated John finally responded:

"Well, lemme tell you the God's honest truth. See, what we do is, we meet each morning at the base of the Verrazano Bridge. Then we jump into the back of my van, we drop our drawers, and we take care of business. Then she gets into her car, I get behind the wheel of my van, we drive to the office and we sign in. Lunchtime, as long as it's quiet or the banks are closed, so we don't have to worry about any stickups, we leave the office and meet up again under the bridge. Back in the van for the old batta-boom, batta-bang. Lunch is over, we go back to the office. Finish up our paperwork. Sign out. Then, before we both go home for the night, we head back under the bridge for one last naughty hula."

The detective stood openmouthed, his eyes like saucers.

Finally, John told him, "Listen, you jackass, she's my partner. And, no, I'm not doin' her."

Even Bob, my husband, thought the whole thing was absurd. Riding up in the elevator at One Police Plaza, he would repeatedly overhear murmurings of my alleged infidelity with John. Since he himself was the target of similar rumors whenever he worked with an attractive female, all he could do was laugh.

But then, the jokes gave way to something more vicious.

"Hey, skirt!" Sergeant Burton said to me as I was signing in one morning.

I could feel my teeth grinding. I had already heard rumors that Burton had taken to referring to me as "the broad" or "Gaspar's lady" or "that fucking broad." But, so far, I had kept my mouth shut.

"So where's your partner?" he asked.

"How should I know?"

Burton gave me a look. "Whatya mean, how should you know? You guys sleep together on the weekends, don't you?"

That did it. I practically came over the top of the desk to get at him.
"What the hell's the matter with you!" I exploded. "He's married. I'm
married. What the hell do I want to sleep with my partner for! I don't
like that. And I don't want to hear you saying it, you hear me?"

Burton laughed. "Whatsamatter, you don't have a sense of humor?"

"No," I snapped. "I don't have a sense of humor."

Sergeant Burton made no attempt to disguise his contempt for me. And
whenever the opportunity arose, he would trash me.

Shortly after I had arrived in the squad, he told me I ought to put in
for a transfer.

When I took target practice at the department's firing range, I overheard him tell one of the range officers, "You shouldn't even give her a
shotgun."

When a cop got shot in Brooklyn and the other detectives were dispatched to the scene to do the canvassing for possible witnesses, he ordered me to stay in the office and answer the telephones. "That's what
you broads do best," he explained.

When stakeouts were being organized, he told the captain that I had
asked to be excused because I was having problems with my babysitter.
Needless to say, it was a lie.

When we made an arrest in a $500,000 armored-car hijacking—a
case on which I had been the primary investigator—he actually interrupted me in the middle of taking a confession from the suspect.

"Somebody else will handle this," he told me. "You go outside and
count the money."

I was not the only woman on the receiving end of the sergeant's
crude humor or attempts at sabotage. When another woman detective in
the squad, who was black, was promoted to detective second grade, Burton told me, "The nigger got your grade money." Meanwhile, to further
poison the waters, he told the other detective that I was pissed off at her
because she had been promoted while I had not. When I handed this
other detective a congratulatory card and kissed her on the cheek, she
became tearful. "You're happy for me?" she asked, incredulous. "The sergeant told me you were angry." We later became good friends.

Women were hardly the only minorities in the squad to get a taste of
the sergeant's disparagement. For a while, we had a smart and able captain who was Jewish. Burton would routinely refer to him as "Murray the
sock salesman" or "the kike." During the holiday season, when I made it

a point to put up Hanukkah decorations along with the Christmas decorations, he scolded me, saying, "Why are you trying to play up to 'the
kike'?"

Finally, when it came to blacks, be they cops or suspects or civilians,
the sergeant's prejudice knew no bounds. Burton routinely referred to
one black detective who worked in the Bronx and was nearing sixty as
Stepin Fetchit. And he humiliated another black detective, a big, tough,
savvy guy who had, at one point, actually gone undercover into the Black
Liberation Army, by burying him on desk duty.

Then, during one stretch of bank robberies, most of which were committed by black males who passed threatening notes to the tellers, the
sergeant was overheard to jauntily refer to the Major Case Squad as "the
NWN Squad."

When a black detective with whom I was working asked me what
the sergeant meant by *NWN,* I tried to avoid telling him. But the detective insisted, so, with a great deal of embarrassment, I did:

"Niggers With Notes."

One week, John and I were closing in on a guy who had committed
twenty-three bank robberies in the city. After studying his profile and his
family history, I used my witchlike predicting powers and told John, "Bet
this guy comes back to Brooklyn to visit the kid for his birthday."

"Bet you're right," John said.

Figuring the suspect would make the birthday visit under cover of
darkness, we asked if we could change from our regular day tour to a 4
p.m.–midnight tour, in hopes of nabbing our man.

"Whattaya wanna do that for?" Sergeant Burton demanded.

"We figure that's when he's going to show up, Sarge," I replied.

"Oh, yeah? What makes you think that?"

"Instincts."

"Instincts!" he scoffed. "Pshaw! What instincts? You got no instincts.
You guys got nuthin'. Your guy's not gonna show and you ain't gonna do
shit. And I'm not changin' your tour, neither."

So we did an end run around Burton and asked the CO of the squad,
Captain Berger, to change our tour. Now the captain did believe in instincts, but he didn't want to completely undermine Sergeant Burton
and embarrass him. So he compromised with us. Instead of giving us a 4
p.m.–midnight tour, he agreed to a 1 p.m.–9 p.m. tour.

And off we went to Brooklyn, hoping to catch our man.

Sure enough, just as we had anticipated, the suspect showed up that evening, to visit his house for his kid's birthday. Quickly and quietly, we cuffed him. Then took him back to Manhattan to be booked.

By the time we had finished the fingerprinting and processing, it was late at night. But when we got back to the office, Sergeant Burton was all snideness and sarcasm:

"Jeez, what'd you do, fuckin' call this guy and tell him to show up so you could put the cuffs on him?"

"Guess we got lucky," I said.

Sergeant Burton obviously did not remember our conversation about acting on instincts. Or if he did, he pretended not to.

Rather gleefully, the sergeant pointed out that we had made the collar long before midnight. "Well," he said, trying to stick the needle in a little deeper, "you guys obviously didn't need to work a four-to-midnight to make the collar, did you?"

"You're right about the collar, Sarge," I admitted. "But the reason we wanted the four-to-midnight was so we wouldn't have to put in for any overtime."

I pointed up at the clock on the wall.

"It's ten thirty p.m. And guess what? Now we are on overtime."

Burton did a slow, steady burn. He was sure we had deliberately fucked him over yet again.

William Breckner was no ordinary bank robber. He stood six feet nine inches tall. He weighed 250 pounds. For obvious reasons, he was known as the Giant.

The first time I locked Breckner up, he was sent back to Oklahoma, where he had escaped from prison, to serve his time. Three years later, he escaped again from Oklahoma and hightailed it right back to New York to do what he did best. Which was stick up more banks. Only this time, he was using a live hand grenade to persuade the terrified tellers to cooperate.

Thanks to an informant, we had a pretty good hunch about where in the Upper West Side Breckner was hanging out. With the help of some precinct detectives, John and I mapped out a plan for a stakeout.

Just as we started to head out, Sergeant Burton buttonholed us.

"I'm putting Donatello in the car with you," he said. "You spot the Giant, Gaspar and Donatello make the arrest."

"Wait a second," I said. "This is my case. Why don't I get to make the arrest?"

"Gaspar and Donatello make the arrest. You stay in the car with the informant."

"Why are you separating me from my partner?" I demanded.

"I'm not separating you from your partner," Burton replied. "Besides, somebody's gotta stay with the informant."

"It's because I'm a woman, isn't it?"

"Now, let's not go down that road, Detective."

"No, I'm a woman. You don't think women can do the job. And it's not right."

Burton exploded, "Look, I'm the sergeant. Until you pass an exam and get these"—here he made a show of tapping his two fingers across his sleeve, pointing to three imaginary sergeant's stripes on his upper arm—"you'll do as you're told, Detective."

"This is discrimination," I fired back. "How about I file a grievance?"

"Go right ahead."

I stomped out of the squad room. But then I made a U-turn, marched right back in again, and picked up where I had left off.

"Look," I told the sergeant, "he's my partner. You can't separate me from my partner, especially in an arrest situation. That's the one time above all others when cops who are used to working with each other should stay together. For safety reasons."

"And it's for safety reasons that I'm doing this," the sergeant shot back. "I'm responsible for the safety of everyone in this operation. This guy's six feet nine. He's a monster. Somebody could get hurt here."

"All the more reason I shouldn't be separated from my partner."

"I gotta agree with her, Sarge," said John Gaspar, who was standing nearby.

Burton whirled on him like a cobra. "You stay the fuck outta this, Gaspar. Just mind your own fucking business."

John stiffened. "This is my business. She's my partner—she should make the arrest with me. I'm used to working with her. If you want to give us an extra person, an extra ten people, we'll take a caravan. But we're doing this together."

"Look, you just shut the fuck up like I told ya," the sergeant told John.

I jumped back into the middle. "Sergeant, fifteen years ago, I took an oath of office. I was authorized to make arrests. I was given a gun and a shield—"

He cut me off before I could finish. "Yeah, well, I had nothing to do with the decision to give you a gun and shield."

I looked at him. "Wait a second. Are you saying I'm not fit for duty?"

"No. But I am saying I don't think you should have a gun and a shield. You can't stand there and tell me you have the same physical abilities as Gaspar."

"That has nothing to do with this," I said. "Given the same goal, we may get there by different means. But we'll get there just the same. And safely."

Burton responded, "You can't always get there by shooting someone, Detective."

"Sergeant, let me tell you something. I've been on this job fifteen years. And in fifteen years, I have never had to use my weapon."

Just then, Captain Berger entered the room. When he learned that Burton had ordered John to work with a different detective, he rescinded the order.

"Not in my squad," the captain said. "We don't separate partners in my squad. Partners work together."

Grumbling to himself, Sergeant Burton looked down at the list of detectives who had been picked to work the surveillance operation. He crossed Donatello's name off.

"You're the boss," he meekly told the captain.

Later that night, we did nab the Giant.

We surprised him while he was walking up Eighth Avenue with an accomplice. John took a flying leap, sailed fifteen feet through the air, and dumped the Giant on his ass. John looked like a giant bird in flight.

While John handcuffed the stunned Breckner, I held my gun on the Giant's accomplice. But I managed to look over and make eye contact with the Giant.

"Hi, Bill! Howya doin'? Remember me?"

The Giant looked up at me from the sidewalk. He studied my face. Then it hit him.

"Aw, jeez, not you again."

In contrast to my problems with Burton, with Chief Jackson the friction had mostly to do with my attempts to secure my next promotion, to detective second grade, which would have added $10,000 a year to my pay. Eleven long years had elapsed since my last promotion to detective third grade—awarded to me by the police commissioner while I'd sat with a bag over my head. And I was starting to get restless.

Other detectives with less seniority had been getting promoted. While everybody knew there was an unofficial quota on promotions for women, one other woman did get upped to detective second grade. But she was not a very good detective. She was known to have a drinking problem, and what's more, while making an undercover drug buy, she had been caught on audiotape engaging in some highly unusual behavior with a known drug dealer. Listening closely to the tape, a number of cops in her backup team concluded that she had actually performed oral sex on him, which was not exactly in the department's manual of proper police procedure. The whole business was quickly hushed up and the woman quietly transferred to another unit.

Notwithstanding this other detective's less-than-stellar reputation, I couldn't understand why I wasn't being advanced in grade. My case clearance rate was high, I had no disciplinary charges against me, and my record did not reflect excessive sick leave. Two of the other sergeants I had worked for in Major Case had recommended me for promotion. So I decided to lobby Chief Jackson to at least place my name on the list of those to be considered for promotion by the chief of detectives. Unless my name appeared on that list—or the "grid" as it was known in the Detective Bureau—I didn't stand a chance.

Now, Chief Jackson was the same Chief Jackson who had blocked my transfer out of Major Case on the grounds that my clearance rate was too high and the squad could ill afford to lose me. So if any boss should have been willing to back me for promotion, I figured it oughtta be this one. Hell, he had already gone on record as saying my clearance rate was superlative.

When I went up to his office, Chief Jackson leaned his chubby frame back into his swivel chair, extended his short legs out from his desk, and gave me a smug, condescending look. After hearing me out, he toyed for a moment with the small hole in his moth-eaten sweater. Then he assured me that he had passed along a recommendation to the chief of detectives, Frank Cosgrove, that I be given "grade."

Still, I couldn't figure out what was taking so long. So, with Chief Jackson's consent, I decided to take my case personally before Chief Cosgrove. Surely, Chief Cosgrove would be willing to hear me out. After all, he was the same guy who had rescued me from Missing Persons and reassigned me to Major Case in the first place.

In preparation for my meeting, I assembled a dossier containing all my past letters of commendation, my awards, my arrests, my time sheets, my disciplinary records. Then I went up to Chief Cosgrove's office. The cop who was working as his receptionist went in to tell the chief the purpose of my visit.

That instant, Chief Cosgrove picked up his telephone and called downstairs to Chief Jackson. Sitting outside in the waiting area, I could easily overhear the conversation.

"What the hell are you trying to pull down there?" Cosgrove demanded of Jackson. "You better straighten this detective out, Chief. You better explain to her that her name isn't even up here for consideration. And I don't have time for this kinda bullshit."

Angrily, he slammed the receiver down.

I was absolutely mortified. Feeling like the village idiot, I never even went in to plead my case to Chief Cosgrove. Instead, I picked myself up, did a quick about-face, and went straight back down to the Special Investigations Division. I didn't even bother to knock before entering Chief Jackson's office.

"You sonofabitch!" I said to Chief Jackson. "You may be a chief, but you set me up! You knew I wasn't on the grid, yet you let me go upstairs to the chief of detectives' office and make a total fool of myself in front of the chief. You lied to me! Who do you think you are anyway?"

Flicking a fat finger at the edges of the moth hole in his sweater, Chief Jackson narrowed his eyes into little slits and glowered at me. He looked like a rattlesnake that was about to uncoil. "It'll be a cold day in hell before I ever evaluate a woman over a man for grade money," he said to me.

So that was it.

Once again, this bastard had deliberately sabotaged me. He had never even intended to recommend me for promotion.

"You know, Detective," he said, "you'd really be better off at home, changing diapers and baking bread."

I promptly lost it. "Let me tell you something, Chief," I shot back. "I'm a better mother to my children than your wife is to yours."

Chief Jackson bristled noticeably at the comparison.

But I was just getting warmed up.

"As for baking bread, I'd be happy to bake bread. Lots and lots of bread. Great big wheelbarrows full of bread. Rye, white, whole-wheat, rolls, bagels, croissants, whatever the hell you want. Enough loaves for the entire squad. Enough for the division. Hey, enough for the whole damned Police Department, and the Fire and Sanitation departments, too, if that'll make you happy . . .

"... just so long as you keep sending my paychecks to my house each week. Along with all my overtime."

Chief Jackson gave me a long, cold stare.

"That will be all, Detective," said the Chief. "You can leave now."

I was furious. The moment I walked out, I marched straight up to the Office of Employee Relations. When I got up there, I encountered Joe Scott, a detective I knew.

"Whattaya need, Kath?"

"I got a big one for you, Joe. I want to see the commissioner. In person."

Joe nearly fell off his chair. "Are you crazy? You can't see the PC. But tell me what the problem is."

I told him the whole story. I also showed him my file with all my medals, my arrests, my time sheets, and my disciplinary records.

"I'm breaking my ass, I'm wearing the suit, I'm doing the job, yet, after eleven years, I'm not even on the grid," I said. "And I can't even find out why. I tried to ask the chief of detectives, but at this point, he thinks I'm a complete moron. So the only one left for me to appeal to is the commissioner himself."

"Look," Joe said, "you may not get to see the commissioner. But I guarantee that your case will."

Police Commissioner Robert McGuire had known about me long before my personnel folder crossed his desk. Prior to becoming commissioner, McGuire had been a criminal defense attorney in private practice. And he had been impressed with the way I had handled myself at a meeting to negotiate a plea bargain for one of his clients in a criminal case. McGuire also knew my husband, Bob, who had headed up the department's public information office.

When my case came before him, Police Commissioner McGuire told his subordinates, "She's a good detective. She deserves to be promoted." He ordered my name added to the grid.

Then, toward the end of 1983, I heard that my promotion was finally going forward. But at the eleventh hour, my name mysteriously vanished from the grid again. It was bumped for another female detective, who just happened to be the girlfriend of a high-ranking chief.

McGuire, however, was not about to be hoodwinked under his own roof. In the last week before he was due to leave office and return to civilian life, McGuire got hold of the promotion list. "Where's Burke's name?" he demanded.

It didn't take him long to put two and two together. With just seven days left until he officially departed, he knocked the chief's girlfriend off the grid. And put my name back on.

I was in court on the day I got the telephone call tipping me that I was finally going to be promoted. The boss who would be giving me the official notification, I was informed, was none other than Chief Jackson.

I practically split my sides with laughter. Of all the bosses they could have picked to break the news to me, they had to pick my nemesis, Chief Jackson.

When I arrived at his office, one of my other detective friends, George Kennedy, was inside chatting with the chief. To my great joy, George was going to be promoted to detective second grade, too.

But I played dumb. "Yeah, Chief?" I said as I stepped inside "You wanted to see me about something?"

With a grandiose gesture, Chief Jackson waved his hand in my direction, knuckles facing out. "You should kiss my ring, Detective. I just got you your promotion."

I stared at him, incredulous. I looked over at George, who simply rolled his eyes. Then I turned back to face the Chief. And I said:

"You should kiss my ass, Chief. I got it myself."

CHAPTER FIFTEEN

The day of my promotion, in December of 1983, I arrived at Police Headquarters all decked out in my dress blue uniform, peaked blue cap, and white gloves. With me were Bob and my two daughters, Veronica and Cathrine, as well as my aunt Marie and my babysitter Rita. All would be sitting in the auditorium to share my big moment when the police commissioner summoned me up to the stage and elevated me to detective second grade. I was bursting with excitement.

Prior to the ceremony, Bob disappeared to attend to some business. I took everyone else up to the Major Case Squad, where I posed for photos with the other detectives who were being promoted, such as Peggy Hopkins, who was assigned to the Special Frauds Squad, and George Kennedy, who worked with me in Major Case. John Gaspar sat thumb-wrestling with my kids. At one point, George and I wandered back to the coffee room to look for some juice for my girls.

Just then, Sergeant Burton walked in and said, "You two can kiss your future overtime good-bye. Nobody makes more money in this squad than me next year."

I couldn't believe what I was hearing. This was our day to celebrate. To rejoice about our promotions, our accomplishments, our careers. To take pride in front of our husbands and wives, our kids and our friends. But Sergeant Burton was determined to piss on our parade.

"You're a sick person," I told him.

Whatever the reason for Burton's continued resentment and animosity, things went from bad to worse after my promotion.

For starters, the sergeant made sure that I earned no more overtime. Then he began bad-mouthing me as a union delegate, taunting the male detectives over their having chosen a woman to represent them with the

Detectives' Endowment Association. When I first came into Major Case, I was an alternate delegate to the union. About three months later, after the long-standing full-time delegate was transferred to another unit, I was elected to succeed him.

While I was attending a DEA picnic, Sergeant Burton reportedly told several of the detectives, "What kind of men are you, you let a cunt broad be your leader and do your fighting for you?" For a man who habitually talked trash to my face, as well as behind my back, that had to be an all-time low.

But the worst part was that Sergeant Burton began accusing me of botching my case reports, known as DD-5s.

"Burke," Sergeant Burton would say to me, "the captain is looking for that case folder, that last DD-5. Where the hell is it?"

"I already did it," I would invariably say.

"Oh, yeah? Then where is it? I can't find it anywhere. You're falling down on the job, Detective. You gotta have your paperwork up-to-date in this squad."

Day in and day out, the sergeant was on me about my DD-5 reports. I knew I had completed them, but they seemed to keep disappearing.

Finally, I went to see the detective analyst in charge of keeping the squad's case folders. Maybe he had mislaid my DD-5s.

"Haven't touched 'em, Kath," the analyst said.

"Do me a favor," I said. "Show me one of my case folders."

He pulled one out of his file cabinet. When I looked inside, I found that the report was missing.

"Show me a few more of my cases," I said to the analyst.

He pulled out a whole bunch of case folders. The reports I had filed were missing from these folders, too. What the hell was going on here, anyway?

I went down to the department's records section. Duplicates of all case reports were routinely sent to this office. I pulled the duplicates of my case reports and studied them carefully. Each had been signed by the captain and the sergeant, as required by the department. This meant that both the captain and the sergeant had seen my reports, had read them, and, by virtue of their signatures, had acknowledged reading them. I grabbed one of the duplicate DD-5s—one on which the sergeant had scolded me for my tardiness—and went back up to the captain's office.

"Captain," I began. "I understand you're looking for one of my cases. Here it is."

Captain Stengel looked at me blankly. "What are you talking about, Detective?"

By now it was pretty obvious that somebody was deliberately screwing around with my reports.

Sergeant Burton called me into his office. One more time, he reamed me for not having my paperwork up-to-date.

It didn't take me long to put two and two together. By accusing me of bungling my case reports, Sergeant Burton was laying the groundwork to give me a lousy job evaluation. One poor evaluation, and the department would put me on probation. A second poor evaluation several months down the line, and it would demote me. Clearly, the sergeant was looking for a ruse to take away my promotion to detective second grade and my grade money. At the same time, he was lobbying the men in the squad to vote me out as the union delegate. Stripped of my union status and its attendant protections (i.e., the prohibition against arbitrarily transferring a detective to another squad because he or she chooses to engage in union business), I would become even more vulnerable to his twisted machinations.

Clearly, this guy was gunning for me.

For a fleeting moment, I wondered if I might be paranoid, imagining wild plots and conspiracies where none existed. Just to make certain I was not letting my imagination run amok, I decided I ought to find some piece of concrete evidence corroborating Sergeant Burton's treachery before I took any further action.

So that's when I pulled a Watergate.

It was well past three in the morning when I showed up at Police Headquarters.

After showing my detective shield to the cops at the front door, I made my way up to the floor where the Major Case Squad was located. I knew the office would be locked and no one would be on duty at this time of night, so I casually drifted into the Missing Persons Squad next door. A detective I knew was manning the overnight desk.

"Hi, Sam," I said.

"Hey, Kath," said the cop. "What's shakin'?"

"Um, I need to get into the squad. I left something in the office."

"Go ahead." He handed me a key. I went back outside and unlocked the door to the Major Case Squad.

Once I was inside, I turned on the lights. I glanced back behind me. The detective in Missing Persons was not able to see me.

Then I went straight to Sergeant Burton's private office. The door was open. I made a beeline for his desk. In no time at all, I had the lock on his top drawer picked. Inside the top drawer, I found a pad. Attached to it was a piece of paper with a list of dates. Each of those dates coincided with a day on which Sergeant Burton had scolded me about not doing my DD-5s. To the untrained eye, this list would appear to be a meticulously documented chronology of my malfeasance and ineptitude.

Attached to the list, however, were all my DD-5s, the same DD-5s that Sergeant Burton had claimed were missing. He had secretly removed them from the case folders. Then, with my case reports safely tucked inside his desk, he had called me into his office to chew my ass out for not doing them.

That realization that the sergeant had purloined my case reports sickened me. What made it worse was that there was nothing I could do about it. I would have to keep it to myself. If I told any of the bosses that I had broken into Burton's desk, they would have brought me up on departmental charges for breaking and entering. Once he found out, Burton might have been wily enough to add to my crime by claiming he had left a $50 bill inside his desk—and it was now missing.

I placed the pad and the DD-5s back where I'd found them. I locked the drawer. Turned off the lights. Returned the key to the Missing Persons Squad.

Then I left Police Headquarters, got into my car, and went home for the night.

Clearly, I was heading for a tumble.

What worried me most was that I was due to be away from the squad for a long stretch of time, first for vacation and then for a three-month training stint at the FBI Academy in Quantico, Virginia. During this time, Sergeant Burton would be writing up his job performance evaluations of all the detectives who worked under him. With me out of the way, he would undoubtedly look to put the screws to me.

The notion that he might trash me on my job evaluation was nauseating because it would contradict everything I had worked so long and hard to achieve. In all my years with the New York Police Department, I had never been the subject of any civilian complaints nor departmental discipline. My record indicated excellent arrest activity, superior evaluations from all my previous bosses, promotions to detective third grade and detective second grade based on my superior performance, flawless attendance and punctuality, and long tenure as a delegate to the Detectives' Endowment Association (the first female delegate ever to that police union, in fact).

At first, I tried talking to Lieutenant Caro about my difficulties with the sergeant. I did not reveal to him what I had unearthed inside Burton's desk. But I did tell him that the sergeant was falsely accusing me of bungling my paperwork.

Caro promised to look into it.

I wasn't convinced. I went on to complain about Burton's abusive language and antifemale attitudes. Caro tried to laugh it off as piddling banter. "C'mon, Kathy," he said, "you know the sergeant, and that's just the way he is."

"This is no joke," I told the lieutenant. But at this point, I don't think he was even listening.

I soon realized I would have to take more radical measures and file an official complaint against the sergeant. But, at a meeting of the Policewomen's Endowment Association, of which I was a member, a female deputy commissioner warned me that I would need more evidence than just my word to buttress a complaint. "If you go one-on-one with him, you don't have a chance in hell of winning," she said. A couple of my friends in the squad pulled me aside and told me, "You gotta confront Burton, Kath. And get it on tape."

It was an extreme, perilous tactic. The Police Department secretly tape-recorded people routinely every day of the year. But for one cop to tape another cop was a whole different ball of wax, an act of subterfuge and betrayal that could be perceived as high treason. At this point, however, I felt I had no recourse. My career was about to go up in smoke. Few women were working in detective squads in those days, and those that were had to fight tooth and nail to be promoted. Commanding officers rarely put them on the grid—under official consideration for promotion—and in one instance they had actually tried to strip another female detective of grade money that had already been awarded to her. Women who worked in uniform were subjected to different kinds of harassment—pressure to date, sexual innuendo, lockers turned upside down or decorated with condoms. Women who worked in detective squads were vulnerable to reductions in grade money or the loss of their detective shields altogether. And now it was my turn.

I had to act. And act fast.

At a downtown electronics store, I bought a pocket-size tape recorder and batteries. Then I returned to the office.

Back in the Major Case Squad, I flipped on the recorder and tucked it in the breast pocket of my jacket. Sergeant Burton was sitting at the desk inside his office when I walked in.

"I'd like to speak with you in private, Sergeant," I said.

"Close the door," the sergeant replied. When I turned around to face him again, he looked up at me, smiling. For some reason, he seemed to be expecting me. At the outset, he seemed perfectly calm. A paragon of decorum, civility, and good manners. Which immediately aroused my suspicions.

"Sergeant, I'd like to talk to you about some things," I said.

"Which things are those, Detective?" he asked.

I carefully avoided any mention of the case reports I had found inside his desk. Instead, I said, "We seem to have a problem, and I don't understand why. What's wrong with my work?"

"Nothing's wrong with your work," he replied.

"So why do you keep doing these things to me?"

"I'm not doing anything to you, Detective. I don't know what you're talking about."

"What about trying to separate me from my partner the night we arrested the Giant?"

"That was to protect the safety of everybody in the squad," Sergeant Burton said.

"Well, why did you pick that particular night to worry about squad safety? There have been at least a dozen other occasions when you didn't stop me from going out with my partner to make a collar."

Sergeant Burton smiled at me, like a patient parent trying to humor a difficult child. "I think you're imagining things, Detective."

Sergeant Burton was playing it cool. Too cool. He was measuring his words carefully, like a clergyman delivering a Sunday sermon. And it was totally out of character. I began to wonder if somebody, perhaps Lieutenant Caro, might have tipped him that I might try to tape-record him. But I couldn't turn back now. There might not be another opportunity.

I had dealt with uncooperative subjects before, during my case interrogations, and I knew that if I stayed with it long enough, kept twisting and probing and prodding, sooner or later I would find that hidden nerve, that hair trigger that would cause him to blow. So I began to needle him about his foul language.

"Why do you keep calling me a 'cunt broad,' Sergeant?"

"I've never used that word, Detective."

"Aw, c'mon, who's kiddin' who? You called me a 'cunt broad.' Everyone in the squad knows you said it about me. A whole bunch of times. You said it when I was at the DEA picnic. You've said it half a dozen other times."

"I'm sorry, Detective, but you are mistaken."

"'Cunt broad.' That's what I keep hearing, Sergeant. And I don't like it."

"I never used the word, Detective."

"C'mon, Sergeant, admit it. You called me a 'cunt broad,' didn't you?"

And then, he snapped. "I called you a fucking broad and I can call you that anytime I want."

Bingo. And I had it on tape.

"What about those other things you've called me, Sergeant?"

"What things are those, Detective?"

"'The skirt,' 'Gaspar's lady,' you know exactly what I'm talking about."

"I never said any of those things, Detective."

I scoffed. "Aw, gimme a break."

Sergeant Burton gave me a real fish-eyed look. "You sure you're not going through the change of life, Burke? You know, you women are very sensitive at these times."

I practically hit the ceiling. "What are you talking about?" I shot back. "I just had a baby. I'm nowhere near the change of life."

When I left Burton's office, I made a beeline for Lieutenant Caro's office. Captain Stengel, the new CO of the Major Case Squad, was with him. Stengel was a creepy character with weird, psycho eyes and an eerie obsession with Ouiji boards, genies, and demonic symbols.

"I just had a conversation with Sergeant Burton," I told them. Then I let the other shoe drop. "And I taped it."

Well, I doubt that you ever saw two grown men move away from a woman so quickly. Both of them took a sudden leap backward, as if I had just admitted to having a communicable social disease.

"Don't you want to hear it?" I asked.

Lieutenant Caro brought his palms up defensively, as if trying to ward off lethal rays. "Uh . . . no thanks. That won't be necessary."

"But he admits to his wrongdoing," I said. "You should listen to this."

"We're conducting our own investigation of this matter," said the lieutenant. "We'll get back to you when it's finished."

And that's when I knew I was really in deep shit.

On September 30 of 1984, I was due to leave for the FBI Academy in Quantico. So I told the lieutenant and the captain that I would wait until September 10 to learn the results of their "investigation" of my feud with Sergeant Burton. After that, if they failed to act, I would bring the entire matter up to the department's Office of Equal Employment Opportunity in the form of an official discrimination complaint.

"And if I go to OEEO," I told them, "I am not going to lose."

What I did not tell the captain and the lieutenant was that I had not switched off my tape recorder. Hey, I was no dummy. Down the line, I knew I would need to prove that I had warned them about taking my complaint to OEEO. I was pretty certain the lieutenant and the captain would develop a sudden case of amnesia and deny ever having heard me say it. So I secretly taped them, too.

The bosses of the Major Case Squad would preferably choose to deal with my complaint in-house. I made it clear to them that filing an OEEO complaint, which would make my allegations public, would be my very last resort. And something I was not eager to do.

I knew they would never transfer Sergeant Burton out of Major Case. Short of his removal, I was willing to settle for an apology. Had the sergeant offered to sit down with me, in front of witnesses, and say, "Okay, look, I pulled all this shit, and I'm sorry for it. What can I tell ya, I'm a Neanderthal. I come out of the old school. Can we just wipe the slate clean and start fresh again?" I would have been satisfied.

The lieutenant and the captain said it would take some time for them to review my allegations. And, indeed, weeks drifted by. Then months. One month, two months, three months . . .

At one point, the lieutenant told me he had "a solution" to the problem. Through the grapevine I learned that they were thinking of shifting Sergeant Burton over to the Missing Persons Squad. But then Missing Persons got wind of the plan and balked. The detectives there knew Burton—and wanted no part of him. So this "solution" fizzled real fast.

Meanwhile, most of the other detectives in the Major Case Squad began to shun me like the plague. Once the captain and the lieutenant told Burton that I had taped him—and spread the word to everyone else in the squad, as well—the reaction was swift. Fierce. And ugly.

Guys were warned to steer clear of me . . . or else. Tough, veteran detectives who had shown not a whit of fear or trepidation on the meanest of New York City's mean streets were now petrified of being seen with me. The scuttlebutt was that I had tape-recorded everybody in the squad, all thirty-five detectives. And that I was looking to hurt somebody, even send one of them to jail.

It was shameful.

Even Bob started to get an earful.

One high-ranking detective chief began haranguing him at a dinner, "Who the fuck is she to tape another cop?"

To which Bob replied, "Hey, you had her working undercover all those years. You trained her how to tape people, so whaddya expect?"

On September 10, the day I had given the lieutenant and the captain as my personal deadline, they called me in to tell me that they had finished their investigation.

Their determination?

They would neither transfer nor punish Sergeant Burton. But out of the goodness of his heart, Sergeant Burton would be willing to shake hands with me and "let bygones be bygones." He would not apologize for anything specific since he believed he had done nothing wrong. If I still felt differently, I was perfectly welcome to leave the squad. And transfer to Queens.

I refused to go to Queens. Nothing was happening in Queens. Queens was a graveyard.

The captain suggested I had a problem with authority.

"It has nothing to do with authority," I fired back. "If Sergeant Burton told me to stand on the corner and whistle 'Yankee Doodle' with a paper bag over my head, I'd do it, 'cause he's the sergeant. But when he steps outta his role as sergeant and starts to abuse people, he just doesn't have that right. And you don't have to side with him, either."

I tried to reason with them. But it was pointless. They felt Sergeant Burton was a good sergeant and a good boss. They would not take any action against him.

So upstairs I marched yet again, this time to file my official complaint with the Office of Equal Employment Opportunity.

"I wondered how long it was gonna take you, Kathy," said one of the female cops in OEEO.

By filing my complaint with OEEO, I was keeping it in-house. I was not going outside the department to influential government leaders and politicians that I had come to know, such as Mayor Ed Koch. Nor was I going to federal court. I was operating within the chain of command, staying within the system. I had sworn an oath of loyalty to the New York Police Department, and I felt obliged to honor that oath. Conversely, I was certain that, in my moment of need, the department would repay that loyalty by coming to my aid and comfort.

I was a complete and utter fool.

Three weeks later, I left New York City for the FBI Academy in Quantico.

The FBI program was terrific, three months of grueling physical training, challenging classroom work, topflight instruction in the use of the newest, state-of-the-art firearms, and invaluable networking with crackerjack detectives, agents, and criminal investigators from all over the world.

At one workshop, I was asked to participate in a psychological study. Based on my answers, the study revealed that I was ethical, truthful, and opinionated. While cautious in my actions, I was too spontaneous with my opinions. I could often be painfully blunt, even to the point that my bluntness might end up hurting my friendships with other people. My rapid-response style might allow for a large group of acquaintances, but only a small circle of true and lasting friends. Finally, the study suggested that while I was quick to perceive things as either all black or all white, other people were inclined to view me in exactly the same way.

"There are no gray areas about you," reported the FBI agent who administered the study.

"Yup," I told him, "folks either love me or hate me."

I should have been less flip. The study revealed something profoundly important about my personality flaws. Something I should have been able to learn from it for the future.

In hindsight, I should have paid a hell of a lot more attention to it.

While I was off at the FBI Academy, I figured things would temporarily simmer down in the Major Case Squad. Unbeknownst to me, they got a thousand times worse. With me out of the picture, Sergeant Burton and his supporters quickly mobilized to exact their revenge. They were determined to make me pay for filing my OEEO complaint. And pay with interest.

For starters, they launched a campaign to unseat me as the squad's delegate to the Detectives' Endowment Association. A petition was circulated calling for a new delegate election. I always suspected that the real instigator behind the move was Lieutenant Caro, but the most visible perpetrators were two old-time detectives who were known to be pals of Sergeant Burton. One of the detectives, Finn, was a guy I had once partnered with briefly. The other detective, Leff, was an overweight, racist bully who had demonstrated, on numerous occasions, a less-than-reverential respect for the Bill of Rights and its guarantees of basic civil liberties for accused suspects. In circulating their petition for a new election, Leff and Finn hardly relied on the velvet-glove approach. When they found that they lacked the required 51 percent to hold a new election, they physically dragged detectives into a back room of the Major Case Squad and warned them they had better sign the petition or they'd be out on their asses, booted from the squad.

Some of the other detectives tried to argue that I had been a competent and dedicated union delegate. Leff and Finn shouted them down. As a result of their strong-arm tactics, they succeeded in getting twenty-two signatures on their petition, enough to legally call for a new vote. They also bullied a detective from the squad into running against me. But, as this detective later confided to me, even he was acting out of fear. Had he not agreed to run, he was told, he'd get thrown out of the squad, too.

And then the pro-Burton faction started to really play dirty. With the new boss of the Major Case Squad, creepy-eyed Captain Stengel, firmly in their camp, they began to put the screws to my partner, John Gaspar.

Now John had not been eager for me to file an official complaint with OEEO. Like most of the other detectives in the squad, he regarded my actions as a violation of the cop's sacrosanct code of the brotherhood in blue. Yet, as distasteful as he found my actions, John felt what the bosses were doing was far more detestable. He saw them as power-drunk, dictatorial, and vindictive.

John knew that once I made an official complaint, he would wind up in the hot seat because he had opted to stay partnered with me. And he certainly had a great deal to lose. He had been welcomed into the Major Case Squad with open arms by the other detectives, who had come to like and respect him. He was next up to go to the FBI National Academy for training as a criminal profiler, perhaps the most prestigious and challenging work an investigator can tackle. He was on the list for promotion to sergeant. He had done well in the Detective Bureau, and he was on the fast track to do even better.

Now, however, because he had chosen to remain loyal to me, it was all being thrown into jeopardy. But as John put it, being loyal to the truth was ingrained in his nature, part and parcel of who he was as a person. It was something he had no control over.

In late summer of 1984, John had been called into the office of a lieutenant who worked in the Special Investigations Division, the umbrella command over the Major Case Squad. The lieutenant tried to pump John for information about my plan to file a formal discrimination complaint against Sergeant Burton. John told the lieutenant if he had any questions, he ought to put them to me directly.

"You know, Gaspar," the lieutenant advised, "if they have to draw up sides on this thing and you pick the wrong side, they'll come after you."

"Hey," John had replied, "if somebody's after me, they're either going to have to use a great deal of imagination, flake me, or get me for bullshit."

To which the lieutenant replied, "It's a big rule book. And the bosses never lose."

The lieutenant changed tacks, telling John how well-liked and respected he was by the other detectives in Major Case.

"But that will all end if you take your partner's side on this thing," the lieutenant added.

The lieutenant's message was loud and clear: Give up the broad. Lie about Burke. Say she's crazy, a nut job, a boss-fighter, and a troublemaker. Or else suffer the consequences.

"I'm not gonna lie, Lieutenant," John said. "No matter what."

Once I went ahead and formally filed my complaint, the pressure on John worsened. Knowing that they would all have to give depositions to the OEEO investigators, the other detectives in the Major Case Squad were on John like horseflies. "What are you gonna do when you get called to testify?" they would ask.

"Tell the truth," John would answer.

"But what is the truth?" the detectives would ask, scared shitless that if he really did tell the truth, he would identify each of them by name and reveal that they knew the truth just as well as he did. Then they would be faced with the choice of going up against Sergeant Burton or lying through their teeth to save their own asses.

"I will not put it on anyone else," John would say. "I am not going to name any other names. I'm only going to testify to what I myself had direct knowledge of."

Despite these assurances, John found himself under constant pressure to throw me to the wolves. Lieutenant Caro continually badgered him to work with a new partner. Other detectives blamed him for allowing me to tape-record Burton in the first place, as if John or anyone else had the power to dictate my actions. Some said I had purposely set John up to take a fall while I went off to the FBI Academy for fun and games.

"You know she's fucking you, don'tcha, Gaspar?" was the typical comment.

One senior detective pulled John aside and confided that he had actually been promised a promotion—to the very highest rank of detective first grade—if he could get John on tape saying that I was a psycho and a boss-fighter. Now this senior detective was not at all happy with what I had done to Sergeant Burton, but to his great credit, he refused to try to ensnare John.

Apart from the face-to-face warnings, John began to receive anonymous threats. Muffled telephone calls. A letter in his office mailbox telling him, "Be careful, John. They're coming after you. A friend."

In time, John learned that he had become the target of an investigation by the department's Internal Affairs Division. The allegation? That sometime earlier in his career, when a relative of John's had been arrested for criminal possession of stolen property, John had improperly attempted to persuade another detective in another squad to ease up on the defendant. John knew that the allegation was completely bogus. The only thing he had ever asked the other detective to do was to treat his relative with respect. Other than that, he had asked for no special favors or breaks. Just so everything was on the up-and-up, he had even notified his superior officer that he wanted to speak with the arresting detective about his relative. The superior officer had given him the okay to go ahead. It didn't take long for the IAD investigators to conclude that the allegation against John was a big bag of stale nothing. John was fully exonerated.

Although the Internal Affairs investigation fizzled, the pressure on John to publicly discredit me did not. The Special Investigations Division lieutenant who had previously tried to strong-arm him into lying about me made another stab at it. One night, while John was working in the Major Case Squad, the lieutenant appeared in the office. This time, he was much more pointed in his warnings.

"You know," the lieutenant told John, "if she does file a complaint, you'll have to say she's a psycho and a boss-fighter. If you side with her, there won't be a rock big enough to hide under or a foxhole deep enough for you to hide in."

The lieutenant told John he was "an asshole" for not changing partners when Lieutenant Caro had offered him the opportunity to dump me and team up with one of the guys.

"Go fuck yourself," John told him.

When they turned up the heat on John, I was still down in Quantico. And I did not have a clue as to what was going on.

CHAPTER SIXTEEN

It was late October when John was called into the back office by Sergeant Burton and Lieutenant Caro.

"Give us your memo book, Detective," they told him.

"Why?" he asked.

"You're being written up for command discipline," the lieutenant replied.

"What have I done?" John demanded.

"You'll be told by the captain at a later date," the lieutenant answered cryptically.

This was not good. Command discipline was an internal punitive measure that could result in the loss of several days' pay and a blemish on one's record. John was flummoxed. Never before in his career had he been written up for anything. His record was spotless. A command discipline could seriously tarnish his reputation as well as his chances for advancement in the department. But when John tried to find out exactly why he was facing disciplinary charges, he ran into a stone wall.

Finally, John went into Captain Stengel's office. "What's this all about, Captain?" he asked.

"It's self-explanatory," the captain answered.

One day, John overheard Captain Stengel on the phone to a sergeant in the Police Department's trial division, the unit responsible for prosecuting more serious infractions by police officers. Captain Stengel was trying to persuade this sergeant to bring John's command discipline directly into the trial room, where it could be goosed up a notch into more official charges. The trial room sergeant, however, was having none of it. The charges against John were piffling bullshit, the sergeant said. If the captain referred the charges to the trial room, the sergeant warned, they would be kicked back down to the Major Case Squad.

And still, the exact nature of these charges was never made clear. John had been notified that he was facing disciplinary charges. But, no matter how often he tried or to whom he spoke, John could never learn precisely what those charges were.

The whole thing was becoming Kafkaesque.

By nosing around, John did learn that his gas-mileage activity sheets—the slips he put in whenever he refueled his car with department gas—were being scrutinized. The rumor being circulated was that John had utilized his department charge card to use more gas than he was entitled to. In fact, he actually overheard Sergeant Burton tell someone, "I'm gonna try to get him for theft of services." The funny thing about all this was that John never used department gas. He always made a point of purchasing nondepartment gas—and paying for it out of his own pocket—since he felt the department's gas was inferior and might damage his car engine.

This harassment of John went on for more than a month. Finally, while I was still away at the FBI Academy, Captain Stengel announced that he would hold a formal command disciplinary hearing in his office on all the mysterious and still unexplained charges that had been leveled at John.

Along with John, the others present at the hearing included Captain Stengel, Lieutenant Caro, and a sergeant. Also present was Detective Bill Crowley, a trustee of the Detectives' Endowment Association. It was customary for detectives to have a union rep present for such proceedings, and Crowley was there to protect John's rights.

At long last, the captain began to spell out the specific charges. First of all, John was accused of changing a work shift without permission. Then he was accused of taking fifteen minutes too long for a meal period. Finally, he was accused of either leaving the office early or speeding through a toll plaza at the Verrazano Bridge.

For several minutes, John went back and forth with the captain over the specifics of the charges, all of which were clearly trumped-up and exaggerated. Finally, John simply interrupted the captain and said:

"Look, let's cut the crap. I know why I'm here. And I know why I've been given charges . . . Kathy Burke." John looked at the captain and the lieutenant. "You guys are on a crusade. You want to get Kathy Burke. And you want to use me to discredit her. You're going to back me into a corner to get me to go along with your crusade. So lemme lay it out for you real simple: You back me into a corner, there are two human responses.

One is flight. The other is fight. Right now, I am attempting to flee. Flight. But if you don't give me that option, I'll have no choice but to fight. And, believe me—fight, I will."

The whole room fell silent.

Bill Crowley, the DEA trustee, asked John to step outside. Once he left, John could hear Crowley screaming at the others, "So you're gonna take this damn fine detective, you're gonna crucify him, put him up on a cross, for your own agenda? And then you're gonna totally sour him? Why don't you cut the bullshit, you don't have this guy on anything!"

A few moments later, Bill Crowley came out again. He told John that if he would be willing to accept three days' loss of pay, for taking too long on his meal period, the captain and the lieutenant would drop the other charges. Of course, if he chose to fight, he could take the entire command-discipline case down to the Police Department's trial room, where he would probably win.

But Crowley cautioned, "If you get an attorney over there that they can reach, they could turn around and try to take your detective shield."

John told Crowley he would accept the three days' loss of pay.

But in his mind, an entirely different course of action had begun to take shape.

For some time, John had been in pain from a spinal injury, which he had incurred when he was still in uniform and had gone to the rescue of a fellow officer who was attacked by a gang of drunks during the St. Patrick's Day Parade. During the melee, John had ended up at the bottom of the pile of bodies and sustained serious back and neck damage. When the Major Case Squad had sent John up to the police shooting range for shotgun practice, he'd aggravated his neck and back injuries. For many years afterward, he suffered constant and continuous pain and needed to be under a doctor's care. Prescription medication and physical therapy became constant necessities.

Accompanied by Bill Crowley, John walked back into the captain's office. He signed the command discipline report, signifying his agreement to the three days' loss of pay. As he did, the others in the room broke into smiles and handshakes. In their minds, they had won, crushed him, beaten him into submission. All of them wore smug, self-satisfied looks of triumph.

Just as they were about to wind things up, John said, "Lieutenant, I have one last question."

"What's that, John?" asked Lieutenant Caro.

"I want to be sure to do this in front of my delegate," John began. Bill Crowley inched closer.

Then John said, "Lieutenant, could you please give me the proper procedure to go line-of-duty sick? Due to my neck injuries, I have headaches, I have continuing pain, and I can't feel my arm. Three of my fingers are numb, and I've lost thirty to forty percent of my grip strength. Therefore, I believe I am no longer able to work as a detective."

Lieutenant Caro turned livid. "Whatya pullin' here?" the lieutenant demanded. "Don't be a wise guy with me, Detective!"

But Bill Crowley quickly stepped between them. "He's within his rights, Lieutenant. Give him the procedure."

John Gaspar went out on sick leave for the next ninety days. During his time at home, he was kept under constant surveillance by plain-clothes officers from Internal Affairs, who seemed eager to catch him in a lie about the severity of his spinal injuries.

When his sick leave came to an end, John returned to work at Police Headquarters, but he was kept on restricted duty. Instead of going back to the Detective Bureau and the Major Case Squad, where he would have worked on bank robberies and other investigations, he was reassigned to a desk in the Legal Division. He also was warned that he was being "watched."

What was done to John was appalling. What made it worse was that, for most of the time, I had no inkling it was even happening.

After arriving at the FBI Academy in Quantico, I immediately began writing letters to John. But, for some reason, I never received a response. And, for the life of me, I couldn't figure out why. Could he have caved to the pressure and turned against me? That didn't seem possible. It was simply not in his nature. I felt abandoned.

As I later would learn, John had never received any of my letters, all of them addressed to him c/o the Major Case Squad. Not a single one of them. I can only guess what happened to them.

Hearing nothing from me, especially at a time when the bosses were trying to break him, John had felt similarly abandoned by me. The poison being spread by the bosses in the Major Case Squad was working its insidious ways on the both of us.

It wasn't until November that I finally got wind of what had been going on behind my back. Two detectives from the Major Case Squad who were down in the Washington, D.C., area on official business stopped by to visit me at Quantico. "You have no idea what's being done to your partner," one told me.

I immediately phoned John, who finally filled me in on all the gory details. I was sickened beyond words. Since the Office of Equal Employment Opportunity had obviously not lifted a finger to protect him, I was boiling mad. After I finished talking to John, I telephoned the people at OEEO and gave them bloody hell.

When I returned to New York in December, the first thing I did was call a prosecutor friend in the Manhattan DA's office and ask him to reactivate all the old criminal cases that John and I had been working before I left for Quantico. The DA then moved to have John temporarily reassigned from the Police Department's Legal Division directly to the DA's office to work on these cases.

Moving these dormant cases to the front burner would require John and me to put in hours upon hours of legwork, relocating and reinterviewing the witnesses, rounding up evidence, serving necessary subpoenas, and attending to myriad other pretrial business. All this extra legwork would generate nearly four hundred hours of overtime for John during his final months on the job. Since a cop's pension was based on his total earnings in his final year of service—that is, base salary plus overtime combined—all this extra overtime would end up handsomely boosting John's retirement pay. After all the suffering he had endured on my account, it was the least I could do for my beleaguered partner.

A month or so later, after his application for a disability pension had finally been approved by the Police Pension Board, John retired from the Police Department. Never again would he be able to call himself a New York City detective.

And that was something that would break John Gaspar's heart.

Meanwhile, back in the Major Case Squad, the Reign of Terror by the pro-Burton faction continued unabated. Once I returned to the office from Quantico, most of the other detectives continued to avoid me like some leper.

During my absence, department investigators had interviewed all the detectives about my OEEO discrimination complaint. Sergeant Burton, needless to say, denied all of my allegations. With the exception of John Gaspar, who supported my story lock, stock, and barrel, the other detectives behaved with appalling ostrichlike timidity. Asked about my allegations, they all pretty much gave the same ambiguous nonresponses: "Wasn't there." "Couldn't say." "Didn't hear." "Not to my knowledge." "Don't remember." "Can't recall."

One of the most disheartening depositions came from another female detective, a woman who had come into Major Case six months before I filed my complaint. When the investigators asked her if she had witnessed any of the abusive behavior I had alleged, she told them that she had seen nothing. All she saw, she added, was "the color blue." She went on to describe herself as "like the sheep that follow the shepherd."

I later confronted this woman. "Tell me, honey," I said to her, "do you know what the shepherd does to the sheep on those long, cold, lonely nights?"

But she rebuffed me and refused to alter her story. (Six months later, after Sergeant Burton began giving her some of the same abusive treatment he had given me, she was driven out of the Major Case Squad altogether.)

Meanwhile, I learned that a new election had been authorized for DEA delegate from the Major Case Squad. Realizing that the pro-Burton forces had pulled out all the stops to unseat me, I sat down and wrote a letter to each and every detective in the squad. In my letter, I talked about my twelve years as a delegate, my familiarity with our health and welfare plans, my efforts to secure financial and medical aid for one detective who had taken seriously ill and maximum death benefits for the widow of another detective who had succumbed to cancer.

Then I tackled the real issue on everyone's mind. The sexual discrimination complaint I had lodged with OEEO.

"I have stood up for the members of this unit when they needed me," I wrote. "As you all know, I recently chose to stand up for myself. And now this sudden election would appear to be a punishment for doing what you would expect me to do for you.

"There have been some rumors circulated to discredit me. I wish to set the record straight. Since I thought I would be pursuing my OEEO complaint alone, for my own credibility and protection I only recorded conversations with the subject of the complaint and no one else. These were the conversations that were 'one-on-ones.' Anyone who says differently is just trying to smear me.

"Most of you know the circumstances that led to this complaint. I ask you: Did I lie? Some of you have heard the remarks. Some of you have seen the deeds. You know I didn't lie.

"Can you really blame me for standing up for my rights? I would not do any less for any one of you. . . . So, when you vote, vote for experience and a proven delegate. You're all intelligent individuals and shouldn't be swayed by the chosen few.

"Your delegate, Kathy."

As the election neared, the tension in the squad room reached an unbearable level. Some detectives nearly got into fistfights with each other right in the Major Case Squad office. And my fate was hanging in the balance.

When the election was finally held, twenty-two votes were cast. Eleven for me. Eleven against me.

A dead heat.

In case of a tie, the union rules stated that the DEA trustee would cast the deciding vote. The DEA trustee was Detective Bill Crowley. The same Bill Crowley who had accompanied John Gaspar to his command-discipline hearing and fought with the bosses when they'd tried to railroad him on trumped-up charges.

Bill Crowley cast his vote for Kathy Burke.

When the final result was tallied, some of the guys actually summoned up the courage to congratulate me. Most of the others continued to snub me. Detective Leff, the gorilla who had tried to strong-arm the others into voting against me by threatening to have them kicked out of the squad, actually picked up a chair and hurled it across the office. "Who are the traitors who sabotaged this election?" he bellowed.

Yes, I had retained my union post. But in the end, it was a hollow victory. The mood in the squad was still tense and angry and divisive, and I had become the lightning rod. With John Gaspar now banished to the Legal Division, treading water until his retirement on disability became official, I was assigned to work with three other detectives. But soon into this new partnership, these three detectives begged off. It was as if I had suddenly become contagious.

"Look, Kathy," said one, "it's not personal, but we really can't ride with you anymore. We can't even go out to eat with you anymore 'cause, if we do, we're in trouble. They're going to be watching you, which means they're going to be watching us. And we don't need the aggravation."

I felt heartbroken. But I was angry, too.

"I am sorry I put you guys in this position," I said. "But if you're men, you'll stand up and be counted. How can you allow someone to do this to you? How can you allow them to do it to me? What kind of men are you? What are you going to do on the street? You're letting the bosses do more to you in the office than you would take on the street from a prisoner."

They hemmed and hawed, ummed and ahhed, erred and awwed. But, in the end, I found myself odd woman out. And, yet again, partnerless.

On my last working day before my Christmas vacation, Captain Stengel summoned me into his office.

"They've requested you out in Queens," he told me. "On a temporary basis."

My antennae perked up. They had tried to shuffle me out to Queens once before. Queens was a graveyard, a no-man's-land. There was nothing going on in Queens. The primary responsibility of the Major Case Squad was investigating bank robberies, yet there were about as many bank robberies in Queens as there were Eskimo igloos in Africa.

"I don't really want to go to Queens," I told the captain.

"You don't have a choice," the captain said. "You don't have a regular partner, so you're not much use to me here. Besides, Queens is shorthanded. Hey, you live in Queens. You'll have a shorter commute."

"Bullshit," I fired back. "The Queens office is actually further away from my house than the Manhattan office."

"Well, either way, Burke, you're going to Queens."

"Look, you're not doing me any favors, Captain. I don't want to be there. So I have to consider this some kind of retaliation."

The captain simply shrugged. "You're goin' anyway, Burke."

Shortly after I left Manhattan, Captain Stengel assembled all of the Manhattan detectives for a meeting. At this meeting, the captain announced that he had chosen a new integrity control officer for the Major Case Squad. The integrity control officer was the person designated to monitor the conduct of all the other detectives in the squad to ensure that they operated strictly by the rule book.

The new integrity control officer was Sergeant Sam Burton.

On his last day of work, I accompanied my partner, Detective John Gaspar, as he did "the walk."

Moving from floor to floor through One Police Plaza, John went from one office to the next to be fingerprinted, fill out his separation papers, have his ID card stamped RETIRED, receive his retired-officer's pistol permit, then surrender his shield, his helmet, his bulletproof vest, and his patrol guide.

It was a terrible, traumatic moment for John. Like stripping yourself naked. I walked side by side with him, trying to provide some small measure of moral support as he made his grim rounds. But the whole business saddened him and sickened me beyond words.

Later that day, about twenty-five cops showed up for a retirement dinner that I had organized for John at a restaurant in Little Italy. Initially, some of these cops, especially the ones from Major Case, were reluctant to attend, knowing that the notorious Kathy Burke was the organizer.

"Hey," I had to tell them, "no matter how you feel about me, John's a good guy. So come to his party, willya?"

In the end, they did.

When I showed up in the Queens office of the Major Case Squad, the sergeant out there, Art Boyer, was quick to set the record straight on my transfer. Boyer was a veteran boss, a tall, grandfatherly type with a reddish complexion, sandy hair, and a strong sense of loyalty and integrity. He was a stand-up guy who would never buckle to the weasels, flatterers, and backstabbers in the department.

"I hear you asked for me," I said to him.

"Not exactly," he leveled. "They called me and said, 'We wanna get rid of her.'"

I screwed up my face. "Swell."

Boyer told me he had no problem working with me. But then he warned, "Be careful, Kathy. They're watching you."

"Boss, I'm not going to do anything to hurt you, I promise you that. And I'll give you a good day's work."

Nevertheless, I knew I was under a magnifying glass. If my memo book indicated I had arrived at court at 0945 hours, then my time slips from the courthouse had damn well better indicate that I had punched in at exactly 0945 hours, as well.

If I said I was going to take an hour for lunch, then I had better take exactly one hour, no more, and my memo book had better indicate the name of the restaurant I ate in, as well as the address of the restaurant, the name of the person or persons I ate with, what time I arrived, what time I left, and whether I traveled there by foot, by bus, by subway, car, ocean liner, or hang glider. Then, when I got back to the office, I had better make sure a supervisor signed my memo book.

If I made an arrest and ran a lineup, then my lineup had better be letter-perfect so that no defense attorney could later raise an objection on legal grounds.

If I brought evidence to the lab, then my evidence had better be properly signed, sealed, and delivered.

Knowing that I was being watched, I lived in constant fear when I was on the streets. I wondered if I might eventually be set up by Internal Affairs for some kind of integrity test. Would the other detectives back me up in an arrest situation? Would I find myself operating alone, without a friend in sight, much as I had done when I was working undercover back in the seventies?

The constant stress took a toll.

My colitis flared up worse than ever, with all its vile symptoms: stabbing pains, cold sweats, shakes, vomiting, diarrhea. Alcoholic drinks with ice, whole milk, ice cream, carbonated beverages, and lettuce became my worst enemies. Despite the constant spasms of knifelike pain through my stomach, I was afraid to take any prescription medication, such as Lomotil or Donnatal, for fear that the department might decide I was addicted to narcotic substances and therefore unfit for duty. So, instead, I gulped down glasses of Metamucil and did yogalike meditation exercises in desperate hopes of unknotting my twisted guts.

When I came home from work, the first thing I would do was ask my kids to give me a few moments of privacy to myself. Then I would go into the bedroom and lie down for ten or fifteen minutes. Remembering my self-hypnosis techniques, I would focus all my attention on a point on the wall, then close my eyes, relax all my muscles, and, slowly working my way down from my head to my toes, try to cleanse my mind and my body, allowing all the negative energy to drain out.

After I calmed down, I would play with my two girls, busying myself with their storybooks, their Play-Doh or their Barbie dolls. Pretty soon, they'd be crawling all over me like puppy dogs, giving me big, wet, sloppy kisses, playing with my hair, tugging at my jewelry. And, for one brief moment, I'd start to forget my troubles.

Later on, I would help the kids with their homework. And make supper for Bob and me.

But I couldn't avoid thinking about the job. Half the time I'd end up wondering if some of the things that were said about me in Major Case might be true. I knew I could be outspoken and confrontational, abrasive, self-righteous even, and sometimes it pissed people off. I knew I did not comfortably fit into the male stereotype—or female stereotype, for that matter—of the compliant or self-deprecating woman, be she a civilian or a cop. I was all sharp edges and tough talk, not fluttering eyelashes, frilly collars, and sweet-smelling perfume. But was I, by nature, a troublemaker and provocateur? Was I a boss-fighter? Was I someone who had some perverse need to provoke ugly and costly battles just to prove a point? Did I really have the right to be a detective in the Major Case Squad? Was I on a misguided crusade? Was I a bad wife and a lousy mother?

Then, in my saner, less neurotic moments, I'd begin to remember that I had gotten along just fine in the past. When partnered up with the right people, I had blossomed . . . and shone. My casework had excelled. I had flourished in the Undercover Unit. In Narcotics, too. Despite my confrontational nature, after I became a union delegate who had to fight on behalf of others, I had learned how to deal with high-ranking male bosses professionally, respectfully, and effectively, without setting everyone else's hair on fire or throwing their more delicate body parts into an uproar. I had won kudos from the other detectives for my union work.

I had also gotten the support of many of the other women in the department. No doubt, some of them frowned on my outspokenness. Others made it clear to me that they would have liked to be more vocal on my behalf, but could simply not afford to take the chance. Most of them had come into the department ten years after me. They did not have the time, the age, the credibility, or the stature that I had, as a well-known detective second grade, to entangle themselves in the kind of battle I had launched. Unlike me, most of them worked in uniform and on patrol, meaning that day in and day out they were out on the street, where they had to rely on male partners to help them do their jobs and get their backs. For these women, speaking out publicly on behalf of Detective Kathy Burke would have been akin to committing professional suicide.

Nevertheless, in the meetings of the Policewomen's Endowment Association, almost all of the other women cops demonstrated that they were very much on my side. And I felt tremendously gratified when the executive board of the Policewomen's Endowment Association voted to authorize its attorney to represent me, pro bono, as I pursued my discrimination complaint through legal channels.

Eventually, notwithstanding my moments of insecurity, I concluded that my terrible problems in the Major Case Squad were not entirely of my own making. Even if I ate humble pie and made peace with Sergeant Burton, he wouldn't have changed. One way or the other, he was determined to destroy my career.

It was difficult for me to discuss my problems in the Major Case Squad with Bob. For one thing, even though he, too, was a New York City cop, my problem was not something he could really relate to or comprehend. It had never been a part of his experience. Each day, when he went to his job in the Police Department, whatever that job might be, nobody challenged him. Nobody tried to undermine him. Nobody started questioning why he was there or whether he had a reason to be there. Nobody suggested to him he'd be better off staying at home, taking care of the children and baking bread. Nobody wondered aloud if he even had the right to make a living by being a cop.

I didn't want to place an extra burden on Bob because of my problems. As the commanding officer of a precinct, Bob already had four hundred other cops to worry about and fret over. The last thing in the world he needed was to come home at the end of his day and find one more. Both of us wanted our house to be our safe place, our escape hatch, our sanctuary from the police force and the world outside, especially for our two little girls. And both of us felt we shouldn't let "the job" intrude on that sanctuary.

In time, because of our conflicting work schedules, we rarely had time to discuss the matter anyway. Reassigned to the department's public information office, Bob began working grueling, breakneck hours. Always on call, he often found himself being summoned from our house in the middle of the night to the scene of some major police activity such as a murder or a bombing or a hostage situation.

Not to suggest that Bob was totally immune to being dragged down by my troubles. On the job, other cops began buttonholing him, haranguing him sometimes, pleading with him to rein me in. Even Bill Crowley, the DEA trustee who had saved my delegate's position with his tie-breaking vote and fought to defend John Gaspar during his own trumped-up disciplinary hearing, thought I had gone too far. "Can't you talk to her?" he said to Bob at a police racket (cop lingo for "party") one night. "Can't you get her to calm down?"

But Bob refused to intervene. "She's got her career, and I got mine," he said. Because of his own strong sense of ethics, he felt it was wrong to intervene on behalf of his wife, either to advance my career or to protect it. Whichever way he chose to get involved, he was certain it would backfire and make matters that much worse.

Nevertheless, with all this nastiness swirling around me, I needed a sympathetic ear. One of the few people who made a great listener was

Felicia Shpritzer, a retired lieutenant whom I had first met when I was still a recruit in training at the Police Academy. Felicia and I would room together whenever we attended out-of-town conferences of the International Association of Women Police, of which we both were members. Often, we would stay up late into the wee hours discussing all the twists and turns of my discrimination complaint.

Many years earlier, Felicia herself had filed her own lawsuit against the department to win a promotion to sergeant. Like me, she had taken a lot of heat for her actions. Felicia counseled me not to lose my focus, become bitter, and blame everybody in the world for my troubles.

"When you boil it all down, Kathy," she told me, "one man caused the problem and one man alone. Not the entire system."

Working for Sergeant Boyer in the Queens office of the Major Case Squad actually turned out to be one of the bright spots in my life during this turbulent period.

Boyer was all business, a real pro as an investigator, and he couldn't have cared less about my sorry history with Sergeant Burton back in the Manhattan office. However, with the Manhattan office of Major Case still calling the shots, Boyer was ordered by Captain Stengel to team me up with Herb Conway, another detective who had the reputation of being an oddball. A graying and bespectacled six-footer, Conway was considerate and unassuming in manner. He was a devoted family man who shunned the drinking, the gossiping, and the cursing indulged in by a lot of the other detectives. Because he declined to be one of the boys, he was regarded as an outsider. In point of fact, he was an excellent detective, a real crackerjack on fraud cases, who was grossly misunderstood and maligned by his peers. At the time we teamed up, he was, like me, considered a black sheep.

Wouldn't you know it, right around the time Conway and I teamed up, Queens got hit with a rash of bank robberies! So many stickups and note jobs that Conway and I found ourselves making collars till they were coming out of our ears. Back in Manhattan, Captain Stengel got one look at our mushrooming clearance rate—and overtime requests—and flipped his wig.

"What the hell did she do?" he screamed at Boyer over the phone. "Round up a string of friends to pull a buncha bank robberies so she can get on the sheet?"

"What are you talking about?" said Boyer.

"For Pete's sake, there's never been anything in Queens! Now, all of a sudden, you got ten bank robberies!"

Captain Stengel went ballistic again on the day I showed up in the Manhattan office of the Major Case Squad, looking to kill time before answering a subpoena from the Manhattan DA's office on one of my old cases. Upon seeing me at one of the desks, he telephoned Queens and began screaming at Sergeant Boyer, "Damn it, Boyer, she's not allowed in this office! We don't want her in here! You keep her out in Queens where she belongs!"

But this time, Sergeant Boyer told him to shove it: "Look, Captain, I don't know what your problem is. Detective Burke works for the Major Case Squad. And that is her office. She was there on legitimate business. And, what do you mean, I should keep her out of there? She's not a prisoner. She's not on modified assignment. She's not under house arrest. I knew where she was. She has permission to be there. She's responding to a subpoena to appear in court. She's doing her job, exactly the way a professional detective should do it. So get off my back. And get off her back. You guys are all fucked-up over there."

When a routine rotation resulted in the transfer of Sergeant Boyer out of the Queens office, he was replaced by Sergeant Asadurian, a guy with whom I had gone to high school and worked in Narcotics. Later, I had worked for him when he was a boss in the Safe, Loft & Truck Squad. So we had some history together. And a friendship.

Asadurian knew full well that I was on the department's shitlist. He, too, warned me that I was being followed. I asked him when I might be able to return to the Manhattan office of the Major Case Squad.

That's when he flat out told me, "Kathy, let me speak to you as a friend, not as a sergeant. You may not wanna hear this, but the truth is, you would be wise to transfer out of the Major Case Squad altogether."

CHAPTER SEVENTEEN

In the spring of 1985, the Office of Equal Employment Opportunity notified me that it had reached a determination on my sexual discrimination complaint.

In a nutshell, Sergeant Burton was found guilty—but not of the sexual discrimination I had alleged. Instead, he was found guilty of the far less serious offense of sexual harassment. His punishment? Loss of three days' vacation, plus the requirement that he receive several hours of "instruction" from superior officers on how to treat females in the Police Department.

All in all, it was chickenshit. A whitewash. A slap on the wrist.

Docking Sergeant Burton three days' vacation was like giving him no fine at all. He had accumulated at least three weeks' vacation time on the books. All he had to do was work some overtime to make up for the loss of income.

When the officials in the Office of Equal Employment Opportunity informed me of their decision, I told them they weren't looking to redress my grievances so much as bury them.

Because my attorney had received copies of all the statements given by the detectives in Major Case, I knew that the OEEO people had either deliberately or inadvertently bungled their interviews. Questions had either been phrased improperly or foolishly directed to the wrong individuals. I had submitted a list of seven detectives for the investigators to interview. Seven people who had witnessed firsthand the treatment I had been subjected to in the Major Case Squad. But, instead of interviewing those seven, the investigators chose to interview all thirty-five detectives in the Major Case Squad, including a whole bunch of people who had never worked with me, hardly knew me from Adam, and had no way in hell of knowing what had gone down between me and Sergeant Burton. It was a sloppy, shotgun approach to an investigation—aim at everything, close your eyes, wind up hitting nothing. What's more, from the start, everyone in the Major Case Squad had known exactly what the OEEO investigators were up to and whom they were talking to. For an investigation that was supposed to be airtight and strictly confidential, this one leaked like a sieve.

(A sergeant in OEEO who was known to be leaking information to the Major Case Squad later took a job working for the police commissioner in Baltimore—where he was indicted and convicted on federal charges of conspiring with the commissioner to use department funds to pay for romantic liaisons, lavish meals, unauthorized trips, and personal gifts.)

I argued back and forth with the OEEO people, suggesting that they reopen their investigation. But it was pointless. So I asked for a transfer.

I was emotionally whipped. Mentally exhausted. And physically ill from all the stress. But the worst part was the sense of betrayal I felt. I had gone through the Police Department's chain of command and played by the rules. I had kept my complaint entirely in-house and, in accord with department regulations, brought it up to OEEO, the Police Department office specifically created to handle such matters. Yet, precisely because I had played by the rules and kept the whole matter in-house, both my partner and I were now paying a terrible, terrible price. John's career had been sabotaged and he had been forced to retire. I had lost my friends, my status, my emotional well-being, and my health. I was Public Enemy Number One in the Special Investigations Division and its offshoot, the Major Case Squad.

For most of my career, I had embraced the Police Department. I had given it my love, my faith, and my loyalty. But my romance with the department had turned sour, and I felt disillusioned and embittered. Never again would I experience that unquestioning loyalty and love that I had felt as a bright-eyed, eager young rookie. Never again would I believe what the department said it stood for. The department had lied to me, deceived me, and abandoned me.

And, for that, I could never, ever forgive it.

I also knew I could never again feel safe in the Detective Bureau or the Special Investigations Division. Yet, I realized that if I asked to leave the Major Case Squad, I would immediately be stripped of my position as the DEA delegate for the squad, along with its various and sundry protections. In addition, I would be forced to give up my status as a member of the department's hostage negotiating team, a role I loved. I would also lose my chance to gain another promotion, to detective first grade, since almost all higher-grade promotions were pretty much ear-marked for detectives who worked exclusively in the Detective Bureau or the Intelligence Division. But, at this point, I had no choice. I had to get out. I asked to be sent back to the Organized Crime Control Bureau, preferably to one of the two existing task forces that handled narcotics investigations. That, after all, had been my stock-in-trade as a street cop for many years.

Instead, in July of 1985, I was given a transfer to the Joint Organized Crime Task Force, which worked out of 26 Federal Plaza.

The Task Force contained thirty-six New York City cops and FBI agents. Why I was being sent there, I had no idea. I had nine years' experience in narcotics enforcement. This federal-city task force was specifically set up to investigate gambling.

I knew about as much about gambling as I knew about cattle ranching.

The strange new world I was about to enter—the world of organized crime—was a murky maelstrom populated by a constantly changing cast of sinister, yet fuzzy characters. Early in 1985, a federal racketeering indictment charged nine men—five of them bosses or acting bosses for the five La Cosa Nostra families—with participating in a ruling commission that effectively governed all mob business in New York City, including narcotics trafficking, loan-sharking, gambling, labor racketeering, and extortion against construction companies. Later that year, one of the men, Paul Castellano, the reputed boss of the Gambino family, was ambushed and killed outside Sparks Steak House in midtown Manhattan in a carefully planned hit carried out by John Gotti and his notorious henchman Sammy "the Bull" Gravano.

But hoping to permanently cleanse the city of mob bosses, either through internal strife or external prosecution, was like trying to clear a grassy meadow of wild mushrooms. As soon as you clipped the head of one, five others cropped up to take its place.

My first few weeks in the Joint Organized Crime Task Force, I was assigned to do surveillance on a known gambling location in Little Italy.

The operation was run by the 250-member Genovese crime family. The titular head of the Genoveses was a guy named Anthony Salerno.

But most investigators had concluded that the real power in the family was Vincent "Chin" Gigante, who had acquired his odd nickname because of his prominent, Jay Leno–like lower jaw. For years, the Chin, as he was known, had eluded prosecution by creating the public perception that he was too loopy to function effectively as the godfather of a major Mafia family. This he accomplished by regularly traipsing through the streets of his Greenwich Village neighborhood in his bathrobe, pajamas, and slippers, muttering to himself and babbling incoherently whenever he was approached by strangers. FBI agents who went to his mother's apartment to serve him with a court subpoena actually discovered him standing naked in the shower, holding an open umbrella over his head. For years, the Chin had gotten away with it, but knowledgeable FBI and NYPD officials regarded his nuttiness as an elaborate and carefully staged deception.

My assignment was to keep tabs on one of the Chin's satellite outposts, a storefront that was known to be doing a brisk business in illegal sports bets. To blend in, I tried to dress exactly the way the locals did: bright summer colors, loose-fitting slacks, sandals, *Miami Vice*–style casual jackets.

At first, I camped out on the park benches or at one of the nearby cappuccino joints, keeping an eye on the shady-looking characters who drifted in and out. I tried to clock their arrival and departure times on a slip of paper and take their photographs. But, by using the camera, I always worried that I might seem too conspicuous and end up blowing my cover.

Then I came up with a better idea. Noticing a couple of Sicilian-grandmother types camped out on their front stoops in plastic folding chairs, fanning themselves in the brutal summer heat, I decided to befriend them. They were watching everyone else's comings and goings like hawks. They probably knew a lot of things. And a lot of people.

"Whew!" I sighed, wiping my brow. "You ladies mind if I sit with you a moment? I'm really tired."

"Have a seat, honey," one of them replied. "What's your name?"

"Marie," I said.

"Marie." The other lady smiled. "That's a nice name. Like Maria. My daughter's name. The Virgin Mary. You live around here?"

"I wish. I'm new in this part of town. I'm looking for a job."

"Any luck yet?" asked one of the ladies.

"Not yet, no. But I'm gonna keep trying."

"Have a nice cold glass of lemonade, honey," offered one of them. "It's fresh."

"Thank you." I took a big gulp. "That's really very nice of you."

"That's okay, Marie," she said. "So where you from, anyway?"

"Queens."

"Queens, eh? I got family in Queens."

"No kidding! Small world! What part of Queens they live in?"

I came back again the next day to find the same two old ladies sitting on their stoop, gossiping and sipping lemonade. And the day after that, too. Each time I came by, I would stop and sit, share a glass of lemonade, some Italian sugar cookies, and lots of small talk. Knowing how much the old ladies liked to gossip about everyone in the neighborhood, I figured this was a surefire way to get my cover story around to all the other folks in this close-knit, predominantly Italian enclave.

Lo and behold, it worked.

In no time at all, the old ladies had warmed to me, taking me under their wing as if I were one of their own children or grandchildren. They began to give me leads on jobs and cheap apartments. Pretty soon everyone in the neighborhood got to know me. They all seemed to like me and want me to succeed. I was becoming a familiar fixture in the community, which was exactly what I was hoping for. Everything seemed to be going well.

Right up until the day I realized that someone was tailing me.

He was in his midthirties, about five feet ten, heavily coiffed blond hair, manicured nails, designer clothes, sharklike eyes.

Wherever I went, he always seemed to be two or three steps behind me. And it scared the you-know-what out of me. One day, he was standing so close that I could see the initials on his diamond pinkie ring. I had to duck into the entrance of a building, then slip out the back door, to shake him.

Now the really troublesome part of being shadowed was that I couldn't be certain whether my tail was a KG—known gambler—or a plainclothes cop. Since they often dressed the same—penny loafers, muscle shirts, high-water polyester slacks, diamond pinkie rings, gold chains, and meticulously coiffed and slicked hair—it was nearly impossible to tell one from the other. For all I knew, my shadow was a plainclothes public morals officer who thought I was a hooker and was looking to take me down on a pros collar.

In any case, I realized that it was no longer safe for me to be walking the streets of Little Italy by myself. I needed a partner, someone who could watch my back. For a while, they tried to team me up with an FBI agent. But when the FBI agent showed up one day wearing kelly green pants, a bright yellow shirt, a plaid jacket, and a huge Japanese camera with a telephoto lens dangling from his neck, I told him, in no uncertain terms, to take a hike. With him by my side, I'd get made in a heartbeat by the wiseguys.

No, I needed someone who could blend in with the locals. Someone who would not stick out like a sore thumb. Someone who talked the talk and walked the walk. Maybe even someone who knew the local players. Someone who might be able to vouch for me with the wiseguys.

And I knew exactly who that someone was.

Augie Renzulli looked like a sewer rat. Smelled like one, too. A real-life, honest-to-goodness Ratso Rizzo.

Barely five feet tall, he had a long, narrow face; a sharp, pointy nose; greasy black hair; and a pallid, pockmarked complexion. Nervously shifting from one foot to the other, he was always lighting up cigarettes, stubbing them out, lighting up fresh ones, stubbing those out, too, fidgeting, fussing, and fumbling with his nicotine-stained fingers, a perpetual jitterbug in motion. Augie was a hard-core heroin addict. He was related, by marriage, to some heavy-duty mob guys. He had once shared a jail cell with Chin Gigante. But because of his chronic drug problem, the mob had forced him to divorce his Mafia-princess wife and steer clear of all their business dealings. He was too much of a risk to them.

To support himself, Augie did burglaries. Augie would boost anything for a buck—shirts, cars, frozen shrimp, you name it. Then Augie discovered that he could make even more money by selling information to the police. As much as a thousand bucks a pop if he could set us up to make an undercover heroin buy. So, when I was still working Narcotics, Augie became one of my prime informants.

Because of Augie, I was eventually able to set up hand-to-hand buys of heroin from drug dealers in Chinatown. Up till then, that sort of thing was unheard of among undercover cops. But that was many years ago. And I had lost touch with Augie in the interim.

Now that I was newly assigned to the Organized Crime Task Force and working Little Italy, however, I needed to locate Augie and persuade him to vouch for me with the wiseguys.

It took me three days of staking out a ratty methadone clinic in lower

Manhattan before I tracked him down. But when he came shuffling around a corner for his regular dose, he recognized me immediately. And his mouth sagged.

"Aw, jeez, no," muttered Augie. "I knew this was gonna be my unlucky day. You. I know you want something from me, right? What? What is it? Come on, out with it."

"Aw, Augie," I said, "my feelings are hurt. And, all this time, I thought you loved me. C'mon, I'll buy you breakfast."

"Awright, awright, but I know I'm gonna regret it. Every time I get involved wit' you, sumpin' bad happens."

Augie told me that, yeah, he was still in tight with the Chin and the rest of the thugs and mugs in the Chin's inner circle. They tolerated him, like an errant child, but didn't give him any grief. Just as long as he behaved himself and didn't try to pull any boosts or heists in their part of town. I asked Augie if he could introduce me to some of the Chin's people.

Okay, he said. But first I would need to change my appearance. Give myself a total makeover.

"What do you mean?" I asked him.

Projecting upon me his fantasy of the ideal woman, he ticked off the requisite alterations: "Well, maybe you gotta make your hair blond instead of dark, you know what I mean? And you gotta start wearin' a skirt. A tight skirt. Real tight. And short. Like above your knee there so you show a little more thigh, which ain't bad at all, if I do say so myself. And what could you do with your chest? No offense, but it's kinda on the skimpy side, y'know what I mean?"

Pretty soon, Augie had me wearing a blond wig along with revealing, skintight outfits that had me ballooning right out of my bodice and looking like a $10-a-trick hooker. Squiring me around Little Italy as though I were the mob moll of the month, Augie paraded me through his favorite gin mills and coffee houses, where he proudly introduced me to all his greaser pals.

"Hey, fellas, say hello to Marie here," he would tell them. "She's my goomatta."

Now, some of the wiseguys had asked Augie to set up a "wire room" or illegal sports betting parlor in his apartment. But, given that he still lived with his mother, who was now in her late nineties and frail, Augie had had to pass on their offer. But then I began to wonder, What if I rented a separate apartment for Augie? Then he could go ahead with the wire room setup and begin taking all those bets. Once it was up and running, I might be able to finagle myself a job on the inside, taking bets, too. And, bingo, just like that, I would have found a kick-ass way to personally infiltrate the Mafia's gambling operations.

Unfortunately, right around the time I started to push my wire room scheme with Augie, a new lieutenant showed up to take charge of the Joint Organized Crime Task Force. Five-foot-ten, pudgy, Irish-looking, Lieutenant John O'Brien had worked some high-level cases in the Detective Bureau, including a Weathermen plot to blow up the Statue of Liberty. He didn't seem to know all that much about the street, but he did have some heavyweight political connections within the department's upper echelons. This hook had blessed him with a charmed career. He clearly was tight with all the right people in the Detective Bureau. He was also an old pal of Sergeant Burton's and the whole slaphappy bunch of kidders back in the Major Case Squad. Right from the get-go, he let it be known that he disapproved of women cops, disapproved of me in particular, and would do everything he could to clip my wings and ice me out of the real action. As soon as he heard about my little scheme to go undercover and work in the mob's gambling operation, he eighty-sixed it.

"You're dreamin', Burke," he scoffed. "No way some broad is gonna get in with the wiseguys. But I got something real special lined up for you. . . . You're goin' on the wire."

Housed in the drab and dingy basement of a luxury apartment building in Greenwich Village, thirteen of us cops and FBI agents sat on *the wire*— a term that collectively referred to all the various court-sanctioned wiretaps that had been set up on Chin Gigante, his crime crew, and their associates. Hour upon hour upon hour, we would sit there and listen. And listen. And listen . . .

Occasionally, we would glean nuggets of information about illegal gambling transactions ("Ayy, this is Charley for Rocky! Dis is da spread"), movements of cash or betting slips, "sit-downs" big and small with assorted Mafia bosses, even threats to "break dat guy's legs." And indeed, our taps eventually led to the conviction of Brooklyn Democratic boss Meade Esposito, one of the most powerful political figures in New York City. A subsequent tap, on Esposito's phone, led to the arrest and conviction of Congressman Mario Biaggi on corruption charges.

But, for the most part, listening to the wires was shit work. Long, tedious, and mind-numbing. Sitting underground in that dank and dreary basement, we felt as if we'd been buried alive.

From talking to the other cops and agents down there, I learned that Lieutenant O'Brien had more or less divided the people in the Task Force into two different groups—the A team and the B team.

The A-team detectives and agents worked aboveground, scoring the plum assignments, doing surveillance, gathering intelligence, fashioning their own cases, and ultimately making the big collars. The members of the A team had posed, tellingly, for a gag group photo underneath the Brooklyn Bridge. For the photo, they had dressed up in swashbuckling G-man style with big cigars, spats, old-fashioned fedoras, trench coats, and replicas of Roaring Twenties–style tommy guns.

Then there were the B-team agents and detectives. These were the guys who got stuck in drab and dingy basements, out of sight, out of mind, working twelve hours on, twelve hours off, doing the boring, stultifying job of listening to the wire. The B-teamers were the drones, the troublemakers, and the losers. They never got to pose for photos with fedoras and trench coats and tommy guns. They were like the kids at the pickup touch-football game who get chosen dead last for the team.

Clearly, Lieutenant O'Brien had banished me to the B team. Even after he buried me down there, he continued to stick it to me. When Thanksgiving rolled around, he told all the FBI agents to take the day off. "My cops will cover the wires," he said.

I balked. "I don't mind if I have to work," I told him. "But I'm not gonna cover for the FBI." He promptly threw a shit-fit, blasting me as insubordinate and a troublemaker. But, quite mysteriously, several FBI "volunteers" were suddenly recruited to work alongside the cops who got stuck doing holiday duty.

Things with the lieutenant soon went from bad to worse. When it came time for him to do his annual performance evaluations, he went out of his way to trash me. There was the usual knock about my personality—too assertive, too pushy, too confrontational. But then he went on to write that I had flubbed and fumbled during my court appearances. I was flabbergasted.

"When have you ever seen me in court?" I asked him. "I haven't gone to court since the day you arrived to take command of the unit!"

The lieutenant didn't try to disguise that he had been gunning for me from the get-go. He just shrugged. "Well, I hadda knock you on something. So what are you gonna do about it? File a grievance?"

I knew he was baiting me, for if I took the bait and filed another complaint, it would only end up making me look like a malcontent, a chronic boss-fighter, and a head case. And that would end up undermining my sexual discrimination claim. So, this time, I sidestepped the challenge.

"No," I said, "but I am gonna make you eat your fucking words."

Back in the wire room, I read books and magazines or watched movie videos. Sometimes I would sew, and once I embroidered a family banner I was making for the mass that would be offered the following spring to celebrate my seven-year-old daughter Cathrine's First Communion.

To make our dank, drab surroundings a little cozier, we outfitted the wire room with a miniature freezer for our frozen TV dinners and a microwave oven. In December, we tried to give our subterranean hovel a more festive air by adding a small Christmas tree. Being one of the few females in the outfit (there were four female FBI agents, but I was the only woman detective assigned to the task force), I made it my job to create tree decorations out of the plastic eating utensils, straws, and paper doilies from the local Greek diner. I cut FBI memos into tiny pieces and made multicolored loops to hang from the tree branches. The crowning touch, however, was the star at the pinnacle, made from a picture of J. Edgar Hoover.

Knowing how much old J. Edgar had hated the idea of women in the FBI—and women in general, for that matter—I decided that he deserved a place of real prominence on our yuletide creation.

Of all the cops I met while working the wire, the one who came to be my favorite was a Public Morals detective named Tony Venditti. Tall, dark, and mustachioed, Tony had been on the job for nearly fourteen years.

Over time, Tony and I discovered that we shared a lot in common. I had two daughters; he had three. What's more, his wife, Patti, was then pregnant with their fourth child. Both of us had wanted to become cops for as long as we could remember, and once we had gotten our appointments to the job, neither of us could imagine ever doing anything else. Although my expertise was narcotics and his was gambling, both of us had been active, aggressive cops who loved to be out on the streets, kicking some butt, making good collars. We each had received the identical number of medals and departmental commendations.

Sure, Tony had heard all the nasty rumors about me. Troublemaker, bigmouth, boss-fighter, smart-ass, yada, yada, yada. But, unlike some of the other cops in the Task Force, including the commanding officer, he was not ready to jump to conclusions. He was willing to give me the benefit of the doubt.

Tony was not just a good cop. He was a genuinely good person.

Toward the end of that year, the Task Force bosses decided to wind down our wiretaps and send us back into the field to do firsthand surveillance on the wiseguys and their gambling operations.

When I came into the wire room to begin my tour one night, Tony pulled me aside.

"When we go back out on the street, I'm putting in for you as my partner," he said.

My head snapped around. "What!"

"I want you in our team."

I knew there was already another cop in his team. A detective named Ted Carter. I also knew I was still a highly undesirable hot potato because of my sexual discrimination complaint against Sergeant Burton.

"What's Ted going to say?" I asked Tony.

"We agreed that we both want you," said Tony.

"But I'm under a big black cloud in the department. I've got a lot of baggage."

"All ancient history."

"You sure about this, Tony? I mean, are you absolutely sure?"

"I'm sure."

Tony's decision to bring me into the team gave me a much needed boost. But he turned out to be dead wrong about one thing . . .

. . . the notion that my troubles with the department were "ancient history."

I was still working the wires when I got the call from a friend inside Police Headquarters. My friend, a cop in a sensitive records section, was taking a huge gamble in calling me. But, given what he had just unearthed, he felt an obligation to risk it.

The cop had come across some Major Case Squad personnel records. The records indicated something pretty shocking. It boiled down to this:

Despite the findings by the Office of Equal Employment Opportunity, Sergeant Burton had never received any punishment. Contrary to what it had promised, the department had not taken away his three days' vacation. In fact, during all this time, Sergeant Burton had not lost a single day's pay. My friend at headquarters promised to mail me a photocopy of the sergeant's time sheets to prove it.

But then came the real bombshell:

No mention of my OEEO complaint, nor the punishment that was to have been meted out as a result, had ever been inserted into Burton's personnel file. And within the next few weeks, the Police Department intended to promote Burton to the rank of sergeant-supervisor of a detective squad. That promotion would boost his salary to the equivalent of lieutenant's pay.

The icing on the cake was that the promotion would be slipped through quietly, without any public fanfare or scrutiny.

I cannot begin to describe the rage and humiliation I felt on hearing this news. In the interests of putting the whole ugly dispute to rest, I had agreed to a transfer I did not desire. I had gone to a squad I didn't want. I had sacrificed my reputation, my prestige, and, in many respects, my future. Not to mention my physical and emotional health. And now, after destroying my partner and tormenting me, the department was pouring vinegar on my wounds.

I called Lillian Braxton, the president of the Policewomen's Endowment Association, and asked her what I should do. She didn't even hesitate with her advice.

It was time to sue the bastards, once and for all.

CHAPTER EIGHTEEN

My lawsuit alleged sexual discrimination under the federal Equal Employment Opportunity Act.

It named as defendants the New York Police Department; the deputy commissioner in charge of the Office of Equal Employment Opportunity; Sergeant Burton; Captain Stengel; Lieutenant Caro; the other lieutenant who had twisted John Gaspar's arm to try to get him to alter his testimony; and Leff and Finn, the two detectives who had tried to unseat me as the squad's delegate to the DEA. Everything about my treatment in the Major Case Squad that I had repeatedly complained about was spelled out in the lawsuit—the failure to assign me a regular partner or to significant cases, the constant barrage of disparaging remarks, the thwarted overtime, the forced transfer outside the Detective Bureau, all of it.

By the end of December 1985, my attorney had notified all the principals that my lawsuit would proceed in U.S. district court. Should my claims be upheld by the court, she intended to ask for:

- A declaration that the defendants had intentionally discriminated against me.
- A declaration that my transfer to the Joint Organized Crime Task Force was an act of retaliation.
- An injunction allowing me to transfer into another command that was commensurate with my training, seniority, and experience.
- Another injunction ordering the Police Department to crack down more vigorously on all future cases of gender-based discrimination.
- Payment of $2 million damages to compensate me for lost wages and career opportunities.
- Payment of my out-of-pocket costs and my attorney's fees.

The shock waves were instantaneous. Down in the Major Case Squad, the defendants went into a full-scale panic. According to one of my sources in the Detective Bureau, Sergeant Burton, Captain Stengel, and Lieutenant Caro began huddling daily and brainstorming on how to protect themselves financially. They actually talked about legally transferring all their assets to their wives . . . because they were convinced I would try to take away their houses!

Up until this point, my new partner, Tony Venditti, had never really pressed me for any of the details of my stormy relationship with the Major Case Squad. But shortly after my lawyer filed the lawsuit, he and I finally had a real heart-to-heart. We had already stopped listening to the wires and had started on our surveillance runs when Tony said to me in the car one night, "Listen, I gotta ask you something, Kathy. What the heck went on over there?"

This time, I omitted none of the gory details. Including the part about deciding to secretly tape-record Sergeant Burton.

He shook his head. "Jeez, I don't know if I coulda done that to another cop."

"I know," I replied. "But you're a guy. A guy can say to the boss, 'Look, let's go outside and settle this. Put the gloves on.' A man reacts differently to another man. But what was I supposed to say to the sergeant, 'Hey, let's go duke it out'? I can't do that. I'm a woman. I don't perform that way. This thing wasn't man-to-man. It was man-to-woman. And, worse than that, it was sergeant to cop."

"I dunno," said Tony. "I guess I woulda put in for a transfer."

"I tried. But they wouldn't let me out."

"Yeah, but to tape a guy—"

I finished the sentence for him:

"—was dirty pool, no question about it. But I had no choice. I knew the whole house of cards was gonna tumble. I knew the other men in the squad wouldn't stand up for me. I was gonna end up standing alone. I had to protect myself. If I went in there without that tape as proof, I woulda been dead in the water."

Tony carefully weighed what I had just told him. Finally, he offered, "Then you had no choice. You did what you had to do."

Trying for a little levity, I suddenly raised my hands in the air, as though I were about to submit to a patdown for a concealed wire. "So, you want to toss me?"

Tony smiled. "I'll pass."

We laughed. Slipped into silence for a while. Then, it came time for me to hit him with a question of my own.

"Tony, of all the people you could have picked to partner with in the Task Force, why me? I mean, really, with all my baggage . . . why me?"

Now that my lawsuit was on the record, I knew that all the old wounds would be reopened, all the simmering hostilities rekindled. People would be forced to line up anew and choose sides, for or against me. So why in the world did Tony want to get stuck with an albatross like Detective Kathy Burke?

"'Cause you're a good cop, Kathy," Tony said. "You're known to be where you're supposed to be. And do what you're supposed to do. I checked around. You've got a good reputation."

Tony confided that some of his other partners in the past had proven unreliable. Some had a bad habit of disappearing for long stretches of time while they were supposed to be on duty, usually to shack up with their girlfriends. They had left Tony hanging, alone on the street and potentially vulnerable.

"I just want you to promise me one thing, Kathy," Tony said.

I turned to him. And waited.

"That as long as we're partners, you'll never leave me alone on the street, no matter what."

"I'll never do that to you, partner," I said. "I promise."

One night after work, Tony invited me for a drink at a bar across from the Task Force offices at 26 Federal Plaza. At the bar, he introduced me to a bunch of his old pals from the Public Morals Division. That he was willing to introduce me to these cops, his closest buddies, was a real milestone in our relationship. In effect, he was vouching for me as a stand-up cop. By bringing me into his inner circle and letting me meet his friends, cops whom he liked and trusted and respected, he was telling them:

"Hey, forget what you've heard—she's okay."

The main target of our surveillance was a longtime capo in the Genovese crime family named Fritzi Giovanelli.

A fleshy, middle-aged man with close-cropped, graying hair, Fritzi had a long record of arrests for gambling, loan-sharking, assault, burglary, and robbery and at least three convictions. Based on our wiretap information, we knew that Fritzi was a principal underling to Chin Gigante, the overall boss of the Genovese family, and ran a gambling and loan-sharking operation for the Chin that grossed $21 million a year.

Additionally, Fritzi was a lifelong pal of Meade Esposito, the longtime chief of the Brooklyn Democratic Party, who would eventually be convicted from evidence gleaned through our wiretaps.

We knew that Fritzi owned several houses in Brooklyn and Queens that he used as policy banks or wire rooms to take illegal bets, so we decided to key on two of his locations in Ridgewood, a working-class community of Italians and Hispanics that straddled the Brooklyn-Queens border. Jammed in among the five-and-dime stores, the auto dealerships, the Italian bakeries, and the sporting goods shops, the two sites we targeted were the Bushwick Democratic Club on St. Nicholas Avenue and the People's Democratic Club on Wyckoff Avenue.

Now these clubs may have had innocuous, good-government-sounding names, but the notion that these joints had anything to do with politics, Democratic, Republican, or otherwise, was pure folly. They were illegal-gambling dens. Each week, they took in thousands and thousands of dollars in bets on horse races, sporting events, and the daily "number."

Working late tours—2 p.m. to 10 p.m. or 4 p.m. to midnight—Tony, Ted Carter, and I would drive over to these clubs and sit on them.

Our usual routine was to start our tours by cruising past the two social clubs to see if anything was going down. Then we would drive over to our office in Manhattan. At the office, we would update our paperwork, brainstorm with the bosses, and huddle with the other cops and FBI agents in the Task Force to swap intelligence, trade photos, and do records searches. After a short dinner break, we would head back out into the field. Often, we would cruise past the social clubs in Greenwich Village that were known haunts of Chin Gigante to see if Fritzi might be paying one of his obligatory calls on the godfather. Then we would head back to Queens. For a while, we might keep watch on Fritzi's private home. Eventually, we would end up back at the social club on St. Nicholas Avenue for a few more hours of surveillance before knocking off for the night.

Whenever we sat on the two Queens clubs, we would park a block away and keep tabs on who walked in and out, log their descriptions in our memo books, take their photos with our long-lensed camera, jot down their license plate numbers, etc.

Over time, we noticed that several faces seemed to show up regularly at the clubs.

One, of course, was Fritzi Giovanelli, who often came to the club on St. Nicholas Avenue. Another familiar face on St. Nicholas Avenue was a short, sad-eyed, middle-aged man whom we identified as Steven Maltese. The most prevalent face at the Wyckoff Avenue club was a short, tubby, melon-shaped guy with a bald head and a penchant for chewing gum. His name was Carmine Gualtiere, but he was known to his pals as Buddy. Based on our surveillance and wiretap information, we concluded that Maltese and Gualtiere ran the two social clubs for Fritzi.

Compared to working Narcotics, I found all this gambling stuff to be a bore and a snore. Nothing much ever seemed to be going on. Just a bunch of old geezers sitting around the two social clubs, smoking cigarettes, drinking cappuccino, talking, walking, listening, looking, laughing . . . and often snoozing. The whole business was mind-numbingly dull. We never saw any action. We never made any collars. All we did was sit in the car, wait, and watch.

What was really unsettling, however, is that much of the time they knew we were watching.

Seedy-looking characters would amble right up to our surveillance car, peer through the windows, and give us snarky looks. Sometimes, they would just point at us and snicker. Since our car had been used in previous surveillance operations on Fritzi's gambling outposts, we figured the wiseguys had to know—from the car alone—that we were plainclothes cops. Or, as cops would put it, they had "made" us. The car most certainly was "hot," and we repeatedly asked Lieutenant O'Brien to give us a different one.

In response, the lieutenant taunted us, "Whatsamatter, you too afraid to do your jobs? You too afraid to go out on the street? There are no other cars available."

But we knew that our car "had taken a burn," so we suggested that the lieutenant bring in a different team of detectives working in a different unmarked vehicle to continue the surveillance. These kinds of suggestions from B-teamers were met with sarcasm and ridicule. "You're detectives," the lieutenant told us. "You're big boys and girls. Why don't you stop all your whining and just go out there and do your jobs like real cops!"

Finally, we came up with the idea of abandoning our burned car altogether and setting up surveillance in a fixed observation post inside a building. We even pinpointed the perfect location—a U.S. military recruitment center opposite the St. Nicholas social club.

But when we asked Lieutenant O'Brien to use his influence with the FBI to help us gain access to the recruitment center, which was a federal facility, he responded, "You're detectives. I'm not gonna do your jobs for you. You figure it out."

So, in the end and despite our growing discomfit, we stayed put in our much too familiar brown, 1977 Lincoln Town Car. We waited. And watched. Watched. And waited. While we waited and watched, we began to talk. Trade war stories. And get to know each other.

Tony and Ted had been Public Morals cops. I had been in Narcotics. Public Morals and Narcotics were like vinegar and oil. They complemented each other, but did not operate by the same rules.

Gambling, the crime targeted by Public Morals, was considered a "clean" vice. Arrests were usually not made until weeks or months after the commission of the crime. The potential for violence was relatively slim. Gamblers were older. If they did have rap sheets, their last arrest was probably a hundred years ago. Though they sometimes carried guns, they did not carry them regularly. Nor were they known to square off with the police (a state of grace that probably carried over from the days when they were paying off cops to look the other way). Even if the gamblers were linked to organized crime, which was most of the time, organized crime was not known to commit acts of violence against police officers or FBI agents. It was not part of the Mafia's code to target cops.

Narcotics, however, operated by different rules. Arrests might occur within seconds after the commission of the crime. And, with those arrests, came the ever-present possibility of violence. Particularly, violence with guns. Everyone was fair game. And cops, particularly undercover cops, were always prime targets.

Narcotics cops operated with the expectation that when they got ready to make a collar, they could be killed. Public Morals cops operated with the expectation that when they got ready to make a collar, they could call up the bad guy and tell him to come into the precinct with his lawyer to surrender and be processed.

So, when it came to doing our jobs, Tony, Ted and, I had very different mind-sets. Hell, you could see it just in the different ways we dressed to go out on our surveillance runs. I always donned my bulletproof vest. And kept my gun—a Smith & Wesson, .38-caliber five-shot revolver—within easy reach, in the outer right-hand pocket of my jacket.

Tony and Ted did not wear their vests unless they were about to make a collar. They kept their guns in ankle holsters. Not as easy to reach in a moment of danger.

But much easier to conceal under their stylish, neatly pressed gabardine trousers.

CHAPTER NINETEEN

The evening of January 21, 1986, was unseasonably mild. Balmy, almost.

Tony and I were working alone that week. Ted was away on vacation, skiing up in Canada.

Because the weather was so temperate, the two of us put aside our heavy winter gear and dressed accordingly. Blue jeans, pink shirt, sneakers, and tan, three-quarter-length cloth jacket for me. Jeans, dark wool vest, open-collared sports shirt for Tony. He wore no overcoat.

We spent the beginning of our tour at the Task Force offices in 26 Federal Plaza, tending to paperwork. For a while, we studied photos of some of the wiseguys. Once again, we asked Lieutenant O'Brien to give us a fresh surveillance car. Or at least put a second car with more cops in it out on the street to back us up. And once again, he mocked us, repeatedly taunting us that we couldn't do our jobs.

It was hopeless. The lieutenant was a dead end. We decided to give up and go to dinner.

In the car, we kicked around the idea of asking one of the FBI agents in the Task Force to pull some strings with army intelligence and help us gain access to that military recruitment center located near the St. Nicholas social club. If it could be done on the sly, without our having to go through Lieutenant O'Brien or the FBI bosses, and we could quietly sneak our spying and photographic equipment into the recruitment center, we might be able to keep tabs on Fritzi's gambling operation without continuing to expose ourselves to jeopardy by using a burned surveillance car. We decided to run the idea by the agent the next time we were back in the office.

"Let's shoot up to the Village," Tony said. "I'm in the mood for Mex." And off we went to a well-known restaurant called El Coyote.

Tony and I finished our Mexican food at 6 p.m. We decided to head back out to the "set"—the two social clubs in Ridgewood, Queens—to sniff around.

That night, unlike most others, I was behind the wheel of the Lincoln Town Car. The camera we were using had a heavy, 200 mm zoom-lens attachment, and I had been having some trouble wielding it. Because he had a stronger grip and was more familiar with the equipment, Tony agreed to ride shotgun and take the surveillance photos. On this particular night, I would be the wheelman.

When we arrived at St. Nicholas Avenue, we spotted several parked cars, including ones we knew belonged to Fritzi and Steven Maltese. The social club itself was brightly lit, but nobody appeared to be inside. Outside, the street was dead. There was no activity at all.

Odd . . .

As we cruised down the block again on a second pass, we spotted Fritzi. He was walking toward his car. He got in and started the engine. Then he drove off, heading for Manhattan. We decided to head for Manhattan, too.

Instead of tailing him in a car we already suspected of being burned, we opted instead to drive down to Greenwich Village. Once we arrived, we would cruise past the social clubs on Thompson and Sullivan streets where Chin Gigante liked to sip cappuccino and talk business. Maybe we'd get lucky and spot Fritzi in the Chin's company.

When we got to Sullivan Street, we saw no sign of Fritzi or his car. But something unsettling did occur. As we neared the Triangle Social Club, the Chin's favorite hangout, we noticed a couple of paunchy-looking wiseguys standing out front, bullshitting with each other. Just as we drove past, one of the wiseguys turned, stared, and pointed straight at us.

This time, there was no doubt whatsoever. They had made us for cops. Or Johnnie Law, as they liked to phrase it. We'd been burned, pure and simple. And we weren't at all happy about it.

Nevertheless, we decided to drive back out to Ridgewood to see if we could pick up Fritzi's trail again. When we got there, we found the St. Nicholas social club still brightly lit. Yet it was still empty, not a wiseguy or a gambler within sight.

It was all starting to feel very, very odd.

Down the block, we did spot Fritzi's BMW parked on the street again. If he had, in fact, driven into Manhattan, he had managed to beat us back to Queens. As we drove past his car, we could see Fritzi sitting behind the steering wheel, peering down at a newspaper spread open in front of him. He appeared to be studying it closely. Yet how could he? No light was on inside his car. Nor was there a streetlamp overhead to provide any illumination.

So what the hell was he doing in there, anyway?

Something was off this night, out of kilter. Both of us could feel it. But we couldn't quite put a finger on what it was. Just a vague sixth sense, telling us that something was amiss. The smart thing, we agreed, was not to push the surveillance, but knock off early. Then head back to our office in Manhattan. We could always pick it up again the next day.

As we headed back into Manhattan, I casually removed my bulletproof vest and flung it over my shoulder into the backseat. What the hell, I figured, we were finished for this night, so why not make myself a little more comfortable? As usual, Tony was not wearing a vest.

I turned the car left, under the elevated train tracks, then left again. Just then, Tony said he needed to stop and use a bathroom. A greasy spoon called the Castillo Diner was just up ahead on our left. Tony told me to pull over and drop him off so he could dash inside.

Just as we neared the diner, I glanced into my rearview mirror. And that's when I saw the other car, tailgating us. So close it was practically kissing my rear bumper. What really spooked me, though, was that it was traveling with its headlights off. I looked more closely. And, despite the darkness, I recognized Fritzi Giovanelli as the driver.

"Tony," I said, "Fritzi's following us."

"Nah, you're crazy."

"No, it's him, I'm sure. And I don't feel good about this. Let's go somewhere else."

But Tony was insistent. "Look, I gotta use the can, so let's just stop here."

"I dunno about this. Something doesn't feel right here."

"C'mon, Kath," said Tony. "What's he gonna do? He's OC. They don't hurt cops. Quit worrying, willya."

Tony and I had a real good thing going, a rapport and friendship that were growing stronger each day, and I sure as hell didn't want to gum it up now by coming across as a pushy contrarian. So I held my tongue. "Alright," I said, "but let's make it real quick."

"Coffee or tea?" Tony asked me.

"Nothing. Just go do what you gotta do, then let's get the hell outta here." I shot another look into my rearview mirror. Fritzi was still on my tail. He was making me real nervous.

As I pulled up parallel to the diner, I double-parked the Lincoln and let Tony out. "Park up the block," he said to me. "I'll meet you over there." Tony jumped out of the car, crossed the street, and bounded up the stairs into the Castillo Diner.

I looked once more into my rearview mirror. Fritzi had stopped behind me, about two car lengths back. He was double-parked, too.

He was just sitting there. Watching me.

Now more than ever, I was convinced that Fritzi had made us.

Rather than park, I decided to keep driving and try to lure Fritzi away from the diner. If I hit the gas, I figured, Fritzi would probably key on our car and begin tailing it again. As I neared the corner, I started to make a right turn. Unbeknownst to me, I was turning the wrong way onto a one-way street. For an instant, Fritzi looked as if he were about to take the bait and follow right behind me onto that one-way street. But suddenly, he threw his car into reverse and backed into a parking space. Hurriedly, I stopped the Lincoln and began to back up, too.

Then, to my horror, I realized I was too late.

For just as I started to back up, another car appeared out of nowhere. It immediately boxed me in from behind, making it impossible for me to back up any farther. At first, I got pissed at the other driver. Then, in a flash, it hit me. A sudden, sickening sensation in the pit of my stomach . . .

This other car's sudden arrival was no accident.

Turning and peering through my rear window, I strained to look beyond the new car that was blocking me. I could make out Fritzi. He had gotten out of his car and was standing beside it. Looking one way, then the other, he started across the street, toward the diner.

"Oh, my God, no," I heard myself saying.

I knew I had to get back to my partner.

Quickly.

Since the other car was still boxing me in from behind, I threw the Lincoln into forward and followed through with my right turn. Gunning it, I sped the wrong way up the one-way street. After several more hard-right turns, I got the Lincoln back on the main drag again, circling back toward the diner. This time, I found a parking spot in the middle of the block, closer to the diner.

Jumping out of the Lincoln, I bolted across the street toward the diner. I could see Tony inside at the cash register, paying for his take-out coffee. Two staircases led up to the diner's entrance vestibule, one approaching from each side. Together, they formed a kind of inverted V, with the entrance at the top. I bounded up the left one. But as I moved higher, I saw through the plate-glass window that Tony was now descending the right one. So I went back down my staircase and circled around the entrance to meet up with him.

Then, just as I came around the corner, I saw them.

Fritzi Giovanelli. Carmine Gualtiere. And Steven Maltese.

Gualtiere and Maltese had Tony pinned up against the wall. Blocking his arms with their bodies, they had wedged him into a small alcove at the base of the staircase. Fritzi stood a few feet back on the sidewalk, facing the others. Standing with his back to the diner, Tony was juggling his bag of take-out coffee, trying to figure out just what the hell was going down.

I lunged toward them. "Tony! Watch out!" I shouted.

Fritzi made a sudden, counterclockwise turn to face me. "You!" he barked. "You get over here, too!" At this instant, he was standing no more than six feet away from me.

Slowly, I started to back up. As I did, my hand groped for the .38-caliber Smith & Wesson revolver in my jacket pocket. "Police!" I barked. "Freeze!"

A sudden, loud noise split the air. It sounded like the crack of a bullwhip.

My whole world felt as if someone had flipped it end over end. My feet flew out from under me.

Somehow, once the shooting began, I must have gone on automatic pilot and let my police training take over. I had fired up and into the air to avoid hitting civilians. In firing skyward, I had been trying to create a diversion that would give Tony enough time to get to his own gun.

I struggled to keep my bearings, but everything was going haywire. My sense of balance and my sense of direction were completely shot, and I could no longer tell if I was standing or sitting or lying down. Rather, I seemed to be floating in suspended animation. My arms had gone slack. My legs were like Jell-O. My brain was stuck in neutral. I couldn't understand why everything looked upside down to me. Gradually, it dawned on me that I must be drifting in and out of consciousness. The bright lights from the diner and the overhead streetlamps made my eyes hurt.

Suddenly, through the glare, a human shape loomed directly above me.

Fritzi.

He was looking down at me now. Expressionless. Eyes as black and as dead as a shark's. Slowly, as I would later testify, he raised his gun. And pointed it at my head. I could actually see the cylinder working inside his gun barrel. "This bastard is gonna shoot me," I thought to myself.

Ever so slowly, he squeezed the trigger. The barrel began to turn. An instant before the flash, I put my hand over my head and turned a fraction of an inch to one side. I must have moved out of harm's way at the last instant. Incredibly, miraculously, absurdly, the bullet missed me. It passed through my hair, singed it actually, but did not hit my skull.

When I looked around again, Fritzi had swung back toward Tony.

Tony was reaching down for the gun in his ankle holster. But before he could get a grip on it, all three of the men opened up on him with their handguns.

That was the last thing I remember. That's how it happened. That's what I told my husband, the police investigators, the prosecutors, and how I recounted it at trial.

When I came to again, the three gunmen were gone.

At first, I was not even aware that I had been shot. Still floating in suspended animation, I felt myself being pulled toward a more tranquil place, and an overwhelming desire to surrender to that pull.

But then, the cold, harsh voice of reason grabbed at my lapels, yanking me back to the present. It commanded me to stop. And think. To move toward that place that seemed so happy and safe would be to toss in the towel. To go to that place would be to let myself die.

The choice was simple, really. I could choose to die. Or I could choose to live. To die would be so much easier, so much less hassle, so much more restful.

But then I remembered something. A fragment of a conversation from several days earlier, when I was riding with Tony.

"I just want you to promise me one thing," Tony had said.

I had turned to him. And waited.

"That as long as we're partners, you'll never leave me alone on the street, no matter what."

And I had given him my word.

Now, as I lay wounded, everything slowly and inexorably slipping away around me, I knew I had to stay by his side. To die would be to break my word to him. To live would be to keep it.

Slowly, woozily, I dragged myself upright, into a sitting position. I spotted Tony. Sprawled on the pavement, just a few feet away. Propping myself up on my hands and knees, I crawled on all fours toward him.

As I got closer, I saw that he was lying faceup and his eyes were open, but they looked glassy. They were not focusing on anything. Blood poured from his head. Dark and red in the pale, cold light from the streetlamp overhead, it was pooling into a halo around his skull.

Nearby was the bag of take-out coffee he'd been carrying when all the shooting had started. The coffee was still steaming. I looked down at Tony's legs. His gun was still in his ankle holster.

"Tony," I said, thinking I could wake him. "Oh, God, no . . . Tony."

I knelt over him, placing my hand on the ground near his head. Only to be hit by the sickening sensation that I was touching something I should not have been touching. As I looked down, I realized what that something was. Bits of Tony's brain tissue. Exposed. On the sidewalk. Touching my fingers.

"Tony . . . Tony . . . Tony . . . Tony . . ."

I knew I had to get help. As I pulled myself to my feet, I felt something trickle down my chest. The inside of my shirt was wet and sticky and warm. With blood. Not somebody else's blood. My blood. "Shit!" I heard myself say. "I've been shot."

A bullet had ripped into my torso, I would later learn, spiraled through my insides, then rocketed right out the other side, exploding through my back.

I picked up my gun. It felt as if it weighed a ton. Pressing the stock to my bleeding chest, I used it like a compress. A half-assed compress, for sure, but it would have to do. I had been shot through the chest. I was fucking bleeding.

Fighting off the dizziness and the nausea, I tried to get my bearings. The thinking part of me somehow divorced itself from the feeling part. Instinctively, I began to utilize techniques I had learned from my training in hypnosis. I slowed my breathing, lowered my pulse rate, and put myself on automatic pilot. Oddly, I felt a kind of euphoria take hold, as though I had entered a whole new dimension, a blissfully peaceful zone totally apart from my everyday world.

I was calm. Catatonic, almost. People and objects floated past me in slow motion, as though they were moving through thick molasses. I found myself watching them with mild curiosity, as if I were observing

them through a telescope from a hilltop several miles away. Yet my observations were crystal clear, my senses ultrakeen.

I could have walked up the steps and into the diner. I could have used
one of the outside pay phones by the side of the diner to call for help.
But for reasons I still cannot explain, I did neither of these things. In the
numbed, unreasoning shock I was floating in, the diner seemed to pose
some kind of threat. Had I seen one or more of the gunmen dart inside
after the shootings? I couldn't be certain. Across the plaza, I spotted a
pizzeria. The lights were on, so I began walking away from the diner and
toward the pizzeria. As I walked, I continued to keep my gun pressed to
my bleeding chest.

Luckily, the pizzeria was still open. A guy behind the counter was
making fresh pies.

"I'm a cop," I told him. "My partner's been shot. Call 911. Tell them to
send help. Tell them, 'Officer down.'"

The pizza man went to the back of the store to make the call. I noticed a pay telephone at the front of the store, so I called 911, too. I was
on the phone with the 911 operator when a patron entered the door next
to me.

"It's okay," he said. "The police are here."

I looked out the front window, saw a uniformed cop near the diner.
So I slowly hung up the pay phone. "I have to go," I told the 911 operator.

A small crowd had gathered around Tony's body by the time I got
back to him. His gun, still wedged in his ankle holster at the instant he'd
got shot, was now lying on the sidewalk, between his feet. But how could
this have happened? Or was I just imagining it?

I plopped myself down next to his body, keeping my own gun pressed
up against my bleeding chest.

From out of the crowd, a uniformed cop stepped forward. He had
been on his meal break at the local McDonald's when he'd heard the report of a 10-13 over his radio, the signal for "officer needs assistance."
The moment I spotted him, I told him what had happened. Who we
were. And what we had been doing.

The cop seemed stunned, almost incredulous. I asked to borrow his
radio. He refused to hand it to me. I asked him to notify my superiors
and my husband, Bob, about the shootings.

"I can't handle this," he said. Then, shockingly, incredibly, he just
turned around and vanished into the crowd. I watched him go without a

word. Had he been a figment of my imagination, a phantom? I couldn't be sure.

In the next instant, a nurse who'd been inside the diner rushed to Tony's side. Dropping to her knees, she began to administer cardiopulmonary resuscitation. A man with her came over to me. Dropping to his knee, he identified himself as a retired detective.

"You on the job?" he asked me.

"Yes," I said. "And he's my partner."

The retired detective turned out to be the boyfriend of the nurse. They had been in the diner when the shooting had begun. He had actually seen one of the shooters. Thank God, this cop did not turn tail and run away from me. He offered to take my gun for safekeeping. I handed it to him and asked him to safeguard Tony's gun, as well. I still couldn't fathom how it had popped free of his ankle holster.

But the retired detective supplied the answer.

After Tony had gone down, three Puerto Rican kids had run up to his body and tried to steal his gun. Emerging from the diner, the retired detective had spotted them and chased them away. They had dropped Tony's gun by his feet.

As the scene began to fill with more cops and emergency medical personnel, I continued to sit in a daze by Tony's side. A uniformed female police officer began helping the nurse with her CPR efforts. Although I was at the epicenter of things, I felt curiously distanced from what they were doing, as though I were an invisible observer rather than a participant.

The shock was working its numbing ways again, slowing my reactions and my thought processes. I found myself alternately tuning in, then tuning out again, to what was happening just a few feet away from me.

My breathing became shallow and labored. I was beginning to feel pain from my wound. At one point, some people tried to pick me up and help me into an ambulance. But I yanked my arm away from them. Remembering, sadly now, the vow I had made to Tony about never, ever, leaving his side, I tore aside the fog rolling over my brain and told them:

"No. He's my partner. I need to stay with him. I promised him."

It wasn't until they got Tony into an ambulance that I finally consented to go to the hospital. But I insisted on going in a police radio car, not an ambulance. I wanted to walk into the emergency room under my own power. I did not want anybody to carry me.

At this moment, I was absolutely terrified of giving up my independence.

Once I lost that, I knew I was a goner.

Bob was working a night tour in Manhattan when he got the word.

"They want you to call operator 137," one of the other cops told him. "There's a message."

When Bob called the operator, she told him, "We have a shooting in Queens."

Bob was baffled. Why in the world was he being told about a shooting in Queens? He was on duty in Manhattan. Queens had its own people to deal with shootings. It didn't add up.

"Who got shot?" Bob asked.

"Two detectives," the operator replied.

Bob looked up suddenly. A queasy feeling began to take hold in his gut. "What are the names?"

"Venditti. And Burke."

"What's the condition of the two officers?"

"Burke is dead. And Venditti looks like he's going out of the picture."

Numbly, Bob took down the name of the hospital where the detectives had been taken. Then he hung up the phone. One of the cops in the office came up to him and asked softly, "Do you need a driver to get out there?"

"Yes, please," said Bob, wondering how in the world he was going to tell his two little girls that their mother had just been shot to death.

CHAPTER TWENTY

When they brought me into the emergency room at Wyckoff Hospital, the modest medical facility nearest the shooting scene, the nurses began stripping off my blood-soaked clothes. The initial shock had begun to wear off, and every little movement, even the simple unbuttoning of my jacket or the removal of my blouse, caused me tremendous pain. Breathing had become extremely difficult—every breath I took felt as if it were being strained through a piece of thick, wet cloth. Whenever I inhaled, a sharp, stabbing pain shot through my chest. My lungs felt like a pair of bellows trying to expand inside a spike-covered straitjacket.

The doctors began to check my vital signs, take my medical history, ask all the pertinent questions. Wincing and gasping through my pain, I spat back bits and pieces of answers.

Another gurney was rolled in close to mine. On top lay Tony. Tubes sprouted from his arms, an oxygen mask was strapped over his mouth, and they were working on his heart. His body was faceup and motionless. A life without any life.

"We gotta move you," said one of the doctors who was attending to Tony. "We need this room."

As they rolled me into a smaller room nearby, I caught sight of the female nurse who had tried to administer CPR to Tony on the sidewalk outside the diner.

"How is he?" I asked.

She tried to put on her best face. "We have a pulse."

"Be straight with me," I insisted.

"It doesn't look good."

In my new examining room, one of the doctors asked me, "Do you know how many times you were shot?"

"Once, I think."

"You think?"

Reverting to the present tense, as is the detective's custom, I gave him a synopsis: "After I go down from the first bullet, the gunman steps up over me, aims down at my head, and fires a second shot. That's when I black out."

The doctor looked up from his clipboard. "At your head?"

"At the last instant, I turned away." (Not until later would I learn that the bullet had singed my hair.)

The doctor listened to my heart and lungs. Took my blood pressure and my temperature. Gave me an X-ray and an EKG, as well as a tetanus shot and a painkiller. And drew plenty of blood for the hospital lab.

Little by little, the full extent of my injuries began to emerge. Fired at close range, the bullet had punched through the left side of my chest, blown out through the upper part of my back, and left me with fractured ribs, a collapsed lung, a pierced aortic valve, and a shattered scapula. A pulmonary specialist would later tell me that if I had not utilized my expertise in self-hypnosis—slowing my breathing, lowering my blood pressure, forcing myself to concentrate elsewhere—I would probably have gone into cardiac arrest and died.

The big worry at this moment, however, was that blood and fluids were hemorrhaging into my chest cavity. If this internal hemorrhaging went unchecked, it could trigger a seizure. The doctors wanted to cut a hole in my side and insert a drainage tube. But they were reluctant to give me anesthesia for fear it might send me back into shock.

"Skip the anesthesia," I told them. "Just do the damned procedure."

"Fine," one of them said. "But first we need you to sign this." He handed me a consent form. I signed it.

Just as they were about to begin cutting me, a tall man in a dark suit and white collar entered.

"I'm Monsignor Connor," he said softly.

I was ready for him.

In my purse, I carried two pairs of rosary beads along with several medals of the Virgin Mary. One set of rosaries, which I had had in my possession since third grade, had personally been blessed by the pope. The doctors and nurses stepped back from my gurney to give us some privacy.

From a small leather case, Monsignor Connor removed his scapular. He blessed it and placed it around his neck. Then, using his thumb, he dabbed a few droplets of holy oil on my hands and my forehead. I couldn't help but notice how clean and white his hands were. Gently tracing his fingertips along my skin, he made the sign of the cross over me. He recited the last rites. I replied by uttering the Act of Contrition.

Once again, the priest made the sign of the cross over me. Raising one hand, I made the sign of the cross over myself. Now, and only now, was I fit to meet my Maker.

The moment the priest retreated, the doctors stepped back in. Using a scalpel, one of them gouged a hole in the left side of my rib cage. I bit down hard on my lower lip as he bore into the raw tissue and muscle. Then, using a corkscrew motion that a wine steward might have employed, he began poking and twisting his rubber-gloved index finger into the incision until he could push a plastic tube through it, between my ribs and directly into my chest cavity. A nurse hooked the other end of the tube up to some kind of motorized suction device. When she flipped on the switch, it sounded like a vacuum cleaner with a bad case of asthma.

Meanwhile, bosses and detectives and FBI agents were swarming into the room and frantically peppering me with questions: "What happened?" "Who did it?" "Did you get a good look at them?" "Can you identify them?"

I named the three mob guys I knew to be the gunmen: Fritzi Giovanelli, Steven Maltese, and Carmine Gualtiere.

More bosses and detectives and agents poured into the room and bombarded me with the same questions: "What happened?" "Who did it?" "Did you get a good look at them?" "Can you identify them?"

So I took it from the top and told the same story all over again.

In came more bosses, more detectives, more agents: "What happened?" "Who did it?" "Did you get a good look at them?" . . .

In the midst of all this questioning, I suddenly became aware of something extremely disconcerting: I was lying there butt naked—exposed to God, the New York Police Department, and the rest of the world—with nothing concealed.

Nobody had bothered to give me a hospital gown. Nor cover me up with a blanket or bedsheet. I looked like some kind of grotesque pinup, Playboy's Wounded Lady Cop of the Month. Trying in their own clumsy way to buck up my spirits, some of the male cops tried to make light of my plight with characteristic delicacy and decorum.

"Hey, Kath," cracked one detective as he ogled my bare boobs, "I always wondered if they were real." And a high-ranking detective chief offered, "You know, Burke, you ain't got a bad ass, not bad at all."

Cop humor, crude, crass, and warped to the core. From all my own years on the job, I knew it was often the only thing that kept a cop sane in the midst of all the insanity.

I was still lying naked when Mayor Koch appeared. Tears welled in his eyes. "I don't wanna know anything about what happened," he said. "I just wanna know how you are."

"Well," I replied. "I'm hurtin'. But Tony's dead."

"I know," he said softly.

I knew the mayor's concern was sincere. He was not just here for the politicking. He had always been a friend of the police.

Finally, a friendly and familiar face appeared through the throng. When he saw me with all those tubes plugged into me, his mouth dropped.

"Aw, Kitty-Kat," he said softly. "What happened to you?"

It was John Gaspar, my retired ex-partner, and one of the few people from the job I still trusted. If there was anyone I knew I could count on at this moment, it was John. Especially John. Tears welled up in my eyes.

I asked the other detectives to leave the room. Once they were out of earshot, I fell apart.

"John, those bastards did it," I said through my tears. "They shot him. They fucking killed my partner."

"Aw, Kitty-Kat ..."

"I got myself in a fine mess, John. Look at this. Just look at this. Me, lying here with my ass half hangin' out. And that's a helluva sight to see."

He talked softly to me, stroking my hand. "Kitty-Kat, tell me, what can I do?"

I begged him, "Just make sure they don't screw it up. Just make sure they do everything right, John."

"You got it, Kitty-Kat," he promised.

John poked his head out the swinging doors and began shouting at the other detectives in the corridor. "Anybody out here remember to take a dying declaration from Detective Burke?" he asked. One of the other detectives assured him that, yes, they had.

Some of the other investigators tried to pump John for information I might have provided about the shootings. But he refused to rise to the bait. "Get your facts from Detective Burke, not me," he told them.

Back inside the emergency room, John hollered at the nurses, "C'mon, let's show this lady some respect! Treat her with some dignity! Let's get her covered up!" At long last, one of the nurses gave me a blanket.

Sticking his head out the door again, John buttonholed the first deputy police commissioner. Worried that the shock from my wounds and the medication might distort my recollection of the night's events, John asked the first-dep to put a halt to any further questioning of me. And to clear any unauthorized personnel from my room.

With good reason.

Amidst all the confusion, it was not totally clear at this moment who were the good guys and who might be bad guys. Perfect strangers might overhear a sensitive conversation between me and the investigators, then drop a dime and leak it to the press. Or, worse, to the mob. Wyckoff Hospital was a small, neighborhood hospital in Queens, nestled in the heart of mob territory, the Mafia's own backyard. I was still in the same damned neighborhood where I had just gotten shot, less than a mile from the scene, in fact. The "unwritten law" about mobsters never trying to kill a police officer had just gone right down the crapper, the myth irrevocably shattered. Two New York City cops had been gunned down in cold blood. And I was the chief eyewitness.

Aware of the danger to me as long as I stayed at this location, John lowered his voice and said, "You gotta get outta this joint, Kath."

Just then, the doors swung open and Bob walked in. He was wearing a dark suit and a black trench coat. His face was ashen. Numbly, he moved to my side. At first, he had trouble even speaking. The words stuck in his throat.

"I thought you were dead," he managed to mumble in a voice barely above a whisper. "They told me you were dead." He reached for my hand and squeezed it tightly.

Then he told me how Police Headquarters had screwed up and notified him that I was DOA.

"I got shot in the chest," I told him. "But I'm okay."

His body heaved a sigh of relief. He struggled with his emotions. "Thank God. Thank God."

"But Tony . . ." My sentence trailed off into empty, awful nothingness. My eyes, however, told the rest of the story.

"I know," Bob said. "I know. And I am so damned sorry."

He squeezed my hand again as I fought back the tears.

"What do you want me to do about the girls?" Bob asked, wondering how he should handle Cathrine and Veronica. "Should I keep them home from school tomorrow?"

"No, let them go to school," I told him. "They need to be with their friends, their teachers."

Bob left the room to phone the babysitter.

At that instant, a nurse entered, carrying a tray of bandages and instruments. The moment the door swung open behind her, the newspaper and TV reporters who had massed together outside got a clear and unobstructed glimpse of me. The juicy photo op they'd been waiting for!

In a feeding frenzy, they began snapping their pictures, thrusting their mikes and sound booms at me and shouting their questions, as if I were running for public office. A moment later, they converged en masse on the doors. One more second, they would have been right inside the emergency room with me.

Bob spun round on his heels, ran back toward the doors, and pushed them away. "Damn it, can't you guys give her some privacy! Get the hell away from here! All of yas, move it back! C'mon, move it back! Let's go! Move it!" Other cops rallied to his side and helped him steer the reporters and cameramen back out of the building before cordoning them off from the entrance.

A moment later, Bob was back at my side.

"I can't stay here," I told him. "It's not safe."

"Where do you want to go?"

"Bellevue," I answered, choosing the best-known hospital in Manhattan and the one with the best emergency and trauma units.

But there was a problem. How could they possibly get me out of Wyckoff without the press bird-dogging my every move? And, quite possibly, an eagle-eyed mob sharpshooter, as well? The minute they rolled me out of the emergency room, I'd be in plain sight, a sitting duck.

Bob and John Gaspar put their heads together.

A few moments later, several orderlies hurriedly pushed a lumpy gurney with a sheet drawn over it out of the emergency room, through the corridor, and down the entrance ramp. Cops surrounding the gurney chased away all onlookers. "Make way!" they shouted. "Stand back!" Attendants quickly loaded the gurney into the back of a waiting ambulance and slammed the doors shut.

The reporters and photographers made a mad dash toward the ambulance, but the uniformed cops got there first and regrouped just in time to block their access. Then, like a bat out of hell, the ambulance went screaming away from the hospital and onto an exit road, its lights flashing, its horn blasting, its siren blaring, and a bevy of wailing police cars riding escort. The reporters and cameramen went scurrying for their own cars. Then they hightailed it after the speeding ambulance.

Sometime later, after everyone had left, a second ambulance quietly eased out from a back alley behind the hospital, into the darkness of night. Only this one deliberately kept its lights and siren off until it hit the expressway.

Inside this second ambulance, I lay on my gurney, lapsing in and out of consciousness. Along with Bob, a couple of Wyckoff Hospital doctors were at my side, plus the New York Police Department surgeon and an Emergency Medical Service technician, all monitoring my vital signs. An oxygen mask was strapped to my face. An IV line was stuck in my arm. My chest tube was rigged up to a portable suction device that continued to noisily hoover all the blood and sputum from my collapsed lung.

As the doctors kept checking my heartbeat and my blood pressure, they also began a blood transfusion. At one point, they worried that they might lose me altogether. I had started to hallucinate.

"Get this bat blood outta me!" I blubbered, trying to rip the tubes from my arms. "Next thing you know, I'm going to be hanging by my tail from the trees!" I began to tussle with the doctors, who had to restrain me.

"Take it easy, Kath," Bob started telling me. "Calm down now, hon."

In my addled brain, I had started to imagine that I was being fed buckets of bad blood, some kind of fatally corrosive cocktail tainted with one part HIV for every two parts of hepatitis. I continue to scream, "And don't let 'em run the damned siren! Sirens freak me out! I hate sirens!"

The doctors shot me up with Valium and Demerol.

In a few moments, as the meds kicked in, I drifted into a stupor.

With rumors flying that I could still be a target for a second mob hit, the Police Department threw a tight security cordon around Bellevue Hospital on the East Side of Manhattan. Uniformed cops and plainclothes detectives flooded the emergency room, the reception area, and the adjoining corridors.

When I was first wheeled inside, a police sergeant ordered a young patrolman to stand guard over me. "Don't take your eyes offa her," the sarge told this kid. "Not even for a second."

My collapsed lung was filling up with fluids again, and I was having more and more difficulty breathing. So the Bellevue doctors made a second incision in my chest and inserted another drainage tube. The pain from my fractured ribs was so excruciating that one of the doctors prescribed even more morphine and Demerol.

I was still in the trauma unit when the doctors told me they wanted to perform an arteriogram. This meant making an incision in my groin, then injecting dye into my bloodstream and monitoring its flow with instruments to detect any arterial bleeding.

Time was of the essence, the doctors said. If they waited too long to do the arteriogram, I might be risking a heart attack.

"Fine," I told them, "but before you do it, I want to talk to my daughters."

I worried that my kids might hear about the shootings on television. Or that they might learn about them from their schoolmates. I needed to reassure them personally that I was okay.

These were the days before cellular phones, so the Police Department had to string a wire into the trauma unit to hook up a telephone for me. At 7 a.m., just as the girls were getting dressed for school, I made my call to our house in Astoria. I tried to sound as cheerful and upbeat as I could.

"I won't be home for breakfast, honey," I told Cathrine. "But I just wanted to tell you that I love you."

"Why aren't you coming home, Mommy?" Cathrine wondered.

"I've had a little accident. I'm in the hospital. I need to stay here for a few days, get some rest. But I'll get better. I promise you. And I will be coming home."

"You sure you're coming home?"

"Scout's honor. I'll be there."

But my girls, being my girls, were still curious. "What happened?" Cathrine asked.

"Daddy will explain the rest."

"Okay," Cathrine said, apparently reassured. "See you soon, Mommy."

It's a good thing I made my call when I did. Shortly after I got off the phone, the cartoon show Cathrine and Veronica were watching was interrupted by a news flash. A grim-faced correspondent broke in to report that two detectives who were surveilling the Mafia had been gunned down outside a diner in Queens.

On the TV screen there were close-ups of the diner. Shots of police officers and detectives poring over the crime scene, using their flashlights and metal detectors to search for bullets, shell casings, and other evidence, while forensic experts dusted for latent fingerprints. Long ribbons of yellow tape cordoning off the shooting site. Lake-sized puddles of fresh, dark blood on the sidewalk. Sobering interviews with the police commissioner, the mayor, and others. And clear, color footage of one of the shooting victims—me—being rushed into the emergency room with an oxygen mask on my face and all those tubes stuck in me.

The bulletin also included the first public announcement that one of the detectives had died.

The correspondent noted that the murdered detective—Tony Venditti—was just thirty-four years old.

That he was a highly decorated cop.

That he was married.

And that he had four young daughters of his own.

After the arteriogram was performed, I was moved upstairs to a private room. The room, rarely used, was away from the rooms that housed the general patients and in an area where visitors were infrequent and access could be closely monitored. But it was also in a wing where homeless people were being treated for alcoholism, drug abuse, AIDS, and other maladies, and it was absolutely filthy. The room smelled like unwashed socks, the walls were spattered with blood, the trash receptacle was filled with bloodstained bandages, and the nurse's call button didn't work.

I was still groggy from painkillers when I heard the voice. Calm, gentle, and soothing.

"Hello, Kathy."

I slowly opened my eyes. To see a tall, black-haired man wearing dark glasses. He was standing just outside the curtain around my bed. A second man stood with him. The second man's face was badly scarred.

"May we come in?" the man with the dark glasses asked softly.

"Sure," I said, my eyes half-closed.

Pulling back the curtain, the second man helped guide the man with the dark glasses toward the chair by my bed. Groping for a grip, the man with the dark glasses sat down next to me. When he grabbed for the railing to bolster himself, I noticed that most of the fingers on his hand were missing.

"How ya feelin'?" Detective Richie Pastorella asked me.

"I'm hurtin', Richie," I said.

"Yeah, I can imagine. But hang in there. You're gonna be okay."

The other cop identified himself as Lieutenant Timothy McCue. "I know what you're going through, Kathy," Tim told me. "I've been there myself. But, believe me, you're gonna make it."

Both Rich Pastorella and Tim McCue were members of the Bomb Squad. And I was well aware of their extraordinary personal sagas.

Pastorella had been severely injured in an explosion outside Police Headquarters on New Year's Eve, 1982. The night of terror began when a bomb placed inside a Kentucky Fried Chicken bag by the Puerto Rican terrorist group known as the FALN blew off the leg of a uniformed cop. Dispatched to the scene, Detective Pastorella and his Bomb Squad partner, Detective Tony Senft, discovered a second bomb nearby. But when they tried to remove it, it blew up in their faces. At the very moment the bomb went off, I was inside Police Headquarters, working on a case with my old partner John Gaspar. When the terrorist device detonated, I actually saw Pastorella's and Senft's bodies propelled through the air.

The blast left Pastorella completely blinded, without most of the fingers on one hand and half-deaf. Senft was blinded in one eye and lost much of his hearing, as well.

In a separate incident, Lieutenant Tim McCue had also been maimed while trying to disarm a terrorist's bomb. What's more, he had seen his partner killed in the very same blast. It was no accident that McCue had come to visit me. Both McCue and I had something in common. Both of us had watched our partners die. Both of us had managed to survive. And both of us would have to live with that memory—and all the other feelings that come with that memory—for the rest of our lives.

"It's the first few days that are the roughest," Pastorella told me. "That's when the pain, the isolation, and the feelings of helplessness are the worst."

Pastorella and McCue had come to let me know I was not alone. Other cops besides me had gone through it. And, down the line, those other cops would reach out to me. "We have a group," they told me. "We get together. We talk. We help each other."

This unique fraternity of police officers who had been shot, stabbed, or otherwise hurt in the line of duty was known as the Police Self-Support Group. But neither Pastorella nor McCue put any pressure on me to join it. Not yet, anyway.

Instead, they simply left a card with a phone number. "When you feel up to it," Pastorella said, "give us a call."

With McCue's help, Pastorella rose to his feet again. Then, McCue guided Pastorella back toward the door.

"Good-bye, Kathy," Tim McCue said.

"God bless you," said Richie Pastorella.

And then, just as quietly and unobtrusively as they had slipped into my room, the two hero Bomb Squad cops were gone.

Lieutenant O'Brien came to visit me. "How's it goin'?" he asked. "Anything you need?"

He made no mention of our burned surveillance car.

Not once did he look me in the eye.

In the immediate aftermath of Tony's death, I wrestled endlessly with my conscience.

I tried to tell myself that I had met all the critical tests of whether a cop performs ably and responsibly in a life-or-death situation. I knew I had identified myself as a police officer. Told the suspects to freeze. Taken a bullet in the front of my chest as opposed to my back, so there could be no suggestion I had turned tail and run. Then I had fired my own weapon—emptied it of all its rounds, in fact—before I fell to the ground and blacked out. I had gotten to my feet again. Called for backup. Returned to the scene. Stayed by my partner's side until the ambulance arrived. And, finally, after making sure my partner had been taken to the hospital, I myself had gone to the emergency room for treatment of my own injuries, which were quite serious.

For all intents and purposes, I had done everything by the numbers. And yet, being human, there was always that kernel of self-doubt that kept eating away at me.

I found myself constantly replaying the events in my head. Could the shoot-out have been prevented in the first place? Probably not. Perhaps it might have been delayed by a few minutes, a few hours, maybe even a few days. But, in the end, I was convinced it would have happened anyway.

Because they had planned it that way.

Nevertheless, the possibilities kept swirling around and around in my brain. If we had not taken the Lincoln Town Car out that night, knowing that it had been burned on the street . . . If we had adamantly insisted on a new surveillance car . . . If I had refused to drop Tony off at the Castillo Diner when I'd spotted Fritzi on our tail . . . If I had parked the car immediately, rather than driving it around the block again . . . If I had darted around that vestibule an instant sooner or drawn my gun a second earlier . . . If Tony had kept his gun in his pocket, where it was more accessible, instead of in his ankle holster . . . If both of us had been wearing our vests . . . if . . . if . . . if . . . if . . . if . . .

The scenarios were endless. And at times, they tortured me. I couldn't make them stop, no matter how hard I tried.

Of one thing, though, I was certain: I would have done anything to save Tony's life that night. Anything. Including giving up my own life.

Which, very nearly, I did.

In the end, I came to believe that I had done all that I could have to protect my partner. Yet, no matter how certain I felt, I knew I would constantly be dogged by the doubts, insinuations, and accusations of others. Doubts, insinuations, and accusations that might never, ever, go away, no matter how many times I answered and re-answered all their questions.

And why?

Because my partner had died. Because I had survived. Because he was a male cop, and I was a woman cop. Because I was not just any woman cop, I was a woman cop under a cloud, a woman cop with a sullied reputation. Because I was a woman cop who had violated the code. Because I was a woman cop who had talked back to bosses and secretly tape-recorded them. Because I was a woman cop who had filed a landmark sexual-discrimination suit against the entire New York Police Department and a bunch of male superior officers in the Major Case Squad.

Because I was Detective Kathy Burke.

One morning, another visitor came to see me.

"How are you feeling?" asked Dr. Marty Symonds, the slight, graying Police Department psychiatrist.

I recognized Dr. Symonds as one of the instructors from the hostage-negotiation course I had taken with John Gaspar several years earlier. He had lectured to us on the abnormal psychology of terrorists, psychotics, drug crazies, and other potential hostage takers.

"Everything hurts, Doc," I told Symonds.

"I'm very sorry about your partner," he told me.

"Thank you."

"How do you feel about all of this?" he wondered.

"Awful. Just awful. I wish to God I could change everything. I wish to God my partner was lying here in the bed next to me right now. That we could have wheelchair races down the hall while we recover together from our wounds. But I know that's not possible. He's dead."

"And how do you feel about the fact that he's dead."

"I am so, so sorry he got killed. But I don't want to trade places with him."

"I see."

Dr. Symonds questioned me a bit more. I knew he was trying to determine whether I might be in the throes of "survivor guilt," so consumed with grief and self-blame that I might become self-destructive, even suicidal.

In the end, he concluded I was neither.

"You're going to be okay, Kathy," he said. "What you are going through is quite normal."

He left me a card with his number on it. "But when the dreams start, give me a call."

Dr. Symonds got up to leave. Just before leaving, he turned and said, "Oh, I met with Patti Venditti, Tony's widow. She wanted me to tell you something."

"Yes?"

"Tony said you were a good partner."

In the hospital, I barely slept.

When I wasn't being kept awake by my pain, I was awakened by the doctors and nurses, who came into my room at all hours to take my temperature, check my pulse, poke me, prod me, turn me, listen to my heartbeat, adjust my IV line, or change my bandages.

The two private nurses hired for me by the Police Department were angels of mercy. When I became enraged, they soothed me. When I cried, they cradled me. When I felt alone, they assured me that people cared about me. When I felt overwhelmed, they tried to share my burdens. They gave me the kind of comfort and nurturing I had not received since my mother was alive. Knowing how much I cherished my hot tea, one of them even brought me a teapot from her home so I could have a nice warming cup whenever I needed one. At night, the two of us would sit together sipping tea and eating cookies, feeding crumbs to the resident mouse, who regularly darted out from the hole in the wall of my dreary room to take his exercise laps around my creaky hospital bed.

Apart from the detectives who came to question me about the shootings, friends and colleagues went out of their way to show their concern and compassion. Many old friends from the International Association of

Women Police came to visit, wrote me cards and letters, and called to provide moral support.

I was especially heartened when a group of women detectives from the Special Investigations Division—the overall detective command that included the Major Case Squad—came to my bedside to show their support. Some of them told me that I had actually done the women in the department a huge favor by getting shot the way I had. As they explained it, I had taken a bullet in the front, not the back; fired my gun, emptying it of all its rounds; held my post; and stayed with my partner after he'd gone down—all of these actions that could help dispel the notion that women cops would routinely freeze, panic, or run away in shooting situations.

I also heard from cops and FBI agents I had met during my stint at the FBI Academy in Quantico, Virginia, and my trips to out-of-state conferences for women in policing. My room quickly filled with boxes of Godiva chocolates, cookies, cakes, magazines, a stuffed Cabbage Patch Kids doll, a teddy bear. One detective brought me baked ziti that his wife had prepared in their kitchen. Baskets of fruit and flowers arrived hourly, so many that I eventually asked my nurses to share them with the other wards.

While most of my phone calls were screened by the three cops who were posted around the clock inside and outside my room, I did receive hundreds of cards and letters. The notes that touched me most were the ones sent by all the little boys and the little girls at my daughters' school in Astoria, St. Francis of Assisi. Most of them were hand-scrawled on scratchy, gray sketch paper. Using their crayons, the kids had lovingly adorned their messages with great big hearts, grinning faces set atop gangly stick figures, giant, blue sunflowers wearing enormous ears and big, toothy smiles, and swirling, green helicopters. Many of the kids still remembered me as Mrs. Burke, the nice mommy who had come to school on career day to talk about what it was like to be a police officer and had, at the urging of the nuns, who always worried about possible abductors or molesters, taken all their little fingerprints.

On the day my own kids were finally allowed to visit me, the first few moments were awkward. Seeing me in my hospital gown, propped up on my egg-crate mattress with an IV line still dripping painkillers and antibiotics into my arm, seven-year-old Cathrine bit her lip and screwed up her little face.

"Why did you want to become a policewoman, Mommy?" she asked. "Will you still be a policewoman when you get better?"

"Well, honey," I told her, "it's a little bit like when you were first learning to ride your bike. You remember how you fell off?"

"Yeah."

"You fell off a whole buncha times, didn't you?"

"Yeah."

"But each time you fell off, you got right back on again, didn't you?"

"Yeah."

"Well, in a way, Mommy fell off her bicycle. But it's okay. 'Cause Mommy's going to get back up again. And Mommy's going to ride her bicycle again, just like you did."

Cathrine seemed able to accept this explanation. Five-year-old Veronica, however, needed no explanation. Nor did she even want one. She was too busy bouncing up and down on my hospital bed and playing with the button that made the mattress go up and down.

The funeral took place on a bitter wintry morning. Despite my wounds, I had wanted badly to attend.

The doctors argued I was not strong enough to travel. I repeatedly begged them to let me go, even if it meant going in an ambulance. They refused, saying I could be risking infection. I was angry about their refusal, but eventually I resigned myself to watching the funeral on television, from my hospital bed.

Snow flurries flecked the sky, and an icy wind rustled through the heavy overcoats of the many mourners who attended. More than five thousand cops lined the streets outside the Catholic church in Queens where Tony was to be eulogized. All of the cops had stretched black bands of mourning across their white and gold shields.

In keeping with tradition, the procession to the church was led by the members of the police Emerald Society band, huge, ruddy-faced, mustachioed men in black kilts, white leggings, and black feather bonnets. As they walked slowly ahead of the hearse bearing Tony's coffin, past the endless blue sea of officers who stood silently in long, long rows that were five, six, and seven deep, they thumped out a solemn, muffled cadence on their black-draped drums. Six police pallbearers lifted the green-and-white-flower-draped casket from the hearse and lowered it to the street. Then they carried the casket up the church steps and into the sanctuary for the funeral service.

Mayor Koch, in an interview with one reporter, characterized the murder of a cop as "the most outrageous, cruel act that one can commit" and renewed his long-standing call for the death penalty for those who committed such heinous crimes. One TV commentator talked of the message this huge turnout would send to the mob. Another mentioned the four children that Tony had left behind and took particular note of their ages—five, three, one, one month.

Inside the church, the Police Department's Catholic chaplain spoke of "those who unselfishly lay down their lives for the good of others." A tenor sang "Be Not Afraid" and "Ave Maria." The coffin was carried back outside into the now swirling snow and placed back on the hearse for the final trip to the cemetery. Dressed in a black-and-gray dress and heavy overcoat, Tony's widow, Patti, watched bravely and stoically from the top of the church steps.

Then, as the crowd fell silent, a lone bugler began to play taps. More than five thousand white-gloved hands snapped a crisp final salute to their fallen comrade. Patti's face finally gave way to the emotions underneath. Her lips quivered. Her eyes filled. She put her forehead to her hand.

And that's when I lost it.

"Why did this have to happen?" I sobbed to the nurse who was changing my IV line. "It's just not fair! Why did Tony have to die? Why? Why? Why? Oh, God, tell me, why?"

The nurse tried to comfort me. But I was inconsolable.

I wept for Tony. I wept for myself. I wept for Tony's newborn baby and his three other little girls, children who would never get to know their father. I wept for Tony's widow. For his parents. I wept for my own husband and kids. I wept for the partnership the two of us had begun to build. And for the genuine friendship that was beginning to take root right alongside it.

I wept for what was past and gone forever. And I wept for a future that would never, ever, be.

"It's okay, honey," said the kindly nurse who had been changing my IV line. She put her arm around me and held me tightly. "It's okay. It's good to get it out. Just let it happen."

But once it did happen, it felt as if it would never, ever, end. A vast reservoir of sadness and grief. A bottomless well of hurt and sorrow from which I could never emerge. My anguish was overwhelming, my pain endless. It was not just my body that was crying, it was my entire being, my very soul. I was wracked by uncontrollable, gut-wrenching sobbing. I tried to make it stop. My God, how I tried. But it was futile.

So, in the end, I gave into it.

And, for what seemed an eternity, I just wept.

CHAPTER TWENTY-ONE

The three shooting suspects were quickly arrested.

Fritzi Giovanelli was nabbed just minutes after Tony and I were gunned down. An eyewitness named Frank Simone flagged down a marked police car, got into the backseat with an officer, was taken on a run around the neighborhood, and pointed Fritzi out as one of the shooters. He was captured just a few blocks from the Castillo Diner, trying to flee the scene.

Two days later, Steven Maltese, knowing he was wanted by the police, gave himself up to detectives at his attorney's office in Manhattan.

Three hours after Maltese surrendered, Carmine Gualtiere was picked up at his home in Queens.

All three men were charged with murdering Tony and attempting to murder me. They were also slapped with gambling and racketeering charges arising from our surveillance of their bookmaking and illegal sports-betting operations. All three proclaimed their innocence. All three offered alibis. And those alibis were doozies.

Fritzi's was this:

Yes, he had been present at the shootings, but—in his words—he was the intended victim, not the perpetrator. En route to an appointment, he had stopped to use a pay phone outside the Castillo Diner. Suddenly, two men jumped him and tried to rob him of his money. One jammed what felt like a gun into his back, then attempted to steer him toward a parked car. At that very moment, Tony emerged from the diner and inadvertently stumbled into the middle of the stickup attempt. Almost simultaneously, I came running around the corner of the diner vestibule. Shouting, "You bastards!" I pulled my gun, igniting a wild shoot-out between the robbers and the cops. Caught in the middle—and still a completely innocent victim, mind you—Fritzi stumbled to the ground, then managed to scramble to his feet again. Ducking the flying bullets, he began running as fast as he could. One of the robbers came running after him. The robber then veered off and disappeared. Fritzi, however, was intercepted almost immediately by a radio car driven by a female police officer, who used her loudspeaker to order him to halt. A male police sergeant, coming from another direction, told Fritzi to stand by the radio car and submit to a search for concealed weapons. While he was being searched, Fritzi protested to this sergeant, "Whaddya searchin' me for? I'm not the robber." He was then handcuffed and taken to the 104th Precinct in Queens, where he was charged—mistakenly—in the shootings.

Steven Maltese's story was that at the time of the shootings, he was somewhere else—at his girlfriend's apartment, where he was seen by several witnesses.

Carmine Gualtiere claimed to have been at home, with his daughter and granddaughter, relaxing in front of the TV set, when the shootings occurred. They were watching the Muppets. (Later, in court, Gualtiere's alibi came to be known as "the Muppet defense.")

My version of what happened was somewhat different: Fritzi shot me in the chest. Then, after I went down, Fritzi, Maltese, and Gualtiere turned and fired their guns point-blank on Tony, killing him.

This was the story I told.

It was the story I told to the first cops who arrived on the scene at the Castillo Diner and found me sitting dazed and bleeding on the sidewalk, next to Tony's body. It was the story I told at the hospital, to my husband, Bob, to my ex-partner John Gaspar, and to countless other bosses and detectives who entered the emergency room and repeatedly hammered me with their questions. It was the story I told to the assistant district attorney and the grand jury foreman who sat at my hospital bedside while a technician videotaped my statement for the grand jury. It was the story I would testify to in court . . . on multiple occasions.

It was the one and only story I ever told about what happened outside the Castillo Diner on the night of January 21, 1986, when I was shot and Tony was killed in cold blood. It was the story I would have told until I turned blue in the face. Because, in the end, it was the true story.

Little did I imagine how difficult it would be to get other people to believe it.

After eleven days, I was released from the hospital. Bob picked me up and drove me home. Lieutenant O'Brien, driving his own car, followed us. I was surprised, and quite touched, by this unexpected display of concern for me on the part of the lieutenant. So I invited him to join us for coffee.

But while he sat sipping coffee at my dining room table, he casually revealed the real reason for his visit: "I need you to give me back your official parking placard. After all, you won't be needing it anymore, will you?"

A few days later, the lieutenant called me up, wanting to know how soon I would be able to come up to the Task Force offices at 26 Federal Plaza and clear out my stuff.

"We got a new guy who needs your desk," he said matter-of-factly.

That first night back home, Bob handed me the telephone. "Call Patti Venditti," he told me.

I had yet to speak to Tony's wife about the shootings.

While I was still in the hospital undergoing treatment, I had not expected Patti to visit me. Not only was she a grieving widow, but she had just given birth to a new baby and had three other little ones to care for, as well. Moreover, Bob had asked Patti not to contact me until I had time to recuperate from my wounds. But Bob had assured Patti, sworn to her in fact, that I would talk to her once I was discharged from Bellevue.

I took the phone from Bob. I composed myself. And I dialed the number.

When I reached her, our conversation was stilted and strained. And painfully difficult.

Patti had so many, many questions about the night of January 21. She wanted to know everything about Tony's actions, all about my actions, all about the actions of the bad guys, all about the actions of the Police Department. Some of her questions I could answer, but many of them I could not. I myself did not have all the answers. The biggest question of all was why it had happened to us in the first place. Sad to say, I could not provide her with a definitive, satisfying, or logical explanation.

There were several theories in circulation, among them . . . Theory No. 1: The wiseguys had mistaken us for members of a rival crime crew intent on sabotaging their operation. Theory No. 2: The wiseguys thought we were low-level street thieves trying to steal their gambling receipts. Theory No. 3: The wiseguys had known all along that we were plainclothes cops and decided to confront us. Theory No. 4: On realizing he was being followed, Fritzi simply blew up and lost his temper.

I offered to meet with Patti so we could discuss all of these theories face-to-face. I also offered to have my babysitter stay with her kids so she could meet with me, either at my house or at a coffee shop. Over the next few months, I would repeat this offer several times. But Patti never seemed eager for this meeting to take place.

When I hung up the phone after our first conversation, I knew that Patti was completely dissatisfied with my responses. And deeply suspicious of everything I had said. She seemed convinced that some kind of department cover-up was going on, and that I had been coerced into secretly aiding and abetting that cover-up. It sickened me to think that I could not be more forthcoming and put her mind at ease. I wish I could have cleared up all those loose ends, filled in all the gaps, answered all her questions. But the truth was that I did not have all the answers. When it came to putting all the pieces in place, I was almost as much in the dark as she was.

Meanwhile, reporters began hounding Bob and me mercilessly for interviews, calling at all hours of the day or night. Many had known Bob on a first-name basis when he was the boss of the department's public information office, the unit that liaises with the press, so they already had our home telephone number. Some of the pushier ones just showed up at our house without even troubling to call, heedlessly trampling my iris beds to come up and bang on our front door. So annoying and intrusive did they become that I had to keep my blinds closed and my curtains drawn to keep them from spying on us.

At first, my kids thought it was "cool" to see their mom on the TV news. But before long, they became agitated and upset by all the phone calls and the unannounced visits. "Mommy, why does the phone keep ringing?" they would ask me. "Why can't we answer the phone? Why can't we open the front door? Why can't we go outside to play? Why can't we walk to school by ourselves anymore?"

Lieutenant O'Brien assigned police bodyguards to accompany my girls to and from school each day, trailing slowly behind them in a radio patrol car. I fibbed to Cathrine and Veronica, telling them that the cops were following them to chase the press away. What I did not tell them was that the Organized Crime Task Force had received intelligence that I or someone else in my family might still be a target for a "mob hit." I had become especially concerned about the girls' safety after Veronica came home from school one day and told me that one of her little classmates had talked about her father, a known associate of the Genovese family, scrutinizing photographs of me in the newspaper.

The pain from my collapsed lung, my shattered scapula, and my broken ribs continued to torment me. Three hundred cubic centimeters of blood were still sloshing around in my damaged lung, and on top of everything else, I contracted a nasty case of bronchitis. Whenever I coughed, which seemed to be every couple of seconds, I thought I would die. To manage the pain, I took massive amounts of codeine.

So I was much relieved when Lieutenant O'Brien assigned a detective to drive me to and from my endless doctors' appointments. It made me feel safer to have him by my side. But then, I began to grow suspicious. He kept asking me questions, too many questions. Such as how I felt personally about the lieutenant in the wake of the shootings. And whether I had hired an attorney.

I began to get the feeling that this detective had been assigned to spy on me. To find out if I intended to sue the department for damages— and sue the lieutenant personally for putting Tony and me in harm's way.

One day, I put the question to the detective straightaway. He smiled and said, "Something like that."

After several weeks at home, I asked the Police Department for permission to accompany Bob and the kids on a trip to Florida. Many months earlier, we had planned a winter vacation in Clearwater Beach, and I didn't want my injuries to ruin our trip. I also thought that the sun and the salt water might actually speed my healing, and my pulmonary specialist seemed to concur. So, once the Police Department gave me the okay, I headed south with my family.

The trip, however, turned out to be something less than pleasurable. In constant pain, I popped my codeine painkillers like M&M's. I wore an Ace bandage tightly wrapped around my torso and kept a folded towel under my armpit, to guard against bruising my broken ribs and to lessen the agony whenever I was overcome by hideous bronchial coughing spasms. Every night, I would have terrible nightmares. Waking up shaking, shivering, and in a cold sweat, I would start to sob.

One night, Bob took all of us to a family-style Italian restaurant for dinner. As we were sitting studying the menu, a man passed our table. He and I happened to make eye contact. I can't remember now if he was a patron or a waiter. What I do remember was that he had a mustache. A thick, black mustache.

Tony had a black mustache.

When I saw this man, saw his mustache, something inside me just snapped. There was that sudden instant of recognition, followed by a tidal wave of sadness. Profound, overwhelming, all-encompassing sadness. Right there in front of my husband, my kids, and all the other startled diners in that restaurant, I burst into tears.

Dr. Symonds, the police psychiatrist, had warned me that something like this might happen. And, from this point on, I often found myself succumbing to sudden, uncontrollable fits of weeping.

I knew I was in trouble. And I knew I needed help.

When I came home from Florida, I immediately went looking for the card from the Police Self-Support Group and called Rich Pastorella, the blinded Bomb Squad detective who had visited me in my hospital bed.

"I'm having problems," I told him.

"Come to our next meeting, Kathy," Rich said.

When I walked in, I was trembling. My upper lip was damp with sweat. I was nervous as all hell.

For there I stood, in a room with a bunch of New York City cops who had been cut down in the line of duty. And many of these guys were real heroes. Cops who had been shot by snipers, bank robbers, and fugitives. Cops whose necks and spines and limbs had been broken in car chases with fleeing fugitives. Cops who had been maimed by terrorist bombs. Cops whose legs had been amputated. Cops who were paralyzed. Cops on crutches. Cops in wheelchairs. Cops who could no longer speak, hear, or see. Cops who could barely breathe.

All of these cops in the room were men. And all of these men had heard the ugly rumors about me. How would these other injured cops react to me? Would they boo me? Would they curse me? Would they spit on me? Would they get up and walk out of the room in protest? Would they turn their backs on me?

When it came time to introduce the new members, Richie asked me to stand up and introduce myself to the group. My heart was pounding in my chest as I slowly rose. I took a deep breath. Cleared my throat. And began to tell them my story.

The others listened quietly.

Then, incredibly, some of them began to talk about their own ordeals. Their nightmares. Their outbursts of sudden and uncontrollable sobbing. Their feelings of shame and helplessness after they had gotten shot or stabbed. Soon, I came to realize something quite remarkable. I was not alone in my anguish. These cops had gone through it, too. All of them were struggling to cope with the trauma from their line-of-duty injuries. All of them had been subjected to the doubting, the blaming, and the second-guessing. All of them had felt abandoned by their peers and their superior officers. As they talked about their ordeals, I began to see that I was not some freak. Even though I was the only woman in the room, I realized that, in our injuries, in our traumas, and, most important, in our feelings, we shared a bond. We were, in a way, family.

In time, the cops in the Self-Support Group would help me to realize that when a cop is hurt, he suffers not one injury, but two. The first injury is the physical wound. The second injury, less apparent, is the feeling of rejection and isolation that accompanies that wound, that queasy, unsettling sense of being shunned by fellow cops and put out to pasture by the department.

What's more, as the others would explain to me, when a cop gets hurt, it isn't just that hurt cop alone who is victimized. It's all the other cops around him who become victims, too. The cops in the squad who begin instinctively thinking to themselves, "My God, that coulda been me." The guilt-ridden commanding officer who sent the cop out on the street in the first place, then is left to wonder if he gave the cop bad orders or inadequate support. The partners who secretly blame themselves for not having been there to back the cop up when he went down. The cops who responded by radio car and worry that they might have arrived on the scene a minute too late. All of these people become victims, too. All of them must wrestle with pain and guilt and shame. And, sometimes, without even being aware of it, these cops, in their desire to keep a lid on their own hurts, begin to distance themselves from their injured colleague, unintentionally leaving him feeling like an outcast.

When a cop is gunned down, the group members would tell me, other cops carry the pain right along with him.

Suddenly, it hit me that one of the people who must be carrying that pain was my own husband, Bob.

While he was working in the 79th Precinct in Brooklyn, Bob had experienced learning that two of his officers had been assassinated by the Black Liberation Army. One of those slain cops had left a widow who was eight months pregnant. Now, Bob was being forced to relive the trauma of a double police shooting all over again. This time, one of the victims left behind a young widow with a newborn infant and three other small children. The other victim happened to be his own wife.

At the end of the Self-Support Group meeting, some of the other injured cops came up to personally welcome me to their ranks.

A few even embraced me.

For the first time in a long time, I began to feel that I was not alone.

One morning, as Bob and I sat having breakfast at our dining room table, I started to say to him, "Maybe if I had been a better shot . . ."

Just then, a news story came over the radio. A wild chase and shootout between the police and some bad guys in the Bronx. The police had fired 136 rounds at the perpetrators. But they had not hit any of them. Not even nicked them. Not a single round had found its mark.

"Did you hear that?" Bob asked me. "Did you? None of those cops could hit anything. You should think about that, Kathy."

I made an appointment to see Dr. Symonds, the Police Department psychiatrist who had come to visit me in the hospital.

I told him about my sudden and unexpected bouts of uncontrollable weeping.

"I pretty much expected that would happen," he said. "And right about this time, too."

In the hospital, he explained, I had managed to numb myself to the full emotional impact of the shootings. But now that I had begun to let my guard down, all those dark, buried feelings were bubbling to the surface.

"It's important to talk about them," Dr. Symonds said.

We agreed to continue meeting regularly, once a week for an hour at a time. Our sessions would continue for the next two years.

For the first few months after the shootings, I was unable to mail thank-you notes to all the people who had sent me cards or gifts in the hospital. Nor was I able to read the news clippings and watch the news videotapes from the night we got shot.

Yet these were things I needed to do, Dr. Symonds said. For myself, for my family. "You have to face the reality of how the rest of the world perceives the events," he explained.

Over time, I was able to focus more on the pain and frustration of my own injuries.

Dr. Symonds told me that because of my injuries, it was unlikely that the Police Department would ever let me return to regular detective work and investigate cases. I might be brought back temporarily and given a desk job, but ultimately, he said, the police medical board would survey me off the job.

"If that's my fate," I told him, "so be it. But, for God's sake, let the department put me out to pasture quickly. I don't want to hang around and linger pathetically, like some of the other deadwood I've seen gathering moss in the department."

I still worried a lot about how all of this was affecting my girls.

"How much should I tell them?" I asked Dr. Symonds.

"Explain everything simply, explain it fully and explain it honestly," he said. "Otherwise, if they sense you are holding back on the truth, they may feel like you're punishing them or excluding them."

He suggested I bring him the drawings my kids had made in school, both before and after the shootings.

After he had had an opportunity to study them, he told me, "I see no evidence of trauma. I think they're coping just fine."

One of the things that came up in our sessions was my anger. I told Symonds I felt angry at my dead partner, Tony. Yes, I felt anger.

I know it sounds irrational, but I was angry at him for dying. Angry at him for leaving me alone in this terrible situation, in which I now had to fend for myself. Angry at him for getting out of the car when I had expressly asked him not to. Angry at him for not having put his gun in his pocket or his waistband, rather than his ankle holster where it was less accessible.

"It's not unusual, you know," Dr. Symonds told me. "Actually, it's somewhat to be expected."

One day, two Queens detectives from the 104th Precinct showed up at my house to discuss the investigation into the shootings.

At first, I was relieved. Nearly five months had elapsed since the shootings, but, since all those interrogations by the police when I was first brought into the hospital, nobody had troubled to reinterview me.

The detectives who came to see me were not exactly heavy hitters. Garner was a tall, skinny gum-chewer with liquor on his breath. Schatz was a stocky guy with glasses who was always whistling.

Right off the bat, their questions took an odd and disturbing turn. It began when they asked if it might have been Steven Maltese who had shot me, not Fritzi Giovanelli.

"No," I said, "it was Fritzi. I was looking right at him."

"Well, could Maltese have fired the shot from behind Fritzi?"

I bristled. It seemed as if they were deliberately trying to plant a whole new scenario in my mind other than the one I knew to be true. "Listen," I said, "why do you care who shot me? I'm telling you who shot me. Why are you looking to put the blame on someone else?"

"Well," said the two detectives, "we don't have corroboration from the other witnesses."

Now, this was the first I was even aware there were other witnesses. But, regardless of what others might have seen or said, I certainly knew I was not mistaken about who had shot me. For Pete's sake, I was standing six feet away when the gunman pulled the trigger and drilled a hole through my chest. And even closer than that when he stood over me and tried to put a second round in my head. "It was Fritzi," I said. "Those are the facts."

"Yes, sure," said the detectives, "but you were a hysterical female."

I started to steam. "Wait just a damned second," I shot back. "Just where do you get that? You weren't even on the scene! So how do you know how I behaved?"

"Well, could it be that someone else shot you, other than Fritzi or Maltese, some stranger maybe?"

"Absolutely not."

"Well, could you at least think about this? I mean, you could have been mistaken."

Now I was really pissed. These guys didn't want to know my story. They wanted me to know their story. And, for the life of me, I couldn't figure out why.

"Why are you two doing this?" I demanded. "You're gonna take some civilian's word over mine? I'm the player here. I'm a trained investigator. I have their pictures with me. I know who these guys are. I've been working these people. This doesn't make sense to me."

"Just think about it," they repeated.

That did it. I stood up abruptly. "Gentlemen, there's nothing to think about. I know who shot me. Now please leave my house."

They left.

The next day, I called my friend Detective Tommy Bruno in the Organized Crime Task Force to report this conversation. I also called the Queens DA's office to notify the prosecutors. I was royally PO'd about this blatant attempt to get me to alter my story. Down the line, if I took the witness stand and altered my story, changing it in any way, shape, or form from what I knew to be the absolute truth, other witnesses might end up contradicting what I said. Then I would look like an out-and-out liar.

For some strange reason, the Queens prosecutors did not seem unduly concerned.

But I, for one, was plenty concerned. I was also damned curious to know who was spoon-feeding these two hooples from the 104th their information. Or rather, their misinformation. It had to be coming from somewhere. Or someone. But who?

Down the line, I learned that the Genovese family had hired a private investigator to assist the attorneys who were defending the three accused gunmen. All well and good, except that this private eye was a former police sergeant who had once worked out of the 104th Precinct, the same precinct that was now investigating the shootings. Still chummy with all the detectives in the 104th squad, the ex-sergeant-turned-private-eye was still hanging out in the squad room with them, drinking coffee and munching doughnuts, schmoozing, trading jokes and gossip.

I had to wonder how this private eye might have influenced the police investigators.

Before long, I began to sense that this entire investigation smelled funny. There were just too many cozy associations between the mob and the police, too many ties, too many old links, too many damned coincidences. From our surveillance runs, I remembered that some of the wiseguys had glossy, laminated Patrolmen's Benevolent Association cards in the dashboard windows of their cars. How in the world did they get these cards, anyway? And from whom? Cops? Although they often parked illegally, they rarely seemed to get tagged with summonses by the local uniformed cops. Why?

As for the ex-sergeant who was now working as a private eye for the Genoveses, he was small potatoes. Turned out that some cops who were still on the job were hobnobbing with the wiseguys.

After the shootings, two of my key possessions—a red spiral notebook containing mounted surveillance photos of the wiseguys and a zippered, black loose-leaf book holding both loose surveillance photos and a steno notepad in which I had jotted down my own intelligence notes—were removed by a detective at the shooting scene from our Lincoln Town Car. Also taken from the car was the surveillance camera Tony and I were using the night we got shot.

While I was still in the hospital recuperating, another detective from the 104th Precinct brought my red, spiral notebook to my bedside and had me make identifications of the shooting suspects. Afterward, as I had expected, that same red book was vouchered as trial evidence. But, for some unexplained reason, nobody ever bothered to return my zippered, black loose-leaf to me. When Lieutenant O'Brien came to visit, I asked him about it.

"The Queens chief of detectives has it," the lieutenant informed me.

"Well, either it's vouchered as evidence or I get it returned to me," I said.

"The chief wants to keep it."

The whole business was starting to sound pretty fishy. For what possible reason would the Queens chief of detectives need to keep my loose-leaf notebook, a piece of evidence that might well become critical during a trial?

"Look," I said, "that book is my personal property."

Lieutenant O'Brien said his hands were tied. So, when I got home from the hospital, I called the 104th Precinct squad and asked for my notebook to be returned. A detective up there told me they no longer had it. So I called the Queens chief of detectives' office and, after getting one of his lieutenants on the phone, made the same demand.

"Chief wantsta hang on to it," he sniffed, without any further explanation.

"Fine," I said. "Tell him that, first thing tomorrow morning, I'm going straight to Internal Affairs."

Lo and behold, that very night a lieutenant from the 104th Precinct showed up at my house with the missing zippered, black loose-leaf in his possession. But even before I opened it, I knew something had been removed. Gone was my steno notepad with my hand-scrawled intelligence notes. Also missing were a bunch of pages from the loose-leaf binder, as well as some of my loose surveillance photos. Meanwhile, although our surveillance camera was returned to the Organized Crime Task Force, the film inside it had mysteriously disappeared.

"Where's the rest of my stuff?" I asked the lieutenant.

"Hey," said the lieutenant, "don't look at me. I'm just the messenger."

I immediately called Lieutenant O'Brien, the boss of the Organized Crime Task Force, and reported the disappearance of these items, all of which could have become critical evidence at trial. This was top-secret stuff, and somebody had been screwing around with it. In the wrong hands, it could compromise not only the upcoming trial, but all our surveillance operations.

Later on, when I felt strong enough, I went up to the 104th Precinct detective squad in person to search for the missing items. Only to be told that there was no trace of them. They were gone.

After checking around, I learned the name of the Queens detective who had removed my red, spiral book, my black, zippered loose-leaf, and our surveillance camera from our Lincoln Town Car. But I was unable to track him down.

And, further down the line, a strange piece of information came to light about this detective. According to the FBI, this detective had been spotted at the wedding of a Genovese crime-family member. During the reception, the detective was seen passing police-type documents to one of the Genovese people. Also present at this wedding, coincidentally, were relatives of Steven Maltese, the same Steven Maltese who had just been charged with shooting us.

You'd think the department's higher-ups would have landed like a ton of bricks on this sleazebag. But nothing of the sort ever happened. Not only was this detective never interrogated or fully investigated about his actions—he was allowed to retire from the police force on a full pension!

Apart from the long and spidery reach of the mob, I worried that the investigation into the shootings might be polluted and undermined by my sex discrimination lawsuit, which was slowly moving forward in federal court.

The night Tony and I got shot, a bunch of detectives from the Major Case Squad had shown up at the 104th Precinct. One of them, Joe Leff, promptly announced to the investigators, "We always knew she'd wind up getting somebody killed."

I could only imagine the poisonous effect that crap like that must have had on the detectives assigned to investigate Tony's murder. Pretty soon all of them would be convinced that I had single-handedly been the cause of the shootings.

With all of this venomous nastiness in the air, I spent a lot of time with Dr. Symonds talking about how violated I felt by the Police Department.

"Every cop goes through a sort of romance when he first joins the department," I said to Symonds. "You fall in love with her. You believe in her. You trust her. You put your faith in her. I did all that. But now, I'm being treated like a rejected suitor and a pain in the ass.

"I pledged my love. But the department has been unfaithful to me. I feel betrayed."

Dr. Symonds pondered my words for a moment, then said, "The hurt and the anger might never go away. But you're making a big mistake about one thing."

"What's that?"

"The way you talk about the Police Department—you make it sound like a person. A living, breathing, thinking, feeling, flesh-and-blood person. The Police Department is an institution, not a person. It has no feelings or emotions or conscience. Yet, you keep talking about feeling betrayed. Only human beings are capable of betrayal."

This was something I needed to consider.

Early in March of 1986, a small gathering was planned at the home of Tony's parents. The gathering, timed around what would have been Tony's thirty-fifth birthday, was to honor and remember Tony. I had every intention of attending, along with all the other members of the Joint Organized Crime Task Force.

But right around the time of the birthday gathering, I got some unexpected and terribly sad news. One of my few regular partners from my bumpy days in the Major Case Squad, Terry Carey, was gravely ill. I had known Terry for fifteen years and considered him one of my closest friends. During my time in Major Case, he was the detective who had been so kind to me during my second pregnancy, bringing me cups of hot tea. Later, we had partnered together on bank robbery cases, including the arrest of Kenneth, that bearish, Bible-quoting lunatic who threatened to knock down his holding pen until I calmed him with my magic rosary beads.

Terry's Hodgkin's disease had entered the final stages. Knowing that I might have just one last chance to see him before he died, I had asked permission from the Police Department to travel to Missouri, where Terry was undergoing a last-ditch bone marrow transplant.

But, just before I was due to leave for the airport, I received a telephone call from another Major Case Squad detective.

"You might as well save yourself the trip, Kathy," he told me. "Terry just died. His remains are being flown back to New York. He'll be cremated. They'll have the funeral right after."

Terry's funeral was set for March 11, the same day on which the birthday remembrance for Tony was planned. Which meant I had a real dilemma. I could not possibly attend both events at once.

The whole thing was terrible. I was being forced to choose between my

two deceased partners, Terry or Tony, both of whom I had revered as colleagues and cherished as friends, both of whom I was now grieving in death.
How cruel that one was going to be buried on the other's birthday. But even
worse, how awful that I had to pick which partner to be with in spirit.

I agonized long and hard over the decision. In the end, I felt the right
thing to do was to attend Terry's funeral. So I specifically asked Lieutenant O'Brien, the boss of the Joint Organized Crime Task Force, to
make a point of explaining to the Venditti family why I couldn't attend
the birthday remembrance for Tony. And to extend both my apologies
and my condolences.

Unfortunately, my message was never delivered. Lieutenant O'Brien
never troubled to pass it along.

All the other cops and FBI agents attended the remembrance for
Tony. But I was absent. Conspicuously absent. And, without the benefit
of my explanation, my absence could only have left the impression that
either I had something to hide . . . or I didn't give a damn.

In the spring of 1986, I did finally have an opportunity to meet the
Venditti family in person. A special mass had been scheduled at St. Andrew's Church, near Police Headquarters. The mass was an annual event
to honor all the FBI agents and police officers who had died in the line of
duty while assigned to joint federal-city task forces.

A few days prior to the mass, a major scandal had exploded in a
Brooklyn precinct, where uniformed cops had been caught shaking
down drug dealers for narcotics and cash. The corruption issue was still
very much on everyone's mind. People were upset and edgy and embarrassed. In fact, at the memorial mass, a priest chose for his homily the
subject of criminal wrongdoing by the police.

During his sermon, I happened to glance around the chapel. As the
priest began to excoriate cops who strayed from the path of virtue, I realized that Tony's wife, Patti, and his mother, Anna, had fixed their gaze
upon me. And I began to get the distinct feeling that, in their minds, the
priest must specifically be talking about me.

I knew I had to talk to them face-to-face.

While I had spoken to Patti a few times by phone, I had yet to meet
with her in person. Whenever I had suggested a face-to-face, she had
dodged me. Nor had I been able to extend my condolences to Tony's parents, Anthony and Anna. Once the St. Andrew's ceremony was over,
however, I was determined to walk up to all of them and, though it was
long overdue, pay my personal respects.

Outside the church, I spotted the Vendittis. I started to approach them. My closest friend from the Task Force, Detective Tommy Bruno, intercepted me.

"This might not be the best time, Kathy," he cautioned.

But I persisted. "I gotta do this, Tommy. It's now or never."

I walked up to Patti and greeted her. She remembered me from when I had come to her house to see her new baby. She responded politely and cordially.

Then I introduced myself to Tony's father, Anthony, a kindly, sweet-faced, middle-aged gentleman. "Mr. Venditti," I said softly, "I'm Kathy Burke. I am so, so sorry for your loss."

Mr. Venditti bit his lip, nodded to me, and started to shake my hand. Suddenly, his wife, Anna, stepped between us. She was dark-haired, stern, imposing.

"So you're the woman who killed my son," she said.

The blood drained from my face. I felt as if a knife had just been plunged into my heart. I became hysterical.

Tommy Bruno immediately wrapped his arms around me and whisked me away from the Vendittis. "C'mon, Kath," he said, "time to go."

Patti Venditti came up behind me and tried to make amends. "Please don't take offense," she said to me.

But Patti's words did little to ease the shock and the pain. I knew Tony's mother was suffering, but how could she have said something so cruel and so hurtful? I had taken a bullet, just like her son. My blood was on that sidewalk, right alongside Tony's. I had nearly died that night, too. Would it have been better if I had? Would it have been better if there had been two slain heroes to mourn and memorialize at this mass, rather than just one?

I hadn't been prepared for her attack. And now, my heart was breaking.

By the time Tommy got me across the plaza and away from the other mourners, I was sobbing uncontrollably. Tommy tried his best to console me: "Don't take it personal, Kath. These people are just very, very upset."

And now I realized that, yes, their pain was even more terrible than I could imagine.

But soon after my encounter with the Vendittis, the rumors began . . .

That I had shot Tony.

That I had shot myself.

That I had been shot while trying to run away.

That I had come on the scene while the bad guys were shooting Tony, so I consented to allowing them to shoot me, too, just so I wouldn't get into trouble with the department.

That I hadn't really been shot at all, but was simply put in the hospital to cover up the real facts of the case, which was all part of some vast Police Department conspiracy.

That I had self-inflicted my wound with the point of a Bic pen.

That the mob had paid me to drive around the block so they could ambush Tony.

That I had been on the telephone in the pizzeria, chatting with a friend, at the moment Tony got shot.

That Bob had deliberately removed my bloody clothing from the hospital so it could never be examined as evidence.

That Bob had refused to let me speak to the Venditti family after I'd got shot because we had something incriminating to hide.

That I had refused to attend Tony's funeral.

Gross, malicious, baseless, disgusting rumors, all of them. Particularly ludicrous were the ones about me shooting myself or shooting Tony. Clearly, I had been shot from a distance greater than just a few feet. If I had been shot at closer range—which certainly would have been the case if I had turned my gun on myself—there would have been telltale powder burns on my clothing. But there were no powder burns. What's more, if I had shot myself, I would probably have shot myself in the foot or the arm, where the wound was less likely to inflict life-threatening injuries. I sure as hell wouldn't have put a round in my chest, through my lung, and just inches away from my heart.

As for the rumor that I might have shot Tony, either deliberately or accidentally, the ballistics tests conclusively revealed that none of the bullets taken from his body could have come from my .38-caliber Smith & Wesson revolver. Unfortunately, a lot of people, including one truly shabby and irresponsible freelance writer for *New York* magazine, never bothered to pay attention to any of those test results.

The rumors enraged me. And, from what I was hearing from other detectives in the Task Force and elsewhere, it was the Vendittis who fueled some of them. In their pain, in their suffering, they needed to lash out. Attacking the Mafia was like trying to punch at wisps of smoke. Ditto, going up against the Police Department, another exercise in futility. As I later learned, Anna Venditti had been disparaging me in a series of letters she sent to various NYPD and city officials—letters in which she claimed I was responsible for her son's death and which she distributed freely to the media at one of the subsequent trials.

So, in their anger and their frustration, in their grief for their murdered son, they turned on the most visible and most convenient target in the aftermath. Me.

In the face of these rumors, I realized I could neither defend myself nor fire back a countersalvo. I could not get up on my customary soapbox and freely speak my mind. Much as it pained me, much as it went against my nature, I needed to keep silent. Turn the other cheek. And let others speak up on my behalf. Sadly, few were willing to step forward. Lieutenant O'Brien, for example, never once stood up for me, even though he knew the real story about what had happened outside the Castillo Diner. Fearful of getting caught in the cross fire, he left me to fend for myself and take the heat.

And I had to hold my tongue. Now was simply not the time to display that hard-edged, confrontational side of my personality. Now was not the time to play the tough-as-nails detective or the aggrieved victim of new injustices. Now was the time for me to rein myself in, pay more attention to the injustices perpetrated on others, and keep my mouth shut. To do otherwise in the wake of this awful tragedy, so utterly devastating to everyone it touched, would only make matters a hundred times worse.

Both for the Vendittis and for the Burkes.

Still, the rumors mounted. And they took their toll.

There was only one place where I felt free to vent my feelings.

In my weekly visit to Dr. Symonds, the Police Department psychiatrist, I sobbed and ranted and pounded the top of his desk. "What more do they want from me!" I would scream at him. "I was doing what I was supposed to be doing. I wasn't drunk. I wasn't stoned. I was where I was supposed to be. I did exactly what I was trained to do in a life-or-death situation. The moment I screamed, 'Tony! Watch out! Police! Freeze!' I was prepared to give my life so that he might live. I was trying to buy him a moment of time, so he could get to his gun. I knew I might end up getting shot and dying. And I nearly did die, right on the sidewalk next to him. So why—why—are they crucifying me?"

But the rumors continued, without letup. And, as a wise man once said, trying to stop a rumor is like trying to unring a bell.

About a year after the shootings, I attended a cocktail reception at John Jay College.

I sat at a table with several other detectives. A few of us were talking about more recent police shootings when one of the people at the table—a male detective I had never met before nor even heard of—chimed in, "Oh, yeah, and then there's that Burke shooting."

With a knowing and dismissive scoff, he went on to suggest that he knew considerably more than most about what had actually happened outside the Castillo Diner on that fateful night. And he said he had gotten his information straight from the horse's mouth, Detective Kathy Burke herself.

I decided to play along. "Well," I said to the male detective, "then you must have been a pretty close friend of this Burke."

"Friend, hell," the male detective said. "I was her partner. And, lemme tell ya, we broke a lotta bread together."

"Really!" I said. "Well, what did she tell you?"

"She phoned me after it happened. Turns out she wasn't even on the scene when the shooting started. She fucked up."

"No kidding!"

"Oh, yeah. She left her partner unprotected. Panicked. Turned tail. And ran away. She was terrified. Take it from me."

I listened quietly, allowing this guy to babble on and on. Two other women cops who were friends of mine glanced over at me, wondering just how I was going to respond to this guy. Would I scream at him? Smack him? Throw a drink in his face?

Although I was sorely tempted, I did none of these things. Instead, I said to the male cop, "You know, Detective, you seem to know so much about this incident, I'd really be interested in talking further with you. May I meet with you again sometime?"

"Why the hell not?" he said. "Be happy to shoot the shit with you. If anyone can give you the straight story, it's me."

"Why don't I just give you my card?"

"Great. I'll give you a call."

I handed him my card with my name and telephone number on it. Then I watched him turn twelve shades of purple.

He stood up and walked away from the table.

During the first few months after the shootings, I had regular nightmares. Most of them were bloody reenactments of the shootings. But one was quite different.

In it, I saw myself walking down a long hall. The hall was long, deep, and black.

As I inched forward, I found myself more or less stumbling through the darkness. The furnishings, as best I could make out, were sparse. A damp, bitter chill tinged the air. I could feel the coldness right through my clothing, in my hands, my feet, even in my bones.

Walking down this hall, I sensed that I was alone. No one else appeared to be with me. Groping through the darkness, I continued to make my way toward the end of the hall. Suddenly, up ahead, I spotted some light. So I headed toward it. And that's when I spotted the casket.

A flickering candle sat at the foot of the casket. Another candle was at the head, casting a spectral glow off the dark, polished wood. The casket lid was open. And Tony lay inside it.

Suddenly, as I neared the casket, Tony sat up. He turned. And looked at me.

"What's happened, Kathy?" he asked me. "What's happened to me?"

"Tony," I said to him. "Tony, you gotta lie down. You gotta go now. It's over."

But Tony refused. "I can't, Kathy. I don't know what's happened. I can't go yet, not until I know what's happened to me."

I shivered. Icy fingers of terror clutched at my heart. In desperation, I looked around the room for help.

Suddenly, out of the shadows, a familiar face appeared. It was Art Boyer, one of my old sergeants from the Major Case Squad. A good man, kindly, who had actually tried to protect me during some of my worst times in the squad. "You have to give him peace, Kathy," Sergeant Boyer said softly to me. "You have to tell him the truth about what happened that night."

So I steeled myself. And turned back to face Tony. Then I told him about the shootings. All of it. Everything. The whole horrible story.

After I had finished, Tony nodded to me. He lay back down in his casket. He folded his arms across his chest. Closed his eyes. And allowed himself to die, naturally, serenely, peacefully.

And that's when I woke up, shaking and sobbing.

It took me a few moments to realize that I was still in my bed. In my house. In my old neighborhood of Astoria, Queens. I had been dreaming. A terrible, terrible dream, but a dream, nonetheless. Bob did what he could to comfort me. But I was pretty badly shaken.

On my next visit to Dr. Symonds, I told him about my dream. "Hmmm," he said. "Very interesting."

For a while he pondered the significance.

"It's a peaceful dream," he said.

I was startled.

"Yes, I'm convinced that it's a peaceful dream. Because, in it, you've given your partner a final release. So that he can end his suffering in this world and pass on to the next. From this point forward, Kathy, I think your nightmares will end."

And, incredibly, just as he predicted, my nightmares did end. For the first time in a long time, I was able to sleep peacefully through the night.

CHAPTER TWENTY-TWO

The trial against Fritzi Giovanelli, Steven Maltese, and Carmine Gualtiere began in the spring of 1987 in Queens Supreme Court. Prior to the trial, a Queens judge designated all three men "potential threats to the safety of the community" and revoked their bail.

I knew I would be the star witness for the prosecution's case. After all, I was a victim who had witnessed the shooting and could testify to what I saw. But several others also gave eyewitness testimony.

A seventeen-year-old teenager named Edwin Rodriguez identified Carmine Gualtiere and Steven Maltese as two of the men who had shot us. He testified that after Tony was wounded and fell to the ground, Gualtiere knelt down and shot him again, in the head. However, Rodriguez was unable to identify Fritzi Giovanelli as one of the shooters. And the revelation that young Rodriguez had been in and out of psychiatric wards since the age of twelve seriously undermined the credibility of much of his testimony.

Another eyewitness, an unemployed cook named Frank Simone, testified that he saw Giovanelli menace Tony with "a metal object." After he heard a shot, Simone said, he ducked behind a van. But, he testified, he was able to see Gualtiere walk over to Tony's body and pump two more bullets, at point-blank range, into Tony's head. Simone said that he saw all three defendants—Giovanelli, Gualtiere, and Maltese—then flee the scene. Simone flagged down a patrol car, got inside, and pointed out the fleeing Fritzi to the police, who quickly took Fritzi into custody.

Still another witness, retired detective Tom Kosior, who was inside the Castillo Diner when the shooting started and later took my gun for safekeeping, testified that he, too, had seen Maltese run from the scene.

Eventually, it came time for me to take the stand. Unfortunately, I was not ready.

In the months preceding the trial I had been interviewed only a couple of times by the DA's office. But no real effort was made to prep me for the kinds of tricky questions and nasty insinuations I might be hit with on cross-examination. From my past experiences testifying in court, I knew that this kind of pretrial preparation was vital to solidifying my credibility on the stand and bolstering the prosecution's case.

Several times during the months leading up to the trial I had asked the two assistant district attorneys who were prosecuting the case when they would get around to prepping me. Not to worry, they told me. When the time came, they said, all I needed to do was get on the stand and tell my story.

On the morning I was due to testify, one of the DAs called me into his office, where he introduced me to a Police Department ballistics expert. The ballistics expert began to question me about the bullets I had been using on the night of the shootings. Copper-jacketed bullets had been removed from Tony's body. What did I know about copper-jacketed reloads? Might I have been using them in my own gun?

In other words . . . could I have shot my own partner?

I was incredulous. "Are you crazy?" I snapped at the ballistics expert. "You're asking me this five minutes before I have to go on the witness stand? No, I did not kill my partner. I use standard-issue Police Department ammunition, not copper-jacketed bullets. Now get out of my face."

I was furious. I felt as if I had just been ambushed by my own side. Knowing that I was just minutes away from having to get up on the witness stand, I struggled to recompose myself. But when I entered the courtroom and took the oath, I was upset and angry and flustered. I was particularly angry with the two DAs for not protecting me.

Then, partway into my direct testimony, I unexpectedly found myself embroiled in a new controversy. When cops testify in court, they routinely display their police shield, either on their jacket pocket or their lapel. On the breast of my jacket, I was wearing my gold detective shield. And stretched across my detective shield was the black band of mourning I had worn since the day of Tony's death. Suddenly, a defense lawyer leaped to his feet and objected to the black band, saying it might unduly influence the jury. Whereupon, the judge hastily summoned all the attorneys to the bench for a sidebar conference to discuss my black band.

Now, before coming to court, I had made a point of asking the prosecutors whether I should do anything different with my clothes, my hair, my shoes, etc. I had also asked whether I should display my detective shield, and, specifically, whether I should remove my black mourning band.

"Don't change anything," one of the prosecutors had emphatically told me. "You look fine."

However, as I was to learn sometime later, when this same prosecutor was called up to the bench for the sidebar about my black mourning band, he promptly made me the fall guy. "I can't do anything with her, Your Honor," he told the judge. "She insisted on wearing it."

In front of the jury, the judge then asked me to remove the band, which I agreed to do. But in the eyes of the jurors, it must have looked as if I were being scolded for being a showboat or an obstructionist. I was made to appear arrogant, defiant, and difficult. The same DA who had told me not to alter my appearance was now complaining to the judge that I had been uncooperative. I felt as if I had been set up again. And by my own people!

When I did finally take the stand and give my direct testimony, I tried to give a blow-by-blow account of the events of January 21, 1986. When I got to the details of shootings, I broke down and wept.

The real trouble, however, began when the principal defense lawyer, Lawrence Hochheiser, started his cross-examination.

Unbeknownst to me, much of the police paperwork surrounding the investigation was a shambles. The DD-5 reports written by the detectives in the 104th Precinct were incomplete, inconsistent, and inaccurate. Some of them contradicted each other. One of them had curiously been split into two separate reports, with a mysterious gap between their page numberings. Other reports were grossly erroneous. One of the DD-5s described me as a young girl sitting in the middle of the street with a wounded cop who was my boyfriend. Another DD-5 described me as being married to a lieutenant in the 104th Precinct. Some of the carbon copies of the DD-5s did not match their originals, or the photocopies of the originals. Some of the DD-5s indicated that they had been signed by a single investigating officer but, on closer inspection, displayed what appeared to be two completely different signatures. (This last part may sound more sinister than it really was since, in a pinch, harried detectives routinely sign off for each other to speed the crushing flow of paperwork on their cases.)

When I was taken to Wyckoff Hospital, I had given the names of the three shooters to my old partner, John Gaspar; to my husband, Bob; to one of my friends from the Joint Terrorist Task Force; to two other detectives whose names I didn't even know. At Bellevue Hospital, I had given the names to still more detectives and investigators. And, during this trial, my husband, Bob, and my ex-partner John Gaspar would take the witness stand and testify that I had given them.

Unfortunately, the DD-5s did not reflect that I had supplied all three names. According to the DD-5s, all prepared by the detectives in the 104th Precinct, the only name I had supposedly provided as one of the shooters was Fritzi Giovanelli.

The prosecutors were well aware of these gaffes, but they had never informed me about them. When I took the witness stand, I was completely unaware of all the omissions and inconsistencies in the reports. And how could it have been otherwise? Even though I was a cop, I had been one of the victims in this case, not one of the detectives assigned to investigate it and write up a report on it. I was the one who had been answering the questions, not asking them. I was the subject of all these DD-5s, not their author.

Had the DAs been smarter and prepared me better, they would have gotten me to testify right off the bat that I had not written any of these DD-5 reports nor been given them to review. One thing they could certainly have asked was whether my signature appeared at the bottom of any of the report pages (it did not). And, by their questions, they could have made it abundantly clear to the jurors that I should not be held accountable for what was contained in those DD-5s—since I had never seen them in the first place.

Unfortunately, the DAs never did put these questions to me. What's more, I had no idea that the DD-5s would become a hot-button issue on cross-examination. But when defense attorney Hochheiser got me on the stand, he used all this slipshod paperwork to bludgeon me. The thrust of his questions was that the official Police Department reports—the DD-5s written up by the detectives from the 104th Precinct—did not corroborate my version of the events. I maintained that I had given the names of all three shooters to the police. But, pointing to the inconsistent and incomplete DD-5s, Hochheiser suggested that I had not. If I could be shown to be wrong on this point, he suggested, then I must be lying about everything that had happened that night. And that was precisely the portrait he set about painting for the jury. Detective Kathy Burke—the liar.

Sad to admit, I did not help myself in the way I answered his questions.

All of us have our character flaws. And I certainly have mine. I know that I often come across as hard-edged. I'm too analytical, too critical, too quick to find fault. I'm not diplomatic. I'm not soft enough. In fact, I'm not soft at all. People think I should be more of a lady. Hell, I'm no lady. Never was, never will be. What I am, is a cop. And, as a cop, I don't know how to be anything but nuts-and-bolts, black-and-white. I'm matter-of-fact, blunt—in a right-back-at-you, in-your-face, sure-as-hell manner. So much so that when I am challenged by another person, my response can sound as if I'm verbally counterpunching. Sometimes, I interrupt people in the middle of a sentence and finish their sentence for them. And, to a lot of people, that's a turnoff. It's not something I'm proud of. It is, alas, who I am. I wish I could change that aspect of my personality. But sometimes I need help.

When I took the witness stand that day, I needed help. A lot of help. I never got it.

When Hochheiser began to pummel me about the DD-5s, I felt as if my honesty and integrity were being assailed and besmirched, which triggered something deep inside me. Without even thinking about it, I counterattacked with full force. It's as if I must march straight into the fires of hell, trumpets blasting, drums pounding, and swords slashing, to defend myself. Dr. Symonds, the Police Department psychiatrist who had counseled me after the shootings, once warned me that my principles would end up killing me. Little did he realize that the setting for my demise would be the witness stand in a court of law.

With Hochheiser doing what good defense lawyers are paid to do— jousting and jabbing at me, trying to punch holes in my story—I became combative, antagonistic, and argumentative. I allowed myself to be drawn into a dogfight. The more he snapped at me, the more I snapped back. The more he zinged me, the more I wanted to zap him back, give him the smart answer, dismiss him with sarcasm, make him take a few hard lumps of his own. I became much too emphatic in my answers, saying things like "No, Mr. Hochheiser, I never said that" or "Yes, Mr. Hochheiser, I absolutely did this" or "Am I sure? Of course, I'm sure."

The more Hochheiser badgered me, the more I reverted instinctively to my undercover personality, the tough-talking, kick-ass, in-your-face broad I had played all those years on the streets. Because I felt myself under attack, I became rigidly insistent that each and every detail I was testifying to was 100 percent accurate—no, make that 200 percent—and always had been, damn it to hell. And I refused to give an inch.

In the end, it turned out to be a huge blunder.

For one thing, the defense was able to introduce into evidence all those shoddy, error-filled DD-5s, many of which appeared to contradict me. And because I had been so emphatic and cocksure in my initial responses about what I'd done, what I'd seen, and what I'd said—instead of saying something softer and more pliant like "Well, I may have said that" or "I might have done that"—I began to look like a liar.

The other problem was that I appeared to become two different people on the witness stand. A split personality. One minute, I sounded like a sympathetic and vulnerable female, weeping about being shot and seeing my partner murdered. The next minute, I hardened into super-duper cop as I matter-of-factly described emptying my gun at my assailants, getting up from the ground, walking directly into the pizzeria to notify 911, walking back to the crime scene, giving my weapon to another cop, and waiting patiently at my partner's side for help to arrive.

One instant, I was the victim. The next minute, I was the cop.

To the jurors, this transformation must have seemed too extreme to believe. I sounded like a walking contradiction. And the jurors did not like it.

When we broke for lunch, my friend from the Task Force, Tommy Bruno, shook his head. "They did ya, Kath," he said.

For some reason, my thoughts went back to that personality study that was done on me when I was at the FBI Academy in Quantico, Virginia. The one that indicated I could be too spontaneous with my opinions, too blunt, too black-and-white—and that it could piss people off. I wished now that I had paid closer attention to the study before I had taken the witness stand that morning.

Back on the stand after lunch, I tried to tone my act down. But it was too late. The damage had already been done.

My testimony, however, was not the only problem with this trial. Other witnesses were also caught off guard. On the stand, they bumbled and fumbled under cross-examination. Some key witnesses were never even called to testify.

When the defense presented its case, it took the unusual step of putting one of the defendants, Fritzi Giovanelli, on the stand.

Fritzi acknowledged that he had been outside the diner the night we got shot. But he insisted that he had been the intended victim of a stickup by two gunmen, not the perpetrator. When I came upon the scene and pulled my gun, Fritzi maintained, I had triggered a shoot-out between the robbers and the police.

Miraculously, Fritzi had managed to duck all the bullets, run away, and escape without being injured.

What a lucky fellow.

During the testimony of other witnesses, I sat and waited in the DA's office. But one day, I was told to take a hike and wait somewhere else.

The prosecutors told me my presence could adversely influence the testimony of other witnesses. The real reason, however, was that Anna Venditti, Tony's mother, had complained about me being inside the building while she and her family were waiting there, too. She still blamed me for her son's death. She was determined to keep me out of sight.

And it was a real shame. If the forces of organized crime had hoped to weaken us, they could not have dreamed up a more divisive and damaging scenario than the one that played out between Anna and me in the courthouse.

In many ways, Anna Venditti and I were birds of a feather. Both of us were strong, forceful, stubborn women, unwilling to accept defeat or mealymouthed excuses. Both of us were determined, at all costs, to get the answers to our questions about this tragic case. Had we been able to team up and join forces, there would have been no stopping us. As a team, we would have been unbeatable, a real juggernaut. But now that we were at odds, we were working at cross-purposes. As individuals, our questions packed no punch.

United, we might have stood. Divided, we could only fall.

Banished from the DA's office, I relocated to the Municipal Building across the street. There, peering out an upper-floor window, Tommy Bruno and I used a 200 mm lens from one of our surveillance cameras to keep an eye on all the comings and goings at the courthouse. What we saw made us extremely uneasy. One day, during the lunch break, one of the prosecutors walked out in animated conversation with one of the defense attorneys and one of the private investigators working for the three mob defendants. That kind of fraternization seemed to me just a little too comfy-cozy.

Even before the jury returned, I knew what the verdict would be. The behavior of the court officers was the tip-off.

Usually, when the verdict is about to be announced, the court officers will surround the table where the defendants are sitting. Anticipating that a guilty verdict might spur a defendant to become overemotional, or even violent, the court officers try to position themselves to nip any problems in the bud. But as we waited for the jury to return, most of the court officers moved away from the defendants' table.

Instead, they drifted toward the first row of the spectators' gallery. The person they maneuvered to surround was . . . me.

I turned to Tommy Bruno, who was sitting next to me, and murmured, "Tommy, I think we just lost the case."

Just then, the jurors came back in. I prayed to God that I was wrong, but in my gut, I had a very, very bad feeling about the way it was going to turn out. In my hands, I held a mass card I had been carrying with me wherever I went. On the card was a picture of my murdered partner, Tony Venditti. I held on to it tightly.

After fifty hours of deliberations over nine days, the jurors announced that, on most of the lesser charges, they had voted to acquit the three defendants. On the more serious charges against all three of murder, and one remaining count against Giovanelli for attempted murder, they were stymied. Deadlocked. A hung jury.

The judge declared a mistrial.

I was devastated.

On the way out of the courtroom, my legs gave way and I nearly collapsed. All the heartbreak, all the anger, all the pain and sadness I had managed to keep bottled up inside for so many months came surging to the surface. I became hysterical, sobbing like an infant. At one point, I nearly fainted. Tommy Bruno had to grab me under the arms to keep me from hitting the floor. Then, while the photographers pushed and shoved and crowded around to snap my picture for the next day's papers, he hustled me out of the courthouse.

I was still shaking and sobbing as we went back inside the DA's office next door. I wanted to get the hell away from this place as soon as I could, but I still needed to retrieve my pocketbook from the DA's waiting room. When I entered the room, I found myself face-to-face with Tony's parents.

Anna Venditti began to shriek hysterically, "She killed my son! She killed my son!" She started toward me.

Instead of intercepting Anna, the detectives in the hallway pounced on me. Grabbing me roughly, they dragged me out of the room. Anna was the one who had become hysterical, but they were treating me as if I were the person who needed to be held at bay.

I knew Anna was in terrible, terrible pain at this moment, and my heart went out to her and the rest of her family. In effect, the trial verdict had compounded her anguish and her loss. It had to be like seeing her son killed all over again.

But I was in pain, too. Yet, because I was the detective, I was not permitted to feel my pain. I still had to be supercop, thick-skinned, unflinching, in control, above it all. Unlike the others who were decimated and devastated by this terrible, terrible tragedy, now made ten times worse by what we all knew to be a complete miscarriage of justice, I was still not allowed to feel all that I felt. Unlike everyone else, I was still not permitted to be human.

Tommy led me quickly out a back staircase. Just as we reached the bottom, we unexpectedly crossed paths with one of the female members of the jury. Through my tears, I asked her, "How could you let these men walk free?"

She looked at me coolly. "Hey, you're a police officer. You get paid to die."

I couldn't believe it.

For a brief instant, I managed to fight back my hurt and my rage. "You know, ma'am," I said in a quivering voice, "my partner and I can give you our lives. But, no, you cannot buy them. Not for any amount of money."

After we left, some of the jurors lingered behind to talk to the press.

A few said they believed I had resorted to theatrical ploys by weeping on the witness stand and wearing a black mourning band on my detective shield. Some simply did not believe that mobsters would ever have shot two police officers in the first place. It just didn't jibe with their concept of conventional Mafia behavior.

The juror who was most vocal in denouncing me to the press and had apparently been the most vigorous in pushing for a full acquittal of all three defendants was a Transit Authority worker named Anthony Pirozzi. "I just could not believe the woman," Pirozzi told reporters. He was referring, of course, to Detective Kathy Burke, the state's star witness.

During the trial, Pirozzi had actually taken the unprecedented step of sending a letter to the judge urging him to release all three defendants on bail.

A month after the trial ended, the Queens district attorney disclosed that Pirozzi had leveled an earlier police brutality complaint against a

New York City detective. But Pirozzi had never disclosed this complaint to the court during jury selection in our case, when he was asked—under oath—if he had any pending matters before the police or the district attorney's office. The DA announced that it would investigate the matter.

Three months later, Pirozzi was indicted for perjury.

Not only had he failed to reveal his police brutality complaint, it turned out that Pirozzi himself was an associate of organized crime, and he hadn't bothered to tell the court about that little fact, either. One of Pirozzi's brothers-in-law had been convicted in a federal racketeering case that grew out of an undercover investigation of the Bonanno crime family. Another brother-in-law had been accused of stealing several hundred thousand dollars from the company that employed him. Pirozzi himself had testified as a witness at this brother-in-law's trial, just three weeks before our trial had begun, another fact he'd concealed.

As a result of these deliberate deceptions about his past, Pirozzi was later convicted and given a prison sentence.

And this man, Pirozzi, was the very same juror who had been permitted to sit in judgment of three known mob figures accused of killing one detective and trying to kill another. Who had sworn under oath that he had no connections to organized crime. Who had challenged the notion that mobsters would even shoot cops. Who had labeled my testimony unbelievable.

And who had argued so vehemently for a full acquittal of all three defendants.

I was hurt and bitter about the verdict.

Although I had been reluctant to give any press interviews, knowing that the case would go to trial a second time, I did ask one reporter from the *New York Post*, "Just who does the jury think shot me?"

Back home again, I obsessed about the prosecutors' slipshod investigation, their failure to adequately prep me, their sloppiness in the courtroom, their familiarity with key members of the mob's defense team. I also felt that the detectives in the 104th Precinct, as well as certain key higher-ups within the Police Department, had bungled the investigation. I wrote a letter to the police commissioner, detailing my complaints. He, in turn, sent the letter to the chief of the Organized Crime Control Bureau.

After a cursory investigation, the Police Department found that my complaints had no merit.

Meanwhile, throughout the Police Department, I was elevated to the rank of Public Enemy Number One. With our failure to convict the three defendants, and me taking the lion's share of the blame because of my flawed testimony on the stand, the attacks on me turned vicious. Through the grapevine, I learned that much of the animosity was being stoked by the Venditti family and, in particular, Tony's mother, Anna, who now blamed me not only for getting her son killed but for failing to put the killers behind bars.

I tried to keep my mind off things by busying myself with my kids, attending the regular monthly meetings of the Police Self-Support Group, and helping my attorney prepare for my federal lawsuit against Sergeant Burton and the Major Case Squad.

Up until now, my lawsuit had been kept under wraps. Then, right around the time of the verdict in the first trial, a front-page story popped up in the *New York Post*. The timing could not have been worse, and the news landed like a bombshell.

Knowing that their clients would face a retrial, the attorneys for the three mob suspects pounced on it like a big, meaty bone.

In my lawsuit, I claimed that I had suffered "severe mental distress" as well as "headaches, chronic anxiety, physical illness, and emotional distress" as the result of the harassment I had endured in the Major Case Squad. Citing these statements, the defense lawyers sought to eliminate me as a prosecution witness at the next trial. They asked for a hearing to assess whether I was mentally competent to testify. Then they demanded that the judge dismiss all the charges against their clients, arguing that they had never been told in advance about my mental and physical problems.

The judge told them to take a hike.

And ordered the second trial to proceed as scheduled.

Meanwhile, back at Police Headquarters, my old nemesis in the Major Case Squad, Sergeant Sam Burton, began running an office pool and taking bets on which day of the year I would have my nervous breakdown. A female detective who worked with him tipped me off about the sergeant's sadistic little sweepstakes.

When I heard about this, I just laughed. Then I told my friend:

"If I were you, I'd plunk my money down and take a piece of that action. Then you and I will have the biggest steak dinner he's ever seen. 'Cause, despite what he thinks, there's no way in hell I'm gonna have a breakdown."

CHAPTER TWENTY-THREE

One sunny June morning in 1987, not long after the end of the first trial, I sat outside on the steps of City Hall.

I sat in complete silence, upright and unmoving, barely breathing, every muscle taut with anticipation, my body frozen into position like a statue.

I sat remembering the past. And wondering about the future.

I sat waiting to hear my name called.

When the moment came, I would rise from my seat, move forward, remove my police cap, and bow my head. Then, as the police commissioner and all the department brass looked on, the mayor of New York City would gently loop an emerald green ribbon around my neck.

Affixed to the bottom of that green ribbon were twelve gleaming white stars, a solid gold bar, and an eight-pointed, star-shaped gold medal. Together, the ribbon, the bar, and the medal constituted the city's highest award for valor, the Medal of Honor.

On this particular Medal Day, many, many officers from all over the city would be recognized for their bravery. But only four had been chosen to receive the Medal of Honor:

A young patrolman who was mortally wounded in a shoot-out with a gunman in Far Rockaway, Queens.

Another patrolman who was shot by a mugging suspect in Central Park and left paralyzed for the rest of his life.

My slain partner, Tony Venditti.

And me.

Along with the other award recipients, I held myself rigid as the mayor, the police commissioner, all the department chiefs, and a galaxy of dignitaries took their places inside a flag-draped viewing stand positioned directly in front of City Hall. Next to me sat a police officer who had been shot in the head, but had somehow, incredibly, miraculously, managed to survive.

All of us were dressed in our crispest blue shirts, our smartest blue ties, blue uniforms, and blue police caps, our shiniest, spit-polished black shoes, and our purest, whitest gloves. As I looked down at my own carefully pressed and creased uniform, which had meant so much to me for the last two decades, I knew this would be one of the last times in my life I would ever wear it.

"Detail, tennnnn . . . shun!" barked a uniformed sergeant.

All of us rose to our feet. And stood at attention.

"Presennnnt . . . arms!"

Our white-gloved hands snapped sharply to the brims of our caps.

The police band and color guard marched toward the bunting-draped dais where the mayor and the other dignitaries sat. Together, we pledged allegiance to the flag. The band began to play the national anthem. In a deep, velvety baritone, a police officer sang the words.

One of the police chaplains rose to the podium to give the benediction. In the crowd, I spotted my family: Bob, Cathrine, Veronica. I also saw Tony's family. Their heads were bowed in prayer.

From the corner of my eye, I caught a glimpse of the other hero police officers with whom I now stood shoulder to shoulder. Some grimaced as they tried to keep their aching bodies erect. Many of us, myself included, were still recuperating from our battle wounds. Together, we made up a brigade of tattered and creaky heroes who would bear everlasting scars from our line-of-duty injuries.

How much we had all been through, I thought to myself. How much we had suffered and endured. Yet, how wonderfully brave and strong and noble we all looked at this moment, standing here in the bright sunshine in our freshly pressed dark blue uniforms and our gleaming white gloves.

And how strangely remote, for the first time in a long time, were the death and violence and mayhem we had all known so intimately and so brutally over our careers.

The chaplain finished his benediction.

"Detail, aaaaat . . . ease!"

We took our seats again.

Mayor Koch rose to give his opening remarks:

"The Medal of Honor is the New York Police Department's equivalent of the Congressional Medal of Honor. It is bestowed only rarely. The people who have earned this accolade are very rare, very special people....

"Anyone who isn't humbled in your presence is worse than a fool. And anyone who isn't proud of who you represent and what you do is less than human."

And then I heard the roll of names being called for the Medal of Honor:

Police Officer Scott Gadell.

Police Officer Steven McDonald.

Detective Anthony Venditti.

Detective Kathleen Burke.

The mayor spoke eloquently and compassionately about the other three medal recipients.

When he got to me, he said:

"Detective Kathleen Burke was willing to die if that is what she had to do in pursuit of her professional duty. But Kathleen lived, thank God, to tell the story."

CHAPTER TWENTY-FOUR

Unlike the prosecutors who I thought had bumbled and fumbled through the first trial, the two Queens prosecutors assigned to the second trial, Dan McCarthy and Dick Barbuto, were gems.

Knowing how badly I had been burned on the witness stand the first time around, they worked long and hard to prepare me for my testimony. Long before we ever went into court for the retrial, they sat me down. And they did something that had never been done before.

They listened to me.

Allowing me to talk freely, they let me vent my feelings about this case. My hurt. My anger. My fear. My suspicions that the investigation had been bungled by the detectives from the 104th Precinct and the first two prosecutors. As a result, they came to appreciate that, with regard to the shootings, I was not merely a cop. I was a victim. And while I might be the key witness to their case, I deserved some modicum of consideration as a victim.

The prosecutors tried to make me feel like an asset to their investigation. They let me sit with them as they sifted through all the evidence and prior testimony. Rather than keep me in the dark, they made me part of their team. They asked my opinions. They utilized my knowledge of the streets. They capitalized on my expertise as an investigator. They followed up when I produced some useful leads.

For example, during the questioning of one of the detectives from the 104th Precinct, I jumped in and asked the detective flat out if I had, in fact, given him the names of all three shooters.

"Yes," he admitted. "You did."

"So why didn't you put all three names in the DD-5s?"

"Because I was ordered not to by the lieutenant."

Now there was a real bombshell.

When the two new DAs followed up with the lieutenant in question, he acknowledged that, yes, he had instructed his detective not to include all three names in his report. Fearful of possible mistakes in the labeling of the surveillance photos I had kept with me, the lieutenant had taken it upon himself to alter my verbal identifications. So, rather than go to the trouble to sort out the photo captions, he had simply had one of his men alter my statement—a careless and costly decision that ended up undermining my testimony on the witness stand.

Knowing that my flawed testimony from the first trial could be used to impeach me when I took the stand in the second, the prosecutors prepared me by staging mock cross-examinations in their office. During these sessions, they would fire one question after another at me, bombarding me with my earlier inconsistencies and contradictions. Knowing that my federal discrimination lawsuit would also provide potentially damaging ammunition for the defense, especially the parts about my mental and emotional distress, they hammered me with questions about that as well. Sometimes during these mock cross-examinations, they would deliberately taunt, bait, or otherwise try to provoke me. Sometimes they would speed up the pace of their interrogation, rapid-firing their questions at me like poison darts before I even had a chance to answer them. At one point, they brought in a third assistant DA to join in the prosecutorial gang bang. All in all, the whole experience was like witness boot camp, a brutal, torturous ordeal designed to toughen me up for the real thing.

Rather than becoming adamant and combative about my answers, the prosecutors urged me to own up to my inconsistencies or memory lapses. That way, the defense would not be in a position to later put another witness on the stand who might contradict me. They advised me to soften my characterizations, allowing myself some leeway. For example, if I was not clear on some point, they said I should give qualified answers, like "Gee, I don't remember saying that, but I might have" or "I think I told him the names, but I'm not certain."

They also encouraged me to soften my physical appearance.

Wear a nice suit with a high-collared blouse, they advised.

The second trial in Queens Supreme Court began in January 1988.

Thanks to the expert prepping I'd received from prosecutors McCarthy and Barbuto, I kept my cool. On direct examination, I did break down and start to sob when I got to the part about the shootings. But on cross-examination, when defense attorney Hochheiser again attempted to goad and confuse me, once again relying upon the shoddy paperwork from the 104th Precinct to discredit me, I refused to take the bait. I remained calm. Spoke in a soft voice. And was always polite in my responses, even when I knew that the questions were absurd, outrageous, and deliberately provocative.

Afterward, the prosecutors told me I had been an excellent witness. Hochheiser, frustrated by his inability to rile me, conceded to a *New York Times* reporter that this time around I seemed to be a different person on the stand.

In addition to my testimony, Barbuto and McCarthy introduced several new witnesses to buttress their case, which seemed to be going quite well, indeed.

And then somebody dropped the atomic bomb.

At the eleventh hour, just as Barbuto was about to sum up for the prosecution, the defense lawyers asked to put a key prosecution witness back on the stand. The witness had approached them several days earlier, they announced, asking to provide new and vital information. The defense lawyers had even taped their conversation with him and brought the tape with them into court.

That witness was Frank Simone, the unemployed cook who had testified that he had actually seen Carmine Gualtiere shoot Tony. Repeating his testimony from the first trial, Simone had told the jurors in the second trial, "I'll never forget that face."

Now, however, Frank Simone wanted to recant his testimony.

Returning to the stand, Simone said he had been pressured by the police to identify two of the defendants as the men who shot us. After twice identifying Carmine Gualtiere as the man who had pumped two bullets into Tony's head while he was lying on the ground, Simone now said that Gualtiere had not shot Tony. In fact, Simone claimed that Gualtiere was not even at the scene. Simone said the prosecutors had coached him on which men to identify, showing him pictures of the defendants, then warning him not to tell anybody he had been shown these pictures. He also said he had been promised most of a $10,000 reward if the three defendants ended up being convicted.

Now, Simone had always been a risky proposition as a prosecution witness. Unemployed, often in debt, a heavy drinker, and serious cocaine user, he was not exactly a solid citizen. He occasionally had come into the DA's office, reeking of liquor, to demand that the prosecutors give him money in exchange for his cooperation, which they refused to do. At times, he complained that he had become a pariah in his own family because so many of his relatives were organized-crime associates who felt that he was being a rat by testifying against the mob. He even claimed to have suffered a broken leg in a dispute with a bunch of kids and suggested that the attack was carried out in retaliation for his prior testimony against the three mob defendants. More recently, he feared that he was being followed by would-be assailants.

Yet, Simone had actually flagged down a police car, gotten into that car along with an officer, and pointed out the fleeing Fritzi Giovanelli as one of the men who had gunned us down. And Simone had, on four separate occasions, identified Carmine Gualtiere as the shooter who had pumped two bullets into Tony's head—at a police lineup, before a grand jury, and at two different trials, including the one that was now under way.

Now, however, Simone was saying that he had lied about all of this. That he had been coerced. That he had seen nothing.

Had he been intimidated by the mob into recanting his testimony? the prosecution demanded to know. Had he been offered money?

Simone denied having been either threatened or bribed.

Whether Frank Simone's testimony would have swayed the jurors one way or the other was open to speculation. Many observers in the courtroom perceived Simone as a "dirtball," a sleazy, scheming character whose testimony had to be carefully measured against that of other, more reliable witnesses. But one thing was indisputably clear about his startling, eleventh hour turnabout on the witness stand:

If the mob wanted to reach you, it could. Regardless of whether you were a witness . . . or a juror.

It was no secret that Queens County was the bedroom to the Mafia, a borough so densely populated with wiseguys, their families, and their associates that everybody and his uncle seemed to have a relative who had done time, was about to do time, or was connected. In any criminal proceeding against the mob in Queens, the possibility of retaliation was always an unspoken but real threat. And that fact of life, driven home so dramatically by Simone's eleventh hour flip-flop on the witness stand, could not have been lost on the twelve men and women who now sat in the jury box, staring at the three mob defendants accused of cold-bloodedly shooting two cops. After all, each of these twelve jurors lived in Queens, too. And surely, each of these twelve had to be seriously wondering—if the mob had gotten to Frank Simone, how long will it be before they get to me?

So it was, in the wake of Simone's recantation, that the jurors in this second trial acquitted Carmine Gualtiere in Tony's murder. And declared themselves hopelessly deadlocked on the charges against Fritzi Giovanelli and Steven Maltese.

Another defeat. Another hung jury. Once again, the judge declared a mistrial.

When the jury returned its verdict, Anna Venditti went to pieces. Enraged by this second consecutive failure to mete out justice for her son's murder, she leaped to her feet and spat at Fritzi Giovanelli. *"Figlio di puttana!"* she bellowed. "Son of a whore!"

Turning beet red, the then fifty-six-year-old Giovanelli rose from his seat at the defense table and shouted back, "She called my mother a whore! . . . She's a saint!"

One of the defense attorneys threw a headlock on Giovanelli to force him back down into his chair, then plastered his hand over the defendant's mouth. The judge dashed down from the bench. In an effort to calm the aggrieved Giovanelli, he began stroking the defendant's hand. The gesture was so inappropriate that it flabbergasted everyone in the courtroom.

Meanwhile, Patti Venditti, Tony's widow, stepped to the railing that separated her from defendant Steven Maltese and in a loud, quavering voice asked, "Mr. Maltese, why did you do it? Why did you kill him?"

Maltese remained mute.

Sitting next to him, Fritzi Giovanelli angrily grumbled, "I don't judge nobody."

Once the court officers managed to quiet things down, the judge reinstated bail for Fritzi, a move that allowed him to walk out of the courtroom. Steven Maltese was already out on bail.

The third defendant, chubby, gum-cracking Carmine Gualtiere, was now a free man.

Sometime after the second trial ended, Frank Simone was spotted driving around town in a shiny new Corvette.

Then, in October of 1989, a corpse was found at an intersection next to a Bronx park, near a notorious dumping ground for mob victims. The victim had been shot four times—in the chest, back, head, and mouth. Next to the body was a pile of dead fish, a traditional mob warning that anyone who rats out the mob will wind up in a similar condition.

And just about everyone was of the opinion that the dead man on the sidewalk, Frank Simone, had been whacked Mafia-style.

There was never any doubt that the case against Fritzi Giovanelli, Steven Maltese, and Carmine Gualtiere would eventually wind up in federal court.

Even before they'd shot Tony and me, these men had been the targets of an extensive federal-city investigation into their far-flung gambling and racketeering activities. As the result of all the wiretaps and surveillance conducted by the Joint Organized Crime Task Force, the unit in which Tony and I had been working, prosecutors had amassed mountains of compelling evidence against them. And the U.S. Justice Department had no intention of letting that evidence go to waste.

In the spring of 1989, the three defendants were brought to trial yet again, in U.S. district court in Manhattan. This time around, they were charged under a federal statute called the Racketeer Influenced and Corrupt Organizations Act—RICO, for short. Specifically, they were accused of violating RICO by engaging in gambling, extortion, loan-sharking, and tax fraud. In engaging in these lucrative activities, they were further accused of murdering Tony and shooting me.

This third trial, in federal court, would take almost eleven weeks. Nearly 130 witnesses would be called to the stand, a hundred undercover tape recordings would be brought to light, and a hundred surveillance photos would be introduced into evidence.

Once again, I was notified that I would be called to testify. This time around, I was prepped for my testimony by the two federal prosecutors, Assistant U.S. Attorneys Gil Childers and Adam Hoffinger. Both men had been handpicked for this case by then U.S. attorney for the Southern District, Rudolph Giuliani.

Thanks to the expert prepping I received from Childers and Hoffinger, I performed well on the witness stand, telling my story clearly, calmly, and convincingly. On cross-examination by my now familiar nemesis, defense attorney Lawrence Hochheiser, I did not get rattled.

A number of factors distinguished this third trial from the first two.

First of all, it was held in federal court in Manhattan, rather than state court in Queens. This meant that the jurors were drawn from a much larger, wider, and more anonymous jury pool than just Queens County, the nesting ground for so many mobsters. So the all-pervasive fear factor, so clearly and insidiously at work on both the jurors and the witnesses in the first two trials, was somewhat muted.

Second, because this was a federal RICO prosecution, I was no longer the centerpiece for the entire case. I was simply one of many witnesses, not the star of the show. While I did testify about the shootings, other members of the Joint NYPD–FBI Organized Crime Task Force also testified, and they gave tremendously damaging evidence about the other crimes the defendants had committed as part of their gambling and racketeering conspiracy. Meanwhile, the prosecution was able to buttress all their testimony with fifteen hundred hours of taped conversations from wiretaps on Fritzi Giovanelli's phones, as well as a hundred undercover surveillance photos of Fritzi and his mob cronies.

Third, new and highly damaging testimony was introduced into evidence for the first time. It came from the mouth of a shady New York City detective named Hank Campo.

Campo was one of the many detectives who had shown up at the Castillo Diner immediately after the shootings. Campo was also married to Steven Maltese's sister. And his brother, Anthony Campo, also a New York City detective, was married to another sister of Maltese's.

Campo's testimony made jaws drop. Among other things, he testified that Steven Maltese had repeatedly asked to be tipped in advance to police raids or other activities that might harm the mob's gambling operations. Handing Campo slips of paper bearing the license plate numbers from cars the mob believed were police surveillance vehicles, Maltese had asked Campo to run the plates through the Police Department's computers.

And sure enough, one of the numbers Campo was given, according to his testimony, was the license plate on our brown, 1977 Lincoln surveillance car.

Campo insisted he had rebuffed all of Maltese's requests. He also claimed he had refused to do computer checks on any license plate numbers, including the plate on our surveillance car.

In the wake of the shootings, Campo testified, he had tried to alert a detective from the 104th Precinct about the inappropriate approaches made to him by his mobbed-up brother-in-law. But, he said, the 104th Precinct detective blew him off.

"I don't wanna know about it," this detective supposedly told Campo.

The detective who had turned a deaf ear to Campo was none other than Garner, the booze-guzzling cop I had kicked out of my house for trying to get me to change my story about who had actually shot me.

* * *

In his summation, Assistant U.S. Attorney Gil Childers made an eloquent and compelling argument to the jury.

"Ladies and gentlemen," he said as he looked sternly at the three defendants, "let me ask you to do this. Ask yourselves not how Kathy Burke could remember those faces. Ask yourself how she could possibly ever forget them. Those faces will stay in her mind for the rest of her life."

On July 30, 1989, after five days of deliberations, the jury convicted all three defendants of murdering Tony, attempting to murder me, and committing numerous violations of the federal RICO statute by virtue of their gambling and racketeering enterprise. It was a slam dunk for the good guys.

With the verdicts, all of us finally felt as if a big black cloud had lifted. After eluding state prosecutors in the two previous trials, the defendants would finally have to face the music and answer for their crimes. We congratulated the two prosecutors for the masterful job they had done. Patti Venditti thanked the jury. Anna Venditti was subdued, but relieved. When I was interviewed by the reporters, I said, "Tony Venditti can finally rest in peace."

In November, Fritzi Giovanelli, Steven Maltese, and Carmine Gualtiere were each sentenced by federal judge Constance Baker Motley. The prosecutors had requested that the judge stack all the RICO counts on top of each other and sentence the defendants consecutively, to forty years apiece. Instead, she chose to give them concurrent sentences of twenty years each. The judge said she would recommend no parole.

All things considered, the sentence was stiff. And while none of us felt like popping champagne corks, we all believed that justice had finally been served.

But, much like the first two trials, this trial, too, would have its last-minute surprises.

In the summer of 1991, the U.S. Court of Appeals vacated two of the racketeering acts on which the defendants had been found guilty—on the grounds that the trial judge in the federal case had improperly banned the defense attorneys from referring to the prior trials as "prior trials" and restricted them to saying "prior proceedings." The two acts the court deleted from the conviction were the murder of Tony and the attempted murder of me.

By removing the two most serious acts from the list of charges against the defendants, the appeals court effectively gutted the federal jury's verdict.

The appeals court ordered Judge Motley to resentence the three defendants.

The U.S. attorney's office argued vigorously for the judge to maintain the twenty-year federal prison sentences she had originally handed down. If she still thought the defendants were guilty of murder and attempted murder, the prosecutors reasoned, then she ought to throw the book at them again. And indeed, under the statutes, she could have kept them behind bars for the full twenty years.

Instead, the judge gave Fritzi Giovanelli ten years, Steven Maltese seven years, and Carmine Gualtiere five years. With parole, they would be out even sooner.

Demoralized, the prosecutors conceded it was only fitting that the appeals court had handed down its disappointing ruling on September 13, 1991—a Friday the thirteenth.

CHAPTER TWENTY-FIVE

After the shootings, it was pretty clear to everyone that I could not return to full duty in the Police Department.

As a result of my injuries, my left arm and fingers were numb. I couldn't run. I frequently stumbled or fell while walking, had constant pain in my back and under my breast line, and was always short of breath. Clearly, I would never be able perform all the responsibilities of an able-bodied cop.

For two and a half years after the shootings, I did not go back to work at all. Then in 1988, after the second state trial had ended, I did return to the department. But on limited duty.

I was assigned to do clerical work in a new unit that had been set up to track drug offenders. This turned out to be one of the best experiences of my career. The lieutenant in charge was a gentleman, and we succeeded in bringing some top-notch investigators over from the Organized Crime Control Bureau. Many of the other cops in the unit were much younger than me, just kids really. They often came to me for advice. Given my seniority on the job and my rank, detective second grade, they took to calling me Mom. I loved it.

For the first time, I began to feel as if I had finally put the pieces of my career back together. I was working in a place where I was liked and respected. The new unit operated with a sense of professionalism and camaraderie. I was happy, busy, and productive. Notwithstanding my federal lawsuit alleging sexual discrimination, which was still pending, and the reputation I had gained as a result of the shootings, I once again felt a part of the brotherhood of cops.

Outside the department, I became active in the Fraternal Order of Police. I organized a local lodge, while helping to administer scholarship programs for the children of other cops. The president of our state order, a New York City cop named Bob Lucente, had been one of my most loyal and steadfast supporters. In 1988, I was also elected president of the International Association of Women Police, which has three thousand law-enforcement members worldwide. It was a tremendous honor.

However, in the overall scheme of things, I knew that my time as a New York City cop was running out. The Police Department had already begun to push me out of the job, initiating what is known as a police commissioner's survey.

Rather than fight it, I decided it was probably wise for me to mentally prepare for my retirement.

Since I had sustained a line-of-duty injury, I was eligible to retire on a disability pension. This pension would be tax-free, equivalent to three-quarters of my final year's pay. But to qualify for that pension, I would have to appear before a Police Department medical board, which would review my medical history and decide whether I was, in fact, disabled. The board would then have to certify my disability before I could take things to the next level and apply for my tax-free pension.

The board consisted of three doctors, and they conducted their examinations at the Police Department's Health Services Division in Queens. The first time I went before these doctors, I was roundly humiliated. One of the physicians, whom I'll call Dr. Shatz, was a gruff, dyspeptic man of about seventy. I told him that I was experiencing numbness, stabbing chest pains, labored breathing, and difficulties with my balance.

As he examined my gunshot wounds, he screwed up his face and snorted, "You sure your pain is not in your mind?"

I made it clear I didn't like the way this interrogation was going. At that point, the other two doctors on the board came in to examine me. One of them, a former detective, tried to convince me that he was on my side. "Look," he said, "I know what you're going through. I was in a few shootings myself when I was on the job, you know."

"Oh, yeah?" I said. "Where'd you get shot?"

He cleared his throat. "Well, uh, I didn't, actually. I was the shooter."

I told him, "Then you have absolutely no idea what I'm going through, no idea at all, do you?"

And I said to the others, "I'm not here because I'm crazy. I'm here because I have pain in my chest."

Ultimately, the medical board rejected my request for a determination of permanent disability. Instead, it sent my paperwork back to the city's pension board. The pension board, which included representatives from the city's various police unions, kicked it right back to the medical board, which, in turn, ordered me to go for more tests. This dance went on for four years. Six times I appeared before the medical board. And six times Dr. Shatz sent me for more tests, the results of which he routinely rejected.

What made me especially angry about the whole business was that I knew I was not the only retiring police officer being subjected to this kind of humiliating and dehumanizing treatment. Cop after cop would go before this same medical board, only to be doubted, demeaned, insulted, and subjected to painful, humiliating, and pointless tests that never seemed to end and never seemed to be accepted. Hero cops who had taken bullets in the line of duty or sustained serious, career-ending injuries were being treated no better than cattle. One woman, shot twice, had been forced to appear before the board thirteen times before finally being approved for disability. Other cops had been compelled to hire attorneys to do battle with the board. Meanwhile, high-ranking chiefs and inspectors who went before the board seeking three-quarters disability pensions for their "heart conditions" would be in and out the door in a single day. Never doubted, never questioned, never asked to go for additional tests. All they needed to do was present the doctors with one EKG chart or one bullshit X-ray and, presto, they were home free.

The perks of power, the spoils of mutual butt-scratching.

At one point, I went to see Dr. Symonds, the kindly psychiatrist who had been counseling me in the aftermath of the shootings and had indicated to me that the Police Department would never let me go back to investigating cases.

"Kathy," he asked me, "have you applied to the department for a psychological disability?"

My head snapped around. "Absolutely not. Why do you ask?"

"Because I've been approached to sign off on it if you should."

And then it hit me.

All this inexplicable stalling by the medical board. All the silly tests. All the rejected results. All the wasted time and money spent. All the runarounds and seeming pointlessness of the process. In truth, it had not been pointless at all. It had all been part of a deliberate plan.

They wanted me to leave the department, all right. But not on my terms. On their terms. Not on a line-of-duty disability. But on a psychological disability.

Because if I agreed to go out on a psychological disability, it would provide the department with the perfect legal defense to rebut my lawsuit. If I went out on a psychological disability, the city could photocopy my retirement papers and use them to debunk my allegations of sexual discrimination by Sergeant Burton and the other bosses in the Major Case Squad. By retiring on a psychological disability, I would be handing the city proof that none of this discrimination or harassment had ever occurred. That it had all been in my head. And that I was nuts.

Well, I was having none of it.

After the sixth go-around with the medical board, Dr. Shatz and his colleagues had once again bounced my case back to the city's pension board. And the pension board, still believing I was disabled and should be retired, continued this endless volley by sending it right back again to the medical board. Once again, for the seventh time, I was told to appear before the medical board at the department's Health Services Division offices. But this time, no specific tests were ordered before I came for my appointment.

When I showed up, Dr. Shatz wouldn't even let me into his office. Spotting me in the waiting room, he stepped outside and began yelling at me. In front of all the other injured cops who were waiting to be examined, he went out of his way to make my personal and private business before him a matter of public interest. And ridicule.

"What are you coming in here for, Detective!" he shouted. "You don't have any new tests scheduled. I'm sick and tired of dealing with you. Just what the hell are you trying to pull here?"

That did it.

Rising from my seat, I walked right up to him. Nose to nose. And I told him:

"Listen, you fucking son of a bitch, who do you think you're yelling at?" But I was just getting warmed up. "You sent me for all these tests knowing you wouldn't accept the results? Well, lemme tell you something, mister, if somebody's gonna be under the microscope, from now on it's gonna be you. 'Cause I wanna find out how much kickback you're getting. Come on, Doc, whose payroll are you on anyway? Tell me. And, while you're at it, why don't you share that bit of information with all the other injured cops in this room who you're trying to fuck over."

I continued shouting at the doctor until some guy darted out from another office. He stepped between the doctor and me. "Officer," he scolded, "you're out of control here. What's going on?"

"Who the fuck are you?" I screamed at him.

"I'm the sergeant here. And if you keep this up, I'm gonna write you up."

"Well," I replied, "if you're the sergeant, then you're in big trouble, aren't you, since you don't happen to be wearing your shield. So you better put it on, Sergeant. Because if you're not ready to fight with the alligator, you better get out of the water!"

When I left Health Services that day, I was convinced the sergeant would write me up with a formal complaint, charging me with insubordination. But almost immediately afterward, I got phone calls assuring me that all of the police unions had gotten wind of my little brouhaha. And would back me to the hilt if formal charges were lodged against me.

In the meantime, I sat down and wrote a letter to the chief surgeon of the Police Department, demanding that an entirely new medical board be convened to review my case. The chief surgeon called to say that this could simply not be done. So I told the chief surgeon that I intended to go back to work on full duty, as a detective in the Narcotics Division. The chief surgeon, well aware of my medical condition, said this was out of the question. Everybody knew I was not fit to work full duty.

"Tell that to the medical board," I said, adding that I had already made all the arrangements. A friend who was the commanding officer of a narcotics squad had agreed to take me into his team.

Soon after, I received another call from the chief surgeon. A new medical board had been convened to review my case. Three brand-new doctors. I made an appointment immediately.

When I met with the new doctors, they were civil, professional, and polite. Nor did they ever insinuate that I was a shirker, a malingerer, or a con artist looking to get over on the system. They simply examined me, reviewed my test results, and asked me straightforward questions. Within a matter of weeks, my disability request was approved.

And I was able to begin planning for my retirement.

CHAPTER TWENTY-SIX

Long after they experience a trauma, the victims often feel a need to reshape their lives.

Some people become hermits. They go into self-imposed isolation, building walls between themselves and their spouses, their families, their friends, their coworkers, and the rest of the world. Others engage in long, solitary journeys, adulterous flings, thrill-seeking adventures, or dangerous, death-defying stunts. Still others go on wild spending sprees. In many of these instances, they are struggling to cleanse themselves of their painful past. By ending prior relationships, changing the way they look, reinventing their lives, and breaking away from old, familiar routines, they believe they will have the chance to heal.

I, too, found the need to separate from my past.

For me, the overriding need was personal freedom. With the shootings and the trials that followed them, I had felt violated. My private space had been invaded, my professional reputation sullied, my entire life trampled. Neither my body nor my mind had been left unscarred. Physically, I had been poked, prodded, probed, scoped, and cut. Emotionally, I had been questioned, analyzed, second-guessed, cross-examined, and dissected. After a while, I felt like a bug in a jar. Bit by bit, pieces of me had been ripped away, never to be restored. Yet I wanted those pieces back. I wanted to be whole again, my own person, not merely the person that everyone else said I could or ought to be.

To be my own person, I felt I needed to be independent. Totally on my own. Operating solo. Not responsible to any person other than myself (and my girls, of course). A big part of me simply did not want to have to worry about whether the meal was on time, the laundry was done, or I had permission to go someplace I wanted to go. Unattached, I knew I could simply take off on a whim, shoot for the horizon, follow my dream, do my thing. Unattached, I might be able to put myself back together, reassembling all those lost pieces. Unattached, I could be free to be me.

So it was that I ended my marriage.

Certainly our relationship had not been helped by the strain from the shootings, all the finger-pointing and the recriminations, the trials and the traumas, which left such an indelible mark on each of us. Perhaps it was the glare of endless publicity, which had become so invasive and corrosive in our lives. Perhaps it was our common desire to escape the limelight. Being together as a police couple—and a controversial police couple, at that—had made us even more high-profile in the media. Perhaps being apart might bring each of us some small measure of the peace and privacy we both longed for.

Then again, it could simply have been the job itself. Most cop marriages are risky propositions at best. And that's just when one of the spouses is a police officer. Psychological studies have shown that 60 to 75 percent of all marriages involving police officers end in divorce. The reasons for these breakups are many—the long and unpredictable hours, the partying, the stresses and the traumas, the inability to talk with one's spouse about those stresses and traumas, etc. But here was a marriage in which both spouses were cops. Double the pleasure, double the pitfalls.

Both of us had been ferociously dedicated to our police careers. Both of us had been married to our jobs. At the same time, our work schedules were often wildly at odds with each other. One of us would usually be walking in the door after finishing a tour of duty just as the other one was walking out to start one. On those rare occasions when we would find ourselves at home at the same time, it was an unspoken rule that we wouldn't talk shop. We didn't want "the job" to invade our sanctuary.

Ultimately, however, our moratorium on shop talk may have done more harm than good, eroding some of the intimacy between us as a couple, creating a short-circuit in our connection. Slowly but surely, we became strangers who happened to be living under the same roof. We began to drift further and further apart. In the end, we simply fell out of love. In 1991, we separated.

While I wanted freedom from the marriage, I, in no way, wanted freedom from my children. At the time of our separation, Cathrine was twelve and Veronica ten, and they continued to be my number one priority. The girls were terribly saddened by our decision not to live together as one family, but, in time, they came to accept that their parents needed to be apart. While they would continue to live with me in Astoria, Bob and I agreed to share custody. Over the years to come, we knew we could remain friends and that the girls would be in both our lives.

After our breakup, I did what I had always done whenever I'd broken up with a guy who had been a part of my life.

I went out, got myself a haircut, and bought a brand-new hat.

For a long time after my marriage fell apart, I had no interest whatsoever in meeting new men. Just having friends was the only thing that really mattered.

One of the people who became a friend was Sergeant Tom Fox, who worked out of the same office as the Drug Offender Tracking Unit to which I had most recently been assigned.

Every day, Tom used to buy a big hero sandwich for lunch, then give me half. Sometimes he would need to drive over to the Navy Yard in Brooklyn to pick up equipment for his tours with the U.S. Naval Reserve. "Hey, Burke," he'd say to me, "you're not doing anything. Come on along, keep me company." And I would happily tag along.

On the drives, we'd chat about our lives, our families, our experiences on the job. I had worked Narcotics. Tom had been with the Warrant Squad. As we swapped war stories, I began to feel as if I were partnering up all over again.

One day, I had a big blowout in the office with the lieutenant over some minor clerical matter. Shouting over to Tom, the lieutenant said, "Take her outta here. Go get her lunch."

Tom grabbed me by the elbow. "C'mon, Burke. Let's go."

We drove to a downtown pub called Jeremy's, tucked inside an old warehouse close by the water. Beer, fried shrimp, french fries, nachos, sawdust on the floor, still plenty of Old New York atmosphere, but seriously in peril of being usurped and ruined by the Wall Street yuppies. Dozens of severed neckties dangled from the ceiling, vestiges of Jeremy's long-standing house rule that if you were inside the bar after 6 p.m. and you still had your necktie on, the other patrons had a right to cut that tie off you (the place kept a giant pair of scissors behind the bar for just this purpose) and tack it up as a memento of your pathetic self-importance and stuffiness.

As we settled in at a table, I pointed up at one particular clump of neckties. In the middle of the clump was something that did not look like a necktie at all. "See that?" I asked Tom.

"Yeah," he said, squinting to get a better look. "What the hell is it?"

"My bra."

"What!"

I told him the story.

When I had first arrived in the Joint Organized Crime Task Force, some of the detectives had thrown a going-away party for one of the FBI agents who was about to be transferred back to Washington. Since the rule was that nobody could leave these "rackets" until the pile of used paper beer cups from the revelers reached clear up to the ceiling, everyone that night got completely shit-faced. Noticing that the guest of honor was not wearing a tie, but was wearing an Izod shirt, with its snooty alligator emblem, the revelers wanted to cut the alligator right off his chest.

But the indignant FBI agent had fired back, "Hey, if you're gonna take the alligator off of me, then what are you gonna take offa her?"

All eyes then turned to me. And pretty soon a chorus of drunken cops and FBI agents began chanting, "Her bra! Her bra! Her bra!"

Well, no way I was gonna let this bunch start pawing me for that trophy, so I decided that the best defense was a little offense. "Look," I told the others, "if he gives up his alligator, I'll give you my bra."

With that, three Task Force members jumped the FBI guy and sliced off his Izod alligator.

Grinning in the face of defeat, I had reached behind under my blouse, unhooked my bra—and pulled it out through my sleeve. A roar of approval went up from the drunken crowd. Somebody snipped my bra in two. One-half was furtively and maliciously tucked in the jacket pocket of the now thoroughly soused and totally unsuspecting FBI agent, who would have to explain it all in the morning to his poor wife. The other half was pinned to the ceiling, in the company of all those severed ties.

When I told the story to Tom, he laughed. This was hardly the businesslike image I presented each day in the Drug Offender Tracking Unit, where I would regularly show up for work in a tailored suit and heels. But Tom didn't seem at all put off by my boisterous and unconventional past. In fact, on one occasion, when another sergeant in our office started to bad-mouth me because of the shootings, Tom jumped to my defense, verbally lacing into the sergeant on my behalf.

Why he defended me was a mystery. At this point in my career, I was still a highly controversial figure in the Police Department. Yet, Tom was willing, even eager, to be my friend. And, for the longest time, I couldn't figure it out.

Tom and I continued to break bread regularly. One day at lunch, I blurted out with my customary in-your-face bluntness, "Hey, what's going on here, Fox? What's with you? Why are you being my friend? I'm Kathy Burke. *The* Kathy Burke. Remember? I don't get it."

And that's when Tom let me in on his little secret:

Many years earlier, he had been involved in a controversial shooting of his own.

While doing some off-duty carpentry in Brooklyn, Tom and his partner spotted three kids trying to steal their van. They ran out of the building to confront the thieves. Suddenly, one kid pulled a gun and started shooting at them. Tom and his partner returned fire. Tom's partner was wounded. The kid, who was seventeen, was killed.

At one point, Tom and his partner had actually seen the shooter toss his gun away. But in the aftermath of all the gunplay, that weapon had mysteriously disappeared from the scene.

Soon after, witnesses came forward and declared that the kid had not fired any shots at the cops. In fact, they maintained, he had not even been armed. There was no gun at all, they insisted. Others began suggesting that the shooting was a case of police brutality and cold-blooded murder. Even though the seventeen-year-old victim had a long criminal record—so long that the police commissioner dubbed him "a one-man crime wave"—it was Tom and his partner who came under the most intense, and often critical, scrutiny. One of the city's best-known newspaper columnists seized upon the shooting and suggested that the police were either unable—or unwilling—to explain why the seventeen-year-old had been killed. The public clamor to punish the two cops grew louder and louder. A real bloodlust permeated the atmosphere.

Down the line, the gun used by the seventeen-year-old was recovered—from one of his pals who had swiped it from the crime scene. A grand jury completely exonerated Tom and his partner. The shooting was ruled justifiable self-defense. But long after the matter was laid to rest, the pain from all the accusations and the allegations continued to linger.

Like me, Tom knew firsthand what it felt like to be doubted and second-guessed when you knew you were telling the truth.

As the day of my retirement neared, I got a surprise visit from my lawyer. I was sitting at my desk in Police Headquarters when she came up to give me the news.

"They want to settle," she told me. "The city wants to settle your lawsuit against the Major Case Squad."

"What are they offering?" I demanded.

Knowing that my retirement was imminent, the city had offered to pay my attorney's $85,000 fee and quietly promote me to detective first grade, the highest detective rank in the Police Department. Since I would soon depart from the job, this eleventh hour promotion would boost my pension by $5,000 a year.

But I was suspicious about the proposed settlement terms. Just where would the $85,000 come from? I wanted to know. Would it come from the city's coffers? Or would it come out of the pocket of Sergeant Burton?

My attorney made a call and learned that none of the $85,000 would come from Sergeant Burton. The city was indemnifying him.

I was ready to gag.

After all this time, all the pain and heartache, Sergeant Burton would be allowed to wriggle off the hook scot-free, with no real punishment or public censure. Although my lawsuit had originally asked for $2 million in damages to compensate me for lost wages, lost overtime, and lost career opportunities, the truth was that my lawsuit was never really about money. It was about principle. It was about showing this sergeant that he was wrong, damn it.

I made a counteroffer:

Ten thousand dollars for me to cover my lost wages and overtime. Full payment of my attorney's fees. And, although I had never sought or asked for a promotion, I would accept the promotion to detective first grade the city had offered. Provided it was a public one. Not something quietly slipped through in the middle of the night, on a piece of paper that nobody would ever see. I wanted to be in my uniform when I got my promotion. I wanted to receive my promotion in the auditorium at One Police Plaza, along with all the other cops being promoted. With the police commissioner and the other chiefs present. In front of my family. In front of my peers. In front of an audience. In front of the news media. In short, I wanted a promotion just like every other detective got.

The city came back with a new offer. Ten thousand dollars for me. Seventy-five thousand dollars for my attorney's fees. And a promotion to detective first grade . . . to be made publicly.

I accepted.

After five long years, it was finally over. After all the bitterness, all the acrimony, all the pain.

With the news about my lawsuit, I knew that it was time for me to wind things down. Say good-bye. And move on.

The promotion ceremony took place May 31, 1991, at Police Headquarters. Given that it was a formal ceremony, I wore my regulation dress blue uniform, peaked cap, and white gloves.

While the day was meant to be proud and festive, it was not without its painful side. Still blaming me for Tony's death, Anna Venditti showed up at the ceremony and tried to disrupt it. But as much as Tony's death still haunted me, this day was really about something else. It was about my lawsuit. It was about a five-year battle to win vindication. It was about one woman in the Police Department and all women in the Police Department who had been subjected to the worst kind of harassment, abuse, and discrimination because of their gender. It was about making the Police Department admit that such abuse did occur. That it was wrong. And that, hopefully, it would not be allowed to happen again.

This was my day, my triumph. After all I had been through, I would just not allow anybody to ruin it, no matter what.

Many of the cops being promoted that day were minorities. People who, over the years, had encountered prejudices and stumbling blocks in making their way through the ranks. Blacks. Hispanics. Jews. Asians. And, of course, other women. Stories about the settlement of my lawsuit had cropped up in the newspapers a few days before, so all the other cops in the auditorium that day knew exactly who I was. As I sat in the audience waiting to be called up to the dais, I wondered how these other cops in their dress blue uniforms would react to my promotion. And how would the assembled brass react? Given my reputation, would they continue to treat me like a pariah? Would they give me the cold shoulder? Turn their backs? Would they even acknowledge me?

Up onstage, Police Commissioner Lee Brown, himself a black man, began handing out the promotions. Only three detectives were being promoted to detective first grade this day. The commissioner took note of how rare it was for any detective to achieve this exalted rank. Then, to my astonishment, he began talking about me.

"I'd like to give special attention to Kathy Burke," Brown said. "She has demonstrated that standing by her principles, bringing a suit of sexual harassment, will help insure fair treatment to all women of the New York City Police Department."

A moment later, I heard my name called. "Kathleen Burke, Detective First Grade."

I took a deep breath. Rose from my chair. Walked stiffly down the aisle. And ascended the dais. At the center of the stage, Commissioner Brown handed me a certificate. He shook my hand. Somebody handed me a bouquet of roses. I turned around to face the audience. And that's when I saw something truly amazing.

Almost every cop out there was standing on his feet and cheering me.

A month later, I did "the walk."

Tom Fox accompanied me.

With Tom at my side to provide moral support, I went from office to office in headquarters, divesting myself of all the trappings of my twenty-three-year police career. I surrendered my swipe card that I had used to gain admission to the building. I turned in my helmet. I donated my bulletproof vest to the firearms unit so they could use it for target practice. I gave my ID card to the pension section so a clerk could perforate it with a mark that said RETIRED. I had myself fingerprinted for a pistol permit, then filled out the application to continue carrying my gun as a retired police officer. I surrendered my patrol guide. I also turned in my Mace and my department parking placard.

Back in my office, I packed up all my files and personal effects in cardboard boxes. Later, I took them down to the garage and put them in my car. I gave my desktop AM-FM radio to one of the other women cops in the unit. Somebody else took possession of my special chair, which I had used because of my bad back.

The toughest part of all, of course, was my detective shield.

Detective shield number 341.

Twenty years earlier, I had been handed that very same shield by the police commissioner after I'd nearly got my brains blown out while making an undercover drug buy. At the promotion ceremony, I had been disguised to conceal my identity.

I was a girl then, just a kid.

All those years, all those battles, all those windmills I had tilted at. All the victories, the defeats, the fires of hell I had walked through.

So much had changed in the city; so much had changed in the world.

All during those difficult years when I was doing battle with the Major Case Squad, women were crucified if they so much as uttered the words *sexual discrimination*. In 1991, however, the year of my retirement, the New York City Human Rights Commission found that the New York Police Department had discriminated against 124 women officers. As a result of the ruling, the women or their estates were deemed eligible for monetary damages. Included among those 124 officers, I eventually gained three and a half years of seniority toward my pension.

Meanwhile, down in Washington, D.C., that very same year, a woman law professor named Anita Hill was publicly testifying at the behest of the U.S. Senate about what she considered to be sexual harassment by Clarence Thomas, who was about to be confirmed to the U.S. Supreme Court.

Yes, a great deal had changed.

As I replayed my personal struggles in my head, I kept turning my shield over and over in the palm of my hand, again and again and again. No, I was not at all eager to part with it. It said so much about who I was.

Through it all, Detective shield number 341 had given me my power. It's what had got me through the door. It's what had made the good guys take notice and the bad guys back down. It was that thing I would stick out in front of me that said, "Look out, world, I'm a cop."

Detective shield number 341 had given me my identity.

When I removed the shield from its case, I could still see the contours of the imprint in the soft leather of the case.

I handed the shield to an administrative aide. He tossed it on top of a specially constructed box with a cutout hole on top. The cutout hole, also in the shape of a shield, was designed to separate phony shields from real ones. Sometimes, at the end of their careers, cops tried to stick the department with phony shields and squirrel away their real ones as souvenirs. If the shield slipped through the cutout hole, it was a phony. If it remained on top, it was the real McCoy. One last department integrity test before you left the job.

My shield did not fall through. It was authentic. (Some years ago, a female detective working in this office made a pillow for officers to place their shields on before they were tossed onto the box, adding a preliminary step to the process that, quite literally, would soften the fall.)

"Good luck, Burke," said the administrative aide as he retrieved the shield and put it in a drawer.

That I was no longer being addressed inside Police Headquarters as "Detective Burke" was not lost on me. It stung like hell.

As I left the office, I started to choke up. Tom tried to console me, but it wasn't much use. The book was closed. And I felt completely empty. This had to be one of the worst days of my life.

After twenty-three years, I was no longer a cop.

* * *

In 1992, Bob and I divorced. One day, long after my divorce became finalized, Tom called me up. He was about to get divorced, as well. But this time, he was not looking for a friendly lunch.

"So, Burke," he began, "would you like to have dinner sometime?"

"Sure," I said.

At that point Tom ended our friendship. And began dating.

We have been together ever since.

CHAPTER TWENTY-SEVEN

By the summer of 1994, Steven Maltese and Carmine Gualtiere had completed their federal prison sentences for racketeering, while Fritzi Giovanelli was nearing the end of his. That all three would soon go free—and had never done a single day's time for the shootings—did not sit well with the new DA in Queens, Richard Brown, an ex-judge and a strong supporter of the police. Regardless of what the Feds might or might not choose to do with the three mobsters, Brown was itching to give it another shot in his bailiwick, Queens State Supreme Court.

Gualtiere had been acquitted of murder charges at the second state trial in Queens. But the jurors had deadlocked on similar charges against Maltese and Giovanelli, which meant that Brown had the right to retry Maltese and Giovanelli for Tony's murder and the attempt to murder me. So DA Brown ordered his office to gear up for one more try. This time around, for what would be trial number four (three in state court and one in federal court), Brown tapped Dan Saunders and Richard Schaefer, two of his most skilled and trusted prosecutors, to make the state's case.

The prospect of having to testify at a fourth trial filled me with dread. In my heart of hearts, I had serious doubts that we could ever win. There was just so much excess baggage attached to this case.

I also worried what a fourth trial would do to me and my family. After the three prior trials, I felt burnt-out and exhausted. Since the end of the third trial, I had managed to avoid the limelight, but a fourth trial would surely put an end to my low profile. My two girls, Cathrine and Veronica, were teenagers now, and I hated the idea of exposing them to the pain of fresh media coverage and malicious gossip about their mom. Each time the case had gone to trial, my youngest, Veronica, had suffered nightmares.

During the three prior trials, weird things had happened around our house—break-ins, burglaries of my car, crank calls bringing uniformed cops to our doorstep, strange men following me when I went out shopping. I was not eager for a recurrence.

Notwithstanding all of my concerns, I knew that I had a responsibility to see the prosecution of this case to its conclusion. So I tried to give the new team of prosecutors my fullest cooperation.

In the first few weeks of trial prep, we spent hours upon hours sifting through notes and documents and going over my story. Prosecutors Saunders and Schaefer worked long and hard to gain my confidence. In their dealings with me, they treated me with respect, courtesy, professionalism, and compassion. At times, as we went back over the same old familiar ground, my emotions got the better of me and I lost my temper. To their credit, the two prosecutors neither scolded nor abandoned me. They tolerated my outbursts with saintlike patience. They let me blow my stack. They allowed me my anger.

Nevertheless, I found all the days and weeks of trial prep physically draining and emotionally grueling. As the trial date neared and the tension began to build, my body seemed to turn against me, as though it were staging some kind of rebellion. I began experiencing abdominal swelling and vaginal bleeding. I was past menopause, so the bleeding was somewhat irregular.

I attributed the symptoms to the stress of the upcoming trial and my impending testimony. As best I could, I tried to put them out of my head.

The fourth trial began in the summer of 1994.

It was held in the same dark-wood-paneled Queens courtroom that had been the setting for the second trial. The atmosphere in the courtroom was a study in contrasts. On one side of the courtroom sat the members of the law enforcement community—grim-faced detectives, FBI agents, squad commanders, prosecutors, and police union officials, most of whom wore white shirts, dark suits, and dark ties. Here, too, sat Tony's family: his mother, Anna, his sad-faced father, Anthony, his widow, Patti, as well as their relatives, friends, and supporters, which included the parents of several other New York City police officers who had been murdered in the line of duty. These grieving parents had come to court to provide the Vendittis with moral support.

On the other side of the courtroom sat the friends and relatives of the two defendants, a veritable cheering section for the New York Mafia. The cast of characters was straight out of *The Sopranos*. There were gum-cracking young men in short-sleeved muscle shirts and slicked-back, duck's-ass haircuts who gave the witnesses and the jurors the iciest of stares. There were married-to-the-mob molls with tight pants, high heels, frosted-blond hair, gold-lamé shoulder bags, and great glitzy gobs of jangling jewelry. There were older, grayer, more conservatively dressed matrons and grandmas, clutching their rosary beads and dutifully mouthing the prayers in their dog-eared Bibles. And there was a bevy of paunchy old guys wearing open-collared leisure shirts, polyester slacks, and nylon jogging suits. Many of them wore dark-tinted glasses. These old-timers looked almost grandfatherly and, to the uninitiated, benign. But looks could be deceiving. For most, if not all of them, had been the subjects of our undercover wiretaps. They were dangerous criminals, the real piranhas in this pond. Based on what we had overheard on the wires, we even recognized one of them as a stone-cold killer.

The defendants, Federico "Fritzi" Giovanelli and Steven Maltese, looked more like accountants than murder suspects. Both men were in their sixties now. Wearing his reading glasses as he perused court papers or transcripts, his hair now short and gone totally white, Fritzi Gio-vanelli was the taller and fleshier of the two. Steven Maltese, shorter, sad-eyed, with a full head of dark, graying hair, resembled everybody's favorite Dutch uncle, peering over the tops of his bifocals.

Dressed neatly and conservatively in tweed jackets or dark suits and ties, both defendants looked harmless. How could either of these aging men possibly hurt anybody, you'd have to wonder, much less cold-bloodedly gun down two New York City cops? Walking into the court-room for the first time, one of the spectators actually mistook the two defendants for the defense attorneys.

To the experienced investigators in that courtroom, however, there was one telltale giveaway about the true natures of the defendants. It was their eyes. They were sharks' eyes. Cold, hard, and utterly lifeless.

Once again, Fritzi Giovanelli was represented by attorney Lawrence Hochheiser, a heavyset, middle-aged man with a dark, shaggy Afro-styled hairdo and a thick black mustache. Hochheiser bore a distinct re-semblance to the TV movie critic Gene Shalit. His courtroom manner varied from a folksy, gee-whiz, good-ol'-boy style of yarn-spinning to a casual, howdy-do banter when talking to the jury.

In making the prosecution's case, Assistant DAs Saunders and Schaefer would call to the stand many of the same witnesses who had appeared at the three prior trials. But the star witness, yet one more time, would be Kathy Burke, who would once again evoke nasty insinuations and intense emotions.

When I was called to the stand, Assistant DA Saunders led me slowly and methodically through the events of January 21, 1986—the night I was supposed to have died.

When defense attorney Hochheiser got his chance to cross-examine me, he went straight for the jugular. He did everything he could to impugn my character, my motives, my integrity, and even my very sanity, asking numerous negative and rhetorical questions having nothing to do with the specifics of the case.

Now, in our system of justice, defense attorneys have no obligation whatsoever to prove the truth. Nor do they even have to prove their clients' innocence. They merely need establish "reasonable doubt" in the jury's mind about the version of the events as presented during the trial by the prosecution. Clearly, the purpose of these kinds of questions was not to get at the truth about the events of January 21, 1986. None of his questions were designed to cast light on who shot us, why they shot us, or how they shot us. None of his questions even spoke to the issue of what had happened that night outside the Castillo Diner. No, they had a whole different purpose—namely, to depict me, the state's chief eyewitness to the shootings, in the most unflattering light and cast doubt on my testimony.

But that was the system. And, under the ground rules of our system, all of these questions by the defense were entirely permissible. So I had to answer them.

In my mind, however the most telling exchange between the two of us came toward the end of his cross-examination. "Detective Burke," Hochheiser began, "isn't it true that you would like to see this case go to a successful conclusion because you have a vested interest in the outcome?"

"Yes, sir," I replied.

At this moment, Hochheiser had his back turned toward me. He seemed to have concluded his line of questioning and was walking away from me, back toward his seat at the defense table. Suddenly, halfway across the floor, he stopped in his tracks and whirled around to face me.

Then, in his most theatrically indignant and self-righteous tone of voice, he thundered:

"Detective Burke, isn't it true that you want to see this case go to a successful conclusion because you feel responsible for Detective Venditti's death?"

At that moment, I knew that every eye in that courtroom was fixed upon me, waiting to see how I would respond. How I comported myself and responded to this question could mean a great deal to the prosecution's case. So I took a sip of water to calm myself down and buy some time. Then, looking directly at Hochheiser, I calmly responded:

"No, sir. Because I was not responsible for Detective Venditti's death."

With that, I turned to face the two defendants, Fritzi Giovanelli and Steven Maltese. I raised my hand, extended my finger, and pointed directly at them. "Those two men, sitting over there—your clients, Mr. Giovanelli and Mr. Maltese, along with Mr. Gualtiere—they were the people responsible for Detective Venditti's death."

On this point, Mr. Hochheiser had nothing further to say.

When the defense got its turn to present its case, the most dramatic witness it put on the stand had to be Fritzi Giovanelli himself. Wearing a brown sports jacket and tie, brown pants, and white tennis shoes, he looked tanned and fit. His voice was tough and gravelly. But his eyes were as cold, black, and lifeless as ever.

With Hochheiser doing the questioning, Fritzi once again maintained that he had been an innocent victim in all of this, caught in the middle of a wild shoot-out between the cops and a team of neighborhood stickup men. "I didn't have a gun," he told the jurors. "I didn't shoot anyone. I went to keep an appointment, to make a telephone call. There was an attempted robbery on me, and I got caught between the shooting."

All during Hochheiser's direct examination, Fritzi was on his best behavior. But once Assistant DA Saunders began his cross-examination, that mask of civility dropped like a lead balloon. And it happened with the prosecutor's very first question.

"I guess after four trials, you've got the routine down pretty well, don't you?" Assistant DA Saunders asked Fritzi.

Fritzi's head snapped around. His face flushed red and his eyes bulged in fury. His body jerked spasmodically and he swiveled around in the witness chair to confront his accuser.

"What'd you say?" he shot back at Saunders. "You call this a 'routine'? Hey, this ain't no routine. This is my life."

Later, when Saunders asked Fritzi if he had shot me, the mob boss ex-

ploded anew. "I didn't shoot Kathy Burke," he snapped, practically spit-
ting his denial in Saunders's face. "I didn't shoot Anthony Venditti.
Maybe Kathy Burke shot Anthony Venditti. Howd'ya like that?"

Saunders asked Fritzi a series of questions about his gambling business and his mob associations.

"I ain't gonna answer that," Fritzi snarled at one point.

From that point on, he refused to answer any other questions about
gambling or loan-sharking by citing his Fifth Amendment right against
self-incrimination.

In their summations, defense lawyers Hochheiser and Horlick characterized the prosecution's witnesses as "liars," "creeps," and "thieves." But
they saved their nastiest broadsides for me.

Contending that I had never fully identified the men who shot us,
Horlick sarcastically referred to me as "a woman you may think is nuts,
crazy, insane" or "the greatest police officer since Wonder Bread." Meanwhile, Hochheiser described me as a person given to "confabulation" or
altering the facts when under stress, a person whom other cops had accused of "hallucinating," a witness who, over four trials, had "prepared,
overprepared, and rehearsed her testimony," a person who was "angry"
and "consumed" with a mission. At one point, he told the jurors they
could rightfully compare me to the lunatic, paranoid Captain Queeg
character played by Humphrey Bogart in The Caine Mutiny.

When Assistant DA Saunders finally got his chance to sum up, he
dealt head-on with these assaults on my character. "What is it about this
woman that so upsets Mr. Hochheiser and Mr. Giovanelli?" he asked the
jurors. "I'll tell you what it is. She survived."

Saunders went on to say, "She is dissatisfied with certain aspects of
this case. The police work could have been better. Better DAs could have
been assigned at the first trial. For that, she's been labeled 'crazy.'"

Alluding to my lawsuit against the Major Case Squad, Saunders
added, "She doesn't take crap from anyone, including a sergeant. And
that makes her an unpopular person. But in four days of testimony, she
answered every question that was put to her." Saunders asked the jurors
to compare my testimony with the testimony of Fritzi Giovanelli. "She
never once took the Fifth Amendment," he pointedly noted.

Saunders walked up to the jury box and eyeballed the jurors, one by
one.

"I ask you to walk in her shoes. And feel what she went through when she got shot that night. I can't find the words. We're not talking about being burglarized or having your car stolen. We're talking about being shot at close range, drilled through the chest by someone you know.

"You see your partner murdered. He never went home that night. That is a burden she must carry with her for the rest of her life. She identified the man who shot her—it's in every report. Yet she's the subject of a bitter and personal attack. She's called a 'lunatic.'"

Once again, Saunders contrasted my testimony with Fritzi's. "But after four days of testimony, she was never rude, never inappropriate, even though she was ridiculed. She was articulate. The evidence shows she has identified Fritzi Giovanelli and Steven Maltese convincingly."

Yet again, Saunders reminded the jurors of Fritzi's angry outbursts when he was on the witness stand. Saunders had made his cross-examination tough, he admitted, deliberately trying to goad Fritzi into losing his temper. But there was a method to his madness. He had wanted the jurors to see firsthand what kind of volatile person Fritzi really was. "There is no doubt that on January twenty-first, 1986, Fritzi was determined to confront the person he thought was trouble to his organization," Saunders said. "He lost his temper. He shot Kathy Burke. The situation got out of hand. They turned on Anthony Venditti and fired repeatedly on Anthony Venditti to cause his death."

Turning one last time to face the twelve men and women in the jury, Saunders concluded:

"There is only one verdict possible in this case. In the name of the people of New York, I ask you to find Federico Giovanelli guilty of assaulting Kathy Burke. And I ask you to find Federico Giovanelli and Steven Maltese guilty of causing the murder of Anthony Venditti."

During the judge's instructions to the jury, I was not permitted to sit in the courtroom. Instead, I sat by myself in a room in the district attorney's office. And my mind began to race.

So much had happened in the nearly nine years since we had been shot.

Subway "vigilante" Bernie Goetz had been acquitted of assault in the shootings of four teenagers who'd tried to rob him. Three white teens had been charged with manslaughter after attacking three black men in Howard Beach, New York, and one of the victims was killed by a car. A jogging investment banker had been gang-raped and nearly killed by a pack of wilding teenagers in Central Park. New York City had elected its first black mayor, David Dinkins. Eighty-seven people had been killed in a social club fire in the Bronx. Police all across the country had come under fire after L.A. officers were videotaped brutally beating a black motorist named Rodney King. Arab terrorists had bombed the World Trade Center, killing six and injuring a thousand. United Nations forces, led by the United States, had attacked and defeated the troops of Iraqi strongman Saddam Hussein . . . and so much more.

Yet, despite the cavalcade of events and the passage of so much time, our case lingered on, still fraught with so many unanswered (and unanswerable) questions. Alone, with time on my hands, I tried to sort it all out.

I thought about the three prior trials.

Yes, the mob had put a hurting on us. But we had put a hurting on them, too. We might have lost the murder trials, but we had succeeded in putting these mob mutts in the slammer for gambling and racketeering. Which, after all, was what we had actually set out to do in the first place. The murder investigation by the 104th Precinct might have failed to produce results, but the investigation by the Joint Organized Crime Task Force had paid off stunningly. We had gotten indictments, convictions, and prison sentences.

Would I have liked to take a bigger piece out of them? Damn right. Still, we had put a crimp in the operations of the Genovese crime family. We had disrupted their business and sent three of their biggest earners to prison. And it had all been the result of a terrific team effort. I was merely one of many investigators among many superb cops and FBI agents. I felt proud to have been a part of that effort.

I thought about this final trial and the remaining two defendants.

Every day, they had come to court in their smartest suits and ties. Dressed to the nines, they looked like aging altar boys. Behind them sat their relatives, visibly reminding the jury that these two men on trial were family men, husbands and fathers with wives and children. What the jurors rarely got to see was that the victims had spouses and children, too. What about Tony's family? His four daughters? And what about my family? Faced with the ever-present threat of mob violence, my two daughters had been forced to maintain an ongoing vigil every day of their lives.

I knew Tony's family still blamed me for much of what had happened. And yet, I would have given anything to sit with them, talk with them, cry with them, console them, and show them that I hurt as much as they did. I wanted so very much to share their pain. If only they could have been willing to share a little bit of mine. . . .

My thoughts turned to another family, one that had been conspicuous in its absence. And that was the family of police itself. The Police Department should have underscored the seriousness of this case by packing the courtroom with uniformed officers and having them sit in the first row of the spectator gallery, where all the jurors could see them. But almost no cops in uniform had showed up. Embarrassed by the results of the first three trials, disheartened and wearied by a criminal case that seemingly had no end, the department seemed eager to forget that two of its own had been gunned down in cold blood.

In the end, however, as I sat waiting for the jury to return with its verdict, I thought about Tony. The real friendship that had started to build between us. The bond of trust that was beginning to take hold.

And, one more time, I began to weep.

And then, finally, we got the word. After four days of deliberations, the jury had reached its verdict. At long last, I was permitted to return to the courtroom and hear firsthand its decision.

As I sat waiting in the first row of the spectators' gallery, with my good friend Detective Tommy Bruno at my side, I clutched tightly to the mass card I always kept with me, the one with Tony's picture on it. An eerie silence filled the chamber.

In my ears, I could hear my heart pounding. I turned and glanced behind me. In the very next row, Anna Venditti sat with her head bowed and her eyes closed, deep in prayer. Her husband, Anthony, was looking straight ahead, his sweet, sad face mirroring the pain and heartache we had all endured over the passing years. Around them were the parents of other hero police officers who had been slain in the line of duty. They had all come to bear witness.

A dozen court officers slowly began to position themselves throughout the courtroom, along the walls, in the middle of the aisles, close to the exits. I tried to read something from their expressions and body language and positioning, but this time I was too agitated to interpret it.

I turned back to face the bench, then looked over at the two defendants. Fritzi, with his cold, hard eyes, sitting side by side with his mouthpiece, Hochheiser. Steven Maltese, smiling, sharing some private joke with his bald-headed lawyer, Horlick.

At 4:35 p.m., a door at the rear of the courtroom opened, and all of us sat up in our seats. The court officers escorted the jurors back to the jury box. Quietly, they took their seats, too. For an instant, I studied their expressions looking for some hint or indication. But it was just too much for me. I turned away from their faces.

Instead, I looked down at the mass card in my hands, squeezing it even more tightly with my fingers. Bringing it up to my chest, I pressed it tightly to my pounding heart, closed my eyes, and began to pray silently. At this moment, I knew that Tony and I were at our last crossroads together on this long and terrible journey. "Well, partner," I could hear myself saying inside my head, "we're going down for the last time." Tommy Bruno held tightly to my arm and tried to soothe me. But I could no longer maintain the facade. Tears streamed freely down my cheeks.

The judge reentered the courtroom and took his seat on the bench. His expression was blank. He nodded to the clerk. The clerk asked the jurors to rise.

"Ladies and gentlemen of the jury, have you reached a verdict?" the clerk asked.

"We have," replied the forewoman, a short, squat woman in a bright yellow pullover.

And then she announced that the jury had acquitted the defendants on all counts.

"Yes! Yes! Yes!" shouted a jubilant Fritzi.

He pounded his codefendant, Steven Maltese, on the back. Then he pounded the defense table with his fist. The two defendants hugged their lawyers. Behind them, their relatives burst into gasps and sighs, then tears, joyfully collapsing into each others' arms. Some dashed for the pay telephones in the corridor so they could notify the rest of their friends and families.

On the other side of the courtroom, the prosecutors and cops and FBI agents who had been sitting in the gallery rose silently from their seats and, without uttering a word, filed from the courtroom. Tony's family walked out, as well.

I remained in my seat, too numbed to move.

How in the world could this be happening? How could these people have been so totally fooled? These people, whom Tony and I had faithfully served. These people, whom I had taken a bullet for? These people, whom Tony had died for?

It was almost as if the bad guys had pulled the trigger on us all over again.

I continued sitting statuelike for several more minutes as the last remaining spectators cleared from the courtroom. From the corner of my left eye, I noticed that the lead defense attorney, Lawrence Hochheiser, was walking toward me.

As he neared the banister separating us, he stopped and stood opposite me, saying nothing. Then he spoke. His tone was subdued and respectful. "Detective Burke, I just want you to know, you are one hell of a woman."

Why he said it, I do not know. Perhaps it was his way of trying to be a gracious winner. Perhaps he was apologizing to me for all the pain and agony and humiliation he had put me through over the years. Perhaps it was his way of signaling me that, in his heart of hearts, he knew what the real truth about this case was.

The moment he said it, I flashed back to my childhood. I remembered what my mother had told me when I got roughed up by that neighborhood bully who had punched me in the eye and ruined my new Easter Sunday dress. In my mind, I could still hear her words, Mom's credo for survival: "Never let 'em see you cry."

So I steeled myself. Wiped away my tears. I glanced up at Hochheiser. And I said to him:

"Counselor, you have been deceived by your clients. You have been fooled, sir."

Then, nearly nine years after the night that Tony and I had been gunned down by the mob and the four trials that had followed, I got up and walked out of that courthouse . . .

. . . never, please, God, to set foot in it again.

CHAPTER TWENTY-EIGHT

By the end of the fourth trial, the stomach bloating and vaginal bleeding I had experienced at the outset had not subsided. At first I had attributed my symptoms to the stress of the trial. But, with the trial's end, my symptoms got worse instead of better. And I began to experience severe sciatic pains down the sides of my legs, pains that my chiropractor was unable to alleviate.

I made an appointment to see my cardiologist, who discovered that my blood pressure had zoomed to 150 over 90. He prescribed medication for hypertension. Then I went to see my gynecologist. Since he had done a complete gynecological examination six months earlier, and my mammogram and my Pap test had looked normal, he was convinced that my symptoms were simply the result of all the stress of the trials. But to better assess the cause of my bleeding, he wanted to schedule a laparoscopy, a surgical procedure in which an incision is made in the abdomen, a tube is inserted, a miniature camera is extended through the tube, and the surgeon prowls around like a submariner to get a close-up look at your insides.

In the meantime, Helen Iemola, another retired cop in our Police Self-Support Group, suggested that I ask the gynecologist to send me for two additional tests. One, a CA-125 test, was designed to detect ovarian cancer. The other was a sonogram. Although still skeptical that anything could seriously be wrong with me, the gynecologist scheduled both.

The normal range for a CA-125 test is 0 to 35. My gynecologist was shocked when mine came back at a roaring 120. Meanwhile, the sonogram revealed unusual shadows and masses in the vaginal area. Allowing me some time at home for the upcoming Christmas holidays, the gynecologist scheduled exploratory surgery for February. The plan was to do the laparoscopy first, then, if the laparoscopy confirmed what the preliminary tests seemed to indicate, to go ahead and do a complete hysterectomy.

Now I had never been a Pollyanna, so I did not delude myself about what was going on here. Based on my test results, I knew it was ovarian cancer. I also knew that, for women, ovarian can be the most deadly of all cancers. So, in the weeks before my surgery, I prepared for the worst.

At my lawyer's office, I filled out a living will, mandating the doctors not to resuscitate me in the event my body could no longer keep me alive without the help of tubes and machines. Because Bob was the father of my two daughters and the person I still felt knew me best, I signed a proxy authorizing him to enforce the living will and make medical decisions if I lost the capacity to make them for myself. I revised my regular will. Additionally, I specified where my guns should go—five to Bob and a sixth, my six-shot, four-inch service revolver, back to my old partner in the Major Case Squad, John Gaspar.

My surgery was done at Flushing Medical Center in Queens. After my gynecologist performed the laparoscopy, a surgeon stepped in and removed my uterus and ovaries, along with the lymph nodes and the omentum, a fold of the peritoneum connecting the stomach and the abdominal viscera and forming a protective and supportive covering.

When I came to in my hospital room, Sergeant Tom Fox was at my bedside.

"Well?" I asked him.

He smiled. "I'm not supposed to tell you, but they took a lot out. And it was cancerous."

I had already done my crying, so I didn't go to pieces over the news. Instead, I began thinking of all the things I needed to do in the upcoming weeks. Now that the surgery was over, I knew it was time for me to begin digging in for the real battle.

But first I insisted on taking a previously planned trip to Mexico with my two daughters. Tom Fox came, too.

Within a week of my return, I entered the hospital for the first of my twelve chemo treatments. During each one I would be given intravenous doses of cisplatin and Taxol, two extremely aggressive anticancer drugs. Each treatment would require me to be hospitalized for three days at a stretch.

I knew my hair would fall out, so I had gone to the beauty parlor beforehand and gotten it clipped short. I also had specially preordered two wigs. Nevertheless, I wondered—what other side effects would the chemotherapy have on my appearance? Would I turn pallid and gaunt? Would I look as if I were dying?

The first treatment went fairly smoothly. The biggest problem was that my veins kept collapsing, making it difficult for the nurses to insert an IV line. So a doctor implanted an Infuse-a-Port, a bottle-cap-shaped receptacle, just under the skin in my chest to facilitate the flow of the drugs. Blessedly, I experienced no nausea. But, within two weeks, I was bald as a billiard ball.

I also lost the hair on the rest of my body. The toughest part was having no eyelashes. I could use makeup to simulate eyebrows, but the absence of eyelashes made my face look flat, dull, and characterless. Although I would wear my wigs at social functions, most of the time I went without them. They were uncomfortable and unwieldy, and the adhesive tape inside them made my head itch.

For me, the wigs also symbolized a willingness to accept defeat. I had made a decision not to hide from the cancer. In my mind, resorting to a wig was tantamount to giving the disease some kind of power over me, which I was determined never to do. Nothing would change I decided, as long as I didn't change. So, before long, I simply stopped wearing my wigs. I wasn't ashamed. I didn't feel sorry for myself. My biggest concern was how other people might react to my baldness.

Tom took it just fine. He had recently lost a sister to cancer, so he had firsthand knowledge of the rigors. My kids were great about it, too. Sometimes they would bring their friends around, and we would all cut up and laugh and pose for pictures together. Nobody treated me as if I had the plague. The girls would come up to me and rub my bald head for luck, as though it were Buddha's belly.

I hoped that if I was at ease, other people would be at ease, too. So I made a point of treating my condition with humor. "Hey, you go to bed with me," I would joke to them, "and in the middle of the night you can't be sure whether you got me by the head or by the ass."

After a while, I started to leave the house and go out shopping without my wigs. Some people stopped and gawked, but a lot of them reached out to me. They would come up and ask me questions about my condition. Sometimes they would ask because they themselves were facing chemotherapy. Sometimes they would ask on behalf of friends and relatives who were battling cancer. I became a kind of walking Dear Abby in my Astoria neighborhood, dispensing advice. Because I wasn't hiding under a wig, people felt freer to approach me. Given my own ordeal, the thought that I might be helpful to others was tremendously gratifying. It gave me hope for the future.

The chemotherapy treatments did have other side effects, and some of them were not so pleasant. The drugs were so powerful that they made me anemic. To compensate for the destruction of all those red blood cells, I needed transfusions, two pints of blood after each chemo treatment. The combination of chemo and transfusions made me so exhausted that I required at least twelve hours of sleep every night. Sometimes, I would experience numbness in my extremities, from the elbows and knees right on down to my fingertips and my toes. Other times, I would feel weird little twinges and aches skipping lightly up and down my legs. I took to calling them fairy pains.

After my first chemotherapy treatment, my CA-125 count dropped down to normal. Dr. James Vogel, my cancer specialist, was so pleased that he reduced the scheduled number of treatments from twelve to eight.

When I went back for my second treatment, all the nurses were excited to see me. A TV show called *Top Cops* had recently aired a segment about me, and everyone gathered around as if I were a Hollywood celebrity. I began to kid around with the nurses. I also visited other cancer patients and encouraged them to be upbeat and optimistic about their prospects.

With my doctors, however, I could be ornery, difficult, and obstinate. Each month after a chemo session, I would visit Dr. Vogel to see how I was doing.

"How do you feel?" he would ask me.

"Never mind how I feel," I would shoot back. "How I feel doesn't really matter with this disease. You tell me how I am."

He would always reply cautiously, with guarded optimism, "You're doing well."

A funny thing about this disease. I have never deluded myself about the eventual outcome. But, in many ways, I have found it easier to cope with the cancer than the shooting.

When I was still a cop, I had always made certain to secure the scene. Take control. Bring in the safeguards. But when I got shot, all the controls collapsed. I had been given no warnings and no choices. Somebody took charge of my destiny without asking my permission. My partner died, and I couldn't do anything about it. A man put a bullet through my chest, and I couldn't do anything about that, either. All of a sudden, through no action of my own, I lay bleeding on the sidewalk and I could have died. Then, in the aftermath, I was forced to deal with the horror of the trials, the fallout from my discrimination suit, the hatred of my peers, the treachery of the Police Department.

With the cancer, however, I felt as if I were in control. I was dealing with a doctor who had told me, "This is the treatment. But making the treatment work has a lot to do with how you handle things psychologically."

I had been given choices. Now it was up to me to take charge and act upon them.

I had already faced death, so I was no longer afraid to die. From my own experience, sitting outside that diner with a through-and-through bullet wound in my chest, I had realized exactly what death would be like. It would be peaceful. It would be serene. It would be easy to embrace. Now, nine years later, I no longer feared death. Dying would be an inconvenience at worst, not a catastrophe. I just didn't happen to be ready for it yet.

Moreover, although I knew I was sick, I wasn't at the point where I had to grapple with the bitter end. For the time being, I was dealing with something else altogether. That something was a six-letter word called *cancer*. I could handle it. I didn't have to run from it. I was in charge. I had time to stand and make my fight.

The first thing I did was arm myself with all the weapons I would need. I was diligent about my chemotherapy appointments and my monthly follow-up visits to the doctor. I practiced self-hypnosis to keep my stress down. I drank herbal teas, gulped down antioxidant pills and vitamins, consumed pulverized flaxseeds to keep my liver cleansed. I carefully controlled my diet. Sadly, as the result of the chemotherapy, I lost my ability to taste except for tart, vinegary foods like coleslaw, sauerkraut, and green olives.

After the last of my chemotherapy treatments, my hair started to grow back immediately. My eyebrows and eyelashes grew back in their same old dark color. The hair on my head grew back curly and supersoft, like lamb's wool. But, unlike the grayish brown color it had originally been, it was now snow-white. Consequently, the local beauty parlor and Clairol became my new best friends.

As of this writing, it's been ten years since my last chemotherapy treatment, and there's been no recurrence of the cancer. There are no detectable cancer cells in my system. As for the future . . . well, it's too soon to know for certain.

In my mind, I still have cancer. But I'm fighting it. And, right now, I'm winning the fight. Once again, I draw upon my past to find my power. Like every other major battle I have fought in my life, I'm tackling this one as though I were still a cop on the street.

After my retirement and the last of the trials, I sat down and wrote a letter to Lieutenant O'Brien, my old boss in the Joint Organized Crime Task Force. Like me, he had been compelled to testify at all four trials. Like me, he had been pummeled by the defense. He had corroborated my version of the shootings. But I knew, when the questions had touched on our burned surveillance car and his refusal to change it, he must have been wrestling with his own conscience. So I wrote to thank him.

"You were always there when I needed you in my corner," I said. "I know it wasn't easy, with the volume of allegations and rumors that were flying around, and yet you remained unshaken. For this, I will always be grateful.

"So many times in the past, I have wanted to talk you, but the time never seemed right. But now that the trials are over, I feel it is my time to reach out to those people in this nightmare who made a difference. And you are one of those people.

"Saying thank-you can't even scratch the surface. . . . If it was not for you, so often, setting the record straight . . . if it was not for you believing in me . . . well, I guess I might not have survived. So I guess in many ways, I owe you my life. And, in part, what is left of my reputation."

I never received a response.

Periodically, the lieutenant and I would bump into each other at retirement rackets for other cops. Beer, bullshit, belly laughs, the usual. Our encounters were always polite and friendly, but never more than that. I was certainly open to more, hungry for it in fact. But any expression of real feeling seemed beyond his reach. He seemed to feel awkward around me, eager to keep our conversations superficial and brief. The job. The weather. Our kids. Nothing more.

Once, however, I did tell him about my battle with cancer. I knew that, years earlier, he had had his own brush with cancer, but had apparently beaten it. I told him that if he ever wanted to talk about his illness, he should call me. At this point, I was working with a small support group of cops who were fighting cancer and other life-threatening illnesses, acting as the facilitator at the group's meetings. He told me that he had no need of our group, felt fine now, but, hey, thanks anyway.

Clearly, he wanted to play it safe. So I respected his wishes and never pushed it any further. Not once did he mention my letter.

For a while, we lost touch.

And then, one day, the phone rang. It was a boss from the Police Headquarters.

"I got a guy who needs your help," he said.

"What's his problem?" I asked.

"Cancer. And he's in pretty bad shape."

"What's his name?"

"Lieutenant John O'Brien."

The name hit me with a jolt. "Are you aware that he was my lieutenant when I got shot?"

There was a long pause on the other end of the line.

"So you're *the* Kathy Burke?" the boss asked.

"Yes, that's right. I am *the* Kathy Burke."

The boss filled me in on the rest of the details. Lieutenant O'Brien had just undergone surgery for a new melanoma. The cancer had returned, invaded his chest, then spread to his brain. As a result, he had suffered strokelike symptoms. He was about to undergo chemotherapy. But his prospects were not good.

When he had reached out for help, Lieutenant O'Brien had asked the department to find some other cop who could give him comfort. He had not specified who that cop should be, except to say that it should be someone who had gone through what he was going through. He had not asked for me by name. But, remembering our prior discussion of my work in our support group for cops with cancer, I knew I was the person he had wanted the department to send.

After I got off the phone, I discussed the call with a close friend.

"You're not gonna go to see this guy, are you?" he said.

"Of course I'm gonna go," I replied.

"But I thought you didn't get along so great with him."

"No, I didn't. He never liked me."

"So, why are you gonna go then?"

"Because . . . Because I don't have the right not to go."

When I entered his hospital room, Lieutenant O'Brien was lying listlessly in his bed. His head had been shaved from his recent surgery, and a long, half-moon scar curving across his skull was still held together with staples. An IV line hung from his arm.

"Hello, Loo," I said. I went to his side. Touched his arm.

His eyes welled up. "Thank you for coming," he said.

On the wall behind his bed I noticed a child's drawing, done in multicolored crayons. On it was written, *Daddy—get well soon. We love you.* A little girl's name was scrawled in big letters at the bottom.

I sat down next to Lieutenant O'Brien. Took his hand in mine. And squeezed it tightly. He squeezed back, but with barely any strength.

"We've been through a lot together, haven't we, Loo?"

"Yeah," he answered. "We sure have."

I smiled. And squeezed his hand again. "Well, we're gonna get through this, too. I promise you."

The lieutenant tried to muster a smile.

"Hell," I said, "after all you and I have been through, we're bound together forever. Through thick or thin."

While I sat there talking with him, a chief entered the room. Upon seeing me, he recoiled. "What the hell are you doing here?" he snapped.

I fixed him in a long, hard stare. "I'm exactly where I'm supposed to be. This man was my friend. He was my boss. Where else would I be?"

Silently, the chief turned tail and walked out of the room.

Lieutenant O'Brien looked at me. A tear formed at the corner of one eye.

I spent almost the whole day at his side, squeezing his hand, reminiscing about the old days, reassuring him that things would get better. I told him about my own bout with cancer. How I was still fighting it. How it had taught me to alter the priorities in my life.

Lieutenant O'Brien talked of getting out of the hospital. And going back to work. But I noticed how badly garbled his speech was, how his hearing had begun to fail, how his mental faculties had diminished. He kept drifting in and out of a fitful sleep.

I knew he would never go back to work. But I would never tell him that. Instead, during his lucid moments, I tried to gently steer him toward preparing for the inevitable.

"Maybe going back to work is not the best thing for you right now," I suggested. "Maybe it's better for you to stay at home for a while, take some time off, time for yourself, time to be with your wife and your kids."

Not once did the subject of my letter come up in our conversation. But in my heart, I knew it was on his mind. And I knew he was grateful that I had sent it. That was the reason I had been summoned here in the first place. Lieutenant O'Brien wanted to make peace with me. The squeeze of my hand, the tear in his eye—these things told the real story.

When it came time to leave, I wrote my phone numbers on a piece of paper and put the paper on the nightstand next to his bed. "Anything you need, Loo, anything your family needs, anything at all—you just call me," I said.

"I will," he answered.

"I'll be back to see you again."

Then I leaned over and hugged him. "Just remember, Loo—I love you."

Lieutenant O'Brien bit his lip. "I love you, too."

Fighting back my own tears, I left the room and headed for my car.

Three months later, Lieutenant O'Brien was dead.

CHAPTER TWENTY-NINE

Yes, I have "lived to tell" my story.

But not everybody likes the story I tell.

When I first decided to do this book, many people felt that my story did not have a happy ending. My partner died. The outcome of the trials was not totally satisfying. We weren't able to lock up the bad guys forever and ever and ever. While they did time for gambling and racketeering, the defendants repeatedly beat the murder rap. And despite my continuing contention that the Mafia had infiltrated, undermined, and corrupted the criminal justice system, compromising the police investigation, sabotaging the prosecutions, and influencing or intimidating either the witnesses or the jurors in three out of the four trials, I was personally assigned most of the blame.

What's more, I ended up retiring from the Police Department under a cloud. My marriage fell apart. I was diagnosed with an extremely treacherous form of cancer, a disease that may, one day, end up killing me.

To many folks, these are not the things that make for a happy ending. And, as I have learned, people who read novels or watch television or go to the movies love happy endings. Feel-good endings. Hollywood endings. Endings in which every wrong is righted.

My story does not end that way.

But, in my mind, it still has a happy ending, one of a different sort, one a little bit closer to real life.

My happy ending is that I live. I survive. I go on. And maybe, just maybe, I make things a little bit easier for the next guy or gal who must come down this road.

Even though I am now retired from the Police Department, I am still, in my heart of hearts, a New York City cop. Hell, I will always be a New York City cop. And nothing can erase the sense of pride and satisfaction that brings. Knowing all the good you've done, the drug gangs you've run out of business, the bad guys you've put away, the street corners you've cleaned up, the schools you've made safer—hey, that's something I'm damn proud of. And I still have terrific memories of my twenty-three years on the job—the wacky drug-buy contests with my fellow undercover Billy Hannibal, the look on that six-foot-nine bank robber's face when I locked him up for the second time, the loony powder fight in the back of the hijacked truck with John Gaspar, the camaraderie with my first real friend and partner in the Major Case Squad, Terry Carey, the rapport and mutual respect I was beginning to develop with my last partner, Tony Venditti. And the deep bond of trust and friendship I developed with Tommy Bruno after the shootings and all through the trials.

In the scheme of things, these feelings are far bigger than Sergeant Burton. Bigger than my troubles in the Major Case Squad. Bigger, even, than the New York Police Department.

My joy in being a cop is just as strong today as it was thirty-eight years ago, when I first came on the job. Just recently, I flew to Toronto to attend a convention of the International Association of Women Police. As I sat on the bus, waiting to return to my hotel from one of the convention conferences, a trim-looking black woman got on and sat down next to me. We started talking about this and that, and almost instantaneously a real rapport took root. Both of us felt it. Something that clicked. We spoke the same language, had the same sensibilities, the same take on things, the same jaded, streetwise sense of humor. As we continued to swap stories, I learned that she was a cop. From Bermuda. And, for many years, had worked undercover in narcotics. Just like me. We have since become good friends. That instant bond that comes from knowing you have shared the same experiences, fought the same battles, lived through the same triumphs and the same disappointments, is something I wouldn't trade for anything. Only another cop can know the feeling.

This is not to say that I no longer hurt. Twenty years have passed since the night we got shot, but not a day passes that I do not think about my partner, Tony Venditti.

Good, decent, kind, and brave Tony.

In mid-May of each year, I travel with fellow members of our Fraternal Order of Police to Washington, D.C., to participate in a candlelight vigil. We hold our vigil in front of the National Law Enforcement Officers Memorial.

The memorial consists of gently curving, blue-gray marble walls, into which have been etched the names of more than fourteen thousand federal, state, and local law enforcement officers killed in the line of duty. Each year, approximately three hundred new names are added.

The names now include those of a Washington, D.C., police officer who dove into a dangerous river to save a drowning woman. A Mississippi sheriff who volunteered to trade places with the hostage of an armed assailant. A Minnesota officer who set up a roadblock to stop a felon and was struck down by the fugitive, whose car was going ninety miles per hour.

And a valiant New York City detective named Anthony Venditti.

My partner.

When I locate Tony's name on that wall, I stand before it silently for several minutes. I touch it gently with my fingertips. I bring my fingertips gently to my lips. I close my eyes. And, silently, I say a prayer of remembrance.

After I finish my prayer, I open my eyes and look at Tony's name again. Then, invariably, my gaze drifts just to the right of Tony's name. To the small blank space that appears between Tony's name and the name of the next officer who is memorialized on the monument wall.

For a moment, I study that small blank space.

And I think to myself that, yes, that small blank space also has significance.

Because that is the space in which my own name should have appeared.

I often think of Tony when I attend the meetings of the Police Self-Support Group, our unique fraternity of severely injured and traumatized New York City cops.

Once upon a time, when we were all young and eager and fearless, all of us had seen ourselves as superheroes, virtually bulletproof defenders of the rest of society. Then, when we were cut down in the line of duty, when we bled and hurt and cried just like everyone else, we had struggled to come to grips with our mortality. For those of us who had always imagined ourselves to be invincible—because we were cops, because we had been designated the protectors of everyone else—that realization had been devastating. All of us wrestled with the trauma.

Years after we sustained our injuries, all of us, regardless of whether our wounds were physical or emotional, were still grappling with our darkest fears. Fears of being blamed and second-guessed. Fears of being

permanent invalids. Fears of being considered useless. Fears of being forgotten. Fears of being relegated to the human junk pile. Fears of being
stumped when it came time to answer that critical question: "What, in
God's name, are we meant to do with the rest of our lives?"

When I first joined the group, there were a dozen of us. Now we have
well over a hundred.

Some members of the support group are retired. Others are still on
the job. Our monthly meetings are attended by a tattered brigade of forgotten heroes, incredibly courageous men and women in wheelchairs, on
canes or crutches, with artificial arms and legs and eyes, wearing neck
and body braces or dark, concealing sunglasses, sometimes bearing horrible facial and body scars.

Some of us have injuries that are not immediately apparent to the
naked eye, yet we are wrestling with terrible, terrible pain nonetheless.
The pain of watching cop friends and partners gunned down right before our eyes.

We are a selective and exclusive bunch, our support group, as elitist
and snobbish as the members of a hoity-toity, members-only country
club. You see, we have no desire to open up our ranks to others. In fact,
we often like to say that we are the only fraternal organization within the
New York Police Department that does not seek any new members. In
our visits to police precincts, when we caution younger cops to wear their
bulletproof vests and do thorough searches of their prisoners to ferret out
possible concealed weapons, we make a point of telling them, "We do not
want any of you to join our group."

But amongst ourselves, we have a deep and powerful bond. Because,
when push comes to shove, we share something that outsiders will never,
ever, know. We are family.

We visit other hurt cops in their hospital beds. We help spouses face
the realities of life with newly disabled husbands or wives. We arrange
psychiatric treatment for kids who have nightmares about the gunmen
who shot their mommies and daddies. We reach out to other officers
who've been hurt while off-duty, then pushed out of their jobs by the
Police Department. We try to cut through the red tape on medical insur-
ance, line up rehabilitative therapy for those with spinal injuries, locate
wheelchairs for those who are no longer ambulatory, find lawyers for
those who have costly legal battles to fight.

Once a year, in the springtime, we throw a festive dinner-dance to
raise money. In the summer, we hold a big picnic. At Christmastime, we

sponsor a party for all our children, complete with a magician and a Santa Claus.

When we are together, we laugh and party and reminisce, just as regular folks do. We relive all our years on the job—the wild stories and the crazy characters, the close calls and the nasty scrapes, the good times and the bad. We talk about what it meant to become a cop. And we remember exactly what it was that made each of us want to become a cop in the first place.

One of the things that I do within our self-support organization is lead a smaller group for cops with cancer and other life-threatening illnesses.

Each month, after the full self-support group finishes its business, we peel off to have a separate meeting of our own.

There are thirty of us in the smaller group, which we call Officers With Special Needs. We have cops battling brain cancer, breast cancer, colon cancer, stomach cancer, Hodgkin's disease, non-Hodgkin's lymphoma, and prostate cancer. As of this writing, I am the only one in the group who has battled ovarian cancer. Other members of our group are suffering from hepatitis C and multiple sclerosis.

In our meetings, I am the facilitator. I get things up and running. I get everybody involved and talking, each of us taking a turn, telling the group what has happened in his or her life during the past month. We talk about our conditions, our treatments, our fears, our anxieties. Often, the most difficult hurdle for us to overcome is being able to talk about our sexuality, particularly when the cancer, or the treatment for that cancer, affects our sexual organs. I try to lighten things up by joking that, organ-wise, I myself have been "gutted like a deer" and that "if you yell down my throat, you can hear an echo." Once we can get past the old taboos, open up, and discuss our prostate surgeries, our mastectomies, our hysterectomies, or our impotence, the ice is quickly broken. We become friends and confidants. We talk about the happy things in our lives. We let ourselves laugh. We talk about the sad things. We remember those group members whom we have lost. We let ourselves cry.

In our group, when one of us feels down, we try to make him aware of how much he matters to his family, as well as how much he matters to our self-support group. We remind each other that we are in this together. Each of us represents the other. If one of us gives up and falls, then all of us might as well throw in the towel. But if one of us has the strength and determination to forge on, then all the rest of us can go on, too.

Often, I try to talk to the others not as cancer patient to cancer patient or victim to victim, but as cop to cop.

"Were you afraid of that guy who pointed a gun at you?" I'll sometimes say. "You went in that building. It was dark. The building was abandoned. The stairs were falling down. You were going through it with a flashlight and a gun. Well, what did you think then? Were you afraid? Did you run from that fear? No? So, why should the cancer be any different? Don't run from the fear. You've been dealing with fear your entire career. Now handle it the same way. Look at the cancer as a burglar, a felon, an illegal intruder. It doesn't belong in there. So get it the hell out."

If anyone in the group starts talking about "my cancer," I will interrupt them. "It's not your cancer," I tell them. "Did you invite it in? Did you extend an invitation? Is it a guest at your dining room table? Then show it the door—and get rid of it."

When people complain about the rigors of their surgery, their chemotherapy, and their radiation treatments, I try to reinforce their courage. "You knew that the treatments would be hard. You felt better after they were over. But sometimes, you have to walk through the fires of hell before you can enter the gates of heaven."

For me, helping to facilitate our smaller group for cops with cancer and other serious illnesses has many rewards. By helping the others, I'm also helping myself. By helping the others, I can cope with my own illness. By telling people over and over and over that they're gonna be okay, that they're gonna make it, I can begin to believe it about myself.

In our little group, I am tough, blunt, emphatic, and unwavering. I will not permit people to feel sorry for themselves. I will not tolerate any negativity or defeatism. I come across to the others with absolute, unflinching, know-it-all certainty when I tell them that, no matter how bad things get, they are going to make it through. And go on with their lives. And, God bless 'em, they believe me.

Funny thing about our little group . . .

Outside of it, in the Police Department and the world at large, people may be put off by my manner—my strength, my aggressiveness, my abrasiveness, my insistence on always being right about things, my headstrong, never-say-die personality. But inside the group, all of those characteristics are a plus. At long last, I am free to be who I really am as a human being. By being strong, I am not turning people off. By being strong, I am being exactly the way all the other members of our little group want me to be. And need me to be.

While I was still undergoing chemotherapy, I received a late-night telephone call from the president of our full Police Self-Support Group, a hero Bomb Squad cop named Tony Senft. Some months earlier, a distraught female police officer whose partner had been shot to death in the Bronx actually succeeded in starving herself to death. The female cop's suicide was a devastating demonstration of what can happen when partners cannot come to terms with their "survivor guilt."

Now, Tony was calling to alert me that another young cop, whose partner had been killed in a more recent Brooklyn shooting, was in danger of suffering a similar fate.

The young cop, whose name was Kevin Murphy, had come down with a truly horrific case of colitis. Knowing that I, too, had suffered from periodic bouts of colitis over the years, as well as the trauma of seeing my partner die on the sidewalk next to me, Tony told me I was the best person to try to counsel Kevin.

"But, Tony," I said, "I'm not in real great shape myself right now. I'm going through my own crisis. I'm weak, I'm still going for chemo, I've lost all my hair . . ."

Tony wouldn't take no for an answer. "Kathy, if you don't do this, we might very well end up losing another cop."

So, I agreed to go.

Before I drove out to Kevin's house, I made it my business to learn the particulars of his story. It was pretty tragic.

Kevin and his partner, Ray Cannon, had been partners for two years. They were good friends. They had come out of the Police Academy together in 1990. When they found themselves both assigned to the 69th Precinct in Brooklyn, they decided to partner up.

One of five brothers, Ray Cannon was a boisterous, good-looking kid. He had recently been married. Kevin had attended his wedding. On the job, Ray was known as one of the most aggressive, gung ho cops in the entire precinct. The department had already recognized him with numerous citations for bravery.

Then, in December of 1994, Kevin and Ray responded to a report of suspicious males inside a bicycle shop in the Canarsie section of Brooklyn. Even before they got to the scene, the two cops knew that this bike shop was a trouble spot. It had a history of being robbed. In fact, the owner had installed a buzzer system on the front door as a security precaution.

On this day, Ray went in first. Kevin followed, just a step behind him.

A teenage kid came out from behind the counter. "False alarm," the kid told the two cops. "We hit it by mistake."

Later, after it was all over, Kevin remembered the kid's comment about "the false alarm" as somewhat odd. Especially since the police dispatcher had not said anything to the two cops about a store alarm going off.

But, from that point on, things happened so quickly that there was no time to sort it all out. A man suddenly popped out from behind the counter, where he had been rifling the cash register and tying up the store's employees. He began firing a gun. Ray never had a chance even to draw his weapon. Hit twice in the head, he went down immediately.

Taking cover behind a railing and drawing his own gun, Kevin returned fire, touching off a wild fusillade that shattered windows and ricocheted off walls and bike racks. Kevin dropped the man who had shot Ray. But there were other robbers in the stickup team, and Kevin had no idea how many of them had guns.

Backing out of the store, Kevin reloaded his weapon and used his portable radio to call for backup. "Ten-thirteen!" was his frantic message. "Officer down! Officer down!"

Then he crawled back into the store in hopes of rescuing Ray. The moment he reentered, he found himself face-to-face with the wounded gunman. The guy was up on his feet and charging right at him. And firing his gun.

So Kevin shot him again. This time the gunman toppled to the floor, right at Kevin's feet.

Kevin backed out of the building a second time to radio for help and reload. When he reentered the store again, he spotted the wounded gunman crawling along the floor. Meanwhile, from somewhere else in the store, Kevin heard shouts. Although he didn't know it yet, they were coming from the employees who had been tied up by the robbers.

Backing out of the store again, Kevin saw a police car pull up. Two housing cops jumped out and rushed over to back him up. Along with one of the housing cops, Kevin reentered the store to drag Ray out. By now, other cops from Kevin's precinct, the 69th, had arrived on the scene, and they, too, helped pull Ray to safety.

Using a parked car for cover, they peeled off Ray's jacket, ripped open his shirt, removed his bulletproof vest. Along with a nurse who had been shopping in the local supermarket, one of the cops pounded Ray's chest and gave him mouth-to-mouth resuscitation.

Around them, scores of cops began to cordon off the streets. Then, with reinforcements now in place, the police launched a full-scale assault on the bike shop. From the employees who had been tied up, the police raiders learned that the robbers—there were four of them—had fled to the basement. On the stairs leading down to the basement, they found the man with whom Kevin had traded shots. He was dead.

The police sent a search dog down to the basement to sniff out the others. Behind the dog followed helmeted, shotgun-toting Emergency Service cops. In the basement, they found the other three robbers—all teenage boys—cowering under boxes. The kids surrendered without a fight. One of them had been shot in the buttocks. The cops retrieved two handguns that had been used in the bike-shop stickup.

Back up on the street, ambulances arrived to take Ray and Kevin to the hospital. En route, the other cops tried to prepare Kevin for the worst. "Ray's in bad shape," they told him.

About six hours later, after the Police Department had brought Ray's parents to the hospital by helicopter along with his new wife, they gave Kevin the official word: Ray Cannon had died.

He was twenty-six years old.

In the days after the shooting, the mayor and the police commissioner hailed Kevin for his bravery. The news media made a huge fuss over him. People wanted to shake his hand, slap him on the back, honor him at ceremonies and dinners, give him medals and awards. After all, he had shot and killed the man who had murdered his partner. He had wounded one of the other robbers. He had stayed by his partner's side and radioed for backup. Braving a deadly hail of bullets, he had repeatedly risked his life to crawl back into that bike shop and drag his partner's body out. Then, he had tried to revive him.

To the world at large, Kevin Murphy was a hero.

Everyone said so.

But one person didn't believe it. And would never believe it . . .

. . . and that was Kevin himself.

How, in God's name, could he be a hero when he had lived and his partner had died? How could he be a hero when he had not even suffered a scratch, while his partner had taken two bullets to the head? How could he be a hero when he was filled with self-doubts about his own actions? If only he had waited five minutes longer before leaving the precinct . . . if only he had paid more attention when they had been able to enter the store without being buzzed in . . . if only he had taken note of the first kid's comment about the "false alarm" . . . if only he had entered the store in front of Ray instead of behind him . . . if only . . . if only . . . if only . . . if only . . . if only . . .

Kevin couldn't live with all these self-doubts. So, perhaps unconsciously, he willed himself to die with them.

Originally, Kevin had intended to go back to work right away. However, his body wouldn't let him. Three weeks after the shooting, he found himself going to the bathroom with unusual frequency. He began to experience heavy bleeding. A doctor diagnosed his condition as ulcerative colitis. The doctor gave him some pills, told him he would be fine, and sent him back home to recuperate.

A week later, Kevin wound up in Winthrop Hospital on Long Island. The medication wasn't working. He was even sicker than before. Unable to eat or even drink a glass of water, Kevin had to be nourished intravenously for a month. His weight plummeted from 175 to 115 pounds. So frail did he become that his fiancée, Kerrie, had to pick him up, lift him bodily out of his bed, and carry him to and from the bathroom when she needed to bathe him. And she was able to do it with hardly any effort at all. Owing to his terrible weight loss, Kevin was now as light as a feather.

After a month and a half at Winthrop Hospital, Kevin was moved to Mount Sinai Hospital in Manhattan. The doctors there decided to perform surgery. They made a large cut down the center of his abdomen, removed his damaged and bleeding large intestine, and hooked his small intestine up to a colostomy bag. They closed up the incision with forty metal staples.

Later, the doctors performed a second operation, reconstructing his small intestine into a pouch and reversing his colostomy. But the two surgeries took a terrible toll. Unable to eat properly, Kevin continued to lose weight, as well as most of his physical stamina and strength. He held little real hope of ever getting better or going back to work as a cop. His morale was shot. He no longer wanted to survive.

When I went to visit Kevin at his house, Kerrie, his fiancée, let me in the door. She led me up the stairs to their living room. There, I found a sweet-faced young man who looked to be at death's door. Fair-complected, about thirty, Kevin looked so gaunt, so pale, and so lifeless that he resembled a concentration camp survivor. He had no idea who I was.

"Hello, Kevin," I said. "I'm Detective Kathy Burke. I'm from the Police Self-Support Group. And I'm here to tell you that I love you."

With that, I kissed him on the cheek. He seemed totally taken aback. "And that everything is going to be okay, I promise you."

"Yeah, right," he muttered. But without an ounce of conviction in his voice.

I sat down next to him on the sofa. Then I began to tell him about our self-support group. How all of us had suffered terrible injuries and traumas. And how we had made it our mission to help each other through the worst of the worst times.

I knew I had to choose my words carefully. I knew I was talking to someone who was extremely fragile. One wrong word, one slip of the lip, and my entire mission could backfire. It was as if I were back on the job, being a hostage negotiator and trying to talk an emotionally distraught person to come inside from a tenth-story ledge. Only in this instance, I was talking to a traumatized young cop. And he was holding himself hostage.

Speaking softly and gently, I began to tell Kevin about my own experiences on the job. My bouts of colitis when I was under attack in the Major Case Squad. The night I saw my own partner die on the sidewalk, right by my side. The years and years of recriminations and anger and pain and grief that had followed.

I kept telling Kevin that I knew what it was like. I knew what he was going through. But he didn't seem to be buying any of it.

"It's not the same," he said. "You took a bullet. I didn't."

Somehow, my bullet wound was my badge of honor. A badge he did not possess.

"Yeah," I countered, "but you shot one of the perps. I fired all my rounds, emptied my gun in fact. And I hit nobody. Besides, you might as well have taken a bullet, since they just ripped half your guts out."

I tried to steer the conversation away from my specific shooting injury. That could only make him feel worse about not having got shot.

But he still wasn't buying it. He couldn't seem to accept that we shared something in common. "Yeah, but you don't know what I feel like. You don't know the pain I have."

"Well," I countered, "maybe I do know."

With that, I did something completely out of character. I stood up from the sofa, hiked up my blouse, and unzipped my pants, pulling them down well below my abdomen to reveal the deep, long scar from my laparoscopy and my hysterectomy that sluiced down the middle of my gut. It was still raw, pink, and ugly. I lowered my voice as I spoke:

"I know what it's like when they take your dignity from you. I know what it's like when they strip you down and lay you out. I know what it's like when they stick tubes in places you didn't even know you had places. I know what it's like when they go in, move your guts around, and take some of your body parts out. You see, Kevin, I not only got shot. . . .

"I got cancer. And I believe I got that cancer because of the shootings. The death of my partner. The stress of the trials. The terrible things they were saying about me . . . it all ended up making me pretty sick.

"Your injury was different. Maybe you didn't take a bullet or get stabbed or fall down a flight of stairs. But, hell, you hurt just as bad as I do. Your injury is your colitis."

Now I had his attention.

I tried to joke about my little striptease. "You know, I've never really done this before. I'm usually pretty modest when it comes to my own body. And, let me tell you, I don't drop my drawers for just anyone."

But, in my mind, I sensed that I was still groping for a way to connect with this kid. I knew I had to find it soon. Otherwise, I might lose him. If, by dropping my drawers, I could play the role of the old dog that rolls over and bares its belly, making itself totally vulnerable to others, maybe I could succeed. Maybe, just maybe, Kevin would come to believe that the two of us were in the same boat.

Unfortunately, it wasn't working. Kevin was still fighting me.

"Pshaw," he scoffed. "People can't see that scar under your clothes. To the ordinary person, you look fine. But when they look at me, they see someone who looks like shit. Someone who's lost sixty pounds. A walking corpse. They don't see that when they look at you."

"Well, that's not exactly true. You see, Kevin, for me"—I peeled off my wig, revealing to him my completely bald head—"it's still not over."

Kevin's head snapped back. He examined me more closely. It wasn't long before he realized that I had no eyelashes. And that my eyebrows were painted on.

And, now, I had him. So I kept talking:

"I may be up against different odds with the cancer than you are with your emotional disease, but I'm fighting to live, just as much as you are. For a lot of people, my hair was my strength. It was who I was. And now that it's gone, it's a sign of my frailty and my mortality. But I'm not gonna let that happen to me. I'm not gonna give the cancer that kind of power over me. And you can't allow the disease you are fighting to have that kind of power over you."

When I removed my wig, something in that room changed.

After averting his gaze for most of our conversation, Kevin was now looking me straight in the eye. Finally, we had connected. Finally, we were on the same level. And finally, the two of us could talk as equals.

"You can't beat yourself up for surviving, Kevin," I said. "You can't do it to yourself. You can't do it to Kerrie. And you can't do it to your partner. Your partner wouldn't want this for you. They already took one good cop from us when they shot Ray. Whatever you do, don't you dare let them take another."

I could see that Kevin was starting to let my words sink in. So I took things a step further.

"Six months from now, your partner's going to be forgotten. He's just going to be a plaque in the precinct. Guys get transferred, new guys come in, nobody's even going to know who Ray Cannon was. But you, Kevin, you can do something about that. You can keep his name alive, maintain his good reputation, pass on his legacy. You can keep him alive in people's minds. You have a mission to fulfill. If you abandon that mission, if you give up, then Ray's death will have been in vain. God puts all of us here for a reason, Kevin. Including you. You have been put here to keep Ray's memory alive."

At that moment, it was time for me to pass the torch.

"You see, Kevin," I told him, "you *lived to tell* the story."

Just before I left Kevin's house that day, I urged him to come to one of the meetings of our Police Self-Support Group.

He was noncommittal. He said he would think about it. Whether he would actually show up was anyone's guess. I myself had doubts.

I called Kevin several times after my initial visit to try to bolster his spirits. So did Tony Senft. Other members of our group, including another cop who had undergone a reversible colostomy after being shot, stopped by to visit him, as well.

While I struggled to cope with the ravages of my own illness, and my exhausting sessions of chemotherapy, I found myself thinking often about Kevin. He was a terribly sick kid, making himself even sicker. And unless we could somehow get through to him and help him to turn the corner, convincing him that he had a reason to go on living, we could easily wind up with one more dead cop.

A month went by.

It came time for the regular meeting of our self-support group. I ar-

rived early, as I usually do, to help get things set up. I said hello to some
of the other key members of our group. Tony Senft, our president, who
had been partially blinded by a terrorist bomb. Don Rios, whose spine
had been shattered by a mugger's bullet and who had been left paralyzed
for six months. Michael Saxe, whose back was broken in a car accident.
Karen Mullane, who got shot in the hip during a chase. My close friend
and ever-loyal supporter Helen Iemola, a stunningly beautiful cop who
had suffered facial and spinal injuries when her and her police partner's
car was hit head-on by a drunk driver who had run a light—at the very
moment they were rushing a dying baby to the hospital.

Heroic cops, loyal friends, and remarkable human beings, each and
every one.

Other members of the group drifted into the room and began to take
their seats. Tony Senft called the meeting to order. As Tony took up various business matters before the group, I walked toward the back of the
room, then leaned against the wall to listen.

We were several minutes into the meeting when I became aware of
somebody standing just behind me. He must have entered through the
rear door when I wasn't watching. Tony actually spotted him first. From
his position up on the dais, Tony gave me a little nod. I turned around to
see what it was.

He still looked like hell, but God bless him—here he was.

In the flesh.

At our meeting.

Kevin.

I smiled. "So, you finally made it."

"I came to thank all of you . . . for what you did for me."

"You're here," I said. "That's thanks enough."

Weak and emaciated, he seemed nervous and self-conscious. This
being his first time, I knew that he must be feeling terribly awkward
around all these other hero cops. Vulnerable. Exposed. And, of course,
terrified of being blamed, faulted, and second-guessed. Exactly the way I
myself had felt the first time I'd got up my nerve to come to one of these
support group meetings.

"So . . . how's it going, Kevin?" I asked him.

"Aw . . ." He shrugged, trying to force a smile. He laughed, a little,
nervous laugh. "You know . . ."

He never did finish his sentence. Slowly, almost as if he were phrasing
more of a question than an answer, his voice trailed off. His eyes started

to moisten. He lowered his gaze. And bit down hard on his lower lip to keep from losing it. I moved closer to him.

"Yeah," I told him, "I do know."

Then I wrapped my arms around him and hugged him as tightly as I could.

POSTSCRIPT

In June of 1968, the year that Kathy Burke joined the New York Police Department, ten women were appointed to the force.

By the end of that year, 338 women were on the force out of a total of 30,538 sworn personnel, or roughly 1 percent. Of those 338, a total of 261 were policewomen, 59 were detectives, 16 were sergeants, and 2 were lieutenants. There was also one female deputy commissioner.

By comparison, in January of 2005 a total of 246 women were among a class of 1,750 recruits to graduate from the New York City Police Academy and be appointed to the force.

As of March 31, 2005, there were 6,020 women on the force out of a total of 35,688 sworn personnel, or roughly 17 percent. Of those 6,020 women, 4,517 were police officers, 706 were detectives, 608 were sergeants, 143 were lieutenants, 34 were captains, and 12 held ranks higher than captain (deputy inspector, inspector, chief). Among those in the top ranks were five women holding the rank of chief.

The highest-ranking chief, with three stars to her credit, was Joanne Jaffe, commander of the New York City Housing Police.

In an interview, Chief Jaffe cited Kathy Burke as one of her mentors. "She overcame traditional barriers and achieved a true leadership role among her colleagues in the Detective Bureau," Jaffe said. "I found her courage and dedication inspiring."

Many years earlier, when Chief Jaffe was still a student at John Jay College of Criminal Justice in Manhattan, she'd babysat for Kathy Burke's daughters.

Since 1968, the year that Kathy Burke joined the force . . .

1971: The NYPD promoted its first female captain.

1972: The NYPD promoted its first female deputy inspector. The first policewomen were assigned to patrol duty. The first female officer was assigned to attend the FBI Academy.

1973: The NYPD abolished the titles *policewoman* and *patrolman,* replacing them with the single title of *police officer.*

1974: The first female officer was assigned to the NYPD's Emergency Service Unit. Two NYPD officers became the first women to receive the city's Medal of Honor.

1976: The NYPD appointed its first woman precinct commander.

1978: The NYPD appointed its first female deputy chief.

1984: The NYPD assigned its first female highway officer. Irma Lozada became the first female police officer to be killed in the line of duty.

1986: The NYPD assigned the first female officers to the Harbor and K-9 units.

1990: The NYPD assigned the first female officers to the Aviation Unit and to bodyguard the mayor of New York City.

1992: The NYPD promoted the first female officer as commander of the NYPD Mounted Unit and its first African-American female commanding officer. It also assigned the first female officer to the Bomb Squad.

1994: The NYPD promoted the first African-American female to captain (and, six years later, to full inspector).

1995: The NYPD promoted the first woman to the post of assistant chief and borough commander.

2002: The first female officer was elected to a ranking position in one of the NYPD's unions (the Sergeants Benevolent Association). The NYPD appointed its first female officer to command the Police Academy. The NYPD appointed its first female Hispanic captain.

Since 1968, in the nation . . .

Women have been named to run police departments in Portland, Oregon, Atlanta, Boston, San Francisco, Detroit, and Milwaukee.

In October 2000, a federal jury in Manhattan awarded $1.25 million to a former female police officer who had accused the New York Police Department of retaliating against her because she complained that she had been sexually harassed on the job.

In her suit, the former officer, Gloria Gonzalez, alleged that police supervisors had tried to punish her for filing a sexual harassment complaint against a male lieutenant. Gonzalez said she was routinely cited for minor violations, given poor work assignments, and brought up on disciplinary charges.

"I feel vindicated," Ms. Gonzalez told reporters after the verdict. "The retaliation was immense, it was overwhelming, it was something that no human being should go through."

In August of 2001, seven years after the fourth and final trial stemming from the shootings of Detective Anthony Venditti and Detective Kathy Burke, the prime suspect in those shootings, Genovese crime family capo Federico "Fritzi" Giovanelli, was indicted on new federal charges of obstructing justice, racketeering, and extortion.

The charges, which were unrelated to the shootings of the two detectives, stemmed from allegations that Giovanelli had illicitly pirated confidential information from the U.S. attorney's office in Manhattan pertaining to upcoming indictments and pending arrests of organized-crime figures, then leaked that information directly to the overlords of the DeCavalcante crime family. Armed with this top-secret information, the DeCavalcante family allegedly plotted to kill two men whom it suspected of cooperating with the FBI and took other measures to evade law enforcement, including sheltering its financial assets to protect them from the government.

Giovanelli was believed to have been slipped the secret information by an office worker in the U.S. attorney's office. An FBI official described the employee as a woman who worked for a stenographic service that was periodically utilized by the prosecutor's office. Nearly twenty years earlier, Giovanelli had been suspected of sabotaging a major federal heroin probe against the Gambino family when he tipped Mafia don John Gotti's right-hand man, Angelo Ruggiero, that the FBI had planted a bug in Ruggiero's Long Island home. Law enforcement officials speculated that the mole on the Gambino tip may have been the same person who alerted Giovanelli to the DeCavalcante indictments.

Giovanelli was never arrested for the earlier leak. But he was put on trial in Manhattan federal court for the more recent leak to the DeCavalcantes.

During the trial, members of Detective Venditti's family, including his mother and his widow, sat in the spectators' gallery. Objecting strenuously to their presence, Giovanelli demanded that they be removed from the courtroom. U.S. district judge Jed Rakoff refused.

In May of 2004, Giovanelli was convicted on three counts of obstruction of justice arising from the theft of the confidential grand-jury information. In September, Judge Rakoff sentenced the seventy-three-year-old Giovanelli to ten years in prison.

When the sentence was pronounced, members of Detective Venditti's family rejoiced, hugging one another and kissing federal prosecutor John Hillebrecht.

Sometime after the sentencing, Giovanelli's attorney, Vivian Shevitz, told a reporter that she would appeal the conviction, saying, "What they've done here is convict him of the murder for which he was acquitted after four trials, the killing of Detective Venditti."

In March of 2005, in one of the most startling cases of police corruption in recent memory, two retired New York City detectives, Stephen Caracappa and Louis Eppolito, were charged by federal prosecutors in Brooklyn, New York, with taking part in eight murders at the behest of the Mafia.

Most of the murders occurred while one or both of the detectives was still on the force.

The indictment against the two detectives, which also accused them of leaking confidential information about wiretaps and surveillance operations to members of organized crime, racketeering, kidnapping, money laundering, and narcotics trafficking, identified both detectives as "violent associates of La Cosa Nostra."

Most shocking, it alleged that after the detectives had leaked the names of government informants and potential witnesses to organized-crime figures, the Mafia had many of those individuals targeted for execution—sometimes recruiting the two detectives to help expedite the hits.

During the mid-1980s, Detective Caracappa helped form the Organized Crime Homicide Unit in the New York Police Department's Detective Bureau. Within the unit, Caracappa functioned as the coordinator for all information regarding organized-crime informants, homicides, and investigations conducted by both the New York Police Department and the Federal Bureau of Investigation. Although specifically assigned to investigations relating to the Luchese crime family, he had access to confidential information about all of the Mafia families based in and around New York City. It was alleged that he sold much of this information to the mob.

While gathering and reviewing information about Mafia-related homicide investigations, Detective Caracappa was specifically detailed to the Special Investigations Division and its Major Case Squad.

In this capacity, he worked in the same squad and the same office and—for at least one period—during the same time as Detective Kathy Burke.

On April 6, 2006, Caracappa and Eppolito were found guilty of all counts in the Mafia murder-for-hire indictment. In June 2006, the judge tossed out the convictions because the statute of limitations had run out, although he cited overwhelming evidence that the two men had committed "heinous and violent crimes." The U.S. attorney's office said it would appeal his ruling.

ACKNOWLEDGMENTS

Much like its subject, *Detective* was forged from many years of struggle. It was not a book whose birthing was speedy, smooth, or pain-free. *Detective* demanded not just our blood, sweat, and tears, but also our faith—a faith that was tested time and again.

In the end, we believe, that faith has been rewarded. But if not for the help and support of certain individuals, we might never be writing these words. And so we must extend our deepest gratitude to the following people.

Our editor at Scribner, Lisa Drew, whose appreciation and respect for the story and whose genuine understanding of Kathy Burke the person—a truly rare understanding, as we have discovered over the course of our long journey to publication—enabled us to write the book we always wanted to write. And her tireless assistant, Samantha Martin, who provided critical editorial and logistical support, without which the book might never have seen the light of day.

Suzanne Balaban, the director of publicity at Scribner, who had the perception to recognize that the greatest asset in publicizing our story was the subject herself. And Katherine Monaghan, who worked so diligently to make that perception a reality.

Kai Falkenberg, who shared her legal expertise and insight to make the manuscript that much better.

T.E.D. Klein and Helen Eisenbach, two wonderful writers who gave generously of their time, wisdom, and publishing experience.

Meryl Streep and Mary Salter for recognizing early on the value of the story and helping so significantly to advance it. Michael Apted, a gentleman as well as a superb film director, for sticking with it when so many others wilted, waffled, and disappeared. And his assistant, Cort Kristensen, for flouting conventional Hollywood etiquette by always comporting himself in a prompt, courteous, and attentive manner while keeping the channels of communication open across several continents.

Detectives John Gaspar and Tommy Bruno for being true friends through thick and thin. Prosecutors Dan McCarthy and Richard Barbuto, Gil Childers and Adam Hoffinger, and Dan Saunders and Richard Schaefer for standing up for the truth, both in and out of the courtroom. Tony Senft, current president, and Richard Pastorella, past president, of the New York City Police Self-Support Group, for their truly heroic courage and inspiration. And the officers and members of the Self-Support Group, the Policewoman's Endowment Association, the Fraternal Order of the Police, and the International Association of Women Police for their boundless support and encouragement.

Bob Burke, still a good friend and a person whose generosity of spirit was essential to the success of the effort.

Detective Walter Burnes of the New York Police Department, Professor Dorothy Schulz of John Jay College of Criminal Justice, and the New York City Police Museum for assisting with vital research on the history of women in the New York Police Department. Professor Richard J. Blood of New York University's Graduate School of Journalism for being a mentor, cheerleader, and a loyal friend. And for instilling the fundamental truism that as good as the reporting and writing might be, one must always, always strive to do better. Faigi Rosenthal, Bill Boyle, and Ed Fay of the *New York Daily News,* who extended a helping hand to a former colleague on so many occasions.

And last but certainly not least, our agent Frank Weimann, who had the guts, the smarts, and the determination to make it all happen in the first place.

About the Authors

Kathy Burke is a former NYPD police detective with twenty-three years on the force. When she left the NYPD in 1991 she was a detective first grade, the highest rank for a detective. Today she is actively involved in the Police Self-Support Group as a trauma counselor for cops and law enforcement officers.

Neal Hirschfeld was a prize-winning reporter and editor for the *New York Daily News* and has written for many other publications. His first book, *Homicide Cop,* profiled Detective Carolann Natale, one of the first female homicide investigators in the New York Police Department. He lives with his wife in New York City.